Native Americans on Film

Native Americans on Film

Conversations, Teaching, and Theory

Edited by

M. Elise Marubbio and Eric L. Buffalohead

UNIVERSITY PRESS OF KENTUCKY

Paperback edition 2018

Scholarly publisher for the Commonwealth, serving Bellarmine University, Berea College, Centre College of Kentucky, Eastern Kentucky University, The Filson Historical Society, Georgetown College, Kentucky Historical Society, Kentucky State University, Morehead State University, Murray State University, Northern Kentucky University, Transylvania University, University of Kentucky, University of Louisville, and Western Kentucky University.

Editorial and Sales Offices: The University Press of Kentucky
663 South Limestone Street, Lexington, Kentucky, 40508-4008
www.kentuckypress.com

Library of Congress Cataloging-in-Publication Data

Native Americans on film : conversations, teaching, and theory / edited by M. Elise Marubbio and Eric L. Buffalohead.
pages cm
Includes bibliographical references and index.
Includes filmography.
ISBN 978-0-8131-3665-3 (hardcover : alk. paper) — ISBN 978-0-8131-3681-3 (pdf) — ISBN 978-0-8131-4034-6 (epub) 1. Indians in motion pictures. 2. Indians in the motion picture industry—United States. 3. Indigenous films—United States. 4. Indian motion picture producers and directors—United States—Interviews. 5. Stereotypes (Social psychology) in motion pictures. I. Marubbio, M. Elise, 1963– editor of compilation. II. Buffalohead, Eric L., 1965– editor of compilation.
PN1995.9.I48N38 2012
791.43'652997—dc23 2012040562

ISBN 978-0-8131-7579-9 (pbk. : alk. paper)

This book is printed on acid-free paper meeting the requirements of the American National Standard for Permanence in Paper for Printed Library Materials.

Manufactured in the United States of America.

Member of the Association of University Presses

Contents

Illustrations

Introduction

Talking Back, Moving Forward

In the spirit of conversations and relationships, the nurturing heart of *Native Americans on Film*, we introduce ourselves to you and extend an invitation to participate in the growing network of people interested and invested in the burgeoning field of Indigenous film. Our friendship and respect for each other's ideas, approaches to scholarship and teaching, and philosophy of life have flourished over the years that we have been colleagues. *Native Americans on Film* is an expression of this relationship and the ones we share with the extended family of educators, scholars, filmmakers, and artists we have come to know through the process of creating this collaboration of voices. It also mirrors the philosophical and theoretical approach we take in American Indian studies, which is interdisciplinary and Native centered, foregrounding Indigenous ways of knowing, teaching, and telling.

Native Americans on Film developed out of a commitment to providing our students with Native representation in our academic offerings. Over the years we listened to our students' and our own voices calling for more Native-centered material that talks about the representation of Native Americans in Hollywood and mainstream media, and about the rapidly expanding, multifaceted Indigenous film movement. Finding the material to provide a Native-centered approach for a variety of courses has sometimes been very challenging. Wonderful works are in circulation today, many of which we use, but often a suitable piece is merely a fraction of another work, such as an essay within a large edition not necessarily related to what we are teaching. Complicating the process, much of the available printed material adheres to methods of analysis that privilege Western genres, aesthetics, and ways of teaching film. While these methodologies possess great value and provide useful tools, they often fail to capture the innovations many Native films employ in merging aesthetics and reformulating genres. We thus imagined a single text that offers theoretical approaches to understanding Native film, includes pedagogical strategies for teaching particular films, and validates the different voices, approaches, and worldviews that emerge across the Indigenous film movement.[1] We imagined *Native Americans on Film*.

Native Americans on Film takes inspiration from the Indigenous film movement and the conversations around it, focusing on the creative possibility that emerges by bringing together theoretical, pedagogical, and filmmaker perspectives on Native film. Our collection embraces a Native point of view, one we see often in Native communities and through the work of Native filmmakers, and a commitment to film content as presented through a Native lens. Traditionally, such an approach directly contrasts with much of what First Cinema (American cinema or Hollywood), Second Cinema (independent or art house cinema), and Third Cinema (the cinema of the third world)[2] productions and theory present. Fourth Cinema (Indigenous or Native film), however, need not simply reject these other film frameworks. On the contrary, it grew from and works within and against these influences to include a variety of forms from documentary to narrative fiction films. Referencing, morphing, and reaching across all or some of these cinematic forms, Native film in North America moves forward in new directions.

Our text puts Native filmmakers, whose work represents the diversity of Native film, into intertextual conversation with academics working on the theoretical aspects of Indigenous film and teaching Native film in a variety of disciplines. The resulting dialogue across the pages of the collection opens a myriad of possibilities for engaging students with a number of ongoing debates in Indigenous film: about what Indigenous film is, who is an Indigenous filmmaker, and what Native filmmakers are saying about Indigenous film and their own work. We provide access to these complex dialogues by including multiple voices and approaches. Among those on the cutting edge of Native film research, our contributors provide pedagogical and theoretical methods for teaching Native films as well as offer insight into how the culturally specific aspects and ethics of being a Native filmmaker play out in film. A good number of our contributors are educators as well as filmmakers and storytellers; thus, they bring multifaceted responses to the questions asked above.

Choosing to highlight the individual voices and perspectives of our writers, rather than binding all by a common theory, allows our contributors' ideas of teaching, filmmaking, and writing to shine through. Part of our organizational strategy therefore includes constructing a framework that privileges some of the various, and often conflicting, perspectives about what is Native film. The question opens a debate deeply tied to issues of sovereignty and self-determination, the individual strands of which weave in and out of each other. Our goal is to create links between the essays and interviews across the framework in order to raise theoretical questions that promote new ways of thinking about Native and Indigenous film.[3] Like the Native storytelling styles evident in oral tradition narratives, Native writing, and Native film, these chapters cross genre and disciplinary boundaries, and are often highly personal.

The power of *Native Americans on Film* resides in the intertextual conversations that emerge via the tripartite structure of the book: the unique blending of theoretical (section 1), pedagogical (section 2), and personal voices (section 3). Our contributors bring their expertise as teachers, filmmakers, and writers to consideration of the theoretical and pedagogical. They are also some of the voices that have championed Indigenous film in the academic world within and over the last four decades. The interview section highlights a cross section of Native filmmakers instrumental to Indigenous media in the United States and Canada. The voices of pivotal figures in the development of Indigenous film, Sandy Osawa (Makah), Mona Smith (Dakota), and Shelley Niro (Mohawk), mingle across our pages with those of emergent filmmakers Randy Redroad (Cherokee), Blackhorse Lowe (Navajo), and Sterlin Harjo (Seminole/Creek) in speaking about their work and being Native filmmakers. Most compelling, however, is the refusal of all to be confined by Hollywood's representational strategies for depicting Native Americans. In fact, while the vast majority of our contributors refer to Hollywood in their essays or interviews, they move on to focus attention on Native film in North America.

Talking Back to the Hegemony of Cinema Representations

Because the power of First Cinema drives the film market, imbuing viewers with perceptions of what Native film should look like, the need to refuse stereotypical representations of Native peoples still exists in North America. And so we begin with First Cinema's representation of Native people as a site for exploring teaching strategies and as a catalyst for the Native film movement in North America.[4]

Native Americans and First Nations people make up roughly 1 percent of the population in the United States and 3.8 percent in Canada.[5] For a market-driven industry like Hollywood, such a small viewing demographic is invisible. While advocates in Hollywood supporting Indigenous filmmakers exist, it remains more profitable for Hollywood to continue reproducing the stereotypical images of Native people found in blockbuster period films set in the colonial period or the mid- to late nineteenth century, such as *The Last of the Mohicans* (1992) or *Dances with Wolves* (1990). Such productions tend to valorize the actions of the United States against Native nations during these nation-building eras. As a result they validate for viewers a skewed understanding of Native history, Native peoples, and what Native film is and should be.[6]

In addition, non-Native perceptions of Native peoples and what Native film should look like derive from a popular cultural history that predates cinema, tracing back to Christopher Columbus's and Amerigo Vespucci's journal entries describing the "Indians" they encountered: here, the relation to colonialism is direct. Their journals present clashing descriptions of fantastic images of docile, childlike Natives living in an Edenic landscape and images of cannibalistic, hedonistic peoples posing a distinct threat to European colonizing forces. Translated each subsequent generation from 1492 onward in a variety of popular culture formats, the images came to fit the political and social needs of the settler nations in their quest for colonial dominance and stability in North America.

The American film industry codified such representations into the movie western: the noble or ignoble savage, the pronoun-challenged Indian, the savage warrior, the female work drudge, the princess, the sexualized maiden, and the drunken Indian. Carole Gerster provides our readers with an approach to teaching about the historical persistence of these Hollywood stereotypes, using the seminal production for television, *Images of Indians* (1979), as a key text in "Native Resistance to Hollywood's Persistence of Vision: Teaching Films about Contemporary American Indians." As we know, Hollywood film introduced generations of viewers to, on one hand, rampaging hordes of Natives whose lack of individuality and character development ensure their savagery, as in *Drums along the Mohawk* (1939). On the other hand, viewers met peaceful characters willing to assimilate into white culture by giving up their sovereignty, as in *Broken Arrow* (1950), or encountered characters trying desperately to maintain their vanishing lifestyle, as in *Little Big Man* (1970) and *Dances with Wolves*. And, in the case of many westerns that promote cross-cultural love relationships, audiences watched the Indian maiden die, a cinematic move that ensures the destruction of further Indian generations. In the case of most of these examples, the western perpetuates the problematic tradition of using Indians as a backdrop for the telling of a white person's story.[7] Such a narrative structure, so key to the western's message of white American exceptionalism, is equally powerful as a damaging stereotype because it denies Native Americans agency to tell their own histories.[8] Gerster's strategy in teaching *Images of Indians* along with more contemporary films such as *Smoke Signals* (1998), *A Thousand Roads* (2005), and *In Whose Honor? American Indian Mascots in Sports* (1996) recontextualizes the hegemonic power of these stereotypes through American Indian perspectives and films.

Pedagogical work like Gerster's remains fundamentally important because contemporary First Cinema audiences continue to revel in nostalgia for the Wild West promoted by the western. As does Gerster, Angelica Lawson offers our readers pedagogical approaches for extracting stereotypes from a place of popular culture power through their positioning against films by Native filmmakers that illustrate realistic portrayals of Native peoples. In "Teaching Native American Filmmakers: Osawa, Eyre, and Redroad," Lawson shares strategies for teaching Native American film from an American Indian studies perspective. Detailed lesson plans provide readers with methods for contextualizing Native film within American film and American history. Lawson focuses on Sandra Osawa, Chris Eyre (Cheyenne/Arapaho), and Randy Redroad, drawing our attention to the work each has done to challenge the way non-Native viewers see Native people through documentary, shorts, and narrative fiction films. Her units emphasize visual literacy, which enables our understanding of the power of stereotypes and the significance of self-representation for Native filmmakers and their audiences.

The reality of historical trauma endured by Natives through the colonialist process so celebrated by Hollywood, and discussed by Gerster and Lawson, cannot be ignored. In effect, the continual consumption of these reified images of Indians validates a colonialist historic memory and denies critical acknowledgment of the lived reality of Native nations. These images also deny the fact that Native peoples survived the process and thrive as members of tribal, pan-tribal, and national communities. The ramifications of such continual validation of stereotypes on the lives of Native people are palpably felt outside the fantasy world of the theater. All too often, as our examples below exhibit, non-Natives frequently measure Native peoples against the ideal of an Indian they internalize from media;

this ideal forms the base of their reality of what an Indian should look like, act like, or be. Often, traumatic and long-lived effects on the lives of Native people result.

In *Wiping the War Paint off the Lens*, Beverly Singer (Tewa/Navajo) describes her experience in the public elementary school system as one that made her aware of her difference as a Native person going to school in Espanola, New Mexico. As she explains it, "Although I did my best to hide being different by learning to ski and play in the school band, I was identified as a 'squaw' in front of my classmates by a seventh-grade teacher."[9] Here, in "The Dirt Roads of Consciousness: Teaching and Producing Videos with an Indigenous Purpose," she illustrates for our readers still another level of the power of racializing representations. Singer shares her awakening to the inculcation of Native people into Hollywood's stereotypes during the filming of Warner Brothers' *Flap* at Santa Clara Pueblo in 1969. This experience eventually led her to the director's chair as a Native filmmaker and to the decision to omit Hollywood films about Native people from the courses she teaches. Her personal narrative about teaching and filmmaking lends dual experience to our pedagogical conversation and the scholarship begun with *Wiping the War Paint off the Lens*.

Similarly, coeditor Eric Buffalohead's (Ponca) own experience illustrates how stereotyping and mass media misrepresentation manifests in his daily life:

> As a Native person I am often frustrated by mainstream society's failure to recognize me without the benefit of stereotypes. Once discovered as Native, my childhood experiences included being asked where my Indian clothes were, if I lived in a tipi, and how much I liked riding my horse after school. During my adolescence, the tone changed from one of ignorant questioning to outright persecution. For instance, I was greeted regularly with a war whoop followed by "Hey, chief," with right hand raised in stereotypical fashion. This constant mocking of my culture led me to grow up a very angry person. Teaching a course about Hollywood images and their impact has served as therapy for my recovery to a state of nonanger. I have come to understand that Hollywood and other media sources in popular culture have created a situation in terms of Indian imagery where fantasy has replaced reality. We can't put all of the blame on Hollywood, though; the educational system in the United States is also to blame for this

> situation because of its lack of coverage of or completely ignoring of Native people in all facets of the curriculum.

Buffalohead's statement about popular cultural representations of Native Americans, the educational system failings, and our need as educators to "step up" provides the framework for *Native Americans on Film*. The pedagogical work done by our contributors reflects the expanding academic study of Indigenous film with its focus on Native voices and media autonomy. Their recontextualization of First Cinema through the use of Native filmmakers like Sandy Osawa, Chris Eyre, and Randy Redroad destabilizes the hegemony of Hollywood and refocuses us on the power of Native film to move forward toward self-determination in media representation.

Visual Sovereignty and Cinema of Sovereignty: Decolonizing Media

Indigenous communities and filmmakers globally respond through film against representations of them as exotic and vanishing peoples, as innocent or dangerous, or as colonized by more advanced settler cultures. Community media collectives such as Igloolik Isuma Productions, CEFREC and CAIB (Centro de Formacíon y Realizatión Cinematográfica and Coordinadora Audiovisual Indígena de Bolivia), the Chiapas Media Project, and individual filmmakers working within a community and across communities, reposition media articulation and power through the agency of voice and literally, by refocusing the lens.[10]

The underlying current of today's Native film and media movement emerged in the early 1970s, fueled by the civil rights era: a period marked by heightened Indian activism and the burgeoning of independent film and video in both Canada and the United States. As television documented important moments in U.S. Indigenous self-determination—the reclaiming of Alcatraz (1969–71), the Trail of Broken Treaties (1972), the takeover of Wounded Knee (1973)—and as the world became increasingly aware of Indigenous battles for equality and recognition, private and governmental organizations in the United States and Canada responded with institutional training, production, and distribution programs for film and television geared toward underrepresented groups, including Native Americans and First Nations peoples.[11] In Canada, the National

Film Board instituted its Challenge for Change program in 1969 in part to train Native peoples in filmmaking; in the United States, two NBC-sponsored programs provided Native-directed and Native-focused programming: *Indian Country Today* (1973) and the *Native American Series* (1974).[12] Native American and First Nations media activists' work also resulted in the founding in 1977 of the Native American Public Broadcasting Consortium (now Native American Public Telecommunications, Inc.), sponsored by the Corporation for Public Broadcasting and the Public Broadcasting Service to facilitate Native television programming in the United States, and the establishment of the Inuit Broadcasting Corporation in Canada in 1981, two organizations still producing Native media for a primarily Native audience.[13]

The hallmarks of Native film of this era include the documentary format and the highlighting of social and cultural issues facing Native communities, which fit with the structure of television and the programmatic focus of the 1970s media-funding initiatives. The groundbreaking documentaries of Alanis Obomsawin (Abanaki) for the National Film Board of Canada are primary examples from the era that continue to influence Native media today. Globally renowned for her social documentary style, Obomsawin works within the public media system to redefine how Canadians see and learn about marginalized First Nations peoples. She continues to provide Canadian viewers with films that privileged a Native perspective and bring to light issues facing First Nations people.

Obomsawin's work reflects the growing movement toward self-determination politically and in media for Native and First Nations people, which resulted in shifts of media autonomy and power. The decision of who tells the stories, what stories are told, and how these stories are told now resides in the hands of those who traditionally found themselves the subject and object of the camera's gaze. Thus, Indigenous film is anticolonial media based on self-determination that works to break down preconceived ideas about Indigenous people. The concepts of sovereignty and self-determination, the heart of the Indigenous film movement and media autonomy, promote the belief in Indigenous peoples' rights to represent themselves and their histories in ways that reflect their cultures, needs, and ways of telling.

The radical decolonizing of the image, the production, and the viewer that results from the work of Native filmmakers, writers, and producers grew out of Indigenous sovereignty and the global movement of

Indigenous groups. The movement demands recognition of Indigenous communities' inherent right as autonomous peoples whose nations, belief systems, use and stewardship of land, and worldviews predate those of the colonial settler-nations that surround them and whose policies have been that of forced assimilation or eradication.[14] While Indigenous peoples have resisted colonial oppression for centuries, after World War II, social movements formed around the world with clear articulations and political agendas for decolonization and social justice. They focus on reversing the effects of colonialism by reclaiming land and resources, cultural knowledge, languages, and Indigenous governance locally within countries and globally across nations. For instance, the pan-Indigenous collaboration of groups with their supporters have elevated Indigenous rights to the level of international law, pressuring the United Nations to recognize not only human rights but also Indigenous rights. In 2007, the United Nations and a majority of its constituents, with the glaring exceptions of the United States, Canada, Australia, and New Zealand, ratified the Declaration on the Rights of Indigenous Peoples. This act, as does the case of Bolivia's election for a second term of an Indigenous government, validates Indigenous rights.

In 1995, Jolene Rickard applied the activism of political Indigenous sovereignty to the realm of cultural production in her essay "Sovereignty: A Line in the Sand."[15] We see her assertion that the issue of sovereignty belonged not only to the political realm but to the cultural as well as tied to two terms, *cinema of sovereignty* and *visual sovereignty*. Both terms promote the belief in Indigenous people's right to represent themselves and their histories in ways that reflect their cultures, needs, and ways of knowing and telling. Randolph Lewis uses the term cinema of sovereignty to underscore the political aspect of sovereignty. In part, it includes Indigenous rights to access media; to expose racism and deception on the part of local, state, and federal governments in their dealings with Native peoples; to challenge public memory; and to refuse the stereotypes of the Indigenous primitive so cherished by First Cinema. Ultimately, according to Lewis, cinema of sovereignty means complete Indigenous autonomy over every aspect of production, no matter what the genre.[16] Michelle Raheja's term visual sovereignty emerges from the political to encompass Rickard's idea of the cultural.

In her chapter herein, "Reading Nanook's Smile: Visual Sovereignty, Indigenous Revisions of Ethnography, and *Atanarjuat: The Fast Runner*,"

Raheja explains visual sovereignty as a strategy of creative engagement and reformulation of Native representation through a variety of forms, traditional film forms as well as new media.[17] According to Raheja, visual sovereignty takes place at the individual and community level in an act of self-representation and media self-determination. Igloolik Isuma Productions, which produced *Atanarjuat,* brought Zacharias Kanuk's film and the concept of visual sovereignty to a global audience.[18] Based on an ancient Inuit oral tradition narrative and the stunning beauty of the Arctic, the cinematographic epic, according to Raheja, essentially inverted the ethnographic legacy of Robert Flaherty's *Nanook of the North. Atanarjuat* invites non-Inuit audiences in through subtitles, exquisite cinematography, and compelling storytelling. However, the filmic demand that the audience adapt to a visual pacing and attention to landscape that is intrinsically Inuit results in a displacing of non-Inuit viewers as the primary target audience and their culture as the cinematic norm.

Both cinema of sovereignty and visual sovereignty are aspects of media sovereignty: the act of controlling the camera and refocusing the lens to promote Indigenous agency in the media process and in their own image construction. As our preceeding summary on the hegemony of media representations illustrates, narrative First Cinema, and the western genre in particular, creates images of Indians from the point of view of non-Natives, and often in the service of reinforcing stereotypes and nationalist myths of manifest destiny and conquest. All too often, documentaries about Native peoples also participate in using the camera as a way to inform the viewer about Native Americans through an authoritative male voice-over that perpetuates an image of Native peoples as exotic objects of ethnographic interest. On the other hand, Native media, as Raheja's exploration of *Atanarjuat* indicates, deconstruct and challenge these types of disempowering mechanisms through Native-centered narratives, storytelling modes, and cinematic styles that privilege Native heritage, voice, aesthetics, and audience. As such it constitutes its own area, Fourth Cinema, within the First, Second, and Third Cinema framework. Fourth Cinema, a term coined by Māori filmmaker Barry Barclay, destabilizes a media hegemony that privileges a predominantly white, male, Eurocentric historical perspective that erases or rewrites the histories of those marginalized by dominant power systems.[19]

For Barclay, Fourth Cinema is linked to tribal identity, to a particular non-Western worldview and aesthetic, and to a sovereign gaze un-

Harjo's comment brings to the fore some of the very real issues involved in the naming and identity politics connected with Indigenous film. Clearly, the terms used to define it change depending on audience, identity, agenda, and political positioning.

While the majority of essays and interviews in *Native Americans on Film* provide a Native answer to the questions: What is Indigenous film? and Who is an Indigenous filmmaker? Sam Pack's chapter, "'The Native's Point of View' as Seen through the Native's (and Non-Native's) Points of View," offers reactions from non-Native and non-Navajo viewers. His use of viewer-response theories in comparing viewers' reactions to films about Navajos reminds us not only of the heterogeneous nature of Native film but also that insider/outsider positioning relative to a film's content determines its comparative value as Native or non-Native. Furthermore, the viewer's position from a Native cultural perspective may also determine if a film resonates as tribally valid. For example, a film may be an Indigenous film about Navajos, but that does not mean the community will receive it as a Navajo film.

Pack refocuses our attention on the debates in Indigenous film and Indigenous film studies to include non-Native perceptions, which leads us to another strand in the debates that are philosophically woven through *Native Americans on Film*: the role of the academic—both Indigenous and non-Indigenous—in the Indigenous film movement. Should academics be advocates, critics, historians, or a combination of these? The answer to this question differs across disciplines, but for those of us working from American Indian studies and interdisciplinary studies perspectives, it means working toward decolonization on all its levels, including the arts. As Jolene Rickard clarified in 1995, art as an apsect of culture is not divorced from issues of sovereignty: "Sovereignty in the border that shifts indigenous experience from a victimized stance to a strategic one." 33 So, while we might apply classic film analysis to film techniques used by Indigenous filmmakers—camera work, cinematography, lighting, editing techniques, motifs, storytelling strategies—in an Indigenous film course, we must also place each film in historical, cultural, and sociopolitical context. For example, questions that frame our content and methodologies include: Why is *Smoke Signals* such a breakthrough film in talking back to decades of Hollywood stereotypes? How does Alanis Obomsawin use memoir and documentary forms to foreground Indigenous activism in *My Name Is Kahentiiosta* (1995), and what are the historical politics tary film industry in "Dismantling the Master's House: The Feminist Fourth Cinema Documentaries of Alanis Obomsawin and Loretta Todd." As Gauthier elucidates, while Obomsawin's and Todd's approaches differ—Obomsawin employing more observational and participatory modes of documentary, Todd embracing a postmodern, poetic, and reflexive mode—both infuse documentary with an Indigenous aesthetic shaped by accountability and manifested through visual sovereignty. Gauthier's exploration into their work gives shape to what she calls "their unique feminist Fourth Cinema aesthetic as it responds to the [John] Griersonian tradition." Such an aesthetic includes an Indigenous women's gaze, a gaze that disrupts the traditional hierarchies of knowledge residing behind cameras pointed at Indigenous peoples. Their filmic points of view expose national histories of racism, position their Indigenous subjects to speak for themselves, and underscore Indigenous women's experiences through an intimate style that occurs only when cinematic sovereignty is achieved through the language of equals.

Similar to the ways in which Obomsawin and Todd reimagine Western cinematic traditions, Dana Claxton's multimedia productions decolonize Indigenous social memories in order to indigenize them. Carla Taunton describes it as Claxton intertwining "her Indigenous worldviews with contemporary Aboriginal realities to create a visual language that exposes legacies of colonization, critiques settler histories, and asserts previously silenced Indigenous perspectives." According to Taunton's "Indigenous (Re)memory and Resistance: Video Works by Dana Claxton," Claxton's critical reframing of history through documentary and popular culture media blends enables her to destabilize historical Canadian narratives, privileging contemporary and historical Indigenous voices as central to the narrative. Taunton argues that Claxton's videos are part of a process "rooted in sovereignty, self-determination, and survivance."[22] According to Taunton, Claxton's work is not simply about identity politics or historical trauma; it is about Indigenous survivance and the ongoing process of decolonization, self-determination, and reclamation of Indigenous stories as historic truths. The intimate and multimedia aspect of her work also reminds us of the permeability of media forms and the meshing of personal and community voice as testimonial in Indigenous film.

Survivance also aptly describes the media production of Mona Smith, a pathbreaking figure in Native film whose work often flies under the radar in Indigenous film studies. "My focus is not the media world; my focus is Indian country," Mona Smith tells Jennifer Machiorlatti in her interview "Video as Community Ally and Dakota Sense of Place." Smith's earliest films—*Her Giveaway: A Spiritual Journey with AIDS* (1989) and *Honored by the Moon* (1990)—indicate her local activism, examining Indian health issues, particularly HIV/AIDS and the needs of local Ojibwe and Dakota in Minnesota. Like Claxton's, Smith's work also takes a multimedia approach: interactive Web-based art, installation, and video woven with Native philosophy, history, and stories to highlight issues that affect her community. Smith's current works, including *Cloudy Waters* and the *Bdote Memory Map*, concentrate on the history of southern Minnesota and reflect the humor, passion, and traditions of the Dakota people.

The cross-pollination of documentary, installation, multimedia collage, tribal history, and social activism in Claxton's and Smith's productions illustrates an important point made by Beverly Singer, that "terms like 'avant-garde,' 'documentary,' or 'ethnographic' limit the understanding and information contained in Native films and videos, and they are not natural categories within our experience."[23] The result of choices made by Native filmmakers to merge approaches that will illustrate the story or message in the most appropriate way is work that claims the filmic form without fitting easily into traditional genres such as documentary. Instead, it reflects the intricate melding of the historical, political, social, artistic, and verbal aesthetics found intertwined in many Native cultural forms of expression.

Painter, photographer, and multimedia artist Shelley Niro offers a prime example of such artistry in her narrative film. Niro's work in the 1990s, along with Randy Redroad, Beverly Singer, Chris Eyre, Shirley Cheechoo (Cree), and Valerie Redhorse (Cherokee), helped propel independent Native multimedia and narrative film into mainstream consciousness in the United States and Canada. Niro's underscoring of storytelling, music, dance, community, and collective memory in works like *It Starts with a Whisper* (1992) and *Kissed by Lightning* (2009) brings lasting power to her work. Elizabeth Weatherford's interview with Niro, "The Journey's Discovery," teases out the brilliance of Niro's ability to combine elements of storytelling, performance art, and popular culture art forms in her films. *Honey Moccasin* (1998), "one of the first films to try to reinvent Native cinema in terms of pop culture, and to play with the ironies," Weatherford tells us, is "recognized as a modern Native film classic in its irreverence and its deep appreciation of the strength of community." Niro's insight into community and her sharp wit help deconstruct art and media stereotypes of Native people in refreshing and continually innovative ways.

The wide-ranging work represented by these filmmakers provides techniques for achieving cinema of sovereignty by employing visual sovereignty. We might also call this process Indigenizing film. In addition to those already mentioned, such approaches include: the act of listening and using the camera as an attentive witness; the engagement in cross-cultural dialogue that bridges different worldviews, historical realities, and cultural realities; and the weaving of multiple generic conventions (such as the horror film) to evoke mood and visceral reactions to historical and cultural material.[24]

Debates in Indigenous Film

The field of Indigenous film is an expansive global phenomenon in which regional and community aesthetics exist alongside pan-tribal/pan-Indigenous issues, highlighted in the work of groups as distantly located as Canada and Bolivia, Mexico and Australia. Thus, while some common trends exist across Indigenous films, such as issues of sovereignty and centering Native voices in the act of media representation, the resulting diversity in local productions refuses easy compartmentalization into any homogenous category. In "Dimensions of Difference in Indigenous Film," Houston Wood argues against attempts to utilize non-Indigenous film forms, such as genre, to generalize a unified pan-Indigenous method for thinking about Indigenous film. Rather, he explores the diversity across global Indigenous film projects. The importance of Wood's method resides in his construction of an Indigenous film continuum that expands Barclay's idea of Fourth Cinema. For Barclay, Fourth Cinema would "seek to rework the ancient core values to shape a growing Indigenous cinema outside the national orthodoxy."[25] Wood's proposal of an Indigenous film continuum that includes Indigenous filmmakers working across the four areas illustrates the problems of confining Indigenous film within particular parameters. It also highlights strands of the debates about who is an Indigenous filmmaker, what constitutes an Indigenous film, and who decides these matters—strands that filter through the essays and interviews in *Native Americans on Film*.

As is evident, naming Indigenous film necessarily embeds the politics of Indigeneity discussed above, and what it means to call oneself, or be called, Indigenous or Native or First Nations. The pan-Indigenous global activism for sovereignty illustrates one level of identity politics, which turns increasingly more complicated as we move from a pan-Indigenous to a tribally specific level. In the United States, for example, where treaties recognize the inherent sovereignty of tribal nations, but a legacy of laws and policies forcing assimilation continues to hinder full recognition of those rights, we see the complexity of nations-within-a-nation status play out in identity politics and membership status. This dilemma also raises an important question about who is considered Native. Is it a biological question or a cultural question? Or does it depend upon to whom you talk and the reason for claiming or recognizing inclusion?

Similar politics surround Indigenous film. The production of Indigenous or Native film, for some, is linked to tribal identity, to a particular non-Western worldview and aesthetics, and to a sovereign gaze unmediated by outside cultural aesthetics and agendas. This is what Barclay names Fourth Cinema. In 1991, Hopi filmmaker Victor Masayesva Jr. articulated these politics as having "accountability built into [the filmmaker]. . . . Accountability as an individual, as a clan, as a tribal, as a family member."[26] Fourth Cinema in the United States includes much of Masayesva's work, such as *Itam Hakim, Hopiit* (1984). It also encompasses productions done for a community that may or may not be sold or distributed outside that community or may be presented to viewers in ways that contradict the capitalist nature of the cinema industry—a screening that pays viewers to attend or provides free traveling shows to reservation communities.[27] Thus, what constitutes accountability depends on the filmmaker, the community or communities involved, and the focus of the work and its narrative. Importantly, in this context Indigenous film stays committed to Native worldviews, stories, or communities even if the work is shared with those outside the community.

Others, as Wood's chapter illustrates, expand Indigenous film to include productions by filmmakers who identify as Indigenous or Native but whose work embraces multiple audiences, both Indigenous and non-Indigenous. Alanis Obomsawin's and Sandra Osawa's documentary work fits into this definition, as does Arlene Bowman's (Navajo) and George Burdeau's (Blackfeet). However, to intertwine strands of the debate, their work also dovetails with the tribal- or community-specific aspects of Fourth Cinema. A larger framing of Indigenous film includes work by Native filmmakers that embraces a Hollywood narrative style. Our text showcases four in particular whose films destabilize the long-held misconception by many in Hollywood that there is not a substantial market audience for Native film: Sherman Alexie, Randy Redroad, Blackhorse Lowe, and Sterlin Harjo.[28]

Sherman Alexie (Spokane/Coeur d'Alene), well known for his novels, broke through Hollywood hegemony with the release of *Smoke Signals*, which he coproduced with director Chris Eyre. The film marked a decisive moment in Native cinema sovereignty as the "first major release feature" by a Native director since the silent period. Distributed by Miramax, it garnered critical acclaim at the Sundance Film Festival, where it debuted in 1998.[29] The film remains a staple example in college classrooms across the country of a pan-Indian film that takes on Hollywood's stereotypes and addresses them without alienating its non-Native viewers.[30]

While the importance of *Smoke Signals* as the "first feature film written, directed and acted by Native Americans to receive national distribution" cannot be denied,[31] it is Alexie's directorial debut film, *The Business of Fancydancing* (2002), that informs our conversations on Indigenous film and cultural identity. In "Geographies of Identity and Belonging in Sherman Alexie's *The Business of Fancydancing*," Amy Corbin calls our attention to Alexie's techniques that utilize a "nomadic viewing experience" as a destabilizing tactic that forces us to consider how we participate in representing, seeing, or imaging cultures. Corbin's text-centered reading of *Fancydancing* through the lens of cinematic geographies accentuates Alexie's experimentation with representing geographical space and the individual, as spaces, community, and viewer positioning in film shape him. Alexie's work refuses viewers safety in their cultural assumptions about what constitutes a Native film aesthetic and narrative. His multiple foci on issues of gender identity, alcohol and drug abuse, insider/outsider positioning, and social hybridity resist essentializing Native culture just as they defy a facile multiculturalism. For Native critics arguing that mixed-audience Indigenous films should focus on positive aspects of tribal culture to combat generations of negative imagery, Alexie's film represents a decidedly problematic approach. Thus, Alexie's film complicates the debates about accountability to community, particularly for those filmmakers with multiple communities whose Indigenous politics may differ considerably.

Less controversial, but no less poignant, Randy Redroad's films also focus on issues of identity and belonging across geographical space. In this respect, his award-winning early films, *Haircuts Hurt* (1992) and *High Horse* (1994), which mark his time in New York City, provide particularly clear comparison to *Fancydancing*. Redroad's first feature-length film, *The Doe Boy* (2001), garnered him national attention and illustrates his craft as a filmmaker, musician, and writer. Redroad's influence as a filmmaker lies in his ability to integrate stories of everyday people with social and political commentary on issues of identity, urban homelessness, poverty, and alcoholism, issues that bridge communities of viewers and yet contain subtle filmic moments of Native worldview. Marubbio's "Wrestling the Greased Pig" offers a personal perspective on Redroad's films and storytelling influences, his eclectic taste in films and, most importantly for this text, his opinions on the academic study of Indigenous film and the term *Native filmmaker*. As Redroad tells Marubbio, "I don't reject it [the term] as much as resist it. And I don't resist it, except in conversations with academics. In the personal realm, being a Native filmmaker means that I am one of the architects of an emerging cinema and part of a relatively small family of makers who, more often than not, support each other." His interview provides insight into the question raised by Alexie's work about what should be represented in Native film, hinting that there exists an assumption that particular values and ethics should emerge in Native films. Like Alexie, he refuses such essentialism and confinement of Native film to particular communities. He also opposes being confined as a filmmaker to making only "Indian" films, seeing himself as someone who makes films, many of which have Native characters. Redroad does clarify, however, that positioning vis-à-vis community and your choices as a filmmaker to work for your community or for Hollywood shape the type of Native filmmaker you are; the former involves a deeper level of responsibility, particularly if you are "speaking for your tribe and using traditional elements."

Similarly ambivalent about the label "Native filmmaker," Blackhorse Lowe and Sterlin Harjo exhibit an attitude common among many emerging Native filmmakers interested in narrative film who see themselves as influenced by First Cinema and home community, their films as products of their heterogeneous backgrounds, and themselves as participants in national popular cultural forms. Both filmmakers received national exposure for their films, which include, for Lowe, the feature film *5th World* (2005) and the short *Shisasani* (2009) and for Harjo, two feature films, *Four Sheets to the Wind* (2007) and *Barking Water* (2009). As do Redroad's, Harjo's and Lowe's films revolve around personal stories that, while regional (the Southwest for Lowe and Oklahoma for Harjo), engage the global through their references and influences. Joanna Hearne and Zack Shlachter provide us with a unique tandem interview with the two filmmakers in "'Pockets Full of Stories,'" which showcases their humor, connection to family and their regional locations, their filmic and popular culture influences, and their attitude toward such labels as Native filmmaker. As Harjo tells Hearne and Shlachter, "I have sort of a love-hate relationship with the whole 'Native filmmaker' thing. Sometimes I'm like, 'I hate this—what is this? What are you talking about?' But at the same time, I learn to be proud of it." Similarly, for Lowe the concept of being a Native filmmaker did not resonate until he began meeting others; it is this connection to other Native filmmakers who are doing similar work that makes him proud of the label.

Redroad's, Harjo's, and Lowe's interviews and comments on Native film lead us to another strand of the debates on Indigenous film: Who defines Indigenous or Native cinema? The dynamics involved in this are nuanced and complicated. Suzan Harjo articulates clearly two aspects of the debate and the politics of naming who is or is not an Indigenous filmmaker.

> Native Peoples have been so busy with stopping name-calling and reclaiming our traditional names that we haven't paid much attention to a name for ourselves collectively. This collective name issue is mostly for the benefit and convenience of non-Indians, so they don't have to deal with our individual tribal names. There are really only two things about Native film identity—the filmmaker and the subject. So, a film is either made by an Indian filmmaker or it's not. And, it's either about Native Peoples or it's not, whether or not the filmmaker is Native. If it's by an Indian filmmaker, then s/he can be identified by a Native nation (and if s/he cannot, then s/he is not a tribal citizen and should not be identified as a Native filmmaker). If the filmmaker is Māori, then say Māori, or any other tribal name identification.[32]

Harjo's comment brings to the fore some of the very real issues involved in the naming and identity politics connected with Indigenous film. Clearly, the terms used to define it change depending on audience, identity, agenda, and political positioning.

While the majority of essays and interviews in *Taking Back, Moving Forward* provide a Native answer to the questions: What is Indigenous film? and Who is an Indigenous filmmaker? Sam Pack's chapter, "'The Native's Point of View' as Seen through the Native's (and Non-Native's) Points of View," offers reactions from non-Native and non-Navajo viewers. His use of viewer-response theories in comparing viewers' reactions to films about Navajos reminds us not only of the heterogeneous nature of Native film but also that insider/outsider positioning relative to a film's content determines its comparative value as Native or non-Native. Furthermore, the viewer's position from a Native cultural perspective may also determine if a film resonates as tribally valid. For example, a film may be an Indigenous film about Navajos, but that does not mean the community will receive it as a Navajo film.

Pack refocuses our attention on the debates in Indigenous film and Indigenous film studies to include non-Native perceptions, which leads us to another strand in the debates that are philosophically woven through *Native Americans on Film:* the role of the academic—both Indigenous and non-Indigenous—in the Indigenous film movement. Should academics be advocates, critics, historians, or a combination of these? The answer to this question differs across disciplines, but for those of us working from American Indian studies and interdisciplinary studies perspectives, it means working toward decolonization on all its levels, including the arts. As Jolene Rickard clarified in 1995, art as an aspect of culture is not divorced from issues of sovereignty: "Sovereignty is the border that shifts indigenous experience from a victimized stance to a strategic one."[33] So, while we might apply classic film analysis to film techniques used by Indigenous filmmakers—camera work, cinematography, lighting, editing techniques, motifs, storytelling strategies—in an Indigenous film course, we must also place each film in historical, cultural, and sociopolitical context. For example, questions that frame our content and methodologies include: Why is *Smoke Signals* such a breakthrough film in talking back to decades of Hollywood stereotypes? How does Alanis Obomsawin use memoir and documentary forms to foreground Indigenous activism in *My Name Is Kahentiiosta* (1995), and what are the historical politics that led to the Oka crises represented in the film? What cultural information might we need to appropriately teach and also understand specific Indigenous storytelling strategies?[34]

> It seems likely to me that some Indigenous film artists will be interested in shaping films that sit with confidence within the First, Second and Third cinema framework. While not closing the door on that option, others may seek to rework the ancient core values to shape a growing Indigenous cinema outside the national orthodoxy. I hope that, in the not too distant future, some practitioner or academic will be able to . . . begin to talk on Fourth Cinema which begins at this very point, rather than ends on it.[35]

Māori filmmaker Barry Barclay's words mark the blossoming of an invigorating and meaningful movement in global media: a pivotal moment of change in which Indigenous worldviews, channeled through visual storytelling, share equal acceptance within, and in addition to, traditional Western cinematic traditions. It is a time that bears witness to Indigenous film studies, in all its forms, positioned centrally in academia alongside Western humanities and artistic traditions. Such a time will bring about a revolutionary moment when Indigenous film across First, Second, Third, and Fourth Cinema categories is valued as core to the overall education of all our people. This is a moment drastically different from our current era in which Indigenous film still is a topic or side area filtered through the traditions of Western humanities and film.

Barclay's hope manifests itself as an undeniable reality today in the growing number of Indigenous film artists who create "films that sit with confidence within the First, Second and Third cinema framework" or move toward Fourth Cinema. His hope also surfaces in the increasing global accessibility of their films and the expanding scope of film festivals.[36] In addition, we see the movement reaching into the film industry itself through projects such as the Sundance Institute's Native American and Indigenous Initiative and the Walt Disney Company's collaboration with the Institute of American Indian Arts to train Native students in all levels of film and television production.[37]

Barclay's desire for academic response has also been answered in the increasing number of college programs that focus on training Native filmmakers, the expansion of course offerings on Indigenous or Native film, the escalation of academic conferences with Indigenous film areas, and the engaging dialogues flourishing around the topic of Indigenous film.[38] As a result, the ongoing and very rich discussion includes the cultural and artistic aspects of Indigenous film, the continuum of reference for what constitutes Indigenous film and Indigenous filmmakers, and the categorization of Indigenous film by genre, approach, or placement within or across First, Second, Third, and Fourth Cinema categories.

Native Americans on Film participates in Barry Barclay's call to action for those of us working in academia to support Indigenous media sovereignty. We hear him speaking to the deconstruction of media hegemony just as Shohat and Stam do in defining multiculturalism as "seeing world history and contemporary social life from the perspective of the radical equality of peoples in status, potential, and rights. [Such an approach] decolonizes representation not only in terms of cultural artifacts—literary canons, museum exhibits, film series—but also in terms of power relations between communities."[39] Such visions do not absorb Indigenous creativity into a hegemonic whole; instead, they celebrate its multiplicities as equal parts of many autonomous ways of seeing, being, and expressing.

We see this moment calling for a volume that, as indicated by Barclay's words, explores the possibility of change through the confluence of voices working within the film movement itself and in Indigenous film studies. *Native Americans on Film* takes inspiration from these examples, bringing together the voices of Indigenous and non-Indigenous scholars and filmmakers whose theoretical ideas, pedagogical strategies, and lived experiences underscore the diversity of thought across critical and artistic production in the field. The book's structure allows for area study as well as ease in locating interviews, theoretical approaches, or teaching strategies. Section 1, "Theoretical Conversations," includes previously published theoretical articles to facilitate educators' and students' participation in the ongoing dialogue about what is Indigenous film. Section 2, "Pedagogical Conversations," provides an interdisciplinary array of strategies for teaching a variety of readily available Native films, and section 3, "Conversations with Filmmakers," offers interviews with filmmakers conducted especially for this volume. We preface each section with an introduction that summarizes the focus of each chapter and raises questions that emerge from their juxtaposition. Readers may choose to focus on one area and engage with the questions that arise from the conversations within that section, or they may choose to take one essayist's perspective and trace it through from the theoretical to the pedagogical to the individual level. Our inclusion of Native and non-Native voices in theoretical, pedagogical, and conversational forms about Native film aims at decolonizing ourselves as teachers, as learners, and as film viewers trained through primarily Western academic models. The juxtaposition of opinions and views between our theorists, teachers, and filmmakers reminds us that without the filmmakers' visions, there would be no Native cinema for academics to theorize and teach.

Notes

1. As this text goes to press, a number of works have been published recently that participate in a similar vision and are complementary to our work. These include but are not limited to Denise K. Cummings's edited volume, *Visualities: Perspectives on Contemporary American Indian Film and Art* (East Lansing: Michigan State University Press, 2011); Michelle H. Raheja's *Reservation Reelism: Redfacing, Visual Sovereignty, and Representations of Native Americans in Film* (Lincoln: University of Nebraska Press, 2010); and Sigurjón Baldur Hafsteinsson and Marian Bredin's edited volume, *Indigenous Screen Cultures in Canada* (Winnipeg: University of Manitoba Press, 2012).

2. Third Cinema applies generally to the emergence in the 1960s of films connected with the decolonization movements globally that proposed alternatives to commercial and auteuristic cinema. These cinematic forms often include social, cultural, and political critique, a commitment to access to media, and new modes of spectatorship.

3. The term *Native film* is generally used to refer to the group of filmmakers linked with the United States and Canada. It emerges out of a term from the 1990s, *Native cinema*, which applies to the film work of Native American and First Nations people. It includes a variety of forms, from documentary to narrative fiction films, that work within and against traditional First and Second Cinema forms, and are often marketed to multiple audiences. As Indigenous filmmakers around the world took up the struggle for media sovereignty, the terms *Indigenous cinema* and *Indigenous film* took center stage. Thus, academics, critics, and filmmakers alike utilize the terms *Indigenous film* and *Indigenous filmmaker* when the focus broadens more globally or when the politics involved necessitate the terms.

Both *Indigenous film* and *Native film* are used throughout *Native Americans on Film* depending on context. As editors, we use Native film generally to refer to the group of filmmakers linked with the United States and Canada that is the primary focus of the volume. We use *Indigenous film movement, Indigenous film,* and *Indigenous filmmaker* when our conversations take on the more global context, as it does with Houston Wood's chapter and M. Elise Marubbio's interview with Randy Redroad. Our writers use a combination of these terms depending on their training and identity; we support their choices by not editing these terms.

4. There are a number of good texts available for use in teaching about Hollywood's long history of misrepresentation of Native Americans in mainstream media and film. We recommend the following: Angela Aleiss, "A Race Divided: The Indian Westerns of John Ford," *American Indian Culture and Research Journal* 18.3 (1994): 167–86; Aleiss, "From Adversaries to Allies: The American Indian in Hollywood Films, 1930–1950" (PhD diss., Columbia University, 1991); Aleiss, "The Indian in Film," in *The Native American Almanac: A Portrait of Native America Today*, ed. Arlene B. Hirschfelder and Martha Kreipe de Montaño (New York: Prentice Hall, 1993); Aleiss, *Making the White Man's Indian: Native Americans and Hollywood Movies* (Westport, CT: Praeger, 2000); Gretchen M. Bataille and Charles L. P. Silet, *The Pretend Indians: Images of Native Americans in the Movies* (Ames: Iowa State University Press, 1980); S. Elizabeth Bird, *Dressing in Feathers: The Construction of the Indian in American Popular Culture* (Boulder, CO: Westview, 1996); Bird, "Tales of Difference: Representations of American Indian Women in Popular Film and Television," in *Mediated Women: Representations in Popular Culture*, ed. Marian Meyers (Cresskill, NJ: Hampton Press, 1999); Ralph E. Friar and Natasha A. Friar, *The Only Good Indian . . . The Hollywood Gospel* (New York: Drama Book Specialists, 1972); Jacqueline Kilpatrick, *Celluloid Indians: Native Americans in Film* (Lincoln: University of Nebraska Press, 1999); M. Elise Marubbio, *Killing the Indian Maiden: Images of Native American Women in Film* (Lexington: University Press of Kentucky, 2006); Beverly R. Singer, *Wiping the War Paint off the Lens: Native American Film and Video* (Minneapolis: University of Minnesota Press, 2001); Peter C. Rollins and John E. O'Connor, eds., *Hollywood's Indian: The Portrayal of the Native American in Film* (Lexington: University Press of Kentucky, 2003).

5. According to the U.S. Census Web site, in 2009 the number of those claiming Native American or Alaskan Native heritage was 1 percent of the national whole, which was listed as 307,006,550. See U.S. Census, http://quickfacts.census.gov/qfd/states/00000.html (accessed August 19, 2010). According to the Human Resources and Skills Development Canada Web page, in 2006 the Canadian Census indicated that 1,172,790 people claimed to be Aboriginals of Canada (First Nations, Métis, or Inuit)—3.8 percent of the population. See Human Resources and Skills Development Canada, http://www4.hrsdc.gc.ca/.3ndic.1t.4r@-eng.jsp?iid=36 (accessed August 8, 2010).

6. The Canadian film industry and Canadian public television have been more successful than the United States in introducing contemporary images of Native people, many of them created by and produced by First Nations filmmakers through such initiatives as the National Film Board of Canada's *Challenge for Change* series, the Native American Public Broadcasting Consortium/Native American Public Television, the Inukshuk Project and its creation, the Inuit

Broadcasting Company, the Aboriginal Peoples Television Network, and the Native American Entertainment Network. Canada's greater success is partially due to the larger number of First Nation peoples in relation to Canada's overall population, in contrast to the United States, where Native population figures are proportionally smaller. In addition, a visible lack of governmental funding in the United States over the last thirty years to promote Native film production and Native public television adds to the growing gap between the United States and Canada in supporting Native media.

7. We recommend Armando José Prats's work on this phenomenon. See "His Master's Voice(over): Revisionist Ethos and Narrative Dependence from *Broken Arrow* (1950) to *Geronimo: An American Legend* (1993)," *ANQ* 9.3 (1996): 15–30. Also see Prats, *Invisible Natives: Myth and Identity in the American Western* (Ithaca: Cornell University Press, 2002).

8. Recently there has been a modest release of both high- and low-budget mainstream films representing Hollywood and independent filmmakers marketed to youth and adult audiences in which Indians appear as primary characters as opposed to the traditional secondary character or sidekick: *Pocahontas* (1995), *Windtalkers* (2002), *The New World* (2005), and *Frozen River* (2008), for example. This trend hearkens back to the early silent period when films that focused on Indian stories and characters were quite popular and constituted a genre, separate from the western. Hundreds of these Indian films depict images and themes related to Indian subjects: some are romantic portrayals of Native American life, love, and noble spirit; others are decidedly unromantic in their negative portrayals of Native Americans as violent savages and distinct others to whites. Native American women were more prominently featured in these early films than at any other time in history, providing a blueprint of representation for future cinematic generations. However, by the mid-1920s, Indian films become a subgenre of the western, with its focus on the white male hero. Hollywood has never fully returned to narratives that privilege Native actors and scenarios, though occasional attempts are made with such films as Disney's *Pocahontas* and Terrence Malick's *The New World.*

There are a number of in-depth works on these early films. A few we recommend are Andrew Brodie Smith, *Shooting Cowboys and Indians: Silent Western Films, American Culture, and the Birth of Hollywood* (Boulder: University Press of Colorado, 2003); Joanna Hearne, "'The Cross-Heart People' Race and Inheritance in the Silent Western," *Journal of Popular Culture* 30.4 (2003): 181–96; and M. Elise Marubbio, "Death of the Squaw Man's Wife: The Politics of Cecil B. DeMille's Adaptations of Edwin Milton Royal's *The Squaw Man*," in *2003 Film & History: CD-ROM Annual* (Spring 2004).

For a good collection of commentaries against inaccurate media representations of Native Americans that date from the silent period through the mid-1970s, see Bataille and Silet, *The Pretend Indians*. The work also includes an annotated checklist of articles and books on popular images. Historical researchers will find that it pairs nicely with Friar and Friar's *The Only Good Indian*, which also includes an extensive appendix on Indian actors, white actors who played Indians, and film titles categorized by term. In addition, Angela Aleiss's work *Making the White Man's Indian*, sheds new light on the behind-the-scenes making of Hollywood films through her use of scripts, publicity materials, and published critiques.

9. Singer, *Wiping the War Paint off the Lens*, 30.

10. For more information on Latin America's Indigenous film movement, see Freya Schiwy's seminal work, *Indianizing Film: Decolonization, the Andes, and the Question of Technology* (New Brunswick, NJ: Rutgers University Press, 2009). Pamela Wilson and Michelle Stewart's edited collection, *Global Indigenous Media: Cultures, Poetics, and Politics* (Durham: Duke University Press, 2008), provides a well-rounded sample from around the world that focuses on topics such as aesthetics, activism, cultural preservation, and new media. Also see Elizabeth Weatherford, "Indigenous Visual Power: Film and Media in Latin America," *National Museum of the American Indian* (Spring 2010): 18–21.

11. Elizabeth Weatherford and Emelia Seubert, *Native Americans on Film and Video*, vol. 2 (New York: Museum of the American Indian, 1988), 7–8.

12. Singer, *Wiping the War Paint off the Lens*, 33–60.

13. For excellent historical background on Native film and media, see ibid., particularly 33–60 for this early period; and Elizabeth Weatherford's "Currents: Film and Video in Native America," in Weatherford and Seubert, *Native Americans on Film and Video*. Singer's text also provides background on individual programs and an extensive set of short biographies on Native filmmakers in chapter 4, "Native Filmmakers, Programs, and Institutions," and a discussion of early important works by seminal filmmakers such as Victor Masayesva Jr., Sandra Osawa, Randy Redroad, and Beverly Singer in chapter 5, "On the Road to *Smoke Signals*."

14. There are a number of valuable texts for understanding the various aspects of Indigeneity and Indigenous sovereignty globally: Joanne Barker, ed., *Sovereignty Matters: Locations of Contestation and Possibility in Indigenous Struggles for Self-Determination* (Lincoln: University of Nebraska Press, 2005); Ken S. Coates, *A Global History of Indigenous Peoples: Struggle and Survival* (New York: Palgrave Macmillan, 2004); Jeffery Sisson, *First Peoples: Indigenous Cultures and Their Futures* (London: Reaktion, 2005); and Wilson and Stewart's introduction, "Indigeneity and Indigenous Media on a Global Stage," to their *Global Indigenous Media*, 1–38.

15. Jolene Rickard, "Sovereignty: A Line in the Sand," *Aperture* 139 (1995): 50–59.

16. Randolph Lewis, *Alanis Obomsawin: The Vision of a Native Filmmaker* (Lincoln: University of Nebraska Press, 2006), 156–94.

17. Raheja's conception of visual sovereignty stems from concepts of sovereignty outlined by Jolene Rickard and Beverly Singer. See Rickard, "Sover-

eignty." Singer framed a similar idea in *Wiping the War Paint off the Lens* as "part of a social movement" she termed "'cultural sovereignty,' which involves trusting in the older ways and adapting them to our lives in the present" (2). For another articulation of this concept, see Joanna Hearne, *Smoke Signals and the Emergence of Native American Cinema*, forthcoming University of Nebraska Press.

18. Igloolik Isuma Productions founded itself around a particularly sovereign media mission to promote cultural knowledge, to tell Inuit stories locally and globally, and to provide training and jobs for the community. Through its mission, Igloolik Isuma Productions may offer the most powerful example of visual sovereignty and Lewis's cinema of sovereignty in the United States and Canada.

19. Barry Barclay, "Celebrating Fourth Cinema," *Illusions* 35 (Winter 2003): 1–11.

20. See Upstream Productions, http://upstreamvideos.com/wp/about-us/ (accessed October 11, 2010).

21. Sandra Sunrising Osawa, *Native Networks*, http://www.nativenetworks.si.edu/eng/rose/osawa_s.htm#open (accessed October 11, 2010).

22. *Survivance* is a term used by Anishinaabe writer and theorist Gerald Vizenor. It reflects the concept of Indigenous survival, perseverance, and an ongoing "active presence" that cannot be ignored. His work is foundational to American Indian studies and includes poetry, prose, screenplays, and memoirs and semiotic/activist theory. See Gerald Vizenor, *Manifest Manners: Post-Indian Warriors of Survivance* (Middleton, CT: Wesleyan University Press, 1994), 15.

23. Singer, *Wiping the War Paint off the Lens*, 2–3.

24. Schiwy's *Indianizing Film* examines how Indigenous film in South America embraces First Cinema generic forms, such as the horror film, within a narrative that is intrinsically Indigenous as a way to evoke particular visceral and cultural reactions from the audience. A number of North American narrative fiction films, Georgina Lightning's *Older Than America* (2008) in particular, also utilize aspects of the horror genre to evoke the feelings of fear and trauma that accompany memories of the boarding school eras for generations of Indigenous people.

25. Barclay, "Celebrating Fourth Cinema," 11.

26. As quoted in Steven Leuthold, *Indigenous Aesthetics: Native Art, Media, and Identity* (Austin: University of Texas Press, 1998), 1. Victor Masayesva Jr., along with other prominent figures in Native film such as Bob Hicks and George Burdeau, participated in the Two Rivers Native Film and Video Festival in Minneapolis. This seminal conference provided an opportunity for sharing ideas about Native media and the challenges Native filmmakers and video artists face in the marketplace. See also Steven Leuthold, "Social Accountability and the Production of Native American Film and Video," *Wide Angle* 16.1–2 (1994): 41–59.

27. As Barclay notes, it is unimaginable in First, Second, or Third Cinema

structures to imagine a free screening or to think that "the owners and the makers would actually pay people to come and watch the film, pay, for example, for their transport, pay for the venue and the print and the projectionist, and pay for a celebratory communal meal afterwards, at which speeches are made far into the night." This is what he sees as usual practice for Indigenous cinema in many areas of the world ("Celebrating Fourth Cinema," 10). Chris Eyre provides another example from the United States with his Rolling Rez Tour of his film *Skins* (2002), which offered free screenings on Indian reservations throughout the country. While his film would be considered by many to be Indigenous but not Fourth Cinema, his process of screening falls into Fourth Cinema ethics.

28. We also suggest the work of Chris Eyre, Valerie Redhorse, Shirley Cheechoo, Ian Skorodin (Choctaw), Roderick Pocowatchit (Comanche), and Georgina Lightning (Cree).

29. Singer, *Wiping the War Paint off the Lens*, 61.

30. For an excellent article on *Smoke Signals*, see Amanda J. Cobb, "This Is What It Means to Say *Smoke Signals*: Native American Cultural Sovereignty," in Rollins and O'Connor, *Hollywood's Indian*, 206–28.

31. Hearne, *Smoke Signals*. According to Hearne, "While other Native-controlled documentary and feature films came before and after *Smoke Signals*, its claim is substantively accurate, and the film has been taken up on these terms as an identifiable origin point in the unfolding history of Native media."

32. Suzan Harjo, e-mail correspondence on the question, "What is Indigenous film?" June 15, 2010.

33. Rickard, "Sovereignty," 51.

34. Kerstin Knopf's *Decolonizing the Lens of Power: Indigenous Films in North America* (Amsterdam: Rodopi, 2008) provides an excellent American Indian studies' and postcolonial studies' approach to Indigenous film analysis.

35. Barclay, "Celebrating Fourth Cinema," 11.

36. While there are many more film festivals in the Americas and globally doing this good cultural work, three in particular illustrate a long history of building alliances across national boundaries in the Americas, which is the focus of this text, and are notable for their commitment to celebrating a variety of Indigenous approaches to media across the cinematic traditions. The first Latin American Council of Indigenous Film and Communication's festival was organized in Mexico City in 1985. It is now known for innovative awards based on the creative process in filmmaking. (See Juan Francisco Salazar and Amalia Córdova, "Imperfect Media and the Poetics of Indigenous Video in Latin America," in Wilson and Stewart, *Global Indigenous Media*, 39–57.) Organized by the Film and Video Center of the Smithsonian National Museum of the American Indian in 1995, the Native American Film + Video Festival "is the first international indigenous film festival, founded to celebrate the creative energy of Native American directors, producers, writers, actors, musicians, and cultural activists, and all who support their endeavors." (See Native Networks, http://www.nativenetworks

.si.edu/eng/blue/nafvf_11.html [accessed August 8, 2010].) According to its Web site, the imagineNATIVE Film and Media Arts Festival, which was launched in 1999 in Toronto, Canada, as a global festival, "celebrates the latest works by Indigenous peoples on the forefront of innovation in film, video, radio, and new media . . . [that] reflect the diversity of the world's Indigenous nations and illustrate the vitality and excellence of our art and culture in contemporary media" (imagineNATIVE Film and Media Arts Festival, http://www.imaginenative.org [accessed August 8, 2010]).

For more information on the history of Native film festivals in the United States, see Singer's *Wiping the War Paint off the Lens*, which provides an overall history of the Indigenous media movement in the United States and Canada with reference to key filmmakers, organizations, and programs from the 1960s onward that have fueled the expansion of Indigenous film.

37. See the Sundance Institute's Web site and particularly its link to Native Forum: http://www.sundance.org/festival/film_events/native_forum.asp (accessed August 9, 2010). For more information on both the Sundance Institute's work with Native filmmakers and Disney's collaboration with the Institute of American Indian Arts, see Wilson and Stewart, *Global Indigenous Media*, 1–2.

38. In the United States the following conferences have created specific areas in the last decade dedicated to Indigenous or Native film: the Native American Indigenous Studies Association Conference, American Studies Association Conference, Society of Cinema and Media Studies, and various regional and national Popular Culture Association/American Culture Association Conferences.

39. Ella Shohat and Robert Stam, eds., *Unthinking Eurocentrism: Multiculturalism and the Media* (New York: Routledge, 1994), 5.

Section One

Theoretical Conversations

Introduction to Section One

At every good dinner party, numerous conversations take place that sometimes converge, sometimes overlap, and sometimes compete with each other. In the end, fragments of many become one great discussion. Thus it is in this section of the book, where a number of threads from conversations that have been happening throughout Native film circles come together in one fascinating theoretical dialogue. These include issues of representation and Indigenous voice, frameworks or models for Indigenous self-determination and media sovereignty, and the politics of defining what is Native/Indigenous film. The dialogue takes on complexity and nuance as our theorists' analyses of particular filmmakers and films uncover various manifestations of visual sovereignty and media self-determination occurring across the First, Second, Third, and Fourth Cinema framework and across genres.

We begin with a broad theoretical look at the complicated question of what is Indigenous film, a question at the heart of Indigenous film studies and important to understanding the wide variety of often contradictory answers given by theorists, filmmakers, viewers, and distributors. We then narrow our focus to analyses of particular work by Native and First Nations filmmakers working within and against the First and Second Cinema structures that have so long defined Native representations from the outside. What surfaces is a highly diversified manifestation of Barry Barclay's vision of Indigenous filmmakers working across the cinematic traditions and the development of theoretical approaches that allow us to articulate the sovereigntist approaches at work in Native films as they participate in media decolonization. Beverly Singer points out in *Wiping the War Paint off the Lens* that Western film terminology is often arbitrary and irrelevant to Native film and video because it confines our understanding of the information within the films and videos to a Western-centric worldview.[1] Our theorists illuminate the ways in which Indigenous filmmakers subvert and/or combine cinematic genres and approaches with Indigenous aesthetics and storytelling practices to refocus the power of film in the favor of Native peoples.

Houston Wood's provocative chapter "Dimensions of Difference in

Indigenous Film" provides a starting point from which to discuss global, national, and local responses to Indigenous film. His outlining of five dimensions of difference that he sees globally across films marketed as Indigenous productions raises questions of what is Indigenous cinema and who defines it. Wood's piece provides filmic examples with community response but also complicates and perhaps critiques the idea of an easy solution through his Indigenous–non-Indigenous film continuum, which positions completely Indigenous productions in polar opposition to non-Indigenous productions. While not all academics or filmmakers agree with Wood's continuum or the reasoning behind his placement of particular works and filmmakers, his ideas provide an intellectual starting point for understanding the debate about what is Indigenous film.

Narrowing from the global to a North American focus, Michelle Raheja contributes to Wood's conversation through an analysis of the Indigenous model used by Igloolik Isuma Productions. Her chapter, "Reading Nanook's Smile: Visual Sovereignty, Indigenous Revisions of Ethnography, and *Atanarjuat: The Fast Runner*," raises the idea of visual sovereignty, which embeds Indigenous epistemology into the visual work. She sees visual sovereignty as "a creative act of self-representation that has the potential to both undermine stereotypes of Indigenous peoples, and to strengthen the 'intellectual health' of communities in the wake of genocide and colonialism." Her chapter illustrates how Zacharias Kunuk's film *Atanarjuat* talks back to and subverts Robert Flaherty's *Nanook of the North*, a silent-period film heralded for its ethnographic documentation of Inuit people that had ongoing residual effects on the representation of Native people.

Likewise, Jennifer L. Gauthier's chapter explores the ways in which First Nations filmmakers Alanis Obomsawin and Loretta Todd commit to creating documentaries that "seek to empower First Nations people through giving voice to the voiceless, bearing witness to Canada's acts of racism, and challenging official history." Gauthier's "Dismantling the Master's House: The Feminist Fourth Cinema Documentaries of Alanis Obomsawin and Loretta Todd" provides close readings of the work of Obomsawin and Todd to illustrate their techniques for Indigenizing documentary and infusing it with a Fourth Cinema essence, one that includes the act of listening and using the camera as an attentive witness; the engagement in cross-cultural dialogue that bridges different worldviews, historical realities, and cultural realities; and the weaving of multiple generic conventions to evoke mood and visceral reactions to historical and cultural material. The cultural work done by both filmmakers, like that of Igloolik Isuma Productions, embodies Masayesva's conceptualization of Native media as being accountable to Native peoples, their history, and their stories (see introduction).

Providing a slightly different example coming from art house cinema, Carla Taunton highlights the ways in which Dana Claxton's multimedia productions take on the important cultural work of decolonizing Indigenous social memories in order to Indigenize them. Taunton's "Indigenous (Re)memory and Resistance: Video Works by Dana Claxton" explores the ways in which Claxton critically reframes our readings of history through a juxtaposition of traditional documentary forms, such as archival photographs and films, with strategically placed personal interviews and popular cultural texts such as iconic Western imagery, national and Indigenous monuments, burlesque, and popular music. As Taunton's approach illuminates, such a process destabilizes historical Canadian narratives through the foregrounding of Indigenous voices and realities, both past and present.

The concepts of self-determination and visual sovereignty emphasized in the first three chapters of this section also illuminate another concept popular in American Indian studies: that of *survivance*—a term Taunton borrows from Gerald Vizenor to describe Claxton's work.[2] The underlying currents found in the productions of all the filmmakers presented by our theorists are Indigenous survivance and the continual decolonization of media through media sovereignty, reclamation, and healing through storytelling.

The dialogue that emerges across the four chapters in this section illuminates the very real complexities involved in understanding the burgeoning world of Indigenous film as it talks back to ethnographic, documentary, and Hollywood narrative cinema while simultaneously participating in the traditional Western cinematic traditions. What may have started as reactions to non-Native representations of Native peoples evolves into a multiopinionated, multifaceted, politicizing discussion about Indigenous film. These chapters raise a number of questions that are worthy of further consideration. One set of questions revolves around the issue of identity: Who is an Indigenous/Native filmmaker? What is the role of an Indigenous/Native filmmaker? Who are his or her audience? Is it a global community, a pan-Indian community, or a tribally specific community? Should heritage dictate the type of films one makes? Who represents whom? What are the ethical choices involved in working in the mainstream film industries? What ethical choices must be made when working for a Native or Indigenous community?

Another set of questions focuses on the concept of sovereignty: How is sovereignty applied to Native and Indigenous media? Whose voice is foregrounded? Who speaks for whom? Who controls the product? Who is the audience? Does participating in a filmic conversation on sovereignty confine a filmmaker within the dichotomy of colonialist discourse on sovereignty?

A third set of questions weaves between the aforementioned and pertains to the multiple levels of poetics and politics that are Native film: Is there a Native aesthetic and should we even be asking that question at this point in the development of Native cinema history? Does the creation of a Native cinema ghettoize Native filmic/media visions? Or is Native cinema now so enormous a field that it cannot be confined by the term? Where are Native and Indigenous film situated in regard to national cinemas? When do particular examples of Native film break away from the Native cinema label and become subsumed by independent cinema or Hollywood cinema?

Notes

1. Beverly R. Singer, *Wiping the War Paint off the Lens: Native American Film and Video* (Minneapolis: University of Minnesota Press, 2001), 2–3.

2. Gerald Vizenor, *Manifest Manners: Post-Indian Warriors of Survivance* (Middleton, CT: Wesleyan University Press, 1994), 15.

Dimensions of Difference in Indigenous Film

Houston Wood

> We all belong to the story of our people.
>
> —John Trudell, *A Thousand Roads*

Indigenous feature films exhibit so much diversity that it is impossible to generalize about them. Thinking about the collection of Indigenous films as a whole, then, calls for a focus on their differences rather than on their similarities. Many of these films, for example, employ mostly Indigenous people as cast and crew, while many do not. Some adapt traditional cultural practices to filmmaking, but others follow Western production schedules. Many emphasize distinctively Indigenous content, and yet an increasing number do not. The editing and narrative structure of some Indigenous films mimic older oral traditions; many Native features, however, are plotted like mainstream commercial films. Production values are high in some Indigenous features and low in others.

This chapter explores some of the most significant dimensions of difference found in Indigenous films while drawing on examples from films made by dozens of peoples spread around the world. A concluding section examines how this remarkable diversity disturbs attempts to use non-Indigenous ideas as a basis for analyzing Indigenous cinema. The range of differences also makes it unlikely, perhaps impossible, to develop a single Indigenous perspective able to adequately engage with all the work in Indigenous filmmaking now being produced across the globe. The diversity of Indigenous films presents not one but a multitude of separate alternatives to hegemonic commercial filmmaking.

Indigenous Personnel

Great variation exists not only in the Indigeneity of directors, writers, cinematographers, editors, and other members of production crews, but even among the actors who work on films labeled Indigenous. Toa Fraser's *Naming Number Two* (aka *No. 2* [2006]) is a particularly interesting example of the complexities associated with personnel issues. Fraser, a Fijian partly raised in New Zealand, wrote and directed this film, which focuses on a the character of a Fijian matriarch. *Naming Number Two* covers a single day as this matriarch attempts to supervise a traditional feast during which she hopes to pass on the legal title to her house while simultaneously keeping important secrets from her children and grandchildren. Ruby Dee, an African American actor, plays the Fijian matriarch, while the roles of her children and grandchildren are taken mostly by Māori actors. International film festival audiences found few problems with this casting, but when the film was shown in Fiji, the largely Indigenous Fijian audience hissed and booed. It was evident to them that an African American woman and Polynesian actors were not Fijian.

Most audiences outside Fiji, of course, will neither notice nor much care about the differences among Polynesian and Melanesian actors. Outsider audiences, too, are little concerned when an origin story like that of Paikea, the *Whale Rider*, closely connected with one Māori tribe, is acted by people from other Māori tribes who have no genealogical connections to the whale story. In North America, similarly, Indigenous films often rely on actors with various tribal affiliations to tell stories rooted in specific places and tribes. Still, it is good to keep in mind that Indigenous peoples in Fiji, New Zealand, North America, and elsewhere will have different expectations about who may, and may not, pretend onscreen to be one of them.

Different peoples, too, have different expectations about how much of a production crew must be Indigenous in order for the film to seem to belong more to their community than to the commercial circuits of feature films. In many places, first and early Indigenous productions have required substantial assistance from outsiders while, simultaneously, local communities have asked—and sometimes even required—that they be provided training so that subsequent work can be done by the Indigenous people themselves. One impressive example of this occurred with the production of *Ten Canoes* (2006). Though the film was made with substantial contributions and funding from outsiders, the production process was used as an opportunity to teach Indigenous Ramingining community youth technical skills so that future productions would be less dependent on non-Indigenous crews. Planned spin-offs from this training include projects (1) to teach older teens how to shoot, record, and edit video;

(2) to rehabilitate a moribund closed-circuit television station previously abandoned in Ramingining; and (3) to record as many as possible of the traditional Ganalbingu songs that remain.[1] Similar apprenticing strategies have been used during film shoots in Bolivia, Canada, Mexico, and New Zealand.

Though I consider the labels of Indigenous and non-Indigenous films to be opposing poles on a single continuum, pioneering Māori filmmaker Barry Barclay recommends an alternative approach, one that is at once simpler and stricter. Barclay argues that only the dimension of creative control should be used in choosing whether to label a film Indigenous. So Barclay maintains, for example, that *Whale Rider* (2001) is not an Indigenous film since Niki Caro, its director and screenwriter, is not Indigenous.[2] Barclay's criteria would also lead to the exclusion of *Ten Canoes* from the list of Indigenous films, since Rolf de Heer, a non-Indigenous man, is *Ten Canoes*' credited screenwriter and its codirector. Barclay would also have problems labeling *Before Tomorrow* (2007) as an Indigenous film since this Igloolik Isuma coproduction has a non-Inuit, Marie-Hélène Cousineau, as its codirector and coscreenwriter.

Barclay is surely correct that creative control of the final cut is very important in determining whether a film should be called Indigenous. Important, too, however, are factors associated with production methods, film content, and story structure. Māori director Lee Tamahori had creative control of both *Once Were Warriors* (1994) and the James Bond vehicle *Die Another Day* (2002) but, because of their very different actors, content, and story structure, only the former is widely considered to be an Indigenous film. Similarly, Māori director Taika Waititi's (née Cohen) Academy Award–nominated short film, *Two Cars, One Night* (2003), features Māori actors and so seems clearly to be an Indigenous film, while Waititi's later feature film, *Eagle vs Shark* (2007), is likely to seem Indigenous only to those few who know much about this film that does not appear onscreen.

When there are disputes over whether a film should be labeled Indigenous, it seems best to allow the community being represented to decide. So, for example, though directed by a non-Indigenous director (Stephen Johnson) and produced by the Australian Children's Television Foundation, *Yolngu Boy* (2001) tells an Indigenous story using Indigenous actors. It has been widely embraced by the Yolngu people of Australia's northeast Arnhem Land and can thus, it seems to me, rightfully be labeled an Indigenous film. Similarly, if the Māori of the Ngati Porou tribe accept *Whale Rider* as their own, then it, too, is Indigenous.

Indigenous Productions

Indigenous filmmakers frequently rely on their people's distinctive ways of working. Many Indigenous approaches to film production are thus, not surprisingly, quite different from the ways of working associated with commercial cinema.

Differences often manifest themselves even in preproduction. So, for example, Vilsoni Hereniko reports that as he developed ideas for *The Land Has Eyes* (2004), he went back to the island of Rotuma where he had grown up "and I would stand up in the kava circle and tell them the story, act by act. Then I'd ask the people for their reactions and I'd incorporate some of their suggestions into the script."[3]

A similar preproduction process was used on the other side of the world by the makers of *Atanarjuat: The Fast Runner* (2002). The film's official Web site explains, "First we recorded eight elders telling versions of the legend as it had been passed down to them orally by their ancestors. Isuma's team [the production company] of five writers then combined these into a single detailed treatment in Inuktitut and English, consulting with elders for cultural accuracy and with our Toronto-based story consultant, Anne Frank. This same bi-cultural, bilingual process continued through the first and final draft scripts."[4]

Once production begins, working with Indigenous actors also often requires working in culturally appropriate ways. Some Rotumans, for example, were reluctant to perform in *The Land Has Eyes*, as to do so violated the island value of humility. Hereniko overcame these objections by appealing to another Rotuman value, one emphasizing the importance of personal connections and mutual obligations. Rotuman Voi Fesaitu explained, "Vili [Hereniko] came and asked me to try out for the part of Hapati, but I rejected it, refused it. Then we started to discuss it and I found out it's something I had to handle because it's between me and him, so I took the part."[5] As Hereniko's neighbor and cousin, Fesaitu decided personal obligations outweighed the value of humility.

Alan Howard reports that during the shooting of *The Land Has Eyes*, Rotumans sometimes confused pretense with reality. People wanted to continue with their lives, to talk or make other noises and distracting

The Land Has Eyes screened on a hospital veranda in Rotuma. (Courtesy of Alan Howard)

movements while cameras were rolling. Such disturbances sometimes had to be accepted as parts of the shots. In addition, though many of his non-Rotuman crew members did not understand the necessity, for one scene Hereniko produced a real feast, as he knew that for most Rotumans "there was no clear separation between acting and being at a wedding, and at a wedding you are fed, and fed well."[6] Trying to film the wedding without food could have led to an end to further production.

Large-budget as well as smaller-budget Indigenous films can be shaped by the customs of the people for and about whom they are made. *Atanarjuat: The Fast Runner* cost nearly $2 million (Canadian) and, as mentioned earlier, relied on the Inuit community even in its preproduction phase. The shoot itself employed mostly Igloolik Inuit as cast and crew, in part because only natives of the region could be expected to care for themselves and to survive in the frequently extreme subarctic conditions. As filming proceeded, director Kunuk reports,

> All the heads come together, we talk about what it's going to be like and understand each other at length; if we're going to do a scene where tents are—we ask each other "Are they right?" It's everybody's job to get it right, and so we all talk about it: "Should that be there?" "No—I think it should be there. Oh, let's get Anele to tell us where it is." (Chuckle.) We just work like that. And of course, all the actors come from our own little community, and you just tell them when they have to get into their characters and they do. I have very little directing to do. Because the script is already written and people know what to do. I just tell them "start" and "stop" and "wrap" and that's about it.[7]

Indigenous productions often require different sorts of performances from actors from what is common in non-Indigenous cinematic productions. The Aboriginal actors and crew who made *Ten Canoes*, for example, labored to re-create onscreen an entire way of life that more knew through stories and photographs than through direct experience. The photographs had been made in the mid-1930s by the white anthropologist Donald Thomson. Prints of a few of his several thousand plates had found their way back to the Yolngu at Ramingining and been reappropriated as a legacy from the ancestors who lived in what some now call the "Thomson Time." Much of *Ten Canoes* is in black and white precisely because it is widely understood that life in the Thomson Time unfolded in black and white.

Freya Schiwy describes how production practices like those used in Australia and Canada's Northwest Territories were developed independently among Indigenous video makers in Bolivia associated with CEFREC (Center for Cinematographic Training) and CAIB (Organization

Paddling a bark canoe in *Ten Canoes.*

of Indigenous Audiovisual Communicators of Bolivia).[8] Schiwy explains that media productions in Indigenous Bolivia are also commonly organized around principles of reciprocity rather than through wage labor. Even non-Indigenous people who assist or who, like Schiwy, wish to research these media productions must first be woven into the community's webs of reciprocity. Outsiders may be required to assist, for example, in aiding in the distribution of the finished videos. These strategies help maintain what Schiwy describes as the continuing co-presence of both capitalist and reciprocal economies across the rural Andean highland region.

The CEFREC-CAIB community illustrates how Indigenous practices can shape postproduction and also the distribution of Indigenous films. Most of their documentary and fiction videos are distributed to villages throughout the region through existing systems of trade exchange. Some are also sold in existing markets and to foreign NGOs, scholars, festivals, and academic institutions. Increasingly, however, Schiwy reports, Indigenous Bolivian video makers have become wary of allowing their work to circulate as commodities in the global marketplace. There are concerns about who should receive the payments—the video makers or the communities shown? Disagreements arise as well about whether the stories and images in these videos should be allowed to leave the villages in which they are rooted. In 2006, the CEFREC-CAIB video makers decided they would no longer sell their films, at any price.

Few other Indigenous filmmakers have made this choice to restrict sales and distribution, but most do share the Andean filmmakers' desire to provide easy and first access to the communities represented in their films. So, for example, Chris Eyre brought his film *Skins* (2002) to eleven Indigenous communities across North America by creating the Rolling Rez Tour 2002. Eyre offered the film for free viewing inside a large mobile cinema trailer transported from place to place by a semitruck. Audiences sat in luxury seats to watch this film made especially for them.[9]

Most Indigenous filmmakers, of course, lack the resources to create special tours and traveling theaters for their films. Most, especially in Anglo-American settler nations, have to trust that Indigenous people will find their way to watching through the usual distribution channels of film festivals, theaters, rentals, and television. The continuing growth of DVD rentals via mail and of film downloading via broadband Internet connections may one day make it easier to distribute Indigenous films to specialized audiences.

From pre- through postproduction and distribution, then, there is tremendous variation in how Indigenous peoples make and share their films. This is yet another area where it seems fruitless to try to generalize about the archive of Indigenous films.

Screening Indigenous Content

Indigenous filmmakers have made hundreds more documentaries than feature films, in part because producing a documentary is generally cheaper and easier, but also because many filmmakers want most to carefully record the unique cultural practices of their people. Feature films can also represent these practices, of course, but documentaries can do it while less encumbered with the requirements associated with offering a unifying story. Some Indigenous features, nonetheless, emphasize carefully photographed sequences that seem ethnographic. Films like *Atanarjuat: The Fast Runner*, *Seven Songs from the Tundra* (1999), and *Ten Canoes*, for example, seem aimed at helping strengthen and perpetuate precontact traditions. The effect of recording these details can be like that described by an Igloolik elder upon viewing *Atanarjuat: The Fast Runner*. He commented, "We strongly believe this film has helped in keeping our traditional way of life alive and to our future generations it will make them see how our ancestors used to live."[10]

Some Indigenous feature films work at the other extreme. They seem determined to avoid showing behaviors that might emphasize differences between Indigenous and non-Indigenous peoples. *Beneath Clouds* (2002), *Samoan Wedding* (2004), and *Smoke Signals* (1998), from Australia, New Zealand, and North America, respectively, are geographically diverse examples of this approach. Most Indigenous feature films lie somewhere between these extremes. Films such as *Radiance* (1998), *Skins*, and *Whale Rider* linger on a few sequences of distinctive practices but seldom so long that outsider audiences become aware they are witnessing an unfamiliar practice.

Indigenous feature films can include significant Indigenous content merely by casting Indigenous people in prominent roles. Non-Indigenous filmmakers have historically avoided placing Native peoples in these roles, even when the characters onscreen were supposed to be Indigenous. So Dolores del Rio and Debra Paget famously played Polynesian women in, respectively, the original (1932) and the remake (1951) of *Bird of Paradise*. Even decades later, Trevor Howard in *Windwalker* (1980) and various Disney animators in *Pocahontas* (1995) were still assuming they could represent Native Americans better than these Indigenous peoples could represent themselves. The favorable reception of such Indigenous features as *Ngati* (1997), *Ofelas/Pathfinder* (1987), and even *Once Were Warriors* rested to some extent on their pioneering casting of Indigenous actors to play leading roles in films telling Indigenous stories.

In addition to cultural practices and actors, Indigenous films may include a third content element, an Indigenous language, one that has seldom, if ever, been heard before onscreen. *Ten Canoes* relies on several Aboriginal languages; *Sonam, the Fortunate One* (2005) uses the Monpa dialect of India's Himalayas; *The Land Has Eyes* puts Rotuman onscreen for the first time. Māori, the language of *The Māori Merchant of Venice* (2001), had been spoken occasionally in several earlier films, but Don Selwyn's version of Shakespeare's play was the first feature entirely in this Indigenous language. Pei Te Hurinui Jones had translated the play into Māori in 1945. Selwyn worked for ten years to get a film version made. "When I was going to school they brought Shakespeare in to colonise me," Selwyn explains; "now I've put it into Māori language I've colonized Shakespeare."[11]

Shylock with a knife in *The Māori Merchant of Venice.*

Filming in an Indigenous language may discourage wide distribution in English-speaking countries, where audiences avoid movies with subtitles. Still, as mentioned, many Indigenous filmmakers make their films primarily for their own people, foregrounding their Indigenous language in hopes the film will assist in that language's preservation. Sometimes, of course, non-Indigenous filmmakers use Indigenous languages, too, generally in efforts to make their films seem more authentic. So *Windwalker,* for example, uses an English-language voice-over and non-Indigenous actors, but the characters all speak either Cheyenne or Crow. Mel Gibson uses Mayan for similar purposes in *Apocalypto* (2006), hoping to coax audiences into mistakenly believing that they are witnessing a Mayan story.

Non-Indigenous languages are now the first language of many Indigenous peoples. The Māori in *Once Were Warriors* or in *Whale Rider* are no less Māori for speaking English, just as the actors in *Smoke Signals* represent authentic Coeur d'Alene people while speaking English quite as much as if they spoke an Indigenous tongue. Still, it is likely that bilingual Indigenous people will increasingly emphasize their Indigenous languages in the feature films they create. Since many Indigenous languages are currently under threat, in part from the dominance of non-Indigenous media, spotlighting Indigenous languages in feature films can help new generations honor and speak the languages of their ancestors. I do not think anyone, however, would want to claim that a film is less Indigenous because its actors do not speak an Indigenous language. On the other hand, *Windwalker* or *Apocalypto* do not become Indigenous films merely because they rely on Indigenous languages. Degree of Indigenous-language use will just have to be one more of the many dimensions of difference displayed by both Indigenous and non-Indigenous films.

In addition to content differences across cultural practices, actors, and languages, Indigenous films also differ in the degree to which they dwell on Indigenous landscapes, seascapes, symbols, and other related iconography. In many instances, outsiders will not even recognize when significant Indigenous scenes are being shown. Panning across a particular landscape in an Indigenous feature film, for instance, may seem to mainstream audiences as yet another stereotypical establishment shot or an attempt to show the beauties or harshness of nature. These same shots may be seen by Indigenous people as images of their ancestors, or as invocations of spirits or gods, or as a wordless retelling of historical events.

So, for example, while most audiences think it is about two contemporary Indigenous youths, *Beneath Clouds* may also be viewed as a story about Australia's Aboriginal landscape, particularly as connected to a specific cliff; as the film describes it, white "farmers chased all the blackfellas up there a long time ago. They just shot them and pushed them off. Now, no one gives a shit. I suppose they've got their own shit to worry about." Later, beneath this cliff, the two Aborigine protagonists, Lena (Dannielle Hall) and Vaughan (Damian Pitt), confront police officers, contemporary manifestations of those earlier murdering farmers. Lena's surprising subsequent actions are motivated in part by her new understanding of the powers inherent in that site, but audiences who do not recognize that the Aboriginal past persists in places may find her choices unbelievable or, perhaps, "out of character."

Many Indigenous people beyond Australia similarly experience their own places as living stories that contain themselves, families, ancestors, and clans. So, for example, Navajo director Blackhorse Lowe lingers on the western United States' plains landscape in *5th World* (2005) in ways much like director Ivan Sen does in *Beneath Clouds*. Non-Indigenous viewers of *5th World* may share the experience of the reviewer who complained, "Rather than introducing anything as revolutionary as, say, a plot, Lowe gives us endless shots of desert landscapes and blue skies. . . . Something does eventually happen in *5th World,* but it's more than an hour into the film—and the film's only an hour and 15 minutes long. By then it's too late."[12] For viewers who cannot recognize that "the land has eyes and teeth, and knows the truth," as Hereniko's Rotuman characters say in *The Land Has Eyes,* the content of some Indigenous films may, indeed, seem "tiresome." Indigenous filmmakers and viewers, however, likely expect to see their narratives "inscribed on the landscape," as Tongan writer Epeli Hau'ofa explains is common in Oceania. Hau'ofa argues that preservation and study of these landscapes are important to the Indigenous people of the Pacific much as books, libraries, museums, and monuments are important to Oceania's continental colonizers.[13]

Feature films that emphasize Indigenous places are often foregrounding a type of content that only the initiated see. Yet it is clear there are Indigenous feature films, too, at the other end of the continuum, which place their Indigenous characters firmly within non-Indigenous landscapes. *Grand Avenue* (1996) and *Naturally Native* (1998), for example, similarly emphasize that Native Americans continue to be Indians even when living entirely within urban landscapes. An ocean away, two recent New Zealand–made films, *Naming Number Two* and *Samoan Wedding,* correspondingly examine diasporic Pacific Islanders, respectively from Fiji and Samoa. The loss of connection to homelands is part of the stories that all four films tell, but none of them suggests that new generations should try to return to or reclaim their ancestors' land- and island-rooted lives. In their treatment of Indigenous landscapes, symbols, and related content, then, Indigenous features once again exhibit more differences than commonalities.

Screening Indigenous Storytelling Forms

Content and form are notoriously interconnected and confusing concepts; still, it seems useful briefly to consider form separately from content, especially since Indigenous films sometimes mystify audiences accustomed to Western film forms. An emphasis on places, discussed above, is one striking form found in many Indigenous films. These films may, in addition, exhibit Indigenous storytelling forms (1) through translating culture-specific oral tales; (2) by focusing more on groups and communities than on individuals; (3) in presenting time as multidirectional rather than as linear; and (4) through relying on styles of shot selection and editing that differ from dominant film preferences. In each of these four manifestations of form, however, as we shall see, there is so much variation among Indigenous films that it does not seem accurate to claim that any one form characterizes most Indigenous films.

Oral Storytelling Onscreen

Māori filmmaker Merata Mita maintains that "film is very close to an oral tradition."[14] Film invites speech and gesture, so, Mita suggests, translating Indigenous storytelling traditions to film is much easier than translating them to other introduced forms, especially to forms such as print, which reduce the richness of speech to one-dimensional, linear writing. Some Indigenous peoples thus may be able to move their storytelling traditions directly from speech to film, without intermediary steps involving writing and reading.

Freya Schiwy describes this process in the many onscreen fictions produced by Indigenous Andean video makers associated with CEFREC-CAIB in Bolivia. Schiwy maintains these videos adapt Western filmmaking conventions in the service of Andean oral-visual traditions that predate colonialism.[15] Similarly, on the other side of the world, Pacific Islanders Sean Mallon and Pandora Fulimalo Pereira point to the many ways that an older, preliterate, pictorial iconography based in tattooing, jewelry, mat and quilt making, as well as in Indigenous architecture and dance, can guide Pacific Islander filmmakers adapting older visual storytelling traditions to the new screen media.[16]

Atanarjuat: The Fast Runner provides a well-known example of an attempt to translate an oral tale to the screen. Zacharias Kunuk and his collaborators began with an existing allegorical tale, a story Kunuk says "has been passed down from generation to generation. . . . It was taught to me as a little child and I never forgot it."[17] Most of *Atanarjuat* comes directly from the older tale; even the changes made in the ending have been explained as a continuation of the common practice of maintaining multiple versions of oral tales.

Other Indigenous filmmakers have also adapted older stories but revised them for situations associated with more recent times. The opening of *The Land Has Eyes* retells an oral tale, then moves on to near contemporary times, the 1960s, to establish the relevance of this story for a modern Rotuman girl. Marcelina Cárdenas, in her Quechua-language *Llanthupi Munakui/Loving Each Other in the Shadows* (2001), uses a similar mixing of the oral and the modern in an attempt, as she says, to present "the myths and legends of our Quechua existence in a new form of storytelling."[18]

On the other end of this continuum of difference, there are also many Indigenous filmmakers who make little or no use of precinematic oral or visual traditions. Both those who use new media to revitalize older storytelling traditions and those who make films with no traces of culture-specific traditions contribute to the body of Indigenous films.

Collective Stories

At least since Fredric Jameson's well-known introduction of the concept of third world allegory in "Third-World Literature in the Era of Multinational Capitalism," there has been a tendency to interpret non-Western films as if they illustrate stories about entire peoples.[19] While Euro-American protagonists represent individuals, it is said, most third world and Indigenous films should be understood allegorically; their characters represent not autonomous individuals but whole nations and peoples. Allegorical films generally do not develop characters or plots with the complexity common to nonallegorical films. Audiences, then, who do not recognize the allegory in an Indigenous film may judge it as simplistic or underdeveloped. The same film, however, may resonate deeply for viewers who recognize that the history of an entire Indigenous people is being shown.

One can interpret any film allegorically by seeing any one actor as representing not a particular character but, as an example, the proletariat, as in Sergei M. Eisenstein's *Battleship Potemkin* (1925), a self-consciously allegorical film. Darrell Varga has produced just such a thoroughly allegorical reading of *Atanarjuat.* The film is not what it seems on the surface to many, a tale about individuals involved in a revenge adventure, Varga claims, but rather should be understood as offering a moral lesson about the importance of community over individuals.[20]

Even a film such as Chris Eyre's *Skins* can be interpreted allegorically. Nonallegorically inclined audiences would view *Skins* simply as the story of two very different brothers, Rudy and Mogie, living sharply diver-

George Washington cries at the conclusion of *Skins.*

gent lives on the modern Pine Ridge Reservation. Interpreted as allegory, however, the story is less about two individuals than about one Native people. In the spectacularly cinematic ending, when Rudy throws paint across the Mount Rushmore image of George Washington, the resulting long red tear marks no particular pain, not for Mogie's recent death, nor for Rudy's culpability in that death. Rather, the tear, like the film itself, speaks a collective story, a collective grief.

We should be very careful with such allegorical interpretations, however. As critics of Jameson have pointed out, there is something reductive and even condescending about expecting third world and Indigenous films to work allegorically. Some Indigenous films may be allegorical, but surely many others are not. Here we have yet one more dimension of difference across the archive of Indigenous films.

Temporality

Just as Western modernity helped produce a decline in allegorical narratives so, too, has modernity encouraged an exclusively linear conception of time. Western films may sometimes toy with alternative temporalities, but most generally fall back on stories of what Catherine Gallagher labels a linear "undoing."[21] Films such as *Back to the Future* (1985), *The Ter-*

minator (1984), and *Star Trek: Deep Space Nine* (1993) show characters going backward in time to try to undo the past in order to alter the future. These films assume that time flows only one way; a change in the past will thus lead along a single path to determinate consequences. Even a film such as *The Matrix* (1999), while alluding to alternative temporalities, ultimately ties its narrative together by positing a single linear temporality. A more recent spate of commercial and independent films, beginning perhaps with *Pulp Fiction* (1994) and including later releases such as *Memento* (2000), *Eternal Sunshine of the Spotless Mind* (2004), and *Babel* (2006), experiment with temporalities while not attempting any fundamental assertions about the possibly fundamental illusion of linearity.

Indigenous storytelling traditions, however, frequently embrace alternative temporalities, sometimes by offering circular or spiral views, and sometimes by suggesting that, as Lilikalā Kame'elehiwa says of Hawaiian time, the past is out in front leading the present into the future. "It is as if the Hawaiian stands firmly in the present, with his back to the future, and his eyes fixed upon the past, seeking historical answers for present-day dilemmas."[22]

Before there were Indigenous films made by Indigenous peoples, Jorge Sanjinés tried to develop techniques for representing an Indigenous Aymaran sense of time in films. As, for example, John Mowitt notes, while it principally tells the story of a 1967 massacre, Sanjinés's *El coraje del pueblo* (The Courage of the People [1971]) is framed by a sequence drawn from an earlier, 1942 massacre.[23] Showing the earlier massacre first at the beginning of *The Courage of the People* serves to introduce the later massacre; at the end of *The Courage of the People*, showing this earlier massacre a second time points to the circularity of time while, as Schiwy points out, emphasizing that the community has and will survive by offering continuing resistance to such attacks.[24]

Some North American Indigenous feature films have also explored multidirectional temporal perspectives. *Smoke Signals* weaves together parallel events on Fourths of July that are decades apart. The film integrates these multiple time periods so thoroughly that it seems to end simultaneously in 1976, 1988, and 1998, while also suggesting there are no endings—or beginnings—in Coeur d'Alene Indigenous time. *Ten Canoes* uses very different editing and narrating strategies to also mingle three time periods, one contemporaneous with the film audience and narrator, another associated with the Thomson Time frame tale, and yet another with the first Aboriginal ancestors who emerged as time itself began. As with *Smoke Signals*, the effect in *Ten Canoes* is to suggest that Indigenous time is not linear.

And yet, once again, we should not expect all Indigenous films to avoid linear narratives. Alternative temporalities may be more common among Indigenous peoples than among contemporary non-Indigenous peoples, but this does not imply that Indigenous filmmakers can or should only make films rooted in their ancestors' senses of time.

Shot Selection and Editing

Probably more has been written about the shot selection and editing of Indigenous films than about any other element of Indigenous cinematic form. Here again, some claim that a desire to present a specifically Indigenous sense of time and place leads filmmakers to adopt styles of cinematography and editing seldom seen in commercial cinema. Some analysts claim, for instance, that Indigenous filmmakers show a preference for medium to long shots. Close-up views are rejected, it is said, because they force an unnatural intimacy on people that is very different from what is common in their daily lives. Close-ups, too, some claim, tend to emphasize individuals rather than the communities and groups that are the real subjects of Indigenous feature films.

An absence of close-ups, however, is not characteristic of the majority of Indigenous films. Also, an increasing proportion of films are being shot for viewing on smaller screens, such as for television and home viewing. This means that preferences for long and medium shots will likely increasingly fade even for Indigenous filmmakers who have preferred them in the past. Close-ups generally work better for smaller-screen viewing than do medium and, especially, long shots.

Long takes, uninterrupted shots from a single camera, are another form that has frequently been said to be particularly common among Indigenous films. As the anthropological filmmaker David MacDougall points out, any editing of shots, of whatever scale, cuts into fragments what participants themselves experience as continuous.[25] Long takes are thus sometimes claimed to replicate the experience of cultural insiders better than shots edited to compress and otherwise alter filmed events. *Atanarjuat: The Fast Runner*, *The Journals of Knud Rasmussen* (2006), and other works by Igloolik Isuma Productions are often cited as examples of an

Indigenous embrace of the long take. Such diverse films as Navajo director Blackhorse Lowe's *5th World* and the Aborigine *Ten Canoes* also lend some support to the view that Indigenous filmmakers find long takes especially effective. Just as many or more Indigenous filmmakers, however, use long takes no more frequently than do non-Indigenous filmmakers. Indeed, according to Schiwy, the very Andean Indigenous people Sanjinés aspired to represent more accurately through developing his long-take "integral sequence shots" now control the cameras themselves and rely on editing and other techniques that Sanjinés explicitly denounced.[26] Correspondingly, the pioneering Indian political action film *Tushka* (1996) exerts much of its power through frequent and sometimes frenetically edited short takes.

The Sacred Aesthetic

There is yet one further element of form that deserves special mention. Just as some mistakenly claim that frequent depictions of landscapes and emphases on long takes characterize Indigenous films, so others say these films typically manifest onscreen the power of ancestral, spiritual, and other unseen beings. The much-respected and pioneering Hopi filmmaker Victor Masayesva Jr. has said, for example, "There is such a thing as an Indian aesthetic, and it begins in the sacred."[27] Though support for this view can be found in many older Indigenous feature films, recent Indigenous films more often break with this tradition. Films such as *Four Sheets to the Wind* (2007), *Mile Post 398* (2007), *Naming Number Two*, and *Samoan Wedding* may presage a type of secular film that Indigenous filmmakers in settler communities will increasingly make if the integration of Indigenous and non-Indigenous peoples becomes more common. Even in their engagement with the spiritual, then, Indigenous feature films may be becoming too diverse to support any single characterization.

Varied Production Values

Production values are a fifth dimension of difference found in Indigenous films. Some Indigenous films cost millions of dollars, employ experienced crews and actors, rely on elaborate sound and lighting apparatuses, and often shoot scenes on custom-built sets. The result is polished screen images like those shown in Hollywood films. *Once Were Warriors, Whale*

Rider, and *Ten Canoes* are examples of Indigenous films with high production values. Films such as *The Journals of Knud Rasmussen*, *Pathfinder*, *The Land Has Eyes*, and *Smoke Signals* also offer fairly polished scenes, though they do not show off their expensiveness onscreen in the manner of high-end Hollywood films. Further down the continuum of production values are films such as *Beneath Clouds*, *The Business of Fancydancing* (2002), and Barry Barclay's two features *Ngati* and *Te Rua* (1991).

Many Indigenous features exhibit even less of the polish that even a small budget and some professional crew members provide. Films such as the Navajo *5th World*, the Quechua *Llanthupi Munakui/Loving Each Other in the Shadows* and the Aymara *Los angeles de la tierra/Angels of the Earth* (2003), and the Nenets *A Bride of the Seventh Heaven* (2001) were shot with little more equipment than that which thousands of amateurs around the world today rely on in shooting and editing their own home movies.

Production values in themselves are not, of course, the sole predictor of audience engagement. Low production values can, in fact, sometimes work in a filmmaker's favor, as uneven lighting, audio, editing, and similarly inexpensive effects are sometimes associated with "realism," with films that supposedly present the world more as it is actually experienced by its participants than do more expensive films. This sense of reality associated with inexpensive techniques has been exploited by some Indigenous filmmakers who wish to present perspectives that are different from Hollywood's versions of human experience.

The absence of high production values often makes little or no difference to Indigenous audiences hungry to see their own stories onscreen. Many of the short and feature films made by Indigenous people in Latin America have had a strong impact on their local audiences even though, as Schiwy observes, their "visual aesthetic is closer to home video and television" than to commercial films.[28] The pleasure in at last seeing people who look, speak, and act like themselves onscreen can dwarf concerns about the sophistication of the representations being shown. The fact that such a feature film exists at all, after so many decades in which non-Indigenous outsiders controlled most media, can make even the "crudest" Indigenous feature film into an exhilarating viewing experience. Some films by Indigenous people probably will continue to follow commercial trends toward increasingly expensive productions. And many, likely, will not. Important, effective Indigenous films have been and doubtless will continue to be made along all points of the continuum of production values.

Eurocentric Aesthetics

Reviewing these five dimensions of difference underscores the extraordinary diversity to be found in Indigenous films. Even more diversity may well emerge as more Indigenous peoples turn to filmmaking. The range of differences makes it impractical to seek a single perspective for thinking about all Indigenous films. At the least, no such pan-Indigenous perspective should be constructed from ideas rooted mostly in Anglo-European traditions. To do so would be to once again deny Indigenous people the right to interpret and represent themselves.

The peculiarity of using outsider ideas to guide thinking about Indigenous film becomes evident if one considers how this method would work in reverse. Suppose, for example, that the Māori wrote books and sponsored film festivals that evaluated contemporary Anglo-European movies on the basis of how well they fit into Māori traditions of visual representation; or, similarly, suppose that the Hopi produced articles and reviews judging the worth of Hollywood blockbusters from a perspective grounded in centuries of Hopi storytelling. Most audiences would probably declare that Māori and Hopi traditions do not provide sensible criteria for understanding and evaluating European-based cinema. Nonetheless, as Native American poet and anthropologist Wendy Rose explains, just such an ethnocentric perspective grounds most Euro-American thinking about Indigenous art. Euro-American audiences assume that their culture has provided them with a universal viewpoint that makes them "uniquely qualified to explain the rest of humanity, not only to Euroamerica, but to everyone else as well." Rose connects this universalizing way of understanding Indigenous art, including films, within a broader "matrix of contemporary Eurocentric domination."[29] Such an ethnocentric perspective suppresses the probability that much Indigenous art and film rest within cultural traditions that may be incomprehensible to outsiders.

Indigenous films might, at first glance, seem to represent a possible exception to the dangers of conceptual Eurocentrism. Filmmaking, after all, depends on Western technologies, and so all films, wherever produced, might seem amenable to analysis using Western ideas. I suspect not, however, for technologies do not enter new cultures bearing restrictions on their use. Quite the opposite: when new technologies are adapted, new cultures generally forge unique uses that reflect the characteristics of the adopting cultures. So, for example, the colonists' introduction of domesticated horses led to numerous innovative adaptations by different Indigenous peoples across North America. And, similarly, after World War II, the introduction to California of the Hawaiian technology of *he'e nalu* produced, within a few decades, a massive global sport and industry, surfing, that exhibits far more characteristics of its adapting than its originating culture.

In the same way, Indigenous filmmakers frequently adapt film technologies to reflect their own culture's preexisting visual and storytelling traditions. Many—though not all—Indigenous films are thus better understood as instances of specific older visual and oral Indigenous arts than as expressions of aesthetic traditions associated with Western films.

Concepts and experience based on Western aesthetics and cinema can thus as often mislead as help. While it may therefore sometimes be useful to draw upon some Euro-American concepts, it seems best simultaneously to keep open the possibility that each Indigenous film may be different not only from commercial and national cinemas but also from other Indigenous films. Though most feature films commonly work to correct and undermine non-Indigenous cinemas, they do this work in very different ways.

Looking at Indigenous films from across the globe also reveals how difficult it will be to develop inclusive concepts or a pan-Indigenous perspective that provides a unified Indigenous way of thinking about this diverse work. Indigenous peoples on all continents share a common history of more or less successful resistance to modern invasions, genocides, colonialisms, and imperialisms. Many thus share somewhat similar political goals. Contemporary Indigenous cultures, however, at least as manifested in the feature films reviewed in this chapter, seem too different to be reduced to a single category or genre or to be analyzed from a single point of view.

In an important sense, then, while there are an increasing number of Indigenous films, it may seldom be useful to claim there is such an object as Indigenous film. Indigenous peoples are not now creating a unified alternative to the hegemony of commercial cinema but are rather, through film, demonstrating their ability to remain the peoples they have always been, peoples rooted in abundantly distinctive places, customs, and ancestors. The diversity of Indigenous films offers not so much a challenge to non-Indigenous cinema as a reminder of the rich possibilities of what it can mean to be human.

Notes

Reprinted with the permission of the publisher, The Continuum International Publishing Group. Originally published in Houston Wood, *Native Features: Indigenous Films from Around the World* (New York: The Continuum International Publishing Group, 2008). Unless otherwise noted, all photographs are from the author's collection.

1. These and other projects are described on the official *Ten Canoes* Web site, http://www.vertigoproductions.com.au/10canoes.htm (accessed March 27, 2012).

2. Barry Barclay, "Open Letter to John Barnett," *Onfilm*, February 2003, Online Editorial Archives, http://www.archivesearch.co.nz/ViewEditorial.asp?EditorialID=9301&pubcode=ONF (accessed November 16, 2006).

3. Hereniko, quoted in Alan Howard, "Presenting Rotuma to the World: The Making of the film *The Land Has Eyes*," *Visual Anthropology Review* 22.1 (2006): 76.

4. http://www.atanarjuat.com/production_diary/index.html (accessed March 27, 2012).

5. Voi Fesaitu, quoted in Howard, "Presenting Rotuma to the World," 79.

6. Ibid., 82.

7. Kunuk, interview by Michelle Svenson, *Native Networks*, April 1, 2002, http://www.nativenetworks.si.edu/eng/rose/kunuk_z_interview.htm" (accessed on March 27, 2012).

8. Descriptions in following paragraphs are drawn from Freya Schiwy, "Selling Out? Indigenous Media, Ayni, and the Global Market" (paper presented at the annual meeting of the Society for Cinema and Media Studies, Chicago, March 8, 2007); see also Schiwy, "Decolonizing the Frame: Indigenous Video in the Andes," *Framework* 44.1 (2003): 116–32.

9. *Rolling Res*. This documentary is included with the DVD for *Skins*.

10. Quoted in Faye Ginsburg, "Screen Memories: Resignifying the Traditional in Indigenous Media," in *Media Worlds: Anthropology on a New Terrain*, ed. Faye Ginsburg, Lila Abu-Lughod, and Brain Larkin (Berkley: University of California Press, 2002), http://www.ucpress.edu/books/pages/9048/9048.ch01.html (accessed March 27, 2012).

11. Don Selwyn, quoted in Michele Hewitson, "Man Who Colonised Shakespeare," *New Zealand Herald*, November 19, 2005, http://www.nzherald.co.nz/section/1/story.cfm?c_id=1&objectid=10355929 (accessed January 23, 2008).

12. Eric D. Snider, review of *5th World*, directed by Blackhorse Lowe, *eFilm Critic.com*, January 24, 2005, http://efilmcritic.com/review.php?movie=11274 (accessed March 20, 2012).

13. Epeli Hau'ofa, "Epilogue: Pasts to Remember," in *Remembrance of Pacific Pasts: An Invitation to Remake History*, ed. Rob Borofsky (Honolulu: University of Hawaii Press, 2000), 460.

14. Mita, interview by Karin Williams, *Merata Mita*, VHS, directed by Jeff De Ponte (Honolulu: Pacific Islanders in Communications, 1997).

15. Schiwy, "Decolonizing the Frame."

16. Sean Mallon and Pandora Fulimalo Pereira, "Pacific Art Niu Sila: Introduction," in *Pacific Art Niu Sila: The Pacific Dimension of Contemporary New Zealand Arts* (Wellington, New Zealand: Te Papa, 2002), 7–20.

17. Kunuk, quoted in Doug Alexander, "Zacharias Kunuk Q&A," *Geographical* 74.4 (2002): 106.

18. Quoted in Cristina Veran, "Art & Unrest in the Andes," *Colorlines*, Summer 2004, http://colorlines.com/archives/2004/07/art_unrest_in_the_andes.html (accessed March 27, 2012).

19. Fredric Jameson, "Third-World Literature in the Era of Multinational Capitalism," *Social Text* 15 (1986): 65–88.

20. Darrell Varga, "*Atanarjuat: The Fast Runner*," in *The Cinema of Canada*, ed. Jerry White (New York: Columbia University Press, 2006), 225–33.

21. Catherine Gallagher, "Undoing," in *Time and the Literary*, ed. Karen Newman, Jay Clayton, and Marianne Hirsch (New York: Routledge, 2002), 11–30.

22. Lilikalā Kame'elehiwa, *Native Land and Foreign Desires* (Honolulu: Bishop Museum, 1992), 22.

23. John Mowitt, *Re-Takes: Postcoloniality and Foreign Film Languages* (Minneapolis: University of Minnesota Press, 2005).

24. Schiwy, e-mail message to author, July 29, 2007.

25. David MacDougall, *Transcultural Cinema* (Princeton: Princeton University Press, 1998), 205.

26. Schiwy, "Decolonizing the Frame," 124. See, for example, *Jorge Sanjinés y grupo Ukama, Teoría y práctica de un cine junto al pueblo* (Mexico City: Siglo XXI Editores, 1979).

27. Masayesva Jr., quoted in Steven Leuthold, *Indigenous Aesthetics: Native Art, Media and Identity* (Austin: University of Texas Press, 1998), 194.

28. Schiwy, "Selling Out? Indigenous Media, *Ayni*, and the Global Market." Presentation at the Society for Cinema and Media Studies Conference, Chicago, IL (March 8, 2007).

29. Wendy Rose, "The Great Pretenders: Further Reflections on Whiteshamanism," in *The State of Native America: Genocide, Colonization, and Resistance*, ed. Annette Jaimes (Boston: South End, 1992), 406.

Reading Nanook's Smile

Visual Sovereignty, Indigenous Revisions of Ethnography, and *Atanarjuat: The Fast Runner*

Michelle H. Raheja

> I don't think you can make a good film of the love affairs of the Eskimo . . . because they never show much feeling in their faces, but you can make a very good film of Eskimos spearing a walrus.
>
> —Robert Flaherty (1949)

Toward the beginning of Robert Flaherty's *Nanook of the North* (1922), Allakariallak, the Inuit actor who portrays the titular hunter in the film, is introduced to a gramophone by a white trader.[1] Having never seen such a device before, the putatively naïve Nanook inspects all sides of the machine, touches it, laughs at it, seems to ask the trader about its operation, and subsequently bites the record in a haptic effort to understand this new technology. In this well-known scene, the viewer takes these onscreen actions as a cue that Nanook is both unfamiliar with Western technology (and therefore oblivious to the camera's gaze in recording his actions) and primitive (only a guileless person would respond to advances in sound technology—especially in the silent era—with levity). Yet while a non-Inuit audience might register Nanook's smile as a marker of his alterity and childlike nature, Fatimah Tobing Rony asserts, "recent research has shown that the Inuit found Flaherty and the filmmaking a source of great amusement . . . from the Inuit point of view he may be seen as laughing at the camera."[2]

It is tempting to read resistance into films like *Nanook,* created by an amateur white filmmaker formally trained as a mining specialist, that do not seem to permit much, if any, Indigenous agency, especially if the critical apparatuses necessary to read humor as a playful and powerful way of deconstructing audience expectations and the vast matrix of Native American (mis)representations have yet to be fully articulated or understood within their unique cultural contexts.[3] And, since resistance as a category deployed by various colonized peoples is not created equal in all

Nanook (Allakariallak) at the trading post in *Nanook of the North*. (Reproduced courtesy of the Robert and Frances Flaherty Study Center, Claremont, CA)

situations but is located along a spectrum of political and social efficacy, Nanook's response might register one thing to his non-Inuit audience and another to members of an Inuit community who recognize the cultural code of his smile. While Nanook is portrayed as heroic and master of his physical environment in other scenes that situate him outside of Western notions of time and history, when he is compared with the world of the trader, he is depicted as awkward and lacking intelligence, an anachronistic and irrelevant, if quaint, figure in the early twentieth-century context of his original audience.[4]

I explore what it means for Indigenous people "to laugh at the camera" as a tactic of what I call "visual sovereignty," to confront the spectator with the often absurd assumptions that circulate around visual representations of Native Americans, while also flagging their involvement and, to some degree, complicity in these often disempowering structures of cinematic dominance and stereotype. I use *Atanarjuat: The Fast Runner* (2000), the first full-length feature film directed by an Inuit, Zacharias Kunuk, and produced by Igloolik Isuma Productions, a collaborative, majority Inuit production company, as my primary context for analysis to examine the ways this film is embedded within discourses about Arctic peoples that cannot be severed from the larger web of hegemonic discourses of ethnography. I do this first by discussing the pervasive images of Native Americans in ethnographic films and then by theorizing the ways that *Atanarjuat* intervenes into visual sovereignty as a film that successfully addresses a dual Inuit and non-Inuit audience for two different aims. More specifically, I interrogate how the *Atanarjuat* filmmakers strategically adjust and reframe the registers on which Inuit epistemes are considered with the twin, but not necessarily conflicting, aims of operating in the service of their home communities and forcing viewers to reconsider mass-mediated images of the Arctic.

I suggest a reading practice for thinking about the space between resistance and compliance wherein Indigenous filmmakers and actors revisit, contribute to, borrow from, critique, and reconfigure ethnographic film conventions, at the same time operating within and stretching the boundaries created by these conventions. Terming this approach *visual sovereignty*, I demonstrate how this strategy offers up not only the possibility of engaging and deconstructing white-generated representations of Indigenous people, but more broadly and importantly how it intervenes in larger discussions of Native American sovereignty by locating and advocating for Indigenous cultural and political power both within and outside of Western legal jurisprudence.[5] The visual, particularly film, video, and new media, is a germinal and exciting site for exploring how sovereignty is a creative act of self-representation that has the potential to both undermine stereotypes of Indigenous peoples and to strengthen the "intellectual health" of communities in the wake of genocide and colonialism.[6] This is a strategy Indigenous filmmakers have engaged in since at least the 1960s, when North American Indigenous filmmakers began producing televisual, film, and video projects, to the present, with the explosion of hundreds of exciting films by Indigenous filmmakers whose work runs the gamut from short experimental videos to activist documentaries to full-length feature films.[7]

In the case of the Inuit of Canada, visual sovereignty has an earlier history as a result of their involvement in filmmaking projects such as the one that produced *Nanook*. While I find Rony's incisive critique of *Nanook* as "cinematic taxidermy" instructive, I am hesitant to disregard the complicated collaborative nature of the film's production.[8] While Flaherty suffered from the ethnocentric biases and racism of his contemporaries, it is important to foreground the ways in which the Inuit instructed him on working collaboratively, according to their views of social and cultural interaction. Faye Ginsburg has determined that Allakariallak and other Inuit community members worked with Flaherty "as technicians, camera operators, film developers, and production consultants." Jay Ruby has also argued that not only did the Inuit serve as production staff members, they also challenged Flaherty to think differently, even collaboratively, about the project. "The Inuit performed for the camera, reviewed and criticized their performance and were able to offer suggestions for additional scenes in the film—a way of making films that, when tried today, is thought to be 'innovative and original.'"[9] Furthermore, the film and its offscreen stories have had a lasting positive impact on Inuit communities, most likely because of the depth of their participation in its creation. Peter Pitseolak, an Inuit photographer from Cape Dorset, met Flaherty in 1912 and was inspired to learn photography as a result. His stunning, intimate photographs of community members in the 1930s and 1940s militates against images of Arctic people that framed them as archaic, primitive, and doomed peoples.[10]

Even into the 1970s, *Nanook* was employed to empower Inuit communities. At a training workshop in 1979, the Inuit Tapirisat of Canada, a language preservation, land rights, and cultural advocacy organization that later formed the Inuit Broadcast Corporation (IBC), screened the film for an Inuit community.[11] According to Lyndsay Green, operations manager of Inuit Tapirisat, "The film excited great pride in the strength and dignity of their ancestors and they want to share this with their elders and children."[12] Inuit audiences, like those in other communities, have utilized film as a mode of cultural continuity and preservation. This focus on the aspects of the film that reflect their relatives' contributions to the creation of *Nanook* demonstrates how visual sovereignty involves a revision of older films featuring Native American plots in order to reframe a narrative that privileges Indigenous participation and perhaps points to sites of Indigenous knowledge production in a film otherwise understood as a purely Western product, as *Nanook* and Edward Curtis's *In the Land of the Headhunters* (1914) have been.[13] Moreover, by recognizing the imprint of Indigenous people working in various capacities as intellectual and cultural advisors and technical assistants, contemporary Indigenous filmmakers draw from this early motion picture material to frame their own projects that engage with notions of the traditional in order to think about how the past informs the present. Visual sovereignty, then, promotes "intellectual health" on at least two critical registers. By appealing to a mass, intergenerational, and transnational Indigenous audience, visual sovereignty permits the flow of Indigenous knowledge about such key issues as land rights, language acquisition, and preservation by narrativizing local and international struggles. Visual sovereignty, as expressed by Indigenous filmmakers, also involves employing editing technologies that permit filmmakers to stage performances of oral narrative and Indigenous notions of time and space that are not possible through print alone.

Visualizing Sovereignty in Indigenous Films

Sovereignty in its manifold manifestations is what sets Native American studies apart from other critical race discourses. Native Americans have no single shared culture, event, or series of events, no Middle Passage, necessary to imagine a collective group experience. Even the Wounded Knee Massacre of 1890 that resulted in the murders of more than three hundred Lakota tribal members is not an event to which all Native Americans can cathect our communal memories, despite the fact that it is a significant visual register because the bodies of the victims were photographed and these images were widely disseminated as postcards.[14] Sovereignty is an ontological and philosophical concept that unites the experiences of Native Americans with very real practical, political, and cultural ramifications, but it is a difficult idea to define because it is always in motion and is inherently contradictory. As David E. Wilkins and K. Tsianina Lomawaima note, "The political realities of relations with the federal government, relations with state and local governments, competing jurisdictions, complicated local histories, circumscribed land bases, and overlapping citizenships all constrain" contemporary notions of sovereignty.[15]

As a result, sovereignty is perhaps the most important, overused, and often misunderstood term employed in late twentieth-/early twenty-first-century Native American circles.[16] While legal and social science discourses have used the term to describe a peculiar, problematic, and particular relationship between the Anglophone colonies/United States/Canada and Indigenous nations of North America, I would like to suggest a discussion of visual sovereignty as a way of reimagining Native-centered articulations of self-representation and autonomy that engage the powerful ideologies of mass media, but that do not rely solely on the texts and contexts of Western jurisprudence.

Sovereignty is a key term in the lexicon of Native American studies because it demonstrates how Indigenous peoples are different from immigrant communities in the Americas (as well as other Indigenous nations) in terms of political structure, epistemology, and relationships to specific geographical spaces. In Scott Richard Lyon's formulation, sovereignty is "nothing less than our attempt to survive and flourish as a people."[17] Yet while he locates sovereignty within the history of the colonization of the Americas, considerations of the concept of sovereignty should also take into account expressions of sovereignty within traditional Native American aesthetic production prior to European incursion.

Native nations prior to European contact theorized about the concept of sovereignty in order to discursively distinguish themselves from the other human, spirit, animal, and inanimate communities surrounding them through performance, songs, stories, dreams, and visual texts such as wampum, pictographs, and tipi drawings. In a Native American context, the term predates European notions of nation-to-nation political sovereignty even as the Indigenous conceptions have now incorporated these non-Native articulations of the term into their definition. The English word *sovereignty*, then, becomes a placeholder for a multitude of Indigenous designations employed to describe the concept that also takes into account the European origins of the idea. The contradictions of sovereignty are numerous. Its applications vary from Indigenous nation to nation and it often maintains ties to older, Indigenous concepts of self-governance, which are remembered and constructed through oral narrative and a given community's consensus on what constitutes precontact forms and theories of government and social structure. It incorporates as well European notions of recognizing political autonomy and jurisprudence. In other words, *sovereignty* in a Native American context incorporates the paradox of multiple definitions into its genealogy. And the fact that sovereignty is located within and without Indigenous discourse does not make it any less powerful or valid a statement of political, individual, or cultural autonomy.[18]

For example, visual sovereignty can be likened to the Iroquois (Haudenosaunee) Two Row Wampum Belt Treaty. This treaty is a visual representation of a pact based on mutual respect made between the Iroquois and Europeans, stipulating that the communities would coexist and recognize each other's sovereignty, nation to nation. It was first created in the seventeenth century as a pact between the Iroquois and the Dutch. Iroquois interpret it as a visual manifestation of their inherent right to retain their geographic, cultural, political, linguistic, and economic sovereignty.

According to G. Peter Jemison, Seneca Faithkeeper:

> The purple lines represent the Haudenosaunee traveling in their canoe. Parallel to them, but not touching, is the path of the boat of the Europeans that came here. In our canoe is our way of life, our language, our law and our customs and traditions. And in the boat, likewise, are the European language, customs, traditions, and law. We have said, "Please don't get out of your boat and try to steer our canoe. And we won't get out of our canoe and try to steer your boat." We're going to accept each other as sovereign—we're going to travel down the river of life together, side by side.[19]

While European powers, Canada, and the United States have yet to fully honor this covenant, the Iroquois Confederacy continues to abide by the philosophy behind the belt—recognizing European forms of sovereignty, the continuing importance of oral narrative in maintaining a collective identity (the belt depends on "readers" who can decipher and interpret its meaning), and visual artifact as a mnemonic device. It is significant that one of the first treaties made between Indians and whites was recorded using an Indigenous form. From this perspective, visual sovereignty opens up a practice for reading Native American visual culture that incorporates both Indigenous traditions of community representation and non-Indigenous filmmaking practices. As the Two Row Wampum Belt demonstrates, visual sovereignty recognizes the paradox of creating media for multiple audiences, critiquing filmic representations of Native Americans, at the same time that it participates in some of the conventions that have produced these representations.

Sovereignty, because of this diversity of Indigenous relationships to it, has become a kind of collective placeholder term similar to "strategic essentialism."[20] In this sense, sovereignty indicates a powerful way to mobilize social and political action through situational, sometimes temporary, solidarity with the understanding that this solidarity is predicated on consensus that recognizes individual dissent. Likewise, visual sovereignty intervenes in larger discourses on Indigenous sovereignty, but employs a slightly different set of tactics. Visual sovereignty arbitrates in the broader world of Indigenous sovereignty and is not always directly involved in political debates that determine Native American survival and livelihood, as legal sovereignty in the U.S. and Canadian justice system is—there is more room for narrative play. Under visual sovereignty, filmmakers can deploy individual and community assertions of what sovereignty and self-representation mean and, through new media technologies, frame more imaginative renderings of Native American intellectual and cultural paradigms, such as the presentation of the spiritual and dream world, than are often possible in official political contexts. I do not mean, however, to insinuate here that visual sovereignty is outside of or disinterested in political activism and debate. For example, while the film *Atanarjuat* makes no overt reference to local environmental concerns in the Arctic, it "peoples" this particular endangered space. Recent news reports detail how this global catastrophe is adversely affecting all forms of plant and animal life in the Arctic, and simultaneously *Atanarjuat* intimates how human populations on the front line of global warming will also be devastated.

Moreover, Igloolik Isuma Productions employs ethnographic film conventions to serve didactic purposes within the Inuit communities of Canada, forging much-needed economic opportunities in depressed markets; educating younger generations alienated from community elders and tribal epistemologies through diasporic conditions; and addressing the lingering effects of colonization, natural environments in immediate peril, and high mortality, substance abuse, and incarceration rates. Faye Ginsburg notes that as a result of Igloolik Isuma's economic presence in Igloolik, "more than 100 Igloolik Inuit, from the young to the elderly, were employed as actors, hairdressers, and technicians, as well as costume makers, language experts, and hunters who provided food, bringing more than $1.5 million into a local economy that suffers from a 60 percent unemployment rate."[21] According to Zacharias Kunuk, one of Igloolik Isuma's four founding members, "We create traditional artifacts, digital media and desperately needed jobs in the same activity."[22] His statement, coupled with Ginsburg's statistics, points to the important political work of visual sovereignty: making a commercially successful film that foregrounds Inuit epistemes and simultaneously accomplishes collective social justice offscreen by providing job training.

Importantly, Igloolik Isuma is based in Nunavut, Canada's newest territory, established in 1999. With a population of roughly thirteen hundred people, 93 percent of whom are Inuit, and a consensual government system that blends Inuit principles (*qaujimajatuqangit* in Inuktitut) with Canadian parliamentary democracy, Nunavut is the site of a unique and exciting Indigenous political economy and a practicing form of political and cultural sovereignty that provides an ideal site to host a production company that works in the service of visual sovereignty.[23]

Isuma means "to think" in Inuktitut and the members of both Igloolik and its sister company, Arnait Video Productions, which focuses on issues of relevance to Inuit women, are dedicated to a production style that revolves around Inuit worldviews, such as collaborative conceptualizing of the film's diegesis and its incorporation of a subplot based on Inuit spiritual traditions, rather than those borrowed from the West (or, in the Inuit's case, the South).[24] The filmmaking process, as a result, is much slower than that of Hollywood because members attempt to reach consensus on the details of the film (the director, for example, serves more as a contact person than as the director in the conventional sense of the term), and the film is screened before an audience of elders and community members and edited accordingly prior to release.

The work of Igloolik Isuma and Arnait Video Productions aligns with the kinds of work that has been produced in the past three decades by Indigenous filmmakers in sites such as Latin America, Africa, and Oceania.[25] This work is part of a broader historical move from cinema produced by European settler and colonial nations to what Fernando Solanas and Octavio Getino term "Third Cinema" to a variety of Indigenous cinemas that incorporate local epistemes and cultural critiques with new visual technologies.[26] While Third Cinema is a postcolonial movement that grew out of cultural and political changes in the 1960s in formerly colonized parts of the world to denounce Hollywood-style entertainment in favor of a national, popular, and activist vernacular, Indigenous cinema has its roots in specific Indigenous aesthetics with their attendant focus on a particular geographical space; discrete cultural practices; social activist texts; notions of temporality that do not delink the past from the present or future; and spiritual traditions. Barry Barclay has theorized this approach as "Fourth Cinema":

> If we as Māori look closely enough and through the right pair of spectacles, we will find examples at every turn of how the old principles have been reworked to give vitality and richness to the way we conceive, develop, manufacture, and present our films. It seems likely to me that some Indigenous film artists will be interested in shaping films that sit with confidence within the First, Second, and Third cinema framework. While not closing the door on that option, others may seek to rework the ancient core values to shape a growing Indigenous cinema outside the national orthodoxy.[27]

Barclay cites a number of filmmakers, including Zacharias Kunuk and himself, as practitioners of Fourth Cinema. The ways in which these filmmakers operate "outside the national orthodoxy" is not only economically specific—most rely on inconsistent funding sources and shoestring budgets—but culturally specific in their incorporation of an entire Indigenous framework into the filmmaking project from start to finish. In other words, the filmmakers continue their relationship to the film's content and its multiple spectatorship long after the cameras stop rolling. As Barclay notes, "Māori film makers have been insistent on occasion that their films be accompanied to a new venue and be presented to the people of the area with full ceremonial."[28] In North America, this practice can be thought of as visual sovereignty, a practice that takes a holistic approach to the process of creating moving images and that locates Indigenous cinema in a particular historical and social context while leaving room for individual, national, and tribal distinctions.

As in the case with many works that can be called Indigenous cinema, Igloolik Isuma's oeuvre similarly is not solely a vehicle aimed at either an internal or an external audience. *Atanarjuat* compels non-Inuit spectators to think differently about what constitutes Indigenous content in films and more conventional representations of Native Americans in cinematic history and also about Indigenous visual aesthetics. As Michael Leigh argues, Indigenous communities "are ensuring the continuity of their languages and cultures and representations of their views. By making their own films and videos, they speak for themselves, no longer aliens in an industry which for a century has used them for its own ends."[29] Inuit filmmakers do not only employ what have come to be envisioned as Western visual culture technologies to create activist/resistance texts that retell oral narratives in local languages for future generations, however.

Rather, they also engage in dialogue with media communities outside the far North, reconsidering and transforming filmic genres and audience expectations.[30]

Cultural difference, particularly as it relates to a shamanistic plotline, is deployed in *Atanarjuat* to trouble a history of discursive representations of Arctic peoples as simultaneously commensurable and alien. The film reinscribes these scenes of cultural difference as regenerative sites of cultural preservation within a community that understands culture as a locus of fluidity, historical change, and adaptation. Igloolik Isuma filmmakers invert what non-Inuit might consider "aberrant" cultural practices—interacting with supernatural powers, eating raw meat, and engaging in a polygamous, sometimes violent trade in women—through humor and the strategic use of ethnographic film conventions. By doing so, they open up a more subtle, nuanced reading of these practices as a means of entering the debate on sovereignty and rupturing mainstream notions of feminism and aboriginal representation.[31]

Instead, what Igloolik Isuma does is situate the story of *Atanarjuat* on a "virtual reservation"—the space of the film—opening up the narrative for dialogue within and outside the community on a site that is less invested in the traffic in authenticity than in reconsidering the relationship between the visual image, technologies, and larger cultural and political contexts. As an imagined space, the virtual reservation is akin to what Lauren Bertlant would call a "prosthetic body" or an extracorporeal set of identifications onto which dominant national fantasies are projected.[32] Simultaneously, Indigenous people recuperate, regenerate, and begin to heal on the virtual reservation under the direct gaze of the spectator. The virtual reservation is an imagined space, in this instance, for the film industry, but has also been transformed by Indigenous people into something of value, a decolonizing space. Gerald McMaster writes of the historical role of the real-life territorial reserve in Canada: "It is a negotiated space set aside for Indian people by oppressive colonial governments to isolate them, to extricate them from their cultural habits, and to save them from the vices of the outside world. Paradoxically, isolation helped maintain aboriginal languages and many other traditional practices. The reserve continues to be an affirming presence despite being plagued by many historical uncertainties."[33] Lorna Roth has discussed "media reservations" as negative sites of segregation, isolation, and the televisual equivalent of the stereotypes structuring representations of reservation/reserve life in North

America.[34] However, I suggest that virtual reservations are more creative, kinetic, open spaces where Indigenous artists collectively and individually employ technologies and knowledges to rethink the relationship between media and Indigenous communities by, for example, exhibiting art online or by deciding not to distribute videos to non-Indigenous audiences.

"Here Come the Anthros": Sa(l)vages and Ethnographic Representation

In his biting musical indictment of cultural anthropology's intrusion into Indian country, Floyd Red Crow Westerman sings, "Here come the anthros, better hide your past away." Inspired by Vine Deloria Jr.'s groundbreaking work, *Custer Died for Your Sins,* Westerman's song punctures the notion that amateur and professional anthropologists engaging in research projects in Native American communities are universally benevolent and objective.[35] Both Westerman's and Deloria's work responds to statements that assert the primacy for Native Americans of the putatively "lower-order" functions such as attention to the body, action over thought, and doing rather than feeling.

Deloria in particular has questioned the motives of anthropologists who conduct fieldwork in Native American communities and produce "essentially self-confirming, self-referential, and self-reproducing closed systems of arcane 'pure knowledge'—systems with little, if any, empirical relationship to, or practical value for, real Indian people."[36] Although both anthropologists and ethnographers have adopted more self-reflective and sensitive research methodologies in response to critiques launched by Indigenous peoples, Native Americans are still positioned between the proverbial rock and hard place when it comes to ethnographic interpretations of our communities.[37] While it goes without saying that an enduring oral tradition continues within many Indigenous communities, broadening our understanding of the archive, it is also impossible to ignore the important cultural, linguistic, genealogical, and philosophical material in the ethnographic and historical record, especially as this material constructs a mass-mediated view of the Indigenous world.

Since its inception, the commercial motion picture industry in North America has been fascinated with the image of the American Indian.[38] Hundreds of actualities featuring Indians engaging in "traditional" and quotidian practices were shown in nickelodeons from 1894 through 1908.

These actualities and early documentary and ethnographic films simultaneously contributed to the myth of the vanishing Indian and helped to create a form of American spectatorship that coheres around the dichotomous relationship between Indian and white figures. As Miriam Hansen has demonstrated, the idea of the American spectator emerged at the turn of the twentieth century with the perhaps unintended effect of incorporating "outside" social groups, such as Euro-American women and recent immigrants from Europe, into the national body politic as consumers of forms of knowledge, culture, and history through an alternative public sphere "not necessarily anticipated in the context of production."[39] Ironically, while Native Americans and their relationship to specific geographical spaces provided the backdrop for a national origin myth around which immigrant identities could coalesce, Indigenous peoples in the films were erased through both the reenactment of the physical violence of the frontier and the discursive violence that notions of salvage anthropology propagated.[40]

Salvage anthropology in particular inflicted a damaging form of violence on Native American communities as they faced pressure from the government to assimilate and simultaneously received the message from anthropologists and ethnographers that their cultures were becoming increasingly inauthentic, impure, and irrelevant. Salvage anthropology would draw upon older forms of stereotyping found in early colonial texts, captivity narratives, and turn-of-the-century dime novels as well as scientific discourses on race to create the "sa(l)vage"—a doomed, "leftover" figure who, like Flaherty's description of "the Eskimo" in the epigraph above, exists only as a static, flat, protohuman type.

The stagings of "traditional" cultures in actualities and early films provided the kinds of artifacts salvage anthropology hoped to rescue from oblivion. The actualities of the turn of the century are the cinematic source from which representations of Native Americans both in the western and in amateur and professional ethnographic films would take shape. Despite the sense of ethnography as a kind of inescapable frame through which Indigenous lives are screened, Indigenous filmmakers have deployed ethnographic film conventions to assert and revise a sense of visual sovereignty. Critically engaging this seeming paradox—questioning ethnography's tendencies by using the tools and conventions available to the filmmaker—is not entirely new. As Jerry White notes: "Ethnographic filmmaking has undergone a complete transformation in the last two decades. Once the safe vocation of earnest scientists seeking imagery for exotic cultures, ethnographic filmmaking has become fertile ground for revision by Third World and avant-garde filmmakers."[41] However, articulations of this paradox and how it complicates notions of sovereignty on the virtual reservation are unique to Indigenous filmmaking practices.

With few exceptions, contemporary work by Indigenous filmmakers in the United States and Canada is set in the present as a response to films, particularly westerns and ethnographic films, that situate Native Americans in the nineteenth-century past with no viable future. While images of Hollywood Indians have saturated the market since the inception of films, the work of Native American filmmakers and issues of relevance to tribal peoples have been markedly absent from mass-market films, cinema scholarship, and the historical archive.[42] Native Americans in mass media have occupied a twilight zone existence in which they are both hypervisible in ways overdetermined by popular and nostalgic representations and completely invisible because Native American actors are often uncredited, underpaid, and cast in ancillary, sometimes demeaning roles in support of a white protagonist who provides the point of entry for the spectator.[43] As a result, Indigenous filmmakers often create narrative films that strive to overturn stereotypes of Indigenous people by featuring characters experiencing seemingly universal events. For example, the title of Chris Eyre and Sherman Alexie's landmark film, *Smoke Signals* (1998), conjures up images from the western film imaginary, but the action is set on a present-day reservation in the Northwest and centers on a narrative about the complex range of emotions between father and son.

"I Can Only Sing This Song to Someone Who Understands It": Multiple Modes of Address in *Atanarjuat: The Fast Runner*

In the wake of the success generated by *Smoke Signals*, *Atanarjuat: The Fast Runner* promised to serve as a kind of Canadian response to Eyre and Alexie's project. Shot entirely on location in and around Igloolik, *Atanarjuat* is the first Inuit feature-length film. According to an article published in *Nunatsiaq News*, a newspaper based in Nunavut, the film is drawn from a didactic "legend of power, intrigue, love, jealousy, murder, and revenge" more than a thousand years old.[44] It is a visual re-creation of an oral narrative important to the Inuit community and centers on the taboo-breaking romantic relationship between the main protagonist, Atanarjuat (Natar Ungalaaq, one of a handful of professional actors employed by the production company), and Atuat (Sylvia Ivalu), who has been promised in marriage by her family to Oki (Peter-Henry Arnatsiaq). Like most Native American oral stories, there are no absolute binaries in the story or the film. Neither the main protagonist, Atanarjuat, nor his antagonist, Oki, are wholly good or evil, a narrative decision that undermines the expectations of spectators familiar with Hollywood filmic formulas. Both break cultural taboos whose stakes are very high (Atanarjuat's brother is killed by Oki, who in turn kills his own father, and as a result is banished by his grandmother at the film's conclusion), but despite the fact that Atanarjuat performs an act that is socially unacceptable, his actions permit the community to heal from the devastation wrought years ago by the mysterious and ambivalent shaman figure, Tuurngarjuaq (Abraham Ulayuruluk). Yet unlike *Smoke Signals*, with its relatively simple diegesis, English dialogue, and familiar, contemporary references, *Atanarjuat* features an all-Inuit cast speaking Inuktitut (with English subtitles); wearing costumes made of animal skins; performing ostensibly traditional acts, such as hunting walrus and seal with harpoons and eating raw meat; and the film is situated within a shamanistic narrative framework and captured within pre–European invasion time.[45]

At first glance the film appears to be an ethnographic spectacle that seems, like its predecessor *Nanook*, to reinforce Flaherty's contention in the epigraph to this chapter that Arctic people produce a cinema of the Indigenous body and its interaction with the land, but little else. *Atanarjuat*, with its good-natured main protagonist, amateur actors, handheld cameras, teams of sled dogs, and long, slow shots of the frozen land- and seascape (uncredited protagonists in the film), appears to share much in common with Flaherty's classic ethnographic documentary. As Innupiat writer Joseph E. Senungetuk notes, Arctic communities in North America are depicted as "a people without technology, without a culture, lacking intelligence, living in igloos, and at best, a sort of simplistic 'native boy' type of subhuman arctic being."[46] Ann Fienup-Riordan terms these representations "Eskimo orientalism": "Like the representations of the Orient, the representation of the Eskimo is about origins—in this case the origin of society in the 'pure primitive': peaceful, happy, childlike, noble, independent, and free. The Eskimo of the movies is 'essential man,' stripped of social constraint and High Culture. . . . Their position at the geographic and historical fringe of Western Civilization made them the perfect foils for an 'Eskimo orientalism' as potent as its namesake."[47] The filmmakers tap into this "Eskimo orientalist" representational history in the supplementary materials surrounding the film. The companion book to the film opens with a quote by Claude Lévi-Strauss, "I was . . . captivated by many ethnographic details."[48] Even *Isuma: Inuit Studies Reader* (2004), produced by Isuma Publishing, a division of Igloolik Isuma Productions, features ethnographic texts by writers such as Knud Rasmussen and Franz Boas and the companion book demonstrates that the ethnographic verisimilitude of the film, particularly in terms of costuming, is based on drawings by Captain G. F. Lyon, who accompanied explorer William Edward Parry to the Arctic from 1821 to 1823.

Yet an examination of the bookends of the film—its opening scene and nondiegetic production shots shown while the credits roll—demonstrate that the filmmakers self-consciously deploy hallmarks of ethnographic cinematography without interpretive interventions such as the expert talking head. This is done in the service of drawing attention to the film as a film, as opposed to an "authentic" visual record of a vanished past, as part of a larger project of visual sovereignty. Igloolik Isuma Productions, whose team of filmmakers created *Atanarjuat*, declines to narrate the legendary story of Atanarjuat in a contemporary Inuit context, focusing instead on an earlier period that permits the film to forgo representing the white/Inuit colonial equation and the types of nostalgia, what Gerald Vizenor terms "victimry," that often arise out of attempts to portray an unadulterated Indigenous past.[49] Kunuk, the film's primary director, presents his audience with an intact Inuit world, one that does not rely on a binary opposition between Inuit and "southern" communities.[50]

The opening scene and cultural references of the film can be confusing and opaque to a non-Inuit spectator, so perhaps the filmmakers used the marketing materials, the companion book and *Inuit Studies Reader*, to provide the interpretive lens lacking in the film.[51] The film opens with a lone man standing on the snow-packed tundra with his howling dogs. This image is one of isolation and loneliness that hearkens back to what Rony calls Flaherty's "Primitive Everyman," a snapshot of the self-made man in conflict with a desolate and harsh landscape.[52] This image, evocative of *Nanook*, is undercut by the next scene, a tactic that the filmmakers repeatedly employ to challenge audience expectations. The following scene takes place inside a spacious *qaggiq* (large igloo), where a dozen or so adults and children are contemplating a visitor, referred to as an "up North stranger," who has arrived alone in the small community wearing a shaman's necklace made of polar bear claws, designating him as a powerful person; a white fur coat; and white polar bear pants similar to the ones worn by Allakariallak in *Nanook of the North*.[53] We learn later that the events in the opening scene take place approximately twenty years before most of the film's action. The visiting shaman, Tuurngarjuaq, greets the local community leader and shaman, Kumaglak (Apayata Kotierk), who also wears a shaman's walrus teeth necklace and coat decorated with raven feathers to designate his individuality and personal powers.

Tuurngarjuaq sings a song in the qaggiq, which he prefaces by claiming, "I can only sing this song to someone who understands it. When you sing, you laugh at the same time. It must be because you're winning too! It's fun to sing and play a game at the same time." The opening subtitled lines of the film are a cue to the non-Inuit spectator (including non-Inuit Native Americans) that the film's narrative and details may remain incommensurable since a non-Inuktitut speaking person wouldn't understand his song. Tuurngarjuaq's statement makes evident the multiple audiences the film is addressing: Inuit who understand scenes such as the opening one because they are already familiar with the narrative; non-Inuit Native Americans who may read some of the cues from the film and place them in dialogue with their own tribally specific oral narratives and discursive contexts; and non-Inuit who do not understand Inuktitut or the cultural practices represented in the film, but who may be aware of the economy of stereotypes surrounding the Inuit in literature and film. Tuurngarjuaq's lines underscoring the link between humor and play are telling here as they point to how the filmmakers and characters "laugh at the audience," to return to Rony's phrase. Not only does the non-Inuit audience not fully understand the film, the audience is also, unwittingly perhaps, engaged in a game with the filmmakers, one in which the filmmakers obviously have the upper hand.

This idea of narrative play is at work when Tuurngarjuaq and Kumaglak engage in a practice termed *illuriik* (opponents/partners), a public custom, according to the *Atanarjuat* companion book, that tests visiting strangers, particularly shamans, "physically and psychologically" by tying them together and letting their helping spirits (*tuurngait*), often associated with powerful animals such as the walrus and polar bear, encounter each other in the spirit world.[54] Often, if the stranger passes the test, he and the host shaman become friends and exchange their possessions; however, in this case Tuurngarjuaq's helping spirit, which takes the form of a polar bear spirit, kills Kumaglak's, which manifests itself as a walrus spirit, and Kumaglak dies as a result. The two men are tied together and one slumps over, apparently and inexplicably dead.

Although this illuriik has a disastrous ending, the scene is not devoid of humor. When Tuurngarjuaq first stands up to display his shaman's parka, he teases Kumaglak, "Since your clothes are different, take a look at mine. If you show me yours . . ." and the joke trails off here. Kumaglak retorts, "No, I don't want any lessons from some up North stranger." Throughout the film, a more theoretical understanding of illuriik is offered as social and political negotiations and confrontations vacillate between violence and humor. As an expression of a tribally specific episteme, illuriik in the film is a form of visual sovereignty that both places this practice within a local context in the services of linguistic and cultural revitalization and simultaneously makes a broader argument for self-representation and self-determination by involving the spectator in the process of decolonization. This is accomplished by presenting Inuit cultural practices and sensibilities on Inuit terms, without the kinds of explanatory apparatuses that typically accompany ethnographic films.

To decipher exactly what is happening in this scene in its cultural context, the non-Inuit audience has to turn to the texts of ethnography, including Igloolik Isuma's own companion book. Because the illuriik is not a cultural practice that is universally familiar, even among Native North Americans, its decoding points to how Indigenous filmmaking is poised on a grid of representational practices: ethnography, Aboriginal narrative, the lexicon and technology of film.

Upon his death, Kumaglak's wife, Panikpak (Madeline Ivalu), provides voice-over narration: "We never knew what he was or why it happened. Evil came to us like Death. It just happened and we had to live with it." It becomes clear that Tuurngarjuaq occupies an ambivalent position as metaphorical tester of the audience in a kind of extranarrative illuriik, but he also serves as a precursor to the incursion of Europeans on Inuit land, leaving death and destruction in his wake. Read metaphorically as a seductive, foreign presence, the visiting shaman can be seen to represent both an individualized destructive power and the destructive power of Euro-Canadian colonialism. The community struggles over the course of the next two and a half hours to purge itself of the damage caused by the introduction of malevolent forces and begins to heal again. This is instructive for the contemporary community members at Igloolik and its environs who can take these lessons about negotiating the potentially dangerous terrain of the "Other" to apply to the present colonial and environmental context in their homelands.

In the end, an elderly Panikpak is reunited with her brother, Qulitalik (Pauloosie Qulitalik, one of the founding members of Igloolik Isuma and one of the screenplay writers), who had left the community immediately after Kumaglak's death. When Tuurngarjuaq returns, brother and sister work in tandem as complementary forces to force the shaman away permanently. Thereafter, Panikpak banishes her grandchildren, Oki and his followers, from the village: "We are not finished here! Before we can go on we have to forgive some of our family who have done things no one should ever do. For many winters now we have been ruled and frightened just like that evil Tuurngarjuaq was still with us! My own son Sauri's children have led an evil life to others day after day! This has to stop so our future generations can have better lives. Mistreating others, committing murders, telling lies. This has to stop now!" Panikpak's chastisement and call to collective healing reinforce the strength of Inuit women, who hold positions of power that are equal to those of men in the community.[55] This representation of the power of women within Inuit communities is an example of visual sovereignty, a way of subtly demonstrating gender complementarity rather than making more strident, straightforward claims as a documentary or political treatise might.

Another way that visual sovereignty is exhibited is through the film's pacing and attention to landscape. The film has a running time of approximately 161 minutes, much of which is taken up with slow pans of the landscape; the quotidian actions of the characters as they find and prepare food; and shots of things such as feet crunching through the snow that would have been edited out of a conventional Hollywood film. In other words, the film is full of "boring parts" that if skipped over would mean missing the way in which the film constructs a specifically Inuit epistemology.[56] The entire film can be read as a "boring part," as students in my classes on Indigenous film have pointed out, with its attention to ethnographic detail, chaste sex scenes, and relative lack of violence and action. More careful attention to the film, however, demonstrates that what the filmmakers do is take the non-Inuit audience hostage, successfully forcing us to alter our consumption of visual images to an Inuit pace, one that is slower and more attentive to the play of light on a grouping of rocks or the place where the snow meets the ocean. The slowness of the sequencing matches the patience one must have to hunt on the ice, wait for hours at a seal hole, traverse long distances on foot or in a dog sled, or battle over five hundred years of colonialism.

The filmmakers' refusal to edit the film to a more conventional length and decision to "subject" the audience to seemingly interminable long shots of people walking or running on the snow and ice mark a visually sovereign practice. In a geographical site represented as *terra nullius* except for a few large mammals, the filmmakers' insistence upon peopling the land and demonstrating the Inuit's dependence on it is a means of asserting political and representational sovereignty at a time of crisis in terms of the United States' and Canada's history of resource extraction and environmental degradation in the Arctic. As Steven Leuthold attests, "Group identities, especially before the advent of electronic media, were linked, as they still are, to shared but special access to physical locations, a main reason for the continued emphasis on place in Native American documentaries."[57] The land is not something that the characters of the film are in conflict with and attempt to overcome, but a varied and essential backdrop against which the particularities of the narrative are played out. This is especially key to understanding the film since communities in the Arctic continue to rely on the land and its plant and animal population for survival.

The film closes with the expulsion of negative forces and healing in the form of the community singing Kumaglak's *ajaja* (personal) song in the presence of Atanarjuat and Atuat's son Kumaglak (Bernice Ivalu), a kind of reincarnation of the original Kumaglak, making the narrative frame one that is circular rather than linear. The narrative follows the traditional story's plot by expelling the influence of a shaman who caused the community harm, but makes a larger, contemporary claim for repudiating the negative influences of the Western world brought on by colonialism. The cultural and political work of the film within the Igloolik community is to instill a sense of pride in young people through the success of award-winning projects such as *Atanarjuat* and to provide jobs and experience to its members who live in poverty, face substance abuse, and suffer from high suicide rates. Kathleen Fleming notes that both Igloolik Isuma and Arnait Video Productions continue to operate as community-based production companies, helping to stem the tide of violence that began with the advent of colonialism in Arctic villages. She writes that the companies have provided "direct professional experience shooting and editing video, preparing story lines and scripts, and fundraising."[58]

The representation of the film's shamanistic storyline coupled with the cultural and political work it has accomplished offscreen are examples of visual sovereignty, as are the film's production shots included at the end of the film. In these scenes, the audience gets a glimpse into the filmmaking process and the context of the making of the film. As the credits roll and Kumaglak's ajaja song is still heard, camera sleds pulled by actors and the crew film a naked Atanarjuat running on the ice, Oki walks along the beach in hip waders and a motorcycle jacket listening to headphones, and actors out of costume wave to the camera from a modern boat.

These shots, like Nanook's smile, poke fun at the spectator, forcing the viewer (who has the patience to sit through to the film's end) to imagine *Atanarjuat* as a narrative film produced by a vibrant contemporary Inuit community, not a documentary on the mythic past or footage from a bygone era.

These final images lay bare the project of ethnographic film. As Alison Griffiths asserts, "As a discursive category, ethnographic film refers less to a set of unified significatory practices or to the anthropological method of intensive fieldwork than to the looking relations between the initiator of the gaze and the recipient."[59] As a cameraperson sitting on the prow of a boat turns to film another crew member holding a camera, the audience realizes that while the film offers a glimpse into Inuit community life, it also reminds the audience that ethnographic film is often merely a mirror reflecting the gaze of the Western viewer. While Kunuk claims that "the goal of *Atanarjuat* is to make the viewer feel inside the action, looking out rather than outside looking in," the production shots bring the audience back to the present and situate the viewer outside the community, back in the space of the darkened cinema.[60]

Kunuk and the Igloolik Isuma team operate as technological brokers and autoethnographers of sorts, moving between the community from which they hail and the Western world and its overdetermined images of Indigenous people. James C. Faris has argued that Indigenous filmmakers "do not join the global village as equal participants, as just more folks with videocameras. They enter it already situated by the West, which gives them little room to be anything more than what the West will allow" because of the hegemonic effects of capitalism and consumerism.[61] Igloolik

Actors and production crew in *Atanarjuat*'s closing credits. (Reproduced courtesy of Igloolik Isuma Productions, Inc., Igloolik, Nunavut, Canada)

Isuma Productions contradicts Faris's statement by creating a film that incorporates and reworks ethnographic elements to offer up a corrective cultural narrative to combat a century of anthropological monographs and documentaries. The filmmakers present an Inuit oral narrative through a visual register in the service of their community, while at the same time stretching the boundaries of Indigenous representation through the deployment of visual sovereignty. Igloolik Isuma enters the "global village" of media production on its own terms, engaging in a new, metaphorical form of illuriik that retains a sense of humor, laughing, perhaps, like Allakariallak, about the paradoxical nature of the project.

Notes

Originally published as "Reading Nanook's Smile: Visual Sovereignty, Indigenous Revisions of Ethnography, and *Atanarjuat (The Fast Runner)*," *American Quarterly* 59.4 (2007): 1159–85, copyright 2007 The American Studies Association. Reprinted with the permission of The Johns Hopkins University Press.

Earlier versions of this chapter were presented at the Native American Literature Symposium and at Sarai: The New Media Initiative in Delhi, India. I wish to thank Chad Allen, Tiffany Lopez, Vorris Nunley, members of the Race and Independent Media Colloquium at UCLA, Freya Schiwy, Jacqueline Shea Murphy, and Traise Yamamoto for their generous and insightful suggestions on various drafts of this chapter. This article was made possible by financial support provided by an Institute of American Cultures/American Indian Studies Postdoctoral Fellowship at UCLA and a Center for Ideas and Society resident fellowship at UC–Riverside; by the assistance of Jack Coogan at the Robert and Frances Flaherty Study Center in Claremont California; and by the helpful communication of Lucius Barre, Norman Cohn, Marie-Hélène Cousineau, and Katarina Soupkup at Igloolik Isuma Productions, Inc., and Arnait Video Productions.

1. *Nanook of the North* is alternately considered the first documentary and the first ethnographic film, and Flaherty is often credited as the "father of documentary." See Jay Ruby's *Picturing Culture: Explorations of Film and Anthropology* (Chicago: University of Chicago Press, 2000) for a critical analysis of the film's production. For more on the complexities of defining ethnographic film and its relationship to Indigenous media productions, see Peter Ian Crawford and David Turton, *Film as Ethnography* (New York: St. Martin's, 1992); Faye Ginsburg, "Screen Memories: Resignifying the Traditional in Indigenous Media," in *Media Worlds: Anthropology on New Terrain*, ed. Faye Ginsburg, Lila Abu-Lughod, and Brian Larkin (Berkeley: University of California Press, 2002), 39–57; Alison Griffiths, *Wondrous Difference: Cinema, Anthropology, and Turn-of-the-Century Visual Culture* (New York: Columbia University Press, 2002); Karl Heider, *Ethnographic Film* (Austin: University of Texas Press, 1976); and David MacDougall, *The Corporeal Image: Film, Ethnography, and the Senses* (Princeton: Princeton University Press, 2006).

2. Fatimah Tobing Rony, *The Third Eye: Race, Cinema, and Ethnographic Spectacle* (Durham: Duke University Press, 1996), 111. There is some controversy over the use of the terms *Eskimo* and *Inuit*. While Eskimo is still employed as a self-designation in some communities in Alaska, particularly among the Yupik, Canadian Indigenous people prefer the descriptor Inuit as a result of conversations begun at the Inuit Circumpolar Conference in 1977. See Gabriella Golinger, "Inuit to Form World Organization," *Nunatsiaq News*, June 22, 1977. Inuit, in Inuktitut, one of the languages of Nunavut, Canada's newest territory, means "the Living Ones Who Are Here," according to Inuktitut speaker Rachel Qitsualik (Inuk is the singular form), while there is some debate whether Eskimo means the less flattering "Eater of Raw Meat" or the more positive Montagnais "Snowshoe Net-Weaver." See Qitsualik, "Esquimaux," *Nunatsiaq News*, June 27, 2003.

3. In this chapter I use *American Indian* and *Native American* as interchangeable umbrella terms for Indigenous people in the United States, fully aware of the problematic origins of the terms and their homogenizing tendencies, because no better terms yet exist. *First Nations* and *Aboriginal* are terms

that Indigenous people in Canada use to define their communities. Likewise, I employ the terms *white*, *West(ern)*, and *European American* as interchangeable placeholder terms, with the understanding that they represent a broad spectrum of cultural histories and national/ethnic origins.

4. For more on the ways that anthropologists manipulate time in order to make non-Western peoples appear primitive, see Johannes Fabian, *Time and the Other: How Anthropology Makes Its Other* (New York: Columbia University Press, 1983). For more on how the Inuit have been represented in visual and literary culture, see Ann Fienup-Riordan, *Freeze Frame: Alaska Eskimos in the Movies* (Seattle: University of Washington Press, 1995); and Wendell H. Oswalt, *Eskimos and Explorers* (Lincoln: University of Nebraska Press, 1999).

5. My understanding of visual sovereignty is rooted in and expands upon three important discussions of sovereignty that think outside the perimeters of legal discourse: Jolene Rickard's call for expanding the boundaries of discourse around sovereignty to the arts, Beverly R. Singer's notion of "cultural sovereignty" as "trusting the older ways and adapting them to our lives in the present," and Robert Allen Warrior's term "intellectual sovereignty," which in turn draws from Vine Deloria Jr.'s understanding of sovereignty "as an open-ended process" that involves critical and kinetic contemplations of what sovereignty means at different historical and paradigmatic junctures. See Rickard, "Sovereignty: A Line in the Sand," in *Strong Hearts: Native American Visions and Voices* (New York: Aperture, 1995), 51–59; Singer, *Wiping the War Paint off the Lens: Native American Film and Video* (Minneapolis: University of Minnesota Press, 2001), 2; and Warrior, *Tribal Secrets: Recovering American Indian Literary Traditions* (Minneapolis: University of Minnesota Press, 1995), 97. Additionally, Freya Schiwy has called the reworking of technologies of the visual in the service of decolonizing Indigenous Latin American communities "Indianizing," a term that resonates with "visual sovereignty," in her essay "Decolonizing the Frame: Indigenous Video in the Andes," *Framework* 44.1 (2003): 116–32 and in her book, *Indianizing Film: Decolonization, the Andes and the Question of Technology* (New Brunswick: Rutgers University Press, 2009).

6. Robert Allen Warrior, "Native Nationalism and Criticism" (paper presented at the University of California, Riverside, March 2007). See also Wayne Warry, *Unfinished Dreams: Community Healing and the Reality of Aboriginal Self-Government* (Toronto: University of Toronto Press, 1998).

7. The list of contemporary North American Indigenous filmmakers is much too lengthy to give in its entirety here, but it includes artists who work in many different genres, from experimental video to full-length feature films, and who treat a remarkable array of subjects, from gay, lesbian, bisexual, and transgender issues to land rights activism. These include Shelley Niro, Clint Alberta, Chris Eyre, Zachery Longboy, Igloolik Isuma, Arnait Video Productions, Malinda Maynor, Jeff Barnaby, Alanis Obomsawin, Shirley Cheechoo, Victor Masayesva Jr., Sandra Osawa, Thirza Cuthand, and Randy Redroad. There

were at least two Native American directors active during the silent period, Edwin Carewe and James Young Deer, whose work might also be considered as participating in the project of visual sovereignty. For more on Young Deer and representations of Native Americans in early cinema, see Joanna Hearne, "'The Cross-Heart People': Race and Inheritance in the Silent Western," *Journal of Popular Film and Television* 30 (Winter 2003): 181–96.

8. Rony, *Third Eye*, 88.

9. Ginsburg, "Screen Memories," 39; Ruby, *Picturing Culture*, 88–89. Ruby, however, disagrees with Ginsburg and Rony that Inuit working with Flaherty served as camera operators. He argues that there is no evidence to support this claim, although he provides documentation that Inuit consulted with Flaherty about scenes and future film ideas and that their input was valued (283n2).

10. For more on Pitseolak's work, see Peter Pitseolak and Dorothy Eber, *People from Our Side: An Eskimo Life Story in Words and Photographs* (Bloomington: Indiana University Press, 1975).

11. For more on the history of Inuit Tapirisat and early Inuit interventions into satellite broadcasting service, see Faye Ginsburg's "Screen Memories." See also Laila Sorenson, "The Inuit Broadcasting Corporation and Nunavut," in *Nunavut: Inuit Regain Control of Their Land and Their Lives*, ed. Jens Dahl, Jack Hicks, and Peter Jull (Copenhagen: International Working Group for Indigenous Affairs, 2000); Lorna Roth, *Something New in the Air: The Story of First Peoples Television Broadcasting in Canada* (Montreal: McGill-Queens University Press, 2005); and Faye Ginsburg and Lorna Roth, "First Peoples' Television," in *Television Studies*, ed. Toby Miller (London: British Film Institute, 2002), 130–31.

12. Quoted in Ruby, *Picturing Culture*, 92–93.

13. The photographer Edward S. Curtis later changed the name of his film to the more palatable (to twentieth-century white audiences) *In the Land of the War Canoes: A Drama of Kwakiutl Life in the Northwest.* The restored version of a surviving 1972 print was edited by Bill Holm and features new original music and dialogue by Kwakiutl (Kwakwaka'wakw) community members, many of whom consider the film important not only for its visual record of their relatives who were actors in the film, but because of its interpretation of a Kwakiutl story. See also Anne Makepeace's *Coming to Light: Edward S. Curtis and the North American Indians* (coproduction of Anne Makepeace and WNET, 2000), a documentary that discusses Kwakiutl involvement in the production of *In the Land of the Headhunters*, and Pauline Wakeman's "Becoming Documentary: Edward Curtis' *In the Land of the Headhunters* and the Politics of Archival Reconstruction," *Canadian Review of American Studies* 36.3 (2006): 293–309, which argues against reading *In the Land of the Headhunters* as an authentic artifact of unadulterated Native American culture. I do not read these films as fragments of authenticity, but as texts that are, to some extent, collaborative, similar to the "as told to" autobiographies of Indigenous people who worked with white amanuenses.

14. For more on the visual traffic in violence around the Wounded Knee

Massacre, see Richard E. Jensen, Eli Paul, and John E. Carter, eds., *Eyewitness at Wounded Knee* (Lincoln: University of Nebraska Press, 1991). Perhaps more unifying in terms of its effect on thousands of Indigenous families, the federal Indian boarding school period of the late nineteenth and early twentieth centuries, during which thousands of children were forced to attend schools whose goal of assimilation indoctrinated them with mainstream societal precepts and mandatory Christianity, was also a time of intense visual documentation, with its spectacular "before and after" photographs. Yet the boarding school (or residential school, as it is called in Canada) experience was also not a universal one. For more on boarding/residential school history, see David Wallace Adams, *Education for Extinction: American Indians and the Boarding School Experience, 1875–1928* (Lawrence: University of Kansas Press, 1995); Agnes Grant, *No End of Grief: Indian Residential Schools in Canada* (Winnipeg: Pemmican, 1992); K. Tsianina Lomawaima, *They Called It Prairie Light: The Story of Chilocco Indian School* (Lincoln: University of Nebraska Press, 1994); J. R. Miller, *Shingwauk's Vision: A History of Native Residential Schools* (Toronto: University of Toronto Press, 1996); and Clifford Trafzer, Jean Keller, and Lorene Sisquoc, eds., *Boarding School Blues: Revisiting American Indian Educational Experience* (Lincoln: University of Nebraska Press, 2006).

15. David E. Wilkins and K. Tsianina Lomawaima, *Uneven Ground: American Indian Sovereignty and Federal Law* (Norman: University of Oklahoma Press, 2002), 5.

16. For more on sovereignty and its associated discourses, see Vine Deloria Jr. and Clifford M. Lytle, *The Nations Within: The Past, Present, and Future of American Indian Sovereignty* (Austin: University of Texas Press, 1984); David E. Wilkins, *American Indian Sovereignty and the Supreme Court: The Masking of Justice* (Austin: University of Texas Press, 1997); and John R. Wunder, *Native American Sovereignty* (New York: Garland, 1996).

17. Scott Richard Lyons, "Rhetorical Sovereignty: What Do American Indians Want from Writing?" *College Composition and Communication* 51.3 (2000): 449.

18. I find Sandy Grande's discussion in *Red Pedagogy: Native American Social and Political Thought* (Lanham, MD: Rowman and Littlefield, 2004) constructive for the way it calls for such a continued rethinking of sovereignty as grounded only in Western jurisprudence. She suggests that we "detach and dethink the notion of sovereignty from its Western understandings of power and relationships and base it on indigenous notions of power" (52). Grande is in conversation with Gerald Taiaike Alfred, whose *Peace, Power, Righteousness: An Indigenous Manifesto* (Don Mills, Ontario: Oxford University Press, 1999) militated against this dependence on conventional understandings of sovereignty. Other Native American scholars have also called for a broader understanding of sovereignty beyond the relationship of tribes to the U.S. court. Following Singer, Clifford Trafzer and Anthony Madrigal term this understanding "cultural sov-

ereignty" and ground it in Indigenous, specifically Serrano, songs, stories, relationships to plants and animals, and geography. See Trafzer, *The People of San Manuel* (Highland, CA: San Manuel Band of Mission Indians, 2003); and Madrigal, *Sovereignty, Land and Water* (Riverside, CA: Center for California Native Nations, 2008). In addition, see Joanne Barker, *Sovereignty Matters: Locations of Contestation and Possibility in Indigenous Struggles for Self-Determination* (Lincoln: University of Nebraska Press, 2005); and Tharon Weighill, "The Two-Step Tales of Hahashka: Experiences in Corporeality and Embodiment in Aboriginal California" (PhD diss., University of California, Riverside, 2004).

19. G. Peter Jemison, "Two Row Wampum: Symbol of Sovereignty; Metaphor of Life," http://www.pbs.org/warrior/noflash/index.html (accessed July 12, 2005).

20. See Gayatri Chakravorty Spivak's germinal definition of "strategic essentialism" in "Subaltern Studies: Deconstructing Historiography," in *Subaltern Studies IV*, ed. Ranajit Guha (New Delhi: Oxford University Press, 1985), reprinted in *The Spivak Reader: Selected Works of Gayatri Chakravorty Spivak*, ed. Donna Landry and Gerald MacLean (New York: Routledge, 1996).

21. Faye Ginsburg, "*Atanarjuat* Off-screen: From 'Media Reservations' to the World Stage," *American Anthropologist* 105.4 (2004): 828.

22. Zacharias Kunuk, "The Art of Inuit Storytelling," http://www.isuma.ca/about_us/isuma/our_style/kunuk.html (accessed February 12, 2003).

23. Igloolik is a northern village in Nunavut, located to the west of Baffin Island on Melville Peninsula. Igloolik is the cultural hub of Nunavut ("Our Land" in Inuktitut). For more information, see http://www.gov.nu.ca/nunavut. Jens Dahl, Jack Hicks, and Peter Jull have also collected a series of powerful and engaging essays on the creation and future of Nunavut: *Nunavut: Inuit Regain Control of Their Lands and Their Lives* (Copenhagen: International Work Group for Indigenous Affairs, 2000).

24. Igloolik Isuma and Arnait Video Productions have released over twenty documentary, experimental, and dramatic feature films. Inuit refer to mainstream European-Canadian culture as "southern," a geographic rather than racial/ethnic designation.

25. Faye Ginsburg's "Screen Memories," for example, puts Inuit filmmaking practices into productive dialogue with those of Indigenous filmmakers in Australia.

26. See Fernando Solanas and Octavio Getino, "Towards a Third Cinema: Notes and Experiences for the Development of a Cinema of Liberation in the Third World," *Afterimage* 3 (Summer 1971): 16–30. See also Faye Ginsburg, "Indigenous Media: Faustian Dilemma or Global Village?" *Cultural Anthropology* 6.1 (1991): 92–112.

27. Barry Barclay, "Celebrating Fourth Cinema," *Illusions* 35 (Winter 2003): 11.

28. Ibid.

29. Michael Leigh, "Curiouser and Curiouser," in *Back of Beyond: Discovering Australian Film and Television,* ed. Scott Murray (Sydney: Australian Film Commission, 1988), 88.

30. While the Inuit occupy a geographically isolated space and have been perceived as archaic hunter-gatherers, Inuit communities do not conceive of technology and new media as external threats to their culture. According to Joe Mauryama of the Inuit-owned Internet service provider Nunavut WWW Communications, about half the homes in Nunavut's capital, Iqaluit, have Internet access. See Mark Bourrie, "Technology: Internet Heats Up Debate on Arctic Traditions," *Terra Viva Online,* http://www.ipsnews.net/focus/tv_society/viewstory.asp?idn=100 (accessed April 10, 2005). Inuit communities employ the Internet for a variety of uses: language preservation (there are many Web sites that publish in the Inuktitut syllabary and phonetic Inuktitut); for updates on local, national, and international news; medical information; online entrepreneurship; and to link to far-flung villages. Moreover, Neil Blair Christensen writes that the Internet has a "cultural and identity affirming use" among the Inuit. See *Inuit in Cyberspace: Embedding Offline Identities Online* (Copenhagen: Museum Tusculanum, 2003), 12. See also Lucas Bessire's review of *Atanarjuat,* which discusses the film's multiple audiences: "Talking Back to Primitivism: Divided Audiences, Collective Desires," *American Anthropologist* 105.4 (2003): 832–37.

31. I use the term *aberrant* here to signal both the sometimes unintentional way that visual anthropology has represented the non-Western world as "Other" through portrayals of unfamiliar (to the West) sartorial, culinary, familial, etc. cultural mores and Umberto Eco's understanding of the "aberrant decoder" as a potentially liberating site that separates the author/filmmaker's intentions from those of the reader/spectator. See *The Role of the Reader: Explorations in the Semiotics of Texts* (Bloomington: Indiana University Press, 1979). Wilton Martinez has explored the possibilities for spectators of reading the putative "aberrant" in ethnographic film as an invitation to explore the limits of filmic verisimilitude and realism. See "Who Constructs Anthropological Knowledge? Toward a Theory of Ethnographic Film Spectatorship," in *Film as Ethnography,* ed. Peter Ian Crawford and David Turton (New York: St. Martin's, 1992), 131–61.

32. Lauren Berlant, "National Brands/National Body: *Imitation of Life,*" in *Comparative American Identities: Race, Sex, and Nationality in the Modern Text,* ed. Hortense Spillers (New York: Routledge, 1991), 13.

33. Gerald McMaster, "Living on Reservation X," in *Reservation* X, ed. Gerald McMaster (Seattle: University of Washington Press, 1999), 19.

34. Lorna Roth, "The Crossing of Borders and the Building of Bridges: Steps in the Construction of the Aboriginal Peoples Television Network in Canada," *International Journal of Communication Studies* 62.3–4 (2000): 251–69.

35. Floyd Red Crow Westerman, *Here Come the Anthros/The Land Is Your Mother* (Trikont, 1991). Originally released in 1970; Vine Deloria Jr., *Custer Died for Your Sins: An Indian Manifesto* (New York: Avon Books, 1969).

36. Quoted in Thomas Biolsi and Larry Zimmerman's *Indians and Anthropologists: Vine Deloria, Jr. and the Critique of Anthropology* (Tucson: University of Arizona Press, 1997), 3.

37. See James Clifford and George E. Marcus, eds., *Writing Culture: The Poetics and Politics of Ethnography* (Berkeley: University of California Press, 1986) for a collection of essays that rethinks the process of fieldwork and the ethnographer's relationship to the ethnographic subject.

38. For a history of Native American representations in film from its inception to the present, see Angela Aleiss, *Making the White Man's Indian: Native Americans and Hollywood Movies* (Westport, CT: Praeger, 2005); Gretchen M. Bataille and Charles L. P. Silet, *The Pretend Indians: Images of Native Americans in the Movies* (Ames: Iowa State University Press, 1980); Ward Churchill, *Fantasies of the Master Race: Literature, Cinema, and the Colonization of American Indians* (Monroe, ME: Common Courage, 1992); Jacquelyn Kilpatrick, *Celluloid Indians: Native Americans and Film* (Lincoln: University of Nebraska Press, 1999); Peter C. Rollins and John E. O'Connor, eds., *Hollywood's Indian: The Portrayal of the Native American in Film* (Lexington: University Press of Kentucky, 1988); and Singer, *Wiping the War Paint off the Lens.*

39. Miriam Hansen, *Babel and Babylon: Spectatorship in American Silent Film* (Cambridge, MA: Harvard University Press, 1994), 7.

40. Salvage anthropology stressed that Indigenous people were destined to disappear off the face of the earth in a matter of years. Therefore, great pains should be taken to preserve any Indigenous material or linguistic artifact. This anxiety-driven form of anthropology was less concerned with representing Indigenous culture as the Indigenous peoples interpreted themselves than it was with the value of future scientific research on tribal/non-Western cultures. For an important critique of salvage anthropology, see Clifford and Marcus, *Writing Culture*, 98–121.

41. Jerry White, "Arguing with Ethnography: The Films of Bob Quinn and Pierre Perrault," *Cinema Journal* 42.2 (2003): 101.

42. Key exceptions include Jacquelyn Kilpatrick, Randolph Lewis, and Beverly Singer's work.

43. See Victor Masayesva Jr.'s film *Imagining Indians* (1992) and his interviews with Native American actors detailing their treatment by Hollywood filmmakers, as well as the example of Tonto on *The Lone Ranger* television series, and a whole host of relatively recent films such as *The Mission* (1986), *Dances with Wolves* (1990), and *The New World* (2005).

44. "Isuma Feature to Be Launched December 14–16 in Igloolik," *Nunatsiaq News*, December 1, 2000.

45. Ward Churchill argues in *Fantasies of the Master Race: Literature, Cinema, and the Colonization of American Indians* that films with Native American themes must be set in the present in order to do any positive political work. If a film "would alter public perceptions of Native Americans in some meaningful

way," he argues, it must be focus on "the real struggles of living native people to liberate themselves from the oppression which has beset them in the contemporary era" (246). I contend, however, that *Atanarjuat* provides a powerful political message about rethinking ethnography and contemporary notions of visual sovereignty precisely through its setting in the past.

46. Joseph E. Senungetuk, *Give or Take a Century: An Eskimo Chronicle* (San Francisco: Indian Historian, 1971), 25.

47. Fienup-Riordan, *Freeze Frame*, xi–xiii.

48. Claude Lévi-Strauss, quoted in Paul Apak Angilirq, Zacharias Kunuk, Hervé Paniaq, and Pauloosie Qulitalik, eds., *Atanarjuat/The Fast Runner* (Toronto: Coach House Books and Isuma, 2002), 9.

49. Gerald Vizenor, *Fugitive Poses: Native American Scenes of Absence and Presence* (Lincoln: University of Nebraska Press, 2000).

50. Even in its publicity decisions, Igloolik Isuma must contend with the vestiges of colonialism and Western conventions. Kunuk has been identified as the director of the film in most media accounts. But because Igloolik Isuma works collaboratively and attempts to engage with Inuit epistemes of the collective and nonhierarchical production style, it would be more appropriate not to focus on a single director.

51. See Gillian Robinson, ed., *Isuma: Inuit Studies Reader* (Montreal: Isuma, 2004), as well as Shari Huhndorf's discussion of *Atanarjuat*'s reception in her review of the film, "*Atanarjuat, the Fast Runner*: Culture, History, and Politics in Inuit Media," *American Anthropologist* 105.4 (2003): 822–26.

52. Rony, *Third Eye*, 12.

53. As Ted Mala informed me, not all Inuit communities use the term *shaman* to designate a healer or medicine person (conversation with author, Washington, DC, June 22, 2006). However, since Igloolik Isuma Productions employs the term in its press materials, I use it here. The Inuktitut word for shaman is *angakoq* (pl. *angakkuit*) and is not loaded with the kinds of Christian biases associated with the term shaman.

54. Angilirq et al., *Atanarjuat/The Fast Runner*, 37, 39.

55. In her dissertation, "Inuit Postcolonial Gender Relations in Greenland" (University of Edinburgh, 2002), Karla Jessen Williamson, an Inuit scholar from Greenland, asserts that traditional conceptions of gender equality and complementarity among the Inuit inform contemporary structures of gender equality and, among other things, attitudes toward sexual orientation in Arctic communities.

56. In *Sex Objects: Art and the Dialectics of Desire* (Minneapolis: University of Minnesota Press, 2006), Jennifer Doyle locates a queer reading of Herman Melville's *Moby-Dick* in the novel's "boring parts," such as the "Cetology" chapter. I do not find these passages of *Atanarjuat* boring, but have screened the film with students who have found the non–Hollywood action sequences tedious.

57. Steven Leuthold, *Indigenous Aesthetics: Native American Media and Identity* (Austin: University of Texas Press, 1998), 124–25.

58. Kathleen Fleming, "Igloolik Video: An Organic Response from a Culturally Sound Community," *Inuit Art Quarterly* 11.1 (1996): 27.

59. Griffiths, *Wondrous Difference*, xxix.

60. *Igloolik Isuma Production Diary*, http://atanarjuat.com/production_diary/index.html (accessed January 14, 2003).

61. James C. Faris, "Anthropological Transparency: Film, Representation, and Politics," in *Film as Ethnography*, ed. Peter Ian Crawford and David Turton (Manchester: Manchester University Press, 1992), 176.

Dismantling the Master's House

The Feminist Fourth Cinema Documentaries of Alanis Obomsawin and Loretta Todd

JENNIFER L. GAUTHIER

In 2009, Canada's National Film Board (NFB) celebrated its seventieth anniversary. The board was created by John Grierson, a Scot, in 1939 to produce and distribute films to interpret Canada to Canadians and to the world. Funded by the federal government, the NFB was the first such film agency anywhere in the world and has had much success over its history. NFB films have shown at festivals around the world and have received numerous accolades, winning over ninety Genies, twelve Academy Awards, and twenty awards at the Cannes Film Festival. Recently the films of NFB animator Norman McLaren were added to UNESCO's Memory of the World Register, which preserves the most significant world cultural artifacts.[1]

On a CBC broadcast in 1940, Grierson stated, "The National Film Board will be the *eyes of Canada*. It will, through a national use of cinema, see Canada and see it whole—its people and its purposes."[2] Grierson saw the films of the NFB as a "supplementary system of national education" designed to create active and informed citizens.[3] Bill Nichols describes Grierson's philosophy this way: "The filmmaker demonstrated his own civic responsibility by helping others orient themselves to the issues of the day."[4] For Grierson, the National Film Board was to be a major force in the construction of a unified nation, aiding Canadians in creating a distinct Canadian national identity.

The NFB is known for its commitment to representing the diversity of the Canadian nation, and while it has long documented First Nations peoples and issues, it was not until the 1960s that First Nations filmmakers were able to take the camera into their own hands. An Indigenous film crew took shape at the NFB within the "Challenge for Change" program in the 1960s; later Studio One (1990–96) was created to support Aboriginal filmmakers and this became the Aboriginal Filmmaking/Filmmakers

Program.[5] Alanis Obomsawin and Loretta Todd are perhaps the two most recognized inheritors of this legacy.

Obomsawin, a member of the Abenaki Nation, got her start as a composer and singer. In 1967 she was invited to work as a consultant to the NFB and since then she has directed over twenty films, most of which she has also written and produced. She was recognized as an Officer of the Order of Canada and won an Outstanding Achievement Award at the HotDocs Festival in 2009.[6] Todd is a Métis filmmaker from Alberta who studied film at Simon Fraser University and has made film installations, feature-length documentaries, and shorter videos for public service agencies and educational institutions. Her films have won awards at independent festivals around the world, and she is also well respected as a cultural critic.[7]

While both women make documentaries, they have each created a distinct approach to the genre. Despite their differences, Obomsawin and Todd share a strong interest in chronicling the lives of Indigenous peoples, paying specific attention to their struggle for sovereignty and state recognition. Their documentaries seek to empower First Nations people through giving voice to the voiceless, bearing witness to Canada's acts of racism, and challenging official history.[8] This chapter will draw upon examples from Obomsawin's films *Incident at Restigouche* (1984), *Richard Cardinal: Cry from the Diary of a Métis Child* (1986), *Kanehsatake: 270 Years of Resistance* (1993), *My Name Is Kahentiiosta* (1995), *Spudwrench: Kahnawake Man* (1997), *Rocks at Whiskey Trench* (2000), *Is the Crown at War with Us?* (2002), and *Our Nationhood* (2003) and Todd's films *The Learning Path* (1991), *Hands of History* (1994), *Forgotten Warriors* (1997), and *Kainayssini Imanistaisiwa: The People Go On* (2003) to explore the similarities and differences in their unique feminist Fourth Cinema aesthetic as it responds to the Griersonian tradition.

Reinventing the Documentary

Grierson coined the term *documentary* in a 1926 review of Robert Flaherty's *Moana*: "Of course, *Moana* being a visual account of events in the daily life of a Polynesian youth and his family, has documentary value, but that, I believe, is secondary to its value as a soft breath from a sunlit island washed by a marvelous sea as warm as the balmy air. *Moana* is first of all beautiful as nature is beautiful . . . *Moana* achieves greatness primarily through its poetic feeling for natural elements."[9]

In this review, Grierson identifies a dual purpose for documentary film: to make a record of cultural events and to capture the beauty of the world. Although Grierson was influenced by the films of Flaherty, he was also a fan of Russian documentaries, specifically their choice of subject matter. He admired their portrayal of "society on the move" and their attention to contemporary social reality, raw and unscripted.[10] In general, Grierson's conception of the documentary as a mode of social commentary and artistic expression was in sharp contrast to the fictional films made by Hollywood. He highlighted this difference by identifying two distinct moods in society: "moods of relaxation" and "moods of resolution." He argued that too much focus on "moods of relaxation," which he associated with things like Hollywood films, dance halls, and newspaper dope sheets, led to a poor civilization.[11]

The Griersonian documentary style is largely expository, characterized by its voice-over commentary and its logical construction of an argument. Its "voice of God" narration, according to Nichols, addresses the viewer directly, shaping "fragments of the historical world into a more rhetorical frame." Nichols likens it to television news reporting with its balanced, objective approach. Expository documentaries "rely heavily on an informing logic carried by the spoken word." The voice of the filmmaker or narrator is aligned with the voice of a government or society through the shooting and editing process.[12] Nichols suggests that the images serve as illustration or counterpoint to the narration through a technique that he calls "evidentiary editing."[13] The creation of a persuasive argument designed to inform (and ultimately move) the viewer is paramount, thus its "didactic emphasis."[14] Grierson's expository style, while objective on the surface, was in fact intended to advance a specific moral and ethical point of view. The two major series that he produced at the NFB, *Canada Carries On* (1940–45) and *The World in Action* (1942–46), were largely wartime propaganda vehicles.

For Grierson, the filmmaker spoke for his subjects, calling attention to social issues and mobilizing the Canadian public. As Nichols describes it, "A professional corps of filmmakers would go about representing others in accordance with their own ethics and their own institutional mandate as government-sponsored propagandists."[15] This process raises questions about the politics of representation and who can speak for whom in documentary practice. Obomsawin and Todd respond directly to these questions in their films. Moreover, they seek to reinvent the documentary form as it was envisioned by Grierson.

In an oft-quoted passage, writer Audre Lord poses a question and a caveat to cultural workers: "What does it mean when the tools of a racist patriarchy are used to examine the fruits of that same patriarchy? . . . The master's tools will never dismantle the master's house."[16] In their efforts to speak back to national history and renegotiate Indigeneity, both Obomsawin and Todd adapt the "master's tools" for their own use. They are an example of what Leela Gandhi has called "mimic men" (or, more correctly, "mimic women"), whose "generic misappropriations constantly transgress the received and orthodox boundaries." Gandhi suggests that "the paradigmatic moment of anti-colonial counter-textuality is seen to begin with the first indecorous mixing of Western genres with local content."[17] As Homi Bhabha notes, mimicry calls forth hybridity, "at once a mode of appropriation and of resistance."[18] Obomsawin and Todd appropriate the documentary form as means to communicate Indigenous history and culture, but they reimagine this fundamentally Western genre. Their unique brand of feminist Indigenous documentary speaks back to Canadian national identity and national cinema; they refashion Grierson's template for Indigenous purposes.

Grierson recognized that documentary films have two main functions, social criticism and artistic expression. Obomsawin and Todd have embraced these goals to varying degrees, offering two distinct models of First Nations documentary filmmaking. Obomsawin follows in Grierson's footsteps, using a straightforward modernist style and a didactic tone. Todd, in contrast, offers a unique postmodern take on the genre, using experimental techniques to interrogate the act of representation.

Obomsawin's work is rooted in the traditions of Canadian national cinema, but she builds upon Grierson's expository style with her keen powers of observation and an impulse to situate herself within the text. The observational mode, as described by Nichols, chronicles the actions of social actors while the filmmaker recedes into the background.[19] Obomsawin's films focus on events in Canada's history that have been seminal for First Nations people; she captures moments of crisis and conflict for posterity. Her camera becomes a witness to the mistreatment of

Provincial police forcibly remove a Mi'gmaq fisherman from the reserve in *Incident at Restigouche.*

Indigenous Canadians; it sees what the rest of the nation cannot see (or chooses to ignore).

Incident at Restigouche sets the stage for all of her work to follow. It focuses on the property and resource rights of the Mi'gmaq[20] peoples living on the Restigouche Reserve in Quebec. She sets up a tension between First Nations peoples and the Canadian government (both provincial and federal), crystallized by the conflict between national/provincial institutions (police, government, the legal system) and tribal institutions (cultural practices, heritage, traditions, daily life, families, traditional knowledge). The film chronicles the conflict over the Mi'gmaq's very right to exist. In *Richard Cardinal: Cry from the Diary of a Métis Child,* she tackles the child welfare system in Alberta through the case of a young Métis boy. Having lived through sixteen foster homes and twelve group homes, and separated from his eight brothers and sisters, Richard finally committed suicide at age seventeen.

Chronicling these issues, Obomsawin is not content to recede into

Actor Cory Swan plays the young Richard in dramatic reenactments of his life in *Richard Cardinal: Cry from the Diary of a Métis Child.* (©1986 National Film Board of Canada. All rights reserved.)

the background. She adopts a participatory style that enriches the observational aesthetic. She appears in all of her films, seated on a picnic bench interviewing subjects, standing in a cluster of reporters, or barricaded behind the lines during a military battle. Her presence on the screen confirms her intimate connection to the subject matter, so while observational documentaries may labor to elide the filmmaker's presence, Obomsawin intentionally foregrounds it.

One of the most striking examples of this strategy occurs in *Incident at Restigouche* as Obomsawin interviews former Quebec minister of fisheries, Lucien Lessard. Framed with the minister in a two-shot, she becomes irate listening to him reflect on the armed invasion of the Mi'gmaq reserve by provincial police. As she asks him whether he would have done anything differently, the camera slowly pans from her leaning in, awaiting his response, to the minister. She asks him if he consulted Premier Réne Lévesque and he says, "Yes." Then they get into a discussion about sovereignty and what it means, and Lessard remarks that a people cannot have sovereignty without a language and a culture. This comment clearly enrages Obomsawin, who says, "You took, took, took and we share." The interview concludes with Obomsawin asking Lessard if there is anything else he would like to say, and he obtusely apologizes for his actions. Obomsawin's unstinting focus on the minister and his unfortunate comments foregrounds the irony of the situation: Quebecers are unable to see the similarities between their bid for sovereignty and First Nations peoples' desire for recognition by the federal government. In this scene, Obomsawin is wearing a white dress and her hair is plaited in long braids; she plays the role of the beautiful native princess to emphasize her identification with the Mi'gmaq and to establish her credibility as a filmmaker.

In the Oka series (*Kanehsatake: 270 Years of Resistance, My Name Is Kahentiiosta, Spudwrench: Kahnawake Man,* and *Rocks at Whiskey Trench*), Obomsawin is most noticeable in shots of the media gathering at the barricades for interviews with military commanders or documenting the clash between Indigenous people and the soldiers. She is one of the only journalists left behind the lines to record the violence that occurs when the Native warriors and their families surrender and leave the Treatment Center. Her presence in these moments is crucial, as she has noted: "I was told many times that the fact that I was there, especially as a Native person, [meant] that the police and army wouldn't do certain things there with the camera."[21] Obomsawin can be heard asking questions during one-on-one interviews and she is occasionally seen nodding her head or heard encouraging people as they speak. She puts her Native subjects at ease with empathetic sounds and gestures.

In a heartbreaking scene in *Richard Cardinal,* she talks to the foster parents with whom he was living at the time of his suicide. Sitting at a picnic table in an idyllic landscape, she listens and nods as his foster father recounts the painful moment of finding him hanging from a tree.

Her onscreen participation in her films not only enhances her credibility, it also affirms her close emotional investment in the situation. According to Nichols, viewers watching a participatory documentary "have the sense that we are witness to a form of dialogue between filmmaker and subject that stresses situated engagement, negotiated interaction, and emotion-laden encounter."[22] In her unique blend of the observational and participatory modes, Obomsawin builds upon Grierson's commitment to social activism and education, positioning herself as an active citizen who is sharing her knowledge with the rest of Canada. Her goal of advancing

Mohawk warriors and the Canadian Army in a standoff in the Pines in *Kanehsatake: 270 Years of Resistance*. (Courtesy of Shaney Komulainen. ©1993 National Film Board of Canada. All rights reserved.)

a specific moral point of view is evident and rooted in the Griersonian tradition.

In addition to her debt to Grierson, Obomsawin's aesthetic impulses owe much to the *cinéma direct* legacy of the French unit at the NFB. The influences of Michel Brault and Pierre Perrault are evident in her direct engagement with social actors on location in the moment. Her location sound echoes the work of Marcel Carrière; she has said, "I'm very fussy about sound. I come from a place where hearing and listening to people is important."[23] The Québécois pioneers of 1960s cinema used new technology and a more intimate approach to their subjects, forging a radical path for Canadian cinema that blurred the boundaries between fiction and documentary.[24] Just as they used this new aesthetic to shake up Canadian cinema as it had been defined by the NFB, Obomsawin borrows it, makes it her own, and uses it to challenge the status quo twenty years later. She and her camera crew capture unbelievable footage, placing us in the midst of the action as it happens.

Some of the most stunning footage appears in the Oka films. In *My Name Is Kahentiiosta*, a film about one of the Mohawk women who was instrumental in the 1990 uprising, Obomsawin documents her arrest and incarceration at Farnham Military Base. Incredible behind-the-scenes sequences capture the Native people being processed after having been imprisoned on a bus all night. The film offers a powerful glimpse of the mistreatment of First Nations people; Kahentiiosta is the only woman still imprisoned after the others are released because she refuses to give the Quebec lawyer her Canadian name. In *Rocks at Whiskey Trench*, the camera films hordes of white Canadians from the town of Chateauguay, Quebec, throwing rocks at cars full of women, children, and elderly Mohawks as they leave their reserve. Situated on the banks of the highway in the marauding crowd, the camera focuses on random faces twisted in anger, shouting racial slurs while cars drive by with smashed windows. In *Is the Crown at War with Us?* the camera lens is splashed by the wake from a Department of Fisheries and Oceans (DFO) skiff that is being used to try to intimidate Mi'gmaq fishermen. Obomsawin and her camera ride on the small fishing boats, providing dramatic footage of the confrontations between Natives and federal authorities. These sequences heighten the drama of her documentaries, but also offer firsthand evidence of government racism. Obomsawin uses the techniques of cinéma direct to challenge the hegemony of the state, much as the pioneers of this style did in the 1960s.

Obomsawin's films offer alternative truths that challenge official history. Her truth claims are supported by evidence in the form of interviews, historical documents, maps, and location footage. In general, her films utilize a linear, chronological structure, revealing incidents as they unfold. Her editing style is rhetorically straightforward: the images reinforce the voice-over and vice versa; her footage provides illumination or explanation for the opinions that her subjects express. She employs a basic contrast method to lay bare the literal and metaphorical contradictions that characterize Canada's relationship with its Native peoples. Betraying her roots in Griersonian didacticism, she provides viewers with geographical and historical context of the events she chronicles. Obomsawin has said: "History is crucial to me and to all of my work. In whatever I have done, in whatever I have made, I have always included history. History tells the story and educates."[25] She draws heavily upon white Western epistemological forms such as cartography, written history, drawings, paintings,

Mi'gmaq fishermen preparing to set their traps in defiance of the DFO in *Is the Crown at War with Us?* (Courtesy of Pamela Mitchell. ©2002 National Film Board of Canada. All rights reserved.)

and photography to introduce her subjects and their communities. A particularly striking sequence is the seven-minute historical montage in *Our Nationhood,* which documents the history of the Mi'gmaq Nation from its foundation in seven districts to the formation of the thirty-nine-mile Listiguj Reserve. Obomsawin also highlights the white institutions of the military, the legal system, the government, and the penal system through footage of the army, courtroom drawings, and interviews with government officials. Every once in a while she throws the establishment a bone, but a close analysis of her rhetorical structure reveals her intimate connection with her subjects. What inevitably unfolds in these sequences is the complete arrogance, selfishness, and greed of the white man and the fallibility (if not utter negligence) of the state's institutions.

In *Rocks at Whiskey Trench,* a white man states, "That bridge is ours," referring to the Mercier bridge that connects the Mohawk reserve with mainland Canada. Obomsawin counters his assertion with an extended segment about the Mohawk men who labored to construct the bridge, using footage similar to that seen in *Spudwrench: Kahnawake Man.*

Documenting the violence perpetrated against Indigenous peoples, she takes particular aim at the provincial police and the federal military. In the Oka films, both the Quebec Provincial Police (QPP) and the Canadian army come across as war-mongering racists. Moreover, Obomsawin captures the language barrier between the Québécois soldiers and the Native warriors with heartbreaking clarity. In a scene from *Is the Crown at War with Us?* the Royal Canadian Mounted Police (RCMP) become fodder for her cinematic irony. In the year following multiple violent attacks on the Mi'gmaq reserve at Burnt Church, the RCMP establishes an outpost in the community. When a group of elders goes to the office to find out why, an RCMP officer talks about how the previous year was successful because of good communication. The viewer cannot help but laugh, considering the RCMP's use of tear gas and machine guns in the confrontations. Through this kind of ironic editing, it becomes clear that Obomsawin's loyalty is to her subjects; she fully agrees with their negative assessment of the powers that be.

Obomsawin's films make use of the voice-over, a venerated tradition in Griersonian documentary; in NFB films the voice of God narrator provides the viewer with salient facts and observations. However, Obomsawin takes this tradition and turns it on its head. In her films, Obomsawin herself speaks to the viewer, using quiet, measured tones (as many critics have noted, in an unfortunately gendered assessment) that connote an evenhanded objectivity. But the fact that it is her voice underscores her intimate connection to the subject matter; her narration is not aligned with the government, as in the Griersonian tradition, but against it. As Steven Leuthold suggests, this personalized approach is what gives Indigenous documentaries their "truth value."[26] She is not distant; she is not objective—she is enmeshed in the events she chronicles. As an Abenaki woman, her very identity has been shaped by the actions that she documents.

Obomsawin takes the traditional NFB documentary style and adapts it for her own political purposes. She makes films that expose the contradictions within Canadian history and ideology, redressing the wrongs done to First Nations peoples since conquest. She speaks back to official history, speaking with her own voice, but also with the voices of all Native peoples who have been disenfranchised. It is perhaps the greatest irony that her films are produced by the NFB, funded by the very government whose policies and history she interrogates.

Loretta Todd's films are more postmodern in their general rejection of truth claims, although they too highlight the injustices done to Indigenous peoples. Her films rely on multiple voices rather than a single narrator, celebrating polyphony and calling into question the act of representation. Although Obomsawin interviews others, her voice is still predominant as the voice of authority, or "the voice of God." Moreover, Obomsawin generally structures her films around events, while Todd focuses on experiences and memories. Todd's films pose a more overt challenge to the Griersonian style of documentary with their tapestry structure, democratic use of multiple voices, and nondiegetic sequences, including avant-garde inserts and setups that foreground the apparatus.[27]

In *The Learning Path*, *Hands of History*, and *Forgotten Warriors*, Todd's subjects speak directly to the viewer with no intermediary. Although her films include voice-over narration, it is quite understated, acting as an informal guide to knit diverse stories together. The unique stories are united by a common theme; in *The Learning Path* three Cree women reflect on their history and share their current projects in the field of education. Dr. Anne Anderson, Eva Cardinal, and Olive Dickason relate their own learning path and their efforts to mentor young people as they set out on their own path. *Hands of History* documents the work of four Indigenous Canadian artists, Doreen Jensen, Rena Point Bolton, Jane Ash Poitras, and Joane Cardinal-Schubert. The camera captures these artists as they practice their craft (carving, basket weaving, and painting) and discuss their personal and professional development. In *Forgotten Warriors*, Todd celebrates several Indigenous men who served in Canada's armed forces during World War II. Like Obomsawin, she interrogates the racism of government institutions, but her critique is more subtle. It is revealed in the stories told by her subjects.

By allowing Indigenous subjects to take center stage and address the audience directly, Todd gives voice to the voiceless. Their stories demonstrate the impact of history on identity and link the past to the present and the future. The personal narratives serve as a metonym for the experiences of First Nations people in Canada, and the act of sharing helps these individuals to reconstruct their identities and heal old wounds. Moreover, Todd's polyphonous structure calls attention to the multiple versions of history and truth.

Todd's films are best situated in the reflexive and performative modes of documentary. According to Nichols, reflexive documentaries are concerned with issues of representation and realism. They are self-conscious and self-questioning: "From a formal perspective, reflexivity draws our attention to our assumptions and expectations about documentary form itself. From a political perspective, reflexivity points toward our assumptions and expectations about the world around us."[28] In all of her films Todd questions prevailing assumptions about Indigenous peoples, foregrounding the ironies of official history and national policy.

In *The Learning Path,* as Dr. Anne Anderson visits the classroom of an old residential school, the camera alights on various objects: a painting of the Virgin Mary on the wall, a nationalistic slogan written on the blackboard ("One flag, one fleet, one throne"), a Union Jack hanging in the corner, and a book entitled *Chatterbox,* whose cover is adorned with a drawing of a young girl. This patriotic and patriarchal montage makes an ironic counterpoint to Anderson's memories of abuse in the school. In *Forgotten Warriors,* she pairs a shot of Chief Gerry Attachie showing on a map where his people were moved to make way for oil rigs with the singing of "O Canada." Later, the narrator describes the demonstration at Ipperwash, Ontario, which was aimed at preventing a military base from being built on an Indian burial ground, and mentions, almost in passing, that an Indian man was killed by the Ontario police. *The People Go On,* which focuses on the Kainai tribe of the Alberta plains, tackles the subject of representation head-on. Here Todd calls attention to the camera's act of making the film and highlights the problems with museum displays of Indigenous culture.

As a filmmaker and cultural critic, Todd is consumed with existential and metaphysical questions.[29] Her films reflect this concern as they (sometimes indirectly but always lyrically) probe the nature of identity, being, and the construction of meaning. In a recurring dramatic reenactment sequence in *Hands of History,* a white, Western man with glasses evaluates an Indigenous mask for its "value" as art. A similar scene occurs in *The People Go On,* but this time it is real. As a Native man examines an ancient skin painting with a white curator at the British Museum, he explains what the images mean and how the buffalo hunt depicted in the painting would have actually occurred. When he finishes, the Native man goes to roll up the skin, saying, "Why don't I just take this home with me?" Both men respond with nervous laughter. Todd's powerful use of humor heightens her commentary on postcolonial dispossession and diverse ways of knowing.

In their engagement with questions about knowledge, Todd's films are also performative. According to Nichols, performative documentaries are more personal in their tone, making use of embodied and subjective knowledge to move audience members "into subjective alignment or affinity with its specific perspective on the world."[30] Todd is familiar with and connected to her subjects in a way that a non-Native filmmaker would not be, although she is not seen on camera. In contrast, Obomsawin appears on camera with her subjects, but her films, like other participatory documentaries, tend to reinscribe a singular, factual approach to the topic. Using the tapestry style of nonlinear narrative, Todd's films work instead to foreground the subjective qualities of experience.

Nichols suggests that performative documentaries "share a deflection of documentary emphasis away from a realist representation of the historical world and toward poetic liberties, more unconventional narrative structures, and more subjective forms of representation."[31] Todd uses dramatic reenactments to emphasize the subjectivity of the experiences her films document. In a scene from *The Learning Path,* an Indigenous women and her child walk along the road speaking together in their Native language when a car pulls up and a man gets out. "I have to take your child," he says—and he does. As the car pulls away, we see the child looking desperately out of the rear window. The camera then focuses on the mother, lamenting in her Native language. Later in the same film, Todd re-creates scenes from a residential school as her subjects share their memories as students. *Forgotten Warriors* is punctuated with dramatic reenactment scenes from a fictional young man's life as he leaves home for the war, while he is away at war, and when he returns home. In *The People Go On,* Todd includes a repeated sequence of a Kainai family and their horse walking across the prairie. At the close of the film, the family faces the camera and smiles, as if to say, "We are still here, but we are so much more than this idealized, pastoral image suggests." Although dramatic reenactments can be stagy and artificial, these sequences serve to emphasize Todd's experimental approach to the documentary, similar to the work of Errol Morris. She uses these segments to provide an alternative thread of unity to her nonlinear films, and the characters serve as metonyms (occasionally ironic metonyms) for the Indigenous experience in Canada.

Performative documentaries also tend to take advantage of avant-garde aesthetic strategies to offer alternative ways of knowing. Todd real-

One of the recurring images of a Kainai family crossing the prairie in *Kainayssini Imanistaisiwa: The People Go On*. (Courtesy of Morton Molyneux. ©2003 National Film Board of Canada. All rights reserved.)

izes her avant-garde aspirations most fully in *The People Go On*, where she includes multiple nondiegetic sequences that feature archival photos of elders projected on waving flags or televisions placed on the prairie. With these sequences she challenges the traditional use of archival materials, calling attention to the degradation of the image as it is reproduced and further removed from reality. She also foregrounds the multiple versions of reality through her use of split and asymmetrical screens. Her interviews challenge the traditional "talking head" format and cutaway structure. As a filmmaker she did not want to interrupt the story or take attention away from the speaker, so she developed an alternative method of editing: "I had a young emerging filmmaker use a small video camera to shoot extreme close-ups of eyes, mouths, faces." She uses these inserts during the interviews, so while her subjects are speaking we focus on their mouths, their faces, their eyes, or occasionally even their hands. As she notes, "This is one way I wanted to place the speaker as central and the word—more 'important' than the 'documentary.'"[32]

Fourth Cinema

Obomsawin and Todd revise the NFB's traditional documentary form, effectively Indigenizing it. Taking the camera into their own hands and turning it on the white, Western establishment, they are making a distinct form of cinema described as Fourth Cinema by Māori filmmaker Barry Barclay.[33] Made by First Nations or Indigenous peoples, Fourth Cinema has an Indigenous essence to it, according to Barclay. This essence may be grasped only by Indigenous people but, like all cinema, Fourth Cinema works on many different levels. Barclay contrasts this essence, or the inner logic of the film, with its "accidents"—the surface features or elements of mise-en-scène that fill the screen.[34]

Fourth Cinema films take a unique point of view, turning First Cinema on its head. Barclay uses the Hollywood film *The Mutiny on the Bounty* (Lewis Milestone, 1962) to illustrate this idea. In the initial conquest scene, Captain Bligh (Trevor Howard) orders his sailors to go ashore and have sex with a Native woman. The camera sits on the deck of the ship and films the approach of the white men from the invaders' perspective. Barclay asks:

> What happens when the camera is shifted from the deck onto the shore? The camera, cut loose from First Cinema constraints and in the hands of the natives, does not work anything like as well away from the ship's deck (as the ship men see it), because allowing the camera to operate ashore under God knows whose direction would defeat the purposes of those in control of First Cinema, whose more or less exclusive intention has been, over one hundred years of cinema, to show actions and relationships within Western societies and Western ideological landscapes. Furthermore, the First Cinema enterprise is likely to be greatly deflated if there is a camera ashore, a camera outside First Cinema, a camera with a life of its own, watching.[35]

Fourth Cinema reenvisions the act of colonization from an Indigenous point of view, upsetting traditional hierarchies and redistributing power. Indigenous documentaries also "transfer authority to Indigenous people, redefining the 'voiceless victim' as a proactive political participant," calling attention to unequal power relationships.[36]

Obomsawin and Todd accomplish these goals through their acts of listening. Barclay has noted that the camera has to be a listener; it should stay back and observe.[37] Obomsawin has said, "The camera can speak, but it can also listen."[38] This approach recalls Todd's assertions that one important aspect of Indigenous aesthetics is the quality of "attentiveness."[39] She links this quality to the act of witnessing, which both she and Obomsawin do in their films. Both filmmakers seek to encourage attention to people and events that have been forgotten or purposely ignored.

This act of witnessing serves larger political goals as well. Anthropologist Faye Ginsburg sees Indigenous media as "part of broader movements for cultural autonomy and self-determination that exist in complex tension with the structures of national governments, international politics, and the global circulation of communications technology."[40] She suggests that "indigenous people are using screen media not to mask, but to recuperate their own collective histories and stories—some of them traumatic—that have been erased in the national narratives of the dominant culture and are in danger of being forgotten within local worlds as well."[41] In proclaiming Indigenous peoples' continued existence, Indigenous media texts challenge narrow conceptions of the national imaginary, national identity, and national cinema. Moreover, Indigenous films can instigate real social change. Obomsawin's *Richard Cardinal* ultimately brought about changes in Alberta's child welfare system. She has stated, "This is why I make films. To go for change."[42]

Fourth Cinema's radical potential to challenge the status quo depends on cross-cultural communication. Leuthold suggests that Indigenous documentaries initiate a cross-cultural dialogue and in so doing they assert a "dialogic model of truth."[43] Obomsawin has stated that she sees herself as a "bridge between two worlds," the Native and the non-Native, and that her films are intended to start a dialogue.[44] Not only dialogic but polyphonic, Indigenous documentaries foreground the multiple voices that make up the nation and its national cinema. These multiple voices offer different versions of history, often in different languages. As Leuthold notes, the issue of language is fraught for Indigenous filmmakers: do they use the language of the colonizer or their traditional language in their films?[45] Returning to Lord's query, is it possible to dismantle the master's house using his own words? Indigenous filmmakers often choose to incorporate their Native languages into their films, creating multilingual texts that symbolize the hybridity of contemporary Indigeneity. Obomsawin and Todd include Indigenous languages not only to preserve them for the future, but also to assert Indigenous peoples' continued existence and vitality.

As a postcolonial act of rebellion, Obomsawin and Todd's brand of Fourth Cinema is an example of what Laura Marks has called "intercultural cinema." Intercultural cinema is characterized by experimental styles that attempt to "represent the experience of living between two or more cultural regimes of knowledge or living as a minority in the still majority white Euro-American West." According to Marks, intercultural cinema is "constituted around a particular crisis: the directly political discrepancy between official history and 'private memory.'" Intercultural filmmakers perform "acts of excavation," using the cinema to reconstitute their history.[46] Both Obomsawin and Todd create Fourth Cinema documentaries that serve to excavate Indigenous memories and cultural practices that were buried by the colonizer. Marks also suggests that intercultural cinema is "haptic," in that it offers an alternative model of sense perception, appealing to more than just the visual.[47]

The documentaries of both Obomsawin and Todd evoke visceral reactions. Todd has reflected on her use of "the sensual" in her work.[48] Of particular note is her adoption of horror tropes to convey the experience of the residential schools in *The Learning Path.* The camera moves slowly down the halls of a deserted school, then up a set of stairs, to catch a glimpse of a nun from the back. She walks away and the camera follows, peeking through the doorway of a room, empty except for a nun sitting in a chair with her back to us. This eerie sequence, filmed in black and white, is followed by a slow pan across rows of sinks in an institutional bathroom. Todd then cuts to footage of little girls brushing their teeth and getting into bed in a large room full of cots. Over these images we hear Eva Cardinal remember her days in the school, the nun's cruelty and the priest's abuse. A male voice reassuring the children (as he assaults one of them) offers a terrifying counterpoint to the sounds of little girls crying or reciting their catechism. Pairing the conventions of horror films with experimental aesthetics, this segment is evocative of Maya Deren's *Meshes of the Afternoon* (1943) and Sally Potter's *Thriller* (1979). Like Deren and Potter, Todd foregrounds the female body as a site of potential violence and danger, using the tropes of suspense self-consciously for emphasis. In *The People Go On,* Todd films Native artifacts half in shadow over suspenseful music, as if to suggest their terror at being exoticized and trapped in museum displays.

While Obomsawin's films rely primarily on logical appeals, she too borrows from the horror genre occasionally. Her nighttime footage of the Oka confrontation is suspenseful and at times terrifying. The grainy images are almost indecipherable except for a few flashes of gunfire and flares. Paired with shots of wounded Mohawk warriors, these scenes are striking in their documentation of real violence. Zuzana Pick has noted that in these scenes, "the landscape acquires a spectral, almost dreamlike quality . . . the shots of the ghostly forest . . . construct a metaphor of terror."[49] In *Richard Cardinal,* Obomsawin sets up the physical facts of Richard's suicide early in the film, evoking in the audience a morbid fascination with tree where he hanged himself.

The haptic cinema of Obomsawin and Todd foregrounds fear as a visceral response not only to the dangers inherent in being an Indigenous person, but also to the power of Fourth Cinema. As Leslie Marmon Silko explains, "The Hopi with the video camera is frightening for a number of reasons. Euro-Americans desperately need to believe the indigenous people and cultures which were destroyed were somehow less than human; Hopi video makers are proof to the contrary. . . . The Hopi with a video camera is an omen of . . . the time when the indigenous people of the Americas will retake their land."[50] The First Nations woman with the video camera is also frightening.

Fourth Cinema is as varied as the Indigenous peoples who make it, but these diverse texts share common elements. According to Hopi video maker Victor Masayesva Jr., Indigenous cinema is marked by its unique construction of space and time, growing out of distinctly Indigenous conceptions of these elements.[51] Todd has noted this characteristic as well, foregrounding the "timeless" quality of Indigenous culture. She has written, "What does timelessness look like in narrative film?"[52] The tapestry structure of her films is an attempt to portray people's interconnections across both time and space. Moreover, in *The People Go On,* she deliberately disrupts linear time by asking her subjects to respond to the question, "Where were you 200 years ago?"

As is now a well-worn cliché in studies of Indigenous culture, Leuthold identifies the prevalence of nature imagery in Indigenous media: "A profound sense of place, which grows out of the linkage between the spiritual and the natural, is at the center of indigenous aesthetics."[53] Barclay puts it this way, "Māori people too are mindful of where their feet stand. Identifying your tribal land is fundamental to a Māori person because the land gives you your *turanga waewae* ('the place where the feet stand'), your identity."[54] This preoccupation with land is not surprising, given that "control of land has been the single most determinant economic and political issue for Indians throughout the last century and a half."[55]

Nearly all of Obomsawin's films are about the protection of Indigenous land and its resources. She highlights the importance of the land in striking montages that connect birds, water, trees, and humans. Moreover, she contrasts these with footage of bridges, trains, and ships—all man-made technology that has violated nature. In one particularly moving scene from *Is the Crown at War with Us?* a Native fisherman comments that he wishes he were like the great blue heron, who can fish where it wants. The film ends with a shot of a heron, fishing freely in the water. Todd's most evocative nature imagery is seen in *The People Go On,* which is structured around concepts of "home" as rooted in the earth. The first thirteen minutes of the film are devoted to establishing a specific sense of place on the land.[56] The interviews take place outside in natural settings that are important to the subject and they are often intercut with shots of the surrounding land, rocks, and trees.[57] In some instances the subjects hold a handful of grass as they speak to the camera, emphasizing their connection to the earth. Foregrounding Indigenous people's intimate relationship with nature serves to document an important aspect of their culture, but more importantly, it makes a radical political statement: "We are still here living on this land; it is still a part of us."

Feminist Film Theory

Fourth Cinema is act of revolution through which Indigenous filmmakers challenge the politics of the nation and of national cinema. Obomsawin and Todd are even more revolutionary in their disruption of traditional hierarchies, for they are Indigenous women taking the camera into their own hands. Formerly the erotic objects of the gaze, they become instead the powerful wielders of the apparatus. E. Ann Kaplan calls this a "complete reversal of the gaze" in her work on Aboriginal Australian filmmaker Tracey Moffatt's short film, *Nice Coloured Girls* (1987).[58] In their films, Obomsawin and Todd reverse the gaze and compel the non-Native viewer to see the world from an Indigenous perspective.

The woman's active gaze is an anomaly, at least in the history of Hollywood cinema, as feminist film theorists have observed. Following the work of Laura Mulvey in the 1970s, these scholars called for a feminist counter-cinema that would disrupt the pleasure in looking. Using a new language of visual representation, characterized by fragmentation, displacement, and discontinuity, counter-cinema would provoke awareness and critical attention on the part of the audience. Aesthetic strategies like foregrounding the apparatus would break down the illusion of reality, challenging patriarchy and the Hollywood status quo.[59]

Although these descriptions of counter-cinema specifically address fictional films, the aesthetic strategies are also applicable to the documentary form. In their films, Obomsawin and Todd enact a woman's powerful gaze to deconstruct traditional hierarchies of knowledge in both cinema and national history. Their gaze from behind the camera is revolutionary, as is their focus on women as active participants in history. They document the experiences of women who have made significant contributions to the struggle for sovereignty and recognition, helping to shape modern Indigeneity.

Obomsawin takes the traditional documentary form as it has been codified at the NFB and turns the camera back on the nation, exposing its history of racism and deception. Her decision to place herself in the frame with her subjects as an active participant in the conflict at Oka not only foregrounds the cinematic process but also challenges the traditional conceptions of woman as passive object to be looked at. We look at her on the screen, but she is more than mere spectacle. She propels the narrative forward through her work as a filmmaker; she tells the story as a participant in the action; and she interrogates the national imaginary.

While Obomsawin works within the Griersonian aesthetic, Todd's work actively forges a new language of First Nations women's documentary. Hers is a hybrid aesthetic, using the tools of the master against himself. Todd turns the rules upside down and inside out; she challenges them and ignores them. Borrowing aesthetic strategies from both experimental and fictional narrative films, she constructs a new documentary aesthetic. The result is both more intimate and more alienating. In *The People Go On* she distances her audience by calling attention to the apparatus in order to make a self-reflexive statement about the impossibility of portraying a culture on film. But the directness of her interviews compels us to identify with the speakers.

The People Go On is marked by gaps and silences, both of which characterize a political cinema, according to Marks. She suggests that these fissures symbolize "the sites of emergence from these smug sedimented discourses [the official discourse of invisibility, extinction, and racism]. As a result, the film may be less immediately accessible than those of Obomsawin; its messages are not as overtly expressed, nor are the lessons as easily deciphered. This strategy is intentional; as Marks notes: "When postcolonial filmmakers make difficult, hard-to-read works, they are not simply trying to frustrate the viewer, but to acknowledge the fact that the most important things that happened are invisible and unvisualizable." According to Marks, intercultural cinema "assumes the interestedness, engagement, and intelligence of its audience."[60] In other words, it calls for an active spectator who is willing to learn the language of counter-cinema. Todd's film rewards the engaged spectator.

The documentaries of Obomsawin and Todd owe much to the early feminist documentaries of the 1970s, which had their origin in the birth of the women's movement. Julia Lesage suggests that most of these films used a simple format to present the "ordinary details of women's lives." This focus on women's material culture was radical at the time, as was the notion of women talking directly to the camera to share their thoughts. Lesage says of these films, "Women's personal explorations are filmed specifically to combat patriarchy. The filmmaker's and her subjects' intent is political."[61] The link between the filmmaker and her subject is crucial to feminist documentaries, as is the connection between the personal and the political.

Part of the political impact of the women's documentaries comes from their soundtracks. Lesage notes that the stories are "usually told in the subjects' own words, [which] serves the function of rephrasing, criticizing, or articulating for the first time the rules of the game as they have been and as they should be for women."[62] Obomsawin and Todd let their female subjects speak for themselves to interrogate not only the "rules of the game" for women, but also the "rules of the game" for Indigenous Canadians.

Both Obomsawin and Todd foreground Indigenous women's experiences. Obomsawin introduces us to the Mohawk women who fought alongside the male warriors during the Oka crisis, Kahentiiosta, Ellen Gabriel, and Mavis Etienne; the wives and mothers who supported their husbands as they continued to pursue their livelihood in *Incident at Restigouche* and *Our Nationhood*; and the women who were the first to put their lobster traps back into the water in *Is the Crown at War with Us?*

The subjects of Todd's *The Learning Path* and *Hands of History* are all women. Todd shows them in their daily lives, working for change in education, interacting with their families, and sharing their memories. *Hands of History* is perhaps most radical in its close-ups of women working on their art; here Todd redefines "women's work."[63] In *Forgotten Warriors*, the fictional mother and girlfriend take on an important significance as those who bear the burden of the young man's absence. She also profiles Mary Greyeyes Reid, the first Indigenous women to enlist in the military in Canada. It is no accident that I have described her films as "tapestries," considering her focus on women's material culture.

Despite their revolutionary choices in content, early feminist documentary filmmakers deliberately used a traditional "realist" structure for their films because "they saw making these films as an urgent public act" and wanted them to be distributed to libraries, schools, churches, and community centers.[64] Obomsawin has declared a similar intent: "All of my work—whether singing or storytelling or filmmaking has been to fight for inclusion of our history in the educational system in our country."[65] Rather than provoke audiences with an avant-garde aesthetic, the films were intended to provide details of individual women's lives to unite them in the struggle and as "an act of naming previously unarticulated knowledge." Lesage further suggests that early women's documentaries were modeled on the "consciousness-raising" groups of the 1970s. As she observes, "There is a healing in the very act of naming and understanding women's general oppression." These groups harnessed the power of women's conversation as a form of resistance.[66] *The Learning Path* is perhaps the most vivid example of this strategy as Todd's subjects recall in sometimes horrifying detail their experiences in residential schools. Speaking about this trauma allows the women to begin healing and to show others with similar memories that they are not alone.

Alanis Obomsawin and Loretta Todd have forged a new film aesthetic that sits at the nexus of the feminist and the Indigenous; their feminist Fourth Cinema documentaries speak back to the nation and to the history of national cinema. As women filmmakers, their aesthetic choices and approach to Indigenous issues are informed by an embodied knowledge that permeates their work. Their films undertake a radical revision of traditional looking relations, power hierarchies, and cinematic norms. Each with her own unique strategy, Obomsawin and Todd stretch the boundaries of the documentary form as it was imagined by John Grierson for the NFB. Through their work, they have forged a path for other Indigenous filmmakers both in Canada and around the world.

Notes

This article has been reprinted with the permission of *Post Script: Essays in Film and the Humanities. Native American/Indigenous Film, Special Edition,* guest editor, M. Elise Marubbio, *Post Script: Essays in Film and the Humanities* (Texas A&M University–Commerce) 29.3 (Summer 2010).

1. Other artifacts include the Gutenberg Bible, the original manuscript of Beethoven's *Ninth Symphony*, and the films *Metropolis* (Fritz Lang, 1927) and *The Wizard of Oz* (Victor Fleming, 1939). CBC News, "Norman McLaren's Films Added to UNESCO Heritage Collection," December 28, 2009, http://www.cbc.ca/arts/film/story/2009/07/31/norman-mclaren.html (accessed July 31, 2009).

2. D. B. Jones, *Movies and Memoranda: An Interpretive History of the National Film Board of Canada* (Ottawa: Canadian Film Institute, 1981), 30.

3. John Grierson, "A Film Policy for Canada," in *Documents in Canadian Film*, ed. Douglas Fetherling (Peterborough, Ontario: Broadview, 1988), 66.

4. Bill Nichols, *Representing Reality* (Bloomington: Indiana University Press, 1991), 192.

5. Marie de Rosa, "Studio One: Of Storytellers and Stories," in *North of Everything: English-Canadian Cinema since 1980*, ed. William Beard and Jerry White (Edmonton: University of Alberta Press, 2002).

6. Randolph Lewis, *Alanis Obomsawin: The Vision of a Native Filmmaker* (Lincoln: University of Nebraska Press, 2006); and "NFB Portraits—Alanis Obomsawin," n.d., http://www3.nfb.ca/portaits/alanis_obomsawin/ (accessed March 25, 2009).

7. Todd Silverman, "Uncommon Visions: The Films of Loretta Todd," in *North of Everything: English-Canadian Cinema since 1980*, ed. William Beard and Jerry White (Edmonton: University of Alberta Press, 2002).

8. Throughout this chapter I use the term *Indigenous* to denote the original inhabitants of a region. Because Obomsawin and Todd focus on First Nations peoples in Canada, I will often use this phrase and the term *Indigenous* interchangeably. This choice is not meant to obscure the fact that the Inuit are also an Indigenous people of Canada. The capital "I" is intentional, as it distinguishes between indigenous as a general adjective and Indigenous as a proper noun.

9. John Grierson, "Flaherty's Poetic *Moana*," in *Documents in Canadian Film*, ed. Douglas Fetherling (Peterborough, Ontario: Broadview, 1988), 48.

10. Jones, *Movies*, 8.

11. Grierson, "A Film Policy for Canada," 63.

12. Bill Nichols, *Introduction to Documentary* (Bloomington: Indiana University Press, 2001), 105, 107, 97.

13. Nichols, *Representing*, 34–35.

14. Nichols, *Introduction*, 97.

15. Ibid., 140.

16. Audre Lord, *Sister Outsider* (Berkeley: Ten Speed, 1984), 13.

17. Leela Gandhi, *Post-colonial Theory: A Critical Introduction* (New York: Columbia University Press, 1998), 150.

18. Homi Bhabha, *The Location of Culture* (London: Routledge, 1990), 120.

19. Nichols, *Introduction*, 111.

20. Editors' note: Gauthier has chosen to use the spelling Mi'gmaq. Other spellings, which differ by region and group, include Mi'qmaq and Mi'kmaq.

21. Lewis, *Alanis Obomsawin*, 93.

22. Nichols, *Introduction*, 123.

23. Peter Steven, *Brink of Reality: New Canadian Documentary Film and Video* (Toronto: Between the Lines, 1993), 179.

24. Examples include *Les raquetteurs* (Michel Brault and Gilles Groulx, 1958) and *Pour la suite du monde* (Pierre Perrault, 1960).

25. Steve Loft, "Sovereignty, Subjectivity and Social Action: The Films of Alanis Obomsawin," Canada Council for the Arts, n.d., http://conseildesarts.ca/prizes/ggavma/zh127240204281875000.htm (accessed July 21, 2009).

26. Steven Leuthold, "Representing Truth and History in Native American Documentary: Indigenous Efforts to Counter Mass Media Stereotypes," *Film & History* 26.1–4 (1996): 31.

27. It is worth noting that in the book *Our Own Image* (Auckland: Longman Paul, 1990), Māori filmmaker Barry Barclay describes his films as presenting "a tapestry of people" (10).

28. Nichols, *Introduction*, 128.

29. Loretta Todd, "Polemics, Philosophies and a Story: Aboriginal Aesthetics in the Media of This Land," in *Transference, Tradition, Technology: Narrative New Media Exploring Visual and Digital Culture*, ed. Melanie Townsend, Dana Claxton and Steve Loft (Hamilton, Ontario: Art Gallery of Hamilton and the Indigenous Media Arts Group, 2005); Loretta Todd, "What More Do They Want?" in *Indigena*, ed. Gerald McMaster and Lee-Ann Martin (Hull, Quebec: Canadian Museum of Civilization, 1992); and Loretta Todd, "Notes on Appropriation," *Parallelogramme* 16.1 (1990): 24–33.

30. Nichols, *Introduction*, 132.

31. Ibid.

32. Loretta Todd, "A Few Notes about *The People Go On*," e mail message to author, April 6, 2009.

33. His framework is based on the following definitions: First Cinema is American (or Hollywood) cinema, Second Cinema is art house cinema, and

Third Cinema is the cinema of the third world. Third Cinema is specifically associated with 1960s Latin American filmmakers Glauber Rocha, Fernando Solanas, and Octavio Getino. Barry Barclay, "Exploring Fourth Cinema" (lecture, National Endowment for the Humanities Summer Institute, Honolulu, July 2003). See also Paul Willemen, *Looks and Frictions: Essays in Cultural Studies and Film Theory* (London: British Film Institute, 1993). Barclay made the world's first Indigenous feature film, *Ngati*, in 1987.

34. Barry Barclay, "Fourth Cinema" (lecture, Auckland University Film and Media Studies Department, Auckland, NZ, September 17, 2002).

35. Ibid.

36. Steven Leuthold, "Rhetorical Dimensions of Native American Documentary," *Wicazo Sa Review* (Summer 2001): 57, 63.

37. Barclay, *Our Own Image*, 14–15.

38. Merata Mita, "A Woman of Our Times," in *Alanis Obomsawin: 270 Years of Resistance* (DVD booklet), ed. Nancy Barr, Louise Malette, and Judy Yelon (Montreal: National Film Board of Canada, 2008).

39. Todd, "Polemics."

40. Faye Ginsburg, "Aboriginal Media and the Australian Imaginary," *Public Culture* 5 (1993): 558.

41. Faye Ginsburg, "Screen Memories: Resignifying the Traditional in Indigenous Media," in *Media Worlds: Anthropology on New Terrain*, ed. Faye Ginsburg, Lila Abu-Lughod, and Brian Larkin (Berkeley: University of California Press, 2002), 40

42. Lewis, *Alanis Obomsawin*, 55, 58.

43. Leuthold, "Representing," 33.

44. Penny Petrone, ed., *First People, First Voices* (Toronto: University of Toronto Press, 1991), 200.

45. Leuthold, "Representing," 34.

46. Laura Marks, *The Skin of the Film: Intercultural Cinema, Embodiment and the Senses* (Durham: Duke University Press, 2000), 1, 60, 26.

47. Ibid., xi–xiii.

48. Todd, "A Few Notes."

49. Zuzana Pick, "'This Land Is Ours'—Storytelling and History in *Kanehsatake: 270 Years of Resistance*," in *Candid Eyes: Essays on Canadian Documentaries*, ed. Jim Leach and Jeannette Sloniowski (Toronto: University of Toronto Press, 2003), 189.

50. Leslie Marmon Silko, "Videomakers and Basketmakers," *Aperture* 119 (1990): 73.

51. Victor Masayesva, "The Emerging Native American Aesthetics in Film and Video," *Felix* 2.1 (1995): 156.

52. Todd, "Polemics."

53. Steven Leuthold, *Indigenous Aesthetics: Native Art, Media and Identity* (Austin: University of Texas Press, 1998), 199.

54. Barclay, *Our Own Image*, 22.

55. Leuthold, *Indigenous Aesthetics*, 124.

56. This strategy echoes the Indigenous practice of introducing oneself by describing the place whence you and your ancestors came.

57. Todd, "A Few Notes."

58. E. Ann Kaplan, *Looking for the Other: Feminism, Film and the Imperial Gaze* (London: Routledge, 1997), 295.

59. See Laura Mulvey, "Visual Pleasure and Narrative Cinema," in *Feminism and Film*, ed. E. Ann Kaplan (London: Oxford University Press, 2000); Annette Kuhn, "Textual Politics," in *Issues in Feminist Film Criticism*, ed. Patricia Erens (Bloomington: Indiana University Press, 1990); Claire Johnston, "Women's Cinema as Counter-Cinema," in *Feminism and Film*, ed. E. Ann Kaplan (London: Oxford University Press, 2000); and Claire Johnston, "Dorothy Arzner: Critical Strategies," in *Feminism and Film*, ed. E. Ann Kaplan (London: Oxford University Press, 2000).

60. Marks, *Skin of the Film*, 56, 57, 19.

61. Julia Lesage, "The Political Aesthetics of the Feminist Documentary Film," in *Issues in Feminist Film Criticism*, ed. Patricia Erens (Bloomington: Indiana University Press, 1990), 222, 224.

62. Ibid., 234.

63. *Hands of History* was produced by the NFB's Studio D, the first publicly funded women's film production unit anywhere in the world. From 1974 to 1990 it produced films by, for, and about women. Todd was asked to finish the project when Obomsawin left to film the Oka crisis. See Elizabeth Anderson, "Studio D's Imagined Community: From Development (1974) to Realignment (1986–1990)," in *Gendering the Nation: Canadian Women's Cinema*, ed. Kay Armatage, Kass Banning, Brenda Longfellow, and Janine Marchessault (Toronto: University of Toronto Press, 1999).

64. Lesage, "The Political Aesthetics," 223.

65. Loft, "Sovereignty, Subjectivity and Social Action."

66. Lesage, "The Political Aesthetics," 230, 231.

Indigenous (Re)memory and Resistance

Video Works by Dana Claxton

Carla Taunton

> I'm influenced by my own experience as a Lakota woman, as a Canadian, a mixed blood Canadian, and then my own relationship to the natural and supernatural world. So taking that whole bundle of experiences, it all goes in to the artwork, I think that's where the multi-layering comes in because I've had a very multi-layered life. And it's all those experiences that go in to the work.
>
> —Dana Claxton (2010)

> Starting from grandmothers and ancestors, land and sky, rage and beauty, Dana Claxton weaves images, sounds, and ideas together with a sense of balance, subversion, and hope. Dana's work is situated in place, remembering, and history, bringing these elements together in surreal homages and explorations. Dana's work is part of a journey—the journey of identity of self and Nation (both Indigenous nations and Canadian Nationhood), the journey of history, and the journey of the spirit.
>
> —Tanya Willard

The multifaceted artistic practice of Hunkpapa Lakota artist Dana Claxton intertwines her Indigenous[1] worldviews with contemporary Aboriginal realities to create a visual language that exposes legacies of colonization, critiques settler histories, and asserts previously silenced Indigenous perspectives. Although her vast body of work includes films, installations, performances, and photography, her intricately layered video pieces are some of the most salient examples of her activist practices. In this chapter I explore the ways that Claxton re/frames archival photographs and film, personal interviews, contemporary music samples, and iconic images to simultaneously critique and create. A key aspect of her decolonization project is the sharing of Indigenous stories, a strategy that foregrounds (re)memory and resistance. She incorporates Indigenous bodies for the sharing of Indigenous perspectives and mines the archive to assert Indigenous histories. Taken together, I argue, Claxton's videos function as vehicles toward Indigenizing social memory—a role that is rooted in sovereignty, self-determination, and survivance.[2]

The theoretical framework underpinning my chapter draws on the writings of two prominent Indigenous scholars, Steven Loft (Mohawk) and Jolene Rickard (Tuscarora). In his article "Sovereignty, Subjectivity and Social Action: The Films of Alanis Obomsawin," Loft argues that discussions of Aboriginal filmmaking "must take place within a theoretical framework based on the political, social, historic and artistic realities which face Aboriginal people."[3] In "Sovereignty: A Line in the Sand," Rickard suggests, "The work of Indigenous artists needs to be understood through the clarifying lens of sovereignty and self-determination, not just in terms of assimilation, colonization, and identity politics. . . . Sovereignty is the border that shifts Indigenous experience from a victimized stance to a strategic one."[4]

Building on the perspectives of these important scholars, this project explores Claxton's work through frameworks of sovereignty and self-determination. I proceed from the premise that her videos make space for the imperative acknowledgment of the continued negotiations made by contemporary Indigenous peoples, and specifically Indigenous artists of colonial histories and contemporary experiences. More broadly, sovereignty and self-determination are lenses through which contemporary Aboriginal art can be explored in order to highlight Indigenous artists' agency, the autonomy of Native worldviews, and the sophisticated and political artistic strategies of sharing stories and experiences. By approaching Claxton's work within this larger theoretical structure, the complexity of media and meanings in her videos can be understood as tools for responding to and participating in the multifaceted project of reclaiming and revoicing Indigenous histories.

Claxton's *Buffalo Bone China* (1997), a video, performance, and installation, recalls the infinite impact of the extermination of the buffalo on Indigenous life and the historical use of buffalo bone to make fine china. A dynamic interweaving of artistic media, *Buffalo Bone China* is an example of Claxton's use of artistic production to reveal and challenge nationalist narratives and foreground occluded histories and silenced voices. At the same time, it functions as a site for mourning and remembrance of not only the loss of the buffalo but of the way of life the buffalo supported and generated for Plains Aboriginal peoples. This multitude of meanings and messages is made possible through the use of the archive and the body, tools that Claxton strategically employs throughout her work. By juxtaposing imagery from archival film footage with live-feed imagery of the Aboriginal body, Claxton's approach brings the past into the present, complicating settler histories and asserting Indigenous perspectives.

In the twelve-minute video component of *Buffalo Bone China*, Claxton presents archival footage of running buffalo herds intersected with looped and interspaced film images of a white man with a gun, a falling buffalo, and an Indigenous man yelling. These scenes are followed by a photograph of a buffalo skull overlaid on the moving image of stacks of pink, gold, and white china on a table. Later in the work, hands touch and caress the stacks of china, and the scene shifts to an Aboriginal man seated at the table with the china laid out in front of him. Actor Anthony McNab Favell yells at the table of china and then sits mournfully looking at the evidence of the buffalo extermination. After this, the camera follows the long black hair of an unidentified individual as it is slowly swept over the stacks of china on the table. Slow-motion images of running buffalo then return to the screen.

Tanya Willard describes the interconnections between politics, spirituality, memory, and anger in this performance/video installation and in Claxton's work more generally: "Dana smashes pieces of China and later makes four bundles and places them in a sanctified circle while an experimental video of buffalo plays. Feeling the loss of the buffalo, the backbone of Plains spirituality and sustenance, the artist uses a rubber mallet to destroy plates and bowls. The breaking of the china refers to the use of buffalo bones in the making of bone china during the period of exploitation and decimation of the buffalo. This rage can be seen to ebb and flow in Dana's work."[5]

The presence of the china and the buffalo imagery function as documents that allude to colonial histories. Their inclusion introduces audience members to lesser-known events that are then interrogated by the artist through the insertion of individual Indigenous bodies—her own and Favell's. Screaming and breaking of china is set in contrast with more subdued forms of mourning, a juxtaposition that highlights the complexity of individual responses to colonial impact. This pairing of the archive and the contemporary Indigenous body opens up a conversation that complicates existing discussions and asserts Aboriginal self-determination. As a result, Claxton's work calls for the rememory[6] of the past and the creation of new stories in the present. These works are not reactionary; instead, they promote Indigenous perspectives and reframe settler/Indigenous histories in North America.

As described in the preceding example, the archive is an important tool that Claxton uses to reconfigure social memory from Indigenous vantage points. Her videos subvert colonial representation tactics by employing similar strategies in new ways. Both film and photographs were frequently used by colonizers to document, record, produce, and construct Aboriginal peoples according to preconceived Western ideas about identity and race. Marcia Crosby argued over twenty years ago that a large amount of contemporary Aboriginal art is produced as an attempt to reclaim the image of the "Indian" from the ethnographic context of the salvage paradigm. She explains that Indigenous peoples have been collected theoretically and physically by Europeans who "salvaged" their material and visual culture and placed it in museum collections.[7] A number of contemporary Indigenous communities are now mining these archives and using photographs, film, newspaper articles, and objects to critique the past, reclaim histories, and emphasize cultural continuity.

Claxton has drawn heavily on film archives in her reclamation project. Her work, along with that of other Aboriginal filmmakers and artists, asserts Indigenous presence and experience while it also contests and displaces stereotypical imagery produced in mainstream films. In one of the first comprehensive anthologies on Aboriginal peoples and film, *The Pretend Indians: Images of Native Americans in the Movies*, Lakota scholar and activist Vine Deloria Jr. explores the complex relationship of Indigenous peoples with film and video in North America. He writes, "Therein lies the meaning of the white fantasy about Indians—the problem of the Indian image. Underneath all the conflicting images of the Indian one fundamental truth emerges: the white man knows he is alien and he knows that North America is Indian—and he will never let go of the Indian image because he thinks that by some clever manipulation he can achieve an authenticity which can never be his."[8] In other words, the representation and image of Aboriginal peoples in film has a longstanding history, and film and other types of media are strategic vehicles that supported and maintained colonial agendas. Māori scholar Linda Tuhiwai Smith warns, "Western culture constantly reaffirms the West's view of itself as the centre of legitimate knowledge, the arbiter of what counts as knowledge and the source of 'civilized' knowledge."[9] Claxton's practice intervenes in the colonial rhetoric of stereotypes and racist representations by presenting perspectives, histories, and images through an Indigenous lens. In this sense, her film and video work participates in the displacement of colonial and national/ist histories, which historically delegitimated, ignored, erased, and silenced Indigenous experiences.

Claxton's multisensory video strategies challenge colonial historical and stereotypical representations of Aboriginal peoples. She accomplishes this reclaiming of the images of both Indigenous men and women by her inclusions and uses of Aboriginal bodies in her video works. This strategy of inclusion is exemplified by *The Hill* (2004), which includes an Indigenous actor as the focus of the video narrative. The body is the site for articulating Indigenous lived experiences and stories. In a recent interview with the artist, I spoke with Claxton about the role of the body in her video, performance, and photographic works. We discussed how her videos create a space for a very positive representation of the Aboriginal body. Claxton stated that she wanted to create representations that showcased "the beauty of the Aboriginal body and of the beauty of Aboriginal existence."[10] Drawing upon performance artist James Luna's (among other artists and scholars of performance and video art, such as Rebecca Belmore and Lori Blondeau) understanding of body politics and the human body as a "social instrument" for resistance and activism, the inclusion of Indigenous bodies into works by Indigenous artists can vocalize critical discourse.[11] In this regard, Claxton's inclusion of Aboriginal bodies challenges representations and histories of Indigenous peoples presented and maintained by popular culture.

The Hill, a short (three minutes and forty-five seconds) two-channel video, places an Indigenous woman on Parliament Hill in Ottawa. In the right channel, the camera follows a woman, actor Michelle Trush. The audience watches her as she walks the grounds of the Parliament buildings; at one point she attempts to open the doors, but they are locked. This action alludes to the exclusion of Indigenous peoples in Canadian nationalism. The focus on the left channel are the late nineteenth-century neo-Gothic buildings of the Parliament, showcasing the monumentality of the central Peace Tower and other architectural details, such as the carved reliefs of Aboriginal peoples. Claxton's close-ups of these representations allude to the racist and Eurocentric attitudes prevalent during the founding of the nation. Like Edward Curtis's photographs, these stereotypical representations of the Noble Savage created in stone participate in the "collecting" of Indigenous peoples—an example of the erroneous belief in the nineteenth century that the Indigenous peoples of North America were vanishing. Here, in the monumental stonework of the symbol of a nation, the iconic image of an Aboriginal man in headdress is placed on display as a relic of times past. The artist's incorporation of these images through the lens of her camera reclaims and contextualizes their presence, and for the unknowing viewer raises questions as to why these relief representations are on the Parliament buildings. The juxtaposition of the imagery of the Aboriginal woman and the relief carvings alludes to a history: Aboriginal people were not incorporated into the governance of Canada but rather forcibly placed into controlled reserves. As a result, the architectural imagery is continuously contextualized and simultaneously challenged by the presence of the image of the Aboriginal woman. This video places the Indigenous body on the site of Canadian government, a place and space that historically has violently oppressed and attempted to control all aspects of Indigenous life (as exemplified by the Indian Act and the Indian Residential School legislations).

The presence of the Aboriginal woman's body can be seen as Claxton's commentary on the relationship between Aboriginal peoples and the Canadian government. The very fact that she could not open the doors to the Parliament buildings—the site of decision making—overtly elucidates the ongoing struggles and challenges Aboriginal peoples face in relation to Canada, and their ongoing efforts to assert sovereignty over lands and government. *The Hill* is a visual representation of contemporary issues faced by Aboriginal peoples as well as the legacies of colonization. It is an explicit example of Indigenous survivance, which claims rights and visibility in Canadian government and also in Canadian society. Claxton's imagery offers an opportunity for reflecting on Canada as a settler nation and on Indigenous experiences in Canada. Witnessing such a staging, an Aboriginal woman walking Algonquin ancestral land now commonly known as The Hill, which is a site that historically excluded Indigenous peoples, conveys a powerful self-determined message of Indigenous activism. *The Hill* uses the body to emphasize the presence of Aboriginal peoples in Canadian history.

Claxton's inclusion of Indigenous bodies in her video work is an act of re/claiming the image and experiences of Aboriginal peoples that tells an Indigenous story for Indigenous audiences and challenges the representations of the Indian Princess and Noble Savage or, as Marcia Crosby acutely argued, the "Imaginary Indian" of settler society who so frequently appears in popular culture.[12] Claxton's work also asserts an opposition to the history of displaying Indigenous bodies and cultures for settler consumption at World Fairs, Wild West shows, vaudeville and burlesque shows, and in Hollywood films, simultaneously participating in the history of Indigenous peoples' strategic use of performance as a site of sociopolitical resistance and cultural continuance.[13]

Her Sugar Is? (2009), one of Claxton's most recent videos, is linked to the histories of Indigenous performance on settler stages. Although the Aboriginal woman's body is not overtly included, the stereotype is explicitly explored through the use of archival film of burlesque shows. Claxton investigates and complicates the history of white women dressing as Indian Princesses. In this way, *Her Sugar Is?* strategically intervenes and resists stereotypical representations of Aboriginal people by not including the Aboriginal body with this type of iconic imagery. The artist alludes to the relationship between stereotypes of Aboriginal women and their origin, settler narratives and popular culture.

Her Sugar Is? a film of two minutes and forty-one seconds, premiered at the tenth annual imagineNative Media and Film Festival held in Toronto (October 14–19, 2009) in the short-experimental program. This video pointedly and playfully incorporates archival film footage of burlesque shows. Using the iconographic and highly sexualized imagery of the Indian Princess and the Cowgirl alongside other images of showgirls and dancers, Claxton complicates and challenges stereotypical representations of women and the exotification of the Aboriginal woman's body by dominant settler culture.[14] In this short video, a three-channel screen becomes center stage for topless women dancers. The focus in the center screen is black-and-white film footage of an "Indian village" burlesque show. On the stage, white women are dressed up as stereotypical icons of the Indian Princess. A topless woman costumed in a headdress dances in the center channel, the image juxtaposed with mirroring images on the two side panels, which present rotating footage of white women dressed up as Cowgirls; they seem to serve as the backup dancers of the central show, the Indian Princesses. At one point, a blonde naked woman appears, dancing in slow motion and holding a semiautomatic weapon as her stage prop. The juxtaposed images of the "Indian Village" burlesque show and the Cowgirls convey commentary on the interrelated histories of Indigenous and settler peoples. The imagery of *Her Sugar Is?* exemplified by the dancing woman with the gun, also alludes to the violence of both colonialism and stereotypical sexualized representations of Aboriginal women.

The music, produced by Russell Wallace, creates the beat for all the channels' dancers, including the background screen, where a woman dances in a red sequined dress. The archival footage of all the screens is slowed and synchronized so that the women dance to the incorporated music. The imagery of the topless women dancers evokes experiences of Aboriginal performers in burlesque shows, vaudeville theater, and other settler stages, making connections between the history of exhibiting and sexualizing Indigenous women's bodies and violence, colonialism, resistance, and entertainment. This work is quintessential Claxton, as it is a multilayered video that uses the body and archival footage as strategies to reclaim, reveal, critique, and complicate.

Many of Claxton's works, such as *I Want to Know Why* (1994) and *Sitting Bull and the Moose Jaw Sioux* (2003), mine the archive for traces and recorded documents of Indigenous experiences. In her later work, Claxton incorporates live-feed images of the stacks of archival newspapers and other documents that she uncovered during her research. *Sitting Bull and the Moose Jaw Sioux,* one of Claxton's more recent video works, is a four-channel video installation that was commissioned by the Moose Jaw Art Gallery. The video is described as "a contemporary view of a historical story" comprised of interviews, landscape imagery, live-feed images of archival newspapers, stills of historic photographs, and appropriated film footage. The history Claxton explores and reveals is personal as well as communal. As Tanya Willard states, "Dana's family reserve in Wood Mountain, Saskatchewan is an area of Lakota settlement; her family traces its roots to the migration of Sitting Bull and Dana's great-great grandmother's journey."[15] Claxton's great-great grandmother, as asserted in her film *I Want to Know Why,* fled the United States, her ancestral lands, during the Indian wars of the 1880s, which was a period of heightened American land expansion and significant colonial violence against Indigenous peoples. The history of the U.S. federal government's deceptions, the breaking of the Fort Laramie Treaty in 1874 due to the discovery of gold, and the battle of the Little Big Horn in 1876 are intimately explored in the storytelling voice-overs and through the visual imagery of photographs of Sitting Bull and other Lakota men and women who experienced the violence and occupation of the establishing American state. In an interview, Claxton recalls the mass hanging of Dakota men in Minnesota, which remains one of the largest mass hangings in U.S. history. She says, "When the people saw that—if you can imagine seeing 39 men being hung—you just knew it was no longer safe for you and your homeland."[16] *Sitting Bull and the Moose Jaw Sioux* vocalizes this period in American history and the subsequent resettlement of Lakota and Sioux in Saskatchewan and Manitoba.

On the central screen, a black-and-white image of Sitting Bull is flanked by images of Claxton's archival research, piles of newspaper clippings from the *Moose Jaw Times*. Lynne Bell's account of this video installation in "The Post/Colonial Photographic Archive and the Work of Memory" describes in detail the opening scenes of the video:

> As the camera sifts through piles of yellowed newspapers in the side channels, I watch glimpses of banner headlines proclaiming "Custer massacre refugees given aid by Moose Jaw" and "Kingsway Park once site of Hundreds of Wigwams." The grainy news photos depict Lakota men, women, and children. In a voice-over conversation, two Sioux storytellers recall family stories, accounts, and legends of Sitting Bull and the Moose Jaw Sioux. An English translation runs across the bottom of the screens. As the camera pans over a photograph of Sitting Bull on the centre screen, images of the land of the Black Hills of Dakota flash past on the side screens: the voice-over states: "They owned that land of the Black Hills. . . . They called that the heart of the earth. That was their homeland. . . . But gold was discovered. . . . and they broke the treaties.[17]

In *Sitting Bull and the Moose Jaw Sioux*, Claxton makes public the histories of the Moose Jaw Sioux and their migration and subsequent settlement of the Wood Mountain Reserve as well as the experiences of the Sioux people during the late nineteenth century in the United States. The focus of this video on Sioux experience from Sioux perspectives counters the commonly known narratives of this era of North American history.

Such an approach complicates social memory. As David Garneau points out in his review "Dana Claxton: *Sitting Bull and the Moose Jaw Sioux*,"

> Claxton's strategy is both good historical storytelling and creative art. The narrative is layered rather than linear, dialogic rather than authoritarian, and open-ended rather than contained. At least four accounts unspool at

> any one time. While they always complement each other and advance the story, the gentle polyphony encourages repeated viewings and the sense that we can gather only glimpses and should not imagine ourselves completely informed. Unlike conventional documentaries, there is no narrative arc, rising tension, climax, and denouement. In fact, the initiating event, the Battle at Little Bighorn, does not get told until near the end, and its central antagonist, Custer, is barely mentioned. This is the Sioux account of the battle and their subsequent lives. It is eventful, but, until now, only a footnote to settler history.[18]

Claxton achieves this telling of Lakota histories of colonization and the contemporary relevance of these stories through her inclusions of contemporary imagery from Moose Jaw with story voice-overs. In one section of the video, in the center panel, film footage of the original Sioux campsite in Moose Jaw is juxtaposed with images of moose, buffalo, and the iconic architectural details of "Indian heads" that decorate the Fourth Avenue bridge in Moose Jaw. The voice-over states: "They went and saw Father Bernard in Lebret. He gave them food. The RCMP went there and told them not to give them food. Sitting Bull's tribe came back to Moose Jaw. . . . Father Bernard brought some food to them. The RCMP went there and said, 'You're not going to give this tribe anything.'"

The following scene incorporates yet another contemporary image of Moose Jaw, which symbolically evokes a message of the continuing relevance of the history of the Sioux in North America. In the side screens, Claxton's camera shows a close-up view of a city street sign, "Sioux Crescent" juxtaposed with the center panel's images of the Saskatchewan landscape and antelope. These images are further contextualized by Claxton's strategic inclusion of the voice-over, stories from interviews that the artist has conducted. As Bell writes, the work depicts "the Lakota people's migration south in the summer to hunt antelope in the hills and . . . the close and peaceful relations existing between the Sioux and the early settlers in Moose Jaw."[19]

One of the key sites that Claxton turned to in search of documents to reconstruct, retell, and remember the history of the Sioux in Saskatchewan is an archive of late nineteenth- and early twentieth-century photojournalism from the *Moose Jaw Times*. According to Lynne Bell, "This media archive clearly reveals the epistemic violence at the heart of the colonial encounter. In *the Moose Jaw Times* archive, we see how the captioned photograph was used at the turn of the last century to give tangible form to a proliferating set of stereotypes that marked the Sioux as the racialized 'other' of the white settler community in Moose Jaw."[20] Consequently, Claxton's inclusion of these found records with Indigenous-based interviews/oral histories contextualizes the representations of archival photographs and newspaper articles, thereby Indigenizing the historical record of the Moose Jaw Sioux. *Sitting Bull and the Moose Jaw Sioux* complicates understanding and social memory of Sioux experiences by incorporating stories of Moose Jaw Sioux people. The oral memories of the history of violence in the United States, the resulting migration, and the subsequent oppressions, marginalizations, and systemic violence endured in settlement in Canada create a history that is not commonly known. Claxton's engagement with and inclusions of archival film footage and other material documents insert her artistic practice into the larger project of Indigenizing the archive. She combines strategies inherent to the archive in creating and maintaining social memory with tactics of Lakota storytelling. In an interview, curator Tanya Willard and Claxton explored *Sitting Bull and the Moose Jaw Sioux* and discussed the role of the artist as historian within the context of the postcolonial project of decolonization. As Willard notes, "Dana comments on the way many Aboriginal artists become historians in some capacity, uncovering the truths of Aboriginal experience that are buried under layers of colonial histories."[21] Curator Jason St. Laurent's essay *History in Parts: The Work of Dana Claxton* draws similar attention to Claxton's artistic aesthetic and her use of artistic practice to voice histories that are not nationally remembered: "Dana Claxton's work is esthetically innovative, brilliantly written and expertly paced. The thrust of her practice is political, spiritual and social, making it an essential contribution not only to the field of media art, but generally, to a more honest sense of history."[22] Her video works, therefore, visually create history, displacing national narratives while simultaneously creating Indigenous re/memory, a strategy of decolonization.

Claxton's works such as *The Hill*, *Sitting Bull and the Moose Jaw Sioux*, *I Want to Know Why*, and *10* (2003) reveal the many silenced histories of violence and systemic racism in relation to North American colonization and its ongoing legacies. Violence against Indigenous peoples and their bodies is a theme that Claxton explores and gives voice to in both explicit and implicit ways. The visual exploration of violence against Indigenous bodies, minds, cultures, and knowledge is interconnected to the tactics of colonization. Many of these histories of violence are not part of North American social memory and national narratives of nationhood. *10*, a video of seven minutes and twenty seconds, showcases and complicates an Agatha Christie novel and its film adaptations, *10 Little Indians*. The best-selling mystery novel, first published in the United States in 1940 under the title *And Then There Were None*, follows the experiences of ten guests who have been invited to an isolated place only to find that an unknown person is killing them one by one. This video implicates Christie's novel and the commonly known nursery rhyme after which her book is named in the violence against Indigenous peoples and the ongoing silencings around these histories and contemporary experiences. Claxton incorporates the technique of jump-cutting to move between three different movie versions of *10 Little Indians* from three different periods of American film history. During this short experimental work, the nursery rhyme is repeated over and over again. The words become more aggressive through the repetition of the rhyme, revealing their overt racism and violence. *10* exposes the power of language and images and how popular culture and stereotypes are a form of systemic racism and violence.

Dana Claxton's video work, as well as her performances and photographs, draw from the film archive as part of her agenda. The archive, like all colonial entrenched institutions, is currently being decolonized, not only through engagement with its settler/colonial-based structures, as Diana Taylor suggests, but also through cultural continuities and continuance of Indigenous storytellers and artists. In her pivotal study of performance in the Americas and its relationships to memory, history making, and knowledge, *The Archive and the Repertoire*, Diana Taylor defines "archival" as memory that exists as documents, maps, letters, literary texts, archaeological remains, bones, videos, films, CDs, and so on.[23] These understandings of the archive, a tool in national memory making, are related to Western concepts of memory and history writing, whereas within the structures of Indigenous cultures, memory and history writing are connected to oral transmissions of events and stories. As Diane Taylor's work argues, throughout colonization, Indigenous knowledge, oral history, and memory have been rendered invalid—silent and forgotten. The written document and the writing of history as a discipline have served as strategic tools for colonialism's project of conquest, extermination, expansion, and assimilation.

Despite colonial tactics of rendering Indigenous knowledge systems like storytelling subordinate to written knowledge, oral traditions have endured and continue. By revealing the impact of colonization on forms of Indigenous memory making such as storytelling and the oral tradition of history writing, as well as the ways in which settler society constructs memory through films, monuments, archives, and museum collections, the project of decolonizing Indigenous cultural knowledge complicates the history and function of the colonial archive in settler nations. Embodied performance, as Taylor argues, "has always played a central role in conserving memory and consolidating identities in literate, semiliterate, and digital societies. Not everyone comes to 'culture' or modernity through writing. . . . We might look to past practices considered by some to have disappeared. We might look to contemporary practices by populations usually dismissed as 'backward' (Indigenous and marginalized communities)."[24]

In this sense, the oral histories within Indigenous communities, which have largely been delegitimated by colonial agendas, are stories and the performance of stories, which artists like Dana Claxton are continually revealing to both Indigenous and non-Indigenous audiences. In many ways, oral histories are currently being decolonized by acts of reclaiming and retelling. Although the strategies Claxton incorporates, meaning contemporary art, may differ from historic ways of transmitting stories, her use of video (performance and photography) for the telling of histories and experiences links her to the history of storytelling by Lakota elders. The incorporation of Indigenous stories and oral memories into the works of Dana Claxton, therefore, creates visual documents of Indigenous lived experiences.

Claxton's videos contribute to the decolonization of Indigenous social memory as well as national social memory by strategic use of Indigenous stories. Her identity as a Lakota woman and her family's and community's experiences with social injustices in colonial and more current times inform her artistic practice and her strategies of unraveling and revealing silenced histories. Willard extends this point in her description of Claxton's video *I Want to Know Why*, in which the artist's voice is a fundamental part of the work's sound, creating a rhythm that contextualizes the imagery:

> Her heritage is linked to an important historical injustice spanning the US and Canadian colonial borders: the migration of Sitting Bull and his people to Canada. The effects of colonization, discrimination, and systemic

> racism on Aboriginal people and on the artist's own family history fueled her early work. In an early single-channel video work, *I Want to Know Why* (1994), Dana screams, "I want to know why!" In her cry for answers, the injustice and colonial foundation of Canada and the US is revealed within the personal tragedy of her mother's and maternal grandmother's early deaths and her great grandmother's migration to Canada. Dana frames the suffering of her grandmothers and her mother within the context of Canadian colonialism and the injustice of American history.[25]

The recognition of performance or, in the case of Claxton's work, video narratives, as a continued site for transmitting Indigenous experiences and fostering memory and history making lends urgency to acts of Indigenous video art as well as other artistic practices, such as the performance art of artists like Rebecca Belmore, Lori Blondeau, Cheryl L'Hirondelle, and Skeena Reece (as well as other forms of Indigenous performance, such as theater, dance, and music) as viable and contributing media for Indigenous cultural continuance. Indigenous contemporary art such as Claxton's videos, which use strategies of storytelling, can be vehicles for displacing colonial and settler narratives, thereby contributing to the Indigenization of the archive and social memory/ies.

Anishinaabe scholar Gerald Vizenor argues that Native stories are stories of Native survivance, which he defines as being "more than survival, more than endurance or mere response; the stories of survivance are an active presence."[26] In other words, in Vizenor's view, Native stories are the traces of Native experiences and are the evidence of Native survivance. Jean Fisher discusses Coco Fusco's storytelling practice as a site where the act of witness may enable audiences to "rediscover [their] potential as agents of change." Fisher argues that storytelling "has special poignancy for those peoples for whom the trauma of racial violence has yet to be healed and adequately narrativized."[27] Live and/or video-based Indigenous installation art can offer to local, national, and international audiences a site within which to bear witness to the current realities of Indigenous peoples and to take notice of the trauma that marks the Aboriginal body. At the same time, it also contributes to the discourse of Indigenous decolonization, whereby self-determined Aboriginal voices are Indigenizing spaces such as the gallery. The result is a reclaiming of once-victimized bodies, lands, and stories marked by colonial history to a position of Indigenous sovereignty.

It is significant to see the story (the narrative or performance) as a sovereign agent of reclamation and decolonization. In relation to employing Indigenous video and other artistic practices, such as performance art, as a tactic for Indigenous resistance, Steven Loft's argument is very insightful; he states, "The strength lies not in the telling of the story, but in its power to assert meaning."[28] In this sense, the performance of storytelling is a process that can be employed in order to complicate, interrupt, and intervene in colonial histories, to reestablish self-determined representations, and to provoke political resistance. Anishinaabe writer Kateri Akiwenzie-Damm emphasizes the power of telling stories: "When we express ourselves and we listen to the creative and cultural expressions of others, we must do so from an informed position so that we do not contribute to the confusion and oppression but instead bring into sharper focus who we are. By freeing ourselves of the constricting bounds of stereotypes and imposed labels of identity we empower ourselves and our communities."[29] The video works by Claxton that I have explored here are powerful experimental short videos, retellings of shared colonial settler/Indigenous histories as well as of specific Indigenous experience. They successfully displace the legacies of colonial narratives by offering new, multifaceted Indigenous frameworks saturated in conversations of decolonization, sovereignty, self-determination, memory, and resistance.

Arguably, Claxton is a storyteller who intertwines histories, experiences, and stories using visuals from her own directed film footage, popular culture, and the photographic and film archives. *Buffalo Bone China* exemplifies Claxton's aesthetic, established in her earlier works and further pushed and developed in her more recent works. Claxton's visual language, identified by her strategic and sophisticated loopings and layerings of images that contest and reclaim, creates powerful narratives that overtly assert Indigenous perspectives. In her essay "Worlds in Collision: Dana Claxton's Video Installations," Monika Kin Gagnon discusses Claxton's use of storytelling and the collisions between technology and cultures in her video installations *Waterspeak* (2000) and *The Heart of Everything That Is* (2000). According to Gagnon, "Claxton's works evoke such collisions in their exploration of storytelling. Specifically, in their fragmented allusions to Lakota creation stories and relations to the earth, these installations reconfigure and reflect on well-trod tensions in the reception of Native art concerning traditional and contemporary practices. These installations bring the relevance of such stories into the present, and bring for mediation through storytelling and video-making as not simply transparent, but as processes in themselves."[30]

Dana Claxton's re/memory and resistance work is intrinsically connected to acts of reclaiming and revoicing. Within an exhibition space, Claxton's video art and video installations, such as *Sitting Bull and the Moose Jaw Sioux*, create a site from which artist, curators, and audience can participate in the project of decolonization. Her works become a site for witnessing testimony of both contemporary and historic Aboriginal experiences. The stories and histories elucidated in Claxton's work contribute to the postcolonial project by the ways in which they reveal and resist colonial legacies that remain embedded in Canadian dominant culture. For the settler, non-Indigenous audience member, Claxton's video art is a site for displacing many erroneous yet perpetuated understandings of Indigenous peoples, cultures, and artistic production. With this in mind, Claxton's multifaceted art practice is a significant example of contemporary Aboriginal video that presents without compromise her perspectives to explore contemporary and historical stories and experiences. In this way, her videos can be seen as vehicles for Indigenous intervention. By recognizing, as Ruth and Mark Phillips have, that ultimately museums can only be platforms for disruptions of tired stereotypes and spaces for challenging old ways of knowing, we highlight the significant role Indigenous video can play in Indigenizing social memory in North America and in the telling of silenced Aboriginal histories and experiences.[31] The exhibition and screening of videos by Claxton and her contemporaries, such as Shelley Niro's *The Shirt* (2003), which is a live-feed video that explores Indigenous sovereignty and the impacts of colonialism, and Rebecca Belmore's *Vigil* (2002), which exposes the contemporary history of missing Aboriginal women in Canada, in gallery spaces provides sites for bearing witness to contemporary Indigenous realities.

During a second-year course on nineteenth-century Canadian art history that I taught in fall 2011, I incorporated contemporary Aboriginal video art at the beginning of most classes to contextualize the legacies of this era of North American history that we, as scholars of Indigenous art, culture, and politics in Canada, continue to negotiate, confront, and complicate. As a non-Indigenous scholar of contemporary Indigenous art, I am keenly aware of my limitations but also my responsibilities, as both a writer and a university-level instructor, in relation to settler-Indigenous histories and Aboriginal cultural production. During this course at

Queen's University, I attempted to convey to both my Indigenous and non-Indigenous students the ways in which national/ist narratives have silenced, displaced, and erased Indigenous histories of colonization and attempted to claim and collect Indigenous cultural knowledge as a part of Canadian identity without recognition of Indigenous sovereignty, self-determination, autonomy, and agency.

In one lecture, I introduced the students to the concept of revisionist histories and Ian McKay's call for the production of studies of Canada by postnationalist historians who critically reexamine the consequences of instituting a liberal political order in northern North America.[32] With this in mind, I introduced my students to the video work of Dana Claxton, aiming to address the specific effects Canadian nationalism(s) has had on Indigenous nations and their peoples, and how artists have employed artistic practice to respond, intervene, and resist colonial and national rhetoric. I was hoping to convey the contemporary relevance of this era of Canadian history to my students. First, I screened *Buffalo Bone China*, followed by *Sitting Bull and the Moose Jaw Sioux*. My students engaged the knowledge put forth by Claxton's experimental videos to contextualize and complicate several of the late nineteenth-century paintings of Plains Aboriginal peoples by Paul Kane, a settler painter who participated in the salvage paradigm by representing through his Eurocentric lens the life and cultures of North American Aboriginal peoples. The visual strategies incorporated into Claxton's video works were visual examples of the tactic of displacing and complicating histories. Although she was not in my class during the screenings, her voice and the stories she gave testimony to were witnessed and clearly acknowledged.

Notes

Reprinted with the permission of *Post Script: Essays in Film and the Humanities. Native American/Indigenous Film, Special Edition*, guest editor, M. Elise Marubbio, *Post Script: Essays in Film and the Humanities* (Texas A&M University–Commerce) 29.3 (Summer 2010).

1. In this chapter, I will use the commonly recognized terms in Canada, *Aboriginal* and *Indigenous*, interchangeably to discuss the Native peoples of North America.

2. In *Manifest Manners: Post-Indian Warriors of Survivance* (Middleton, CT: Wesleyan University Press, 1994), Vizenor argues that Native stories are sto-

ries of Native survivance, which he defines as being "more than survival, more than endurance or mere response; the stories of survivance are an active presence" (15). In other words, in Vizenor's view, Native stories are the traces of Native experiences and are the evidence of Native survivance.

3. Steven Loft, "Sovereignty, Subjectivity and Social Action: The Films of Alanis Obomsawin," in *Transference, Tradition, Technology: Native New Media Exploring Visual and Digital Culture*, ed. Dana Claxton, Steve Loft, and Melanie Townsend (Banff: Walter Phillips Gallery, 2005), 61.

4. Jolene Rickard, "Sovereignty: A Line in the Sand," *Aperture* 139 (Summer 1995): 51–61, 207.

5. Tanya Willard, "Starting from Home," in *Starting from Home: An Online Retrospective of Dana Claxton* (Vancouver: Grunt Gallery, 2007), http://www.danaclaxton.com/index.html (accessed January 5, 2010).

6. My discussion and concept of Indigenous rememory draws from the writings of several scholars who explore the complex relationships between memory and the writing of history. I have come to understand stagings of rememory as dynamic acts of Indigenous resistance and intervention within the structures of colonial hegemony. See Pierre Nora, "Between Memory and History: Les Lieux de Memoire," *Memory and Counter-Memory: Representations* 26 (Spring 1989): 7–24; Edward W. Said, "Invention, Memory, and Place," *Critical Inquiry* 26.2 (2000): 175–92; Diana Taylor, "Performance and/as History," *Drama Review* 50.1 (2006): 67–81.

7. Marcia Crosby, "Constructing of the Imaginary Indian," in *Vancouver Anthology: The Institutional Politics of Art*, ed. Stan Douglas (Vancouver: Talon Books, 1991), 271.

8. Vine Deloria Jr., introduction to *The Pretend Indians: Images of Native Americans in the Movies*, ed. Gretchen M. Bataille and Charles L. P. Silet (Ames: Iowa State University Press, 1980), xvi.

9. Linda Tuhiwai Smith, *Decolonizing Methodologies: Research and Indigenous Peoples* (Dunedin, New Zealand: University of Otago Press, 1999), 45.

10. Dana Claxton, interview with the author, Vancouver, September 2009.

11. Charlotte Towsend-Gault, "Ritualizing Ritual's Rituals," *Art Journal* 51.3 (1992): 55.

12. Crosby, "Constructing of the Imaginary Indian."

13. For more information on the use of performance as a tool for resistance, see Trudy Nicks, "Indian Villages and Entertainments: Setting the Stage for Tourist Souvenir Sales," in *Unpacking Culture: Art and Commodity in Colonial and Postcolonial Worlds*, ed. Ruth B. Phillips and Christopher B. Steiner (Berkeley: University of California Press, 1999), 301–15; Ruth B. Phillips, "Performing the Native Woman: Primitivism and Mimicry in Early Twentieth-Century Visual Culture," in *Antimodernism and Artistic Experience: Policing the Boundaries of Modernity*, ed. Lynda Jessup (Toronto: University of Toronto Press, 2001), 26–49; and Paige Raibmon, "Theatres of Contact; The Kwakwaka'wakw Meet Colonial-

ism in British Columbia and at the Chicago World's Fair," *Canadian Historical Review* 81.2 (2000): 157–90.

14. For an extensive investigation of Aboriginal women and stereotypical representations in film, see M. Elise Marubbio, *Killing the Indian Maiden: Images of Native American Women in Film* (Lexington: University Press of Kentucky, 2006).

15. Willard "Starting from Home."

16. Ibid.

17. Lynne Bell, "The Post/Colonial Photographic Archive and the Work of Memory," in *Image and Inscription: An Anthology of Contemporary Canadian Photography*, ed. Robert Bean (Toronto: YYZ, 2005), 160–61.

18. David Garneau, "Dana Claxton: *Sitting Bull and the Moose Jaw Sioux*," *Vie des arts* 197 (2004): 93.

19. Bell, "Post/Colonial Photographic Archive," 160–61.

20. Ibid., 162.

21. Willard, "Starting from Home."

22. Jason St. Laurent, *History in Parts: The Work of Dana Claxton* (Ottawa: SAW Gallery, 2005).

23. Diana Taylor, *The Archive and the Repertoire: Performing Cultural Memory in the Americas* (Durham: Duke University Press, 2003), 19.

24. Ibid., xix. Also see Taylor, "Performance and/as History."

25. Willard, "Starting from Home."

26. Vizenor, *Manifest Manners*, 15.

27. Jean Fisher, "Witness for the Prosecution: The Writings of Coco Fusco," in *The Bodies That Were Not Ours, and Other Writings*, ed. Coco Fusco (London: Routledge: 2001), 228.

28. Steven Loft, "Aboriginal Media Art and the Postmodern Conundrum: A Coyote Perspective," in *Transference, Tradition, Technology: Native New Media Exploring Visual and Digital Culture*, ed. Dana Claxton, Steve Loft, and Melanie Townsend (Banff: Walter Phillips Gallery, 2005), 93.

29. Kateri Akiwenzie-Damm, "Says Who: Colonialism, Identity and Defining Indigenous Literature," in *Looking at the Words of Our People: First Nations Analysis of Literature*, ed. Jeanette Amstrong (Penticton, BC: Theytus Books, 1993), 24.

30. Monika Kin Gagnon, "Worlds in Collision: Dana Claxton's Video Installations," in *Transference, Tradition, Technology: Native New Media Exploring Visual and Digital Culture*, ed. Dana Claxton, Steve Loft, and Melanie Townsend (Banff: Walter Phillips Gallery, 2005), 70.

31. Ruth B. Phillips and Mark Salber Phillips, "Double Take: Contesting Time, Place and Nations in the First Peoples Hall of the Canadian Museum of Civilization," *Museum Anthropology* 107.4 (2005): 694–704.

32. Ian McKay, "After Canada: On Amnesia and Apocalypse in the Contemporary Crisis," *Acadiensis* 28.1 (1998): 76–97.

Section Two

Pedagogical Conversations

Introduction to Section Two

A number of years ago at a Native American Film roundtable discussion a recurring question came up around teaching Native film.[1] Many of those participating were educators in American studies, English, ethnic studies, or education who had either limited access to Native films other than those promoted by the motion picture distribution companies—*Smoke Signals*, for example—or who were located in areas of the country that had little interaction with Native communities. Their primary concerns were how to teach the films they could access and where to find other films. Equally important to the discussants was their lack of American Indian studies' resources for supplementing how they taught specific Native films.

The chapters in this section ride the undercurrent of resistance to First and Second Cinema representations of Native peoples and movement forward toward a Native film focus seen in section 1, but bring us back from the theoretical context of the various conversations emerging in the Indigenous film movement to the practical application of teaching Native film. The conversation initiated here highlights pedagogical strategies for reading and teaching across the curriculum and through the lenses of cultural studies, film studies, American Indian studies, and anthropology. The broad strokes and close attention to detail in film analysis in these chapters both provide yet another level to the complexity of the dialogue surrounding Native film and highlight the growing audience desiring to understand that dialogue and apply it to teaching.

We begin with Carole Gerster's chapter, "Native Resistance to Hollywood's Persistence of Vision: Teaching Films about Contemporary American Indians," which directly critiques the Hollywood film industry's Eurocentric approach to Natives onscreen. Initiating a counter-hegemonic trend in Native American film to talk back to Hollywood, Gerster pairs the 1979 documentary series *Images of Indians* with more contemporary Indigenous film productions such as *Smoke Signals*, *A Thousand Roads*, and *In Whose Honor?* to facilitate student learning about the ongoing forms Eurocentrism takes and to outline how they can critique Hollywood stereotypes.

Narrowing our focus to a case study, Amy Corbin's film studies' approach analyzes the filmic styles and cinematographic approaches employed by Sherman Alexie throughout *The Business of Fancydancing* as a way to discuss a "nomadic viewing" perspective versus a Hollywood "touristic point of view." Her chapter highlights how Alexie's shifting hybrid nomadic viewing experience (the various character and viewer positioning in the film) "enhances the creative repertoire of Native feature filmmakers and also puts itself in dialogue with theories of how film form expresses complex cultural identities." Corbin's analysis recalls the chapters in section 1 by calling our attention to how Alexie breaks down "outsider authority" over Native stories. When put into conversation with Raheja's, Gauthier's, and Taunton's chapters, which detail methods of Indigenous visual sovereignty, and Wood's work on dimensions of difference in Indigenous film, an interesting refocusing happens that accentuates the very complexities involved in understanding dimensions of cultural difference across Native and Indigenous film and within a film itself.

Working from an approach similar to Gerster's, Angelica Lawson moves away from a close reading of one particular film to an American Indian studies' approach to teaching a course on Native film. "Teaching Native American Filmmakers: Osawa, Eyre, and Redroad" outlines the pedagogical strategies she employs in teaching three well-known Native filmmakers whose work exhibits the vast difference Wood expressed. Lawson's approach allows students to engage with many of the critical concepts important to the study of Native film and film representation while also introducing them to documentary and feature films. This piece pairs nicely with Gerster's in terms of aiding educators with historical background, information on cultural forms that influenced Hollywood filmic representations of Native Americans, and insights into culturally specific moments in the Native-produced films she discusses. Lawson also brings to the larger conversation the importance of recognizing regional/tribal-specific information within stories in contrast to the pan-Indian or global narratives we often see in feature films.

While our pedagogical conversation has thus far focused on the classroom experience, Sam Pack takes us "into the field" through an anthropological case study of viewer response to Native- and non-Native-produced films on Navajo history and culture. His chapter, "'The Native's Point of View' as Seen through the Native's (and Non-Native's) Points of View," offers an "insider/outsider" perspective on what constitutes Native film, allowing us to apply some of the questions raised by our theoretical conversations: Who speaks for whom? What is a Native film? Does being Native authorize one to speak for all tribal perspectives? Pack's juxtaposition of Native and non-Native viewer responses around easily accessible films returns our conversation to Gerster's call that we reflect on our own positioning in the ongoing representational strategies for depicting and reading "Indians" in film.

The viewer responses in Pack's case studies also point us toward Beverly Singer's chapter, "The Dirt Roads of Consciousness: Teaching and Producing Videos with an Indigenous Purpose," and her comment on the importance of privileging "the complexities of Indigenous history, voices, and stories." Reacting to the undergirding theme of Indigenous representations and treatment by mainstream non-Indigenous film industries, filmmaker and teacher Beverly Singer rejects using commercial films that contribute to Hollywood's narratives even as they talk back to the legacy of Hollywood's Indians. She chooses instead to embrace the Native productions that we would find on the Indigenous end of Wood's continuum in her pedagogical work and that privilege Native media self-determination. Singer's personal chapter also brings this section's conversation full circle, and her perspective as a filmmaker opens the discussions that continue in section 3, "Conversations with Filmmakers."

Our writers provide us with various ways to teach and think about Native film through the use of easily accessible films, such as *Images of Indians, Smoke Signals, The Business of Fancydancing, In Whose Honor? A Thousand Roads, The Doe Boy, Pepper's Pow Wow, On and Off the Res' with Charlie Hill, In the Heart of Big Mountain, Broken Rainbow, Return of Navajo Boy, The Lost Child, Hózhó of Native Women,* and *Hands of History.* They enrich the conversation on pedagogy with insightful approaches to understanding the works of a number of established Native American filmmakers: Sandy Osawa, Chris Eyre, Sherman Alexie, Randy Redroad, and Loretta Todd.

The pedagogical dialogue that emerges around teaching Native film highlights the need for continual self-reflection on the part of students, teachers, filmmakers, and the industry in terms of how we represent Native peoples and Native film. The dialogue also raises the important caution against essentializing Native film as a simple binary reaction to First Cinema; we are reminded that many narrative and documentary Native film productions syncretize genres and classical film techniques with Native and multicultural stories, creating products that may fit into First, Second, Third, or Fourth Cinema definitions or across the spectrum, as Barry Barclay predicted (see introduction). Questions that arise from these chapters include: What are the ramifications of teaching Native film when we don't know the historical/cultural/ontological realities of the communities depicted in the films? What happens when we only have access to films that represent Native people from a generic "Native" level as opposed to culturally specific films populated by actors from those cultures? What happens when we combine pan-Indian narratives with tribally specific or filmmaker-specific narratives? What type of materials and data should we be including in our course curricula to provide cultural and historical context that explicates film narratives? How deeply inculcated are we as a society/societies into culturally stereotyping Native people? This last broad question raises a number of others, including: How do we utilize Native-produced films to respond to stereotypes? Must all Native films do this? What strategies can we employ to move us away from assuming that Native film must teach us about Native America rather than allowing it to teach us about people?

Note

1. Twenty-seventh Annual Southwest/Texas Popular Culture Association/American Culture Association, Albuquerque, NM, February 2006.

Native Resistance to Hollywood's Persistence of Vision

Teaching Films about Contemporary American Indians

Carole Gerster

> Persistence of Vision: the capacity of the eye to maintain an image on the retina for a brief instant after it has disappeared from the screen, thus filling in the gaps between successive images and giving continuity from one to another. [T]he brain is [also] involved to some degree.
>
> —Ira Konigsberg, *The Complete Film Dictionary*

In representing American Indians, as the still-prescient 1979 documentary film series *Images of Indians* illustrates, Hollywood films consistently offer nineteenth-century manifest destiny stories, white male perspectives, and monolithic images of vanishing Indians. To non-Indians, these films convey the impression that American Indians are relics of the past; to Indians, they send a message of cultural and historical misrepresentation and invisibility. "Persistence of Vision" describes how the eye momentarily retains an image until a new image replaces it on the screen. It is also an apt characterization of how viewers collectively retain repeated Hollywood images of vanquished American Indians until new images replace them on movie theater and television screens. *Images of Indians* marks a significant moment in film history by confronting this persistence of vision with its critical review of Hollywood films and its new images of contemporary Indians. Serving as a precursor, this film series helped initiate an alternative independent media movement, wherein both Indians and Indians in collaboration with non-Indians now create films that follow its lead in displacing Hollywood's manifest destiny stories with stories about contemporary American Indians told from Native perspectives.

This chapter focuses on representation issues highlighted in *Images of Indians* and a sampling of other independent media efforts that continue its alternative vision. Teaching all or selected segments of Phil Lucas and Robert Hagopian's *Images of Indians* (1979), followed by Chris Eyre's

Smoke Signals (1998) and *A Thousand Roads* (2005), and Jay Rosenstein's *In Whose Honor?* (1996) serves to illuminate a building visual-media resistance to Hollywood-created invisibility, to visualize the diversity of contemporary Indigenous identities, and to address current and recurrent Indigenous issues important to American Indians and America at large. As these films and videos expand the range of previous representations and representational strategies, they offer students in cultural studies, film studies, and media studies new understandings and inspiration for new forms of Indigenous expression.

Images of Indians

Phil Lucas and Robert Hagopian's five-part film series (each twenty-eight minutes; two hours and thirty minutes altogether) *Images of Indians*[1] is significant as both the first and the most influential documentary film response to the long history of American Indian misrepresentation in Hollywood films.[2] Although now dated (it was released in 1979), this film series effectively records and responds to Hollywood's continuing persistence of vision. In Hollywood's colonial settler films and westerns, repeated stories about heroic Euro-American protagonists require standardized roles of helpful and hostile Natives and manifest destiny plots, wherein both types are doomed to extinction, inevitably relinquishing their lands, cultures, and lives to the always ultimately successful settlers. Working from the history of Hollywood films in *Images of Indians*, students can explore more recent films to see for themselves what has and what has not changed.[3] And knowing the kinds of responses and the new images provided in *Images of Indians* and the other independent films examined here, students can discover and imagine additional representations that update, add to, and continue to revitalize this American Indian independent media movement.

Images of Indians offers a brief history and criticism of both types of vanishing Hollywood Indians. This background is important for students to understand how mainstream mass media creates, maintains, and reinforces images that ensure an entrenched and continuing public perception. A significant topic for students to explore and discuss is how representations of ever-vanishing Indians render contemporary American Indians invisible. As the film series' narrator, Muscogee-Creek film and television actor Will Sampson, reveals in part 3, eighteenth-

and nineteenth-century plays—such as *Pocahontas*, *Hiawatha*, and *Metamora, the Last of the Wampanoags*—popularized the stereotype of the innocent, primitive, and disappearing Noble Savage before its incarnation in films. Sampson notes that images of benign Indians, pictured as "quaint . . . romantic children of nature," appeared onscreen as early as D. W. Griffith's 1911 film *The Squaw's Love*. A part 2 analysis of how Zane Grey's *The Vanishing American* moved from serialized stories to a 1922 novel to a 1925 film notes that the final words describe the friendly Navajo as "vanishing, vanishing, vanishing." Students can study popular repetitions of this type in repeated film versions of *Pocahontas*[4] and *The Last of the Mohicans*[5] as typical of how Hollywood depicts friendly Indian women as temporary love objects for European settlers and portrays helpful Indian men as dying out in the face of other Indians attacking them and Europeans creating a "New World" without them.

The other, even more prominent, standardized role for Indians in Hollywood films, as *Images of Indians* notes in the introductory commentary by Sampson that begins each of its five parts, is that of the "Hostile Savage." This type consistently reappears, in Sampson's words, "as a savage warrior, a renegade, a killer of innocent pioneer women and children, and a merciless scalper who used the most cruel means of torture in his vicious attacks against the white man." In part 1, Sampson notes how popular nineteenth- and twentieth-century western dime novels and Wild West shows set the film stage with Indian antagonists harassing heroic white settlers and, in part 2, scenes from D. W. Griffith's 1924 film *America* provide an early example of Hollywood Indians viciously attacking besieged settlers. A montage of scenes from Hollywood westerns in part 5 shows white male protagonists, who serve as each film's voice of authority on Indians, explaining the savage nature of Indian men to their on- and offscreen audiences alike. They variously claim that Indians "are vicious killers [that] ain't even human," that they are "murdering savages," and that "war is their religion." One proclaims that "Comanche mate their women early" and another asks, "Did you ever see what Indians do when they get a white woman?" Sampson notes in part 4 that Hollywood was not content just to ask such a question, that John Ford imagined such Indian atrocities for his viewers twice: in *Two Rode Together* (1962) and in his critically acclaimed *The Searchers* (1956), which added even more justification, again to on- and offscreen audiences, for eliminating Indians. Victory over the Hostile Savage type occurs in thousands of films where

Euro-American protagonists, with whom viewers are invited to identify, and the U.S. cavalry, which arrives just in time, save innocent women and children from the horrible ravages of Indian antagonists, who typically appear without families, homes of their own, or even motivations.

These highly dramatic attacks and rescues are occasionally supplemented with comic killings, as part 3 illustrates with scenes from the 1948 film *The Paleface* staring comic icon Bob Hope as a tenderfoot. In one scene, his girlfriend shoots attacking Indians so expertly that they fall into what he calls a "neat pile." When one last Indian staggers rather than falls, the tenderfoot hits him on the head to knock him onto the pile and "keep it neat." A film history topic for student discussion is whether the supposedly funny killings in *The Paleface* and its sequels[6] would be thought humorous without the residual audience expectation for Hostile Indians who are, within the context of movie after movie, justifiably eliminated.

Students can examine for themselves, in Kevin Costner's readily available, immensely popular, and frequently televised Academy Award–winning film *Dances with Wolves* (1990) how the Noble Savage and the Hostile Savage types often appear in the same film, remain staples of the still-popular saga of manifest destiny from a white male protagonist's point of view, and continue to be imagined as vanishing. While exploring how Hollywood films encourage viewers to lament the passing of innocent Noble Savages (Lakota Sioux in *Dances with Wolves*) and rejoice in the killing of vicious Hostile Savages (Pawnee in *Dances with Wolves*), students can realize the role of Hollywood films in establishing the invisibility of contemporary Indians. Hollywood is an industry that relies on repeating successful formulas for box office profit. Because these successful formulas include nineteenth-century manifest destiny stories that invite viewing audiences to identify with a sympathetic Euro-American hero and, through his eyes, witness the elimination of Indians, there is no reason for viewers to question repeated film versions of colonial settler and westward expansion history, and there are no obvious openings for subsequent stories about contemporary Indians.

However, with its strategy of recontextualizing Hollywood formulas and formulaic characters by re-viewing them from a variety of contemporary American Indian perspectives, *Images of Indians* creates that opening. This film series begins what has become an ongoing process of hegemonic negotiations in independent media. Following and particularizing the ideas of Italian intellectual Antonio Gramsci, who examined cultural dominance as "hegemony,"[7] students can better understand mass media power and influence. Gramsci explains how mass media are tools that any dominant cultural group (in this case Euro-Americans) can use to perpetuate its own power, wealth, and status by viewing history from its own perspective and popularizing its own culture and interests as past and present ideals to which all other groups should aspire. As owners and managers of media industries, Euro-Americans can produce and reproduce images and ideas favorable to themselves far more easily than any minority group, thereby guaranteeing that their points of view consistently and attractively dominate the public arena. Hegemony also suggests a willing agreement by many outside the dominant group (in this case by some American Indians) to be governed by repeated images of and ideas about themselves that they believe operate in their best (often monetary) interests, even though in actual practice these ideas best serve the interests of the dominant group. Media students can easily understand how encouraging social consent via mass media repetition of images and ideas is a more efficient and effective means of control than coercion or force. And students can also realize that consent and control call for ongoing exposés, corrections, and alternatives in independent media venues until the alternatives effectively rival Hollywood and revise public thinking.

Images of Indians begins this ongoing process of hegemonic negotiations with the dual intention of reeducating viewers and creating an independent alternative to the Hollywood film industry. The process identifies and challenges established film conventions while introducing genuinely divergent views. Each of the five segments of *Images of Indians* opens by announcing its general strategy of hegemonic negotiations, as each begins with Hollywood film images of Indians accompanied by the following song lyrics addressed to the Hollywood film industry:

> We waited years for you to say
> that you were wrong to have pictured us this way.
> But it's too late; the time has come
> for all false images to come undone.

This oppositional resistance and reeducation via recontextualization from contemporary Native points of view forms the foundation for subsequent independent films and videos. Understanding this ongoing process and strategy provides students with a way to read the significance of *Images of*

Indians and of subsequent independent media in their efforts to replace Hollywood's persistence of vision images with images that represent the realities of contemporary Indigenous lives.

Beginning this oppositional movement of counterpoints and counternarratives, *Images of Indians* confronts the basic issue of contemporary American Indian invisibility by juxtaposing Hollywood film caricatures with real people in order to replace old images with new ones and reinform viewers. Rather than continue the standard documentary practice of an off-camera narrator, who serves as a seemingly omniscient voice of authority, each of the film's five parts begins with the series' onscreen host and narrator, American Indian actor Will Sampson (probably best known for his role as Chief Bromden in the 1975 Academy Award–winning film *One Flew over the Cuckoo's Nest*), introducing himself and speaking as himself. Each part opens with Sampson reporting that repeated film images of nineteenth-century Hollywood Indians have made contemporary Indians invisible. Sampson appears in contemporary clothes beside different actors in each part—actors who are variously dressed in buckskin, feathers, and war paint to make the juxtaposition clear. Then, as Sampson declares, "The Native American is invisible unless he looks like the Hollywood Indian," the camera moves until he is out of range and the shot includes only the costumed actor in close up. The point is humorously dramatized again in part 3 of the series, where Sampson advises Indians and non-Indians alike that internalizing Hollywood images of Indians ensures the invisibility of contemporary Indians. Sampson again presents himself as a contemporary Indian who, while walking down the sidewalk, is asked to "step out of the way" so a tourist can "take a picture of the Indian." As Sampson moves aside, viewers see a Euro-American man taking a picture of an Indian dressed in buckskin and full headdress who is posing for photos, and the man's wife saying to their small child, "Look at the Indian; isn't he cute," as if he were an artifact rather than a living human being.

Students can analyze the serious consequences in this humorous scene, including how an older generation educates a younger one to see American Indians only in terms of repeated Hollywood images, and how the tourist-attraction Indian earns a living by helping to perpetuate the idea that Indians are recognizable only as relics of the past made familiar by Hollywood. In these and other scenes, *Images of Indians* dramatizes how Hollywood stereotypes of Indians—even seemingly benign stereo-

A tourist asks Will Sampson to "step out of the way" so he can "take a picture of the Indian" in *Images of Indians.*

types—are not innocent errors of perception, but are a form of social control with the effect that Indians are frozen into relics of the past that appear to have no living presence, no voice in the present, and no future in America.

The invisibility issue is also given serious treatment in *Images of Indians* with Sampson and other contemporary Indian experts appearing onscreen to examine the issue of non-Indians playing Indian roles. As the series illustrates throughout, Euro-American actors performing in redface—the equivalent of the more familiar blackface—was common in Hollywood films.[8] In part 1, Sampson interviews Colonel Tim McCoy, who had his own Wild West show and produced and acted in Hollywood westerns. McCoy testifies that, long after blackface was no longer acceptable, redface continued, because "nobody cared about the Indians." Parts 1–4 each include a different montage of a dozen or so film scenes with non-Indian actors cast in Indian roles, and each part accompanies its montage with the song lyrics that include the line "You were wrong to picture us that way." The film series thus repeatedly suggests that American Indians have historically been kept from participating in their own representation, that Euro-American filmmakers have defined Indians through self-interested representations, and that "the time has come" to expose and challenge those conventions.

Sampson reveals in part 3 what he finds to be a common Hollywood idea. He reads a published statement (by Euro-American filmmaker Alan Hale Sr., director of the 1926 film *Braveheart*): "White men make better motion picture actors than the red men themselves" because "a white man with strong features resembles the Indian more than the Indian does himself," and Sampson comments that Hale was merely "stating a widespread Hollywood belief." Students can explore a more recent example in Iron Eyes Cody, a non-Indian actor who was able to play an Indian onscreen and off because, as reported after Cody's death in 1999, "He looked like what white Americans thought Indians should look like."[9] *Images of Indians* exposes how, by casting Euro-Americans as better representations of Indians than actual Indians, and in attempting to accustom viewers to seeing white actors playing Indians, Hollywood found another means to make Indians invisible while also encouraging viewers to accept Hollywood fantasy creations as more real than reality. This occurred, as part 1 shows, even in featured and title roles, with Anthony Quinn as Crazy Horse in *They Died with Their Boots On* (1941) and with Chuck Connors as Geronimo in *Geronimo* (1962). An appropriation of Indian identity, non-Indians playing Indians is an example of a continuing manifest destiny attitude and of cultural imperialism in practice, as Euro-Americans visually supplant Indians, as if there were no Indians left to represent themselves.

Images of Indians also criticizes Hollywood films for employing Euro-American actors to replace Indians in a particular way. Part 5 includes scenes from the 1970 film *A Man Called Horse* and Sampson's commentary that the film "acts out the fantasy of a white man becoming an Indian chief." In this film, which had two sequels (in 1976 and 1983),[10] British actor Richard Harris plays a nineteenth-century Englishman in America who, in Sampson's words, soon "out-Indians the Indians" to become a better Sioux chief, a superior and thus more real Indian than the Indians. This white male protagonist attracts the most beautiful Indian woman in the tribe, impresses the men by outdoing them with his manliness in a Sundance ritual (misrepresented as an exercise in machismo by Hollywood filmmakers), becomes their chief, and—in showing the men when and how to shoot their arrows (lined up in British fashion and all shooting together on his command to "shoot the bows")—temporarily saves the tribe from another tribe of attacking Indians.

To explore for themselves how accepted and naturalized this white male superiority convention has become, students can review other film renditions of Euro-American male protagonists who out-Indian the Indians.[11] These include a more recent (1990) and familiar version: Kevin Costner as Lieutenant Dunbar in *Dances with Wolves.* Dunbar, who is befriended by a Lakota Sioux tribe, saves a Euro-American woman they have adopted but neglected, discovers buffalo for them while they are too busy dancing to hear the thundering herd, impresses them when he not only successfully participates in his first buffalo hunt but also saves a young Lakota from being killed by an attacking buffalo, and even saves the entire tribe from being wiped out by a group of attacking Pawnee—by supplying the Lakota with guns and even admonishing one of them to "shoot the gun"—at a time when the warriors are away from the village. This appropriation of Indian identity presents the sympathetic Euro-American hero as obviously superior and thus the natural inheritor of a land soon to be emptied of its vanishing Indians. Interested students can also explore how an even more recent film, James Cameron's *Avatar* (2009), to date the highest-grossing film of all time, continues this white male superiority convention in a seemingly well-intentioned science fiction fantasy of Euro-American manifest destiny gone wrong. Here, the Euro-American protagonist, Jake Sully, "out-Indians the Indians" in becoming a mentally and physically superior Na'Vi: he attracts the love of the Na'Vi princess and he saves all the Noble Savage Natives on the planet Pandora. Sully unites them and heroically leads them to victory over the invading Euro-American military antagonists who are attempting to destroy them as "Hostiles" in order to steal the natural resources that sustain them. Another example of cultural hegemony at work in mass media, this Euro-American turned superior Na'Vi hero is the natural inheritor of and is given responsibility for Indigenous lands, cultures, and lives by the Indigenous peoples themselves. American Indian activist Dennis Banks, who appears throughout part 5 of *Images of Indians*, recounts how he and many others have repeatedly approached Hollywood regarding these types of narratives to no avail and condemns the effects of Hollywood images with the strong analogy that what the motion picture industry has attempted to do to Indians is the equivalent of what Hitler attempted to do to the Jews.

To counter Hollywood's attempts at visual genocide and to address recurrent issues important to American Indians and Americans at large, *Images of Indians* recognizes how Eurocentric[12] ideas of racial superiority and racial difference color filmmakers' choices. In part 4, Sampson expresses concern that Hollywood films regularly promote the idea "that the white man is inherently superior." Whether conscious or unconscious, widespread ideas about racial superiority allow filmmakers to keep creating films about vanishing Indians and Euro-American film heroes who visually supplant and "out-Indian the Indians." Even for filmmakers who dismiss erroneous ideas about racial superiority, there remains the even more widespread belief that there are separate races with innate differences. This belief allows depictions of strange Indians with strange customs who stand in stark contrast to supposed Euro-American normality. In part 5, then Euro-American Hollywood producer David Dortort notes that distorted images of Indians are "an insult to an entire race of people," and he suggests that Indians "must take a more prominent part in whatever Hollywood does that involves Indians from now on." Based on his belief in separate races, he also refuses responsibility for producing accurate representations of Indians under the assumption that "the white man cannot really understand the Indian mind," that "the only man that can understand the Indian mind is the Indian." Relying on the now scientifically disproved but still commonly held belief that racial categories are real indicators of essential differences between people,[13] this behind-the-screen producer reveals the often well-intentioned thinking by which Euro-Americans see themselves as an unmarked norm and attribute racial difference to others. While *Images of Indians* certainly calls for Indian participation in the creation of Indian images, it also asks for Hollywood and public understanding of historical and contemporary Indians, and here questions notions of racial difference that claim such understanding is impossible.

An important function of *Images of Indians* is educating viewers about Hollywood's normalized Eurocentric point of view, which historian Vine Deloria Jr. identifies in part 1 as the way Hollywood "projects values of white society onto Indian society." *Images of Indians* exposes Hollywood misrepresentations by pointing to the European origins of what Hollywood depicts as strange and savage Indian customs. Denouncing representations of hostile Indians as vicious scalpers of innocent settlers, part 2 of *Images of Indians* includes a short segment from a 1964 documentary about the Trail of Tears, wherein Johnny Cash shows a U.S. Army–issue tomahawk and offers the correction that scalping was an accepted practice of the British and U.S. armies, whose soldiers were paid for the scalps of Indian men, women, and children. The film makes this point again when, in part 3, Oneida Indian Charley Hill also notes the European origins of scalping. Students can explore how even films outside the western genre can continue old misconceptions by examining how *Inglourious Basterds* (Quentin Tarantino, 2009) suggests that scalping was a distinctly American Indian custom epitomized by Apache practice. In this World War II revenge fantasy, the Euro-American protagonist, Lieutenant Aldo Raine, is the leader of Jewish-American mercenaries in France who becomes known as "Aldo the Apache" because he scalps Nazis.

In part 4 of *Images of Indians*, Eastern Cherokee Lee Piper points to other cultural inaccuracies perpetuated about the Apache. In the 1950 film *Broken Arrow*, for example, the white male protagonist marries an Apache woman (who dies before the end of the film so it does not advocate marriage between them, even though she is played by Euro-American actress Debra Paget in redface) and the two cut themselves to mingle their blood. Piper identifies the blood-mingling ritual as belonging to "male European secret societies" and notes that it was "never practiced by any tribe, including the Apache." Students interested in the psychology of misrepresentations can investigate these Hollywood inaccuracies as projections of Euro-American filmmakers. Their films project onto Indians behaviors that they do not consider acceptable, behaviors they either do not know or do not care to admit as true of their own societies. Revealing the European origins of what Hollywood filmmakers portray as uncivilized Indian behavior suggests that it is only behind the scenes, in their own offscreen history, that Euro Americans actually "out-Indian the Indians" they represent onscreen.

To reeducate viewers and Hollywood filmmakers, *Images of Indians* not only exposes but also corrects misunderstandings about American Indian cultures and American history prominent in Hollywood films. Students can explore how this two-part strategy of exposé and correction becomes standard practice in many independent media that follow. In part 1, Sampson discusses how director John Ford, who was most influential in helping to create the classic western, repeatedly filmed in Monument Valley, actual home to the Navajo Nation, as if it were the place of residence for the vast diversity of American Indians across the continent. Visualizing this diversity as a monolithic entity that perpetuates the idea of Indians as a separate race is also the effect of Hollywood costuming, which, in part 2, Sampson shows as limited to only three: "Sioux, Apache, and Other," the latter an inaccurate combination of important differences in dress "used to represent over four hundred different tribes." Sampson believes that Hollywood's differentiated costumes for the Sioux and Apache are indicative of how films continually represent them as the main stumbling blocks in the path of westward-moving settlers. Noted Sioux historian Vine Deloria Jr. appears in part 1 to correct a basic misconception of Hollywood's manifest destiny films. He laments that Hollywood filmmakers depict fantasies that have "a complete disregard" for the American history they claim to portray and he reports that, if Hollywood "would film actual history, Indians would win most of the time."

Images of Indians also includes a number of other suggestions for new images of Indians that still resonate today. In part 1, Deloria insists that "so many good things could still be done if historically accurate." Regarding women, in part 4, Lee Piper reports that Indian women "were not the slaves of Indian men, without power or authority," as Hollywood portrays them. Instead, women were and are "important members of councils" and (unlike European and Euro-American women) "always had the vote." Women helped to make important decisions, including whether or not a tribe could "go to war," and were and are still "warriors and chiefs." Suggesting new film topics to replace old ones, in part 2, Sampson explains how Euro-Americans emulated Indians in forming a new nation. Viewers see what was for years a popular Saturday morning cartoon illustrating the westward expansion of European settlers as an innocent desire for more "Elbow Room." After dismissing it as a "gross distortion" of reality, Sampson offers a corrective history lesson that includes Indian contributions to American democracy. He explains, for example, how Benjamin Franklin used the democratic constitution of the Iroquois Confederation for the Articles of Confederation, the forerunner of the U.S. Constitution. Sampson also explains, in part 5, how contemporary Indian invisibility in Hollywood films manifests itself in the real lives of Indians today, in how treaty rights—regarding land, fishing, and water and other natural resources on reservation land granted to Indians—are still ignored or threatened and how Indian survival still depends on them. Sampson suggests that Indian battles against manifest destiny have taken a contemporary turn and that, besides providing accurate histories, new films need to depict the realities of contemporary Indian lives. In recognizing the educational function of film, *Images of Indians* offers glimpses of (at the time new) feature films about contemporary Indians (in part 1, *Standing Tall,* in part 3, *Old Fish Hawk,* and in part 5, *One Flew over the Cuckoo's Nest*) as examples of what Sampson hopes is the beginning of "a new trend." Here and throughout, *Images of Indians* calls for the new images of Indians that follow.

Smoke Signals

Directed by (Cheyenne-Arapaho) Chris Eyre, *Smoke Signals* (1998; one hour and thirty minutes) provides viewers with an important alternative to the Hollywood western. It is billed as the first of its kind—the first feature film written, produced, and directed by American Indians, and also starring American Indians as American Indians—to get major distribution. With development assistance from the Sundance Film Institute and several awards from the Sundance Film Festival,[14] it is the kind of film envisioned in *Images of Indians* as part of an alternative media movement to rival Hollywood. Its title signals that it will be a film about American Indians and that it will be told from Native perspectives. The playful title also suggests that the film will play with viewer expectations, and it does so by echoing a number of reeducation and recontextualization strategies used in *Images of Indians* in order to represent the realities of contemporary Indigenous lives in fictional story form. Challenging the Hollywood convention of relegating Indians to some displaced location in America's distant past, and opposed to including Indians as a disappearing backdrop to the heroic adventures of a Euro-American protagonist, *Smoke Signals* presents itself as a convention-reversing feature film alternative to the Hollywood canon. The film takes viewers (via an opening intertitle) to a specific place and time—the Coeur d'Alene Indian Reservation in Idaho in 1998—and introduces viewers to the sometimes troubled, often humorous perspectives of two contemporary American Indian protagonists.

Directly confronting the Hollywood-created invisibility of the contemporary Indian, *Smoke Signals* features two contemporary American Indian protagonists played by American Indian actors: Victor Joseph (Adam Beach) and Thomas Builds-the-Fire (Evan Adams). Immediately and throughout, the film invites viewers to reverse their expectation to find Indians on the verge of disappearing into the past. A local K-REZ radio announcer alludes to a line from an earlier film—"It's a good day to die" (spoken by the character Old Lodge Skins, played by Indian actor Chief Dan George, in Arthur Penn's 1970 film *Little Big Man*)—simultaneously recapturing Old Lodge Skins's humor and challenging his idea with the announcer's revision that "It's a good day to be Indigenous." This new idea becomes a refrain that echoes throughout the film: a basketball-playing friend of Victor's remarks, "Some days it's a good day to die; some days it's a good day to play basketball," and Thomas ends one of his many stories with the observation, "Sometimes it's a good day to die; sometimes it's a good day to have breakfast." Students can research how other, often parodic, allusions throughout the film—to General George Armstrong Custer, Tom Mix, John Wayne,[15] Charles Bronson, Columbus, Geronimo, Jim Thorpe, *The Last of the Mohicans, Dances with Wolves,* and *The Lone Ranger*—also situate *Smoke Signals* as an alternative to Hollywood's persistence of vision and the thinking it encourages. For example, when Thomas tells Victor, "Your dad looks like Charles Bronson," students can recall how *Images of Indians* opposes Euro-Americans playing Indians as an appropriation of Indian identity that makes real Indians invisible and, in parts 1 and 5, shows actor Charles Bronson as one such movie Indian. Thomas's reference to Bronson jokingly suggests that, since non-Indians played Indians based on the Hollywood rationale that they looked more like Indians than real Indians, it must be true that real Indians can now be recognized as Indians only if they look like the non-Indians who played them. Students can also discuss how a casting choice can help viewers shed a specific Hollywood film image and envision the existence of contemporary Indians. Playing Suzy Song, a character who befriends the young men, allows Irene Bedard (whose voice and animated image became the character of Pocahontas for Disney studios and for audiences in 1995) to shed her old association. Here she plays a neighbor and health care administrator, the kind of role that Lois Red Elk and Lahoma Burd in part 4 of *Images of Indians* longed to see replace Hollywood Princesses and Squaws: a professional contemporary Indigenous woman.

To reeducate viewers who have been encouraged by Hollywood to think of American Indians as a monolithic race that shares a similar appearance and (to quote a Hollywood producer in *Images of Indians*) an "Indian mind," *Smoke Signals* portrays its two young protagonists as very different in their physiques, temperaments, and ideas. Thomas is small, wears glasses, and is extremely gregarious, telling spontaneous stories to anyone who will listen and even to those who won't, including Victor. Victor is tall and standoffish, always irritated with Thomas's stories and friendly attitude. He reveals a major difference when he chides Thomas for trusting people: "Don't you know anything?" he says. "People are awful. You can't trust anybody." Students can discuss how, although Thomas and Victor are the same age and were raised on the same reservation, they are about as different as any two individuals can be, and thus help students to visualize the diversity of contemporary Indigenous identities. Students might also want to discuss the poem, titled "Forgiving Our Fathers," that ends the film. Written by Dick Lourie and recited by Thomas Builds-the-Fire in voice-over, it is neither Indian authored nor Indian specific. Its theme is appropriate for *Smoke Signals'* story of two young men coming to know themselves as they come to terms with the death of a man who served as a father figure for both, but it is also applicable to non-Indians. The poem functions as a means to forge links by suggesting similarities between Indians and non-Indians, and it helps to dispel the mistaken notion that because people belong to different races they therefore cannot understand each other.

While *Smoke Signals* challenges ideas about Indians based on notions of racial difference, it promotes the idea of cultural identity. An essential component of this coming-of-age film is how the two young men come to respect each other's differences by discovering commonalities. As flashbacks to their childhoods and their disagreements in the present show, Victor and Thomas have very different ideas about Victor's father, Arnold Joseph (Gary Farmer), who saved Thomas from a July 4, 1976, fire that killed Thomas's parents. Thomas reveres him in numerous stories while Victor condemns him for his alcoholism and for abandoning him and his mother when he was a boy. The film replaces the popular Hollywood plot of a vanishing race with the real problem of a vanishing alcoholic father. As Victor discovers from Suzy Song, his father inadvertently started the fire and left his family and alcoholic life behind as a means to forget. To highlight the different kinds of vanishing, viewers learn via voice-over that, after the fire, "Arnold threatened to vanish. He practiced vanishing until, one day, he jumped in his yellow pickup and did vanish." Arnold's death is the catalyst that sets the two young men on a journey to partially discover and partially create a cultural identity rooted in their heritage and common experiences and in stark contrast to Hollywood Indians.

The film is about Victor and Thomas establishing—for themselves and to inform viewers steeped in Hollywood images—an Indian identity. When Victor's father dies in Arizona, Thomas offers to give Victor the money for the bus trip to collect the ashes, provided he can go along. In explaining to Victor how he knows about the death of Victor's father, Thomas at once parodies and sets himself apart from Hollywood characterizations of what *Images of Indians* calls "romantic children of nature." Thomas says, "I heard it on the wind. I heard it from the birds. I felt it in the sunlight. And your mom was just in here crying." Parodying how Hollywood's Noble Savage types are imagined as part and parcel of the nature that Euro-American settlers sought to overcome in order to civilize the land, Thomas highlights his difference by admitting that he actually heard the news from Victor's mother. By invoking a standard Hollywood characterization and then immediately distancing himself from it, Thomas humorously challenges viewer expectations about Indian identity.

Smoke Signals invites viewers to discard Hollywood images and to discover contemporary American Indians who live according to a cultural heritage that connects past and present. Far from doomed to extinction in the face of Euro-American civilization, Thomas tells stories that are, as one young woman (who accepts a story as barter in exchange for giving Thomas and Victor a ride to the bus station) laughingly concedes, "a fine example of the oral tradition." His stories link a living past to life in the present; they invoke the oral tradition, and they are relevant to the present. They are about contemporary people, including himself and Victor's family, and contemporary places, including Denny's, Taco Bell, and Spokane Falls. Victor's mother, Arlene (Tantoo Cardinal), refers to broken treaties—when she makes Victor promise to return to the reservation but doesn't want him to sign a paper to that effect because they know "how Indians feel about signing papers"—and Thomas refers to the extinction of salmon at Spokane Falls. The references answer Will Sampson's call, in part 5 of *Images of Indians*, for contemporary stories about current and recurring issues. *Smoke Signals* dramatizes how the oral storytelling tradition, continued here in film (today's most popular storytelling medium), remains an important vehicle for expressing an evolving, rather than static, Indian identity. Victor learns that his father told loving stories about him to Suzy Song and comes to appreciate Thomas and Thomas's never-ending stories. Thomas's stories are akin to Victor's mother's famous fry bread. Her fry bread recipe comes from Victor's grandmother, who got it from her grandmother, but she watches Julia Child for new cooking techniques. *Smoke Signals* is about young men who retain their cultural heritage while living in the present.

Smoke Signals illustrates throughout how one of the realities of contemporary American Indian life is living in the shadow of repeated images of Hollywood Indians. Instead of a conventional film about Indians of the past who cannot survive manifest destiny, *Smoke Signals* is about Indians of today who must survive manifest destiny films. Akin to *Images of Indians, Smoke Signals* recontextualizes manifest destiny films by viewing them from a contemporary Native perspective. In a dramatized segment in part 2 of *Images of Indians,* Will Sampson turns off a television over the protests of a group of American Indian children who are watching a western and cheering for the cavalry. Sampson admits that the scene is a dramatization but explains that it is not unusual for Indian children to root for sympathetically portrayed cowboys instead of the Indians. In *Smoke Signals,* Thomas walks by a television showing a western with a cavalry rescue scene similar to the one in *Images of Indians* and remarks, "The only thing more pathetic than Indians on TV is Indians watching Indians on TV."

Using similar strategies, both re-viewings remind viewers that old Hollywood westerns are not safely relegated to the past but are frequently replayed on television and continue to influence and misinform audiences, including Indian youth.

On their journey to retrieve Arnold's ashes, Victor and Thomas rid each other of the ill effects of Hollywood's influence. They criticize each other for their differing ideas and discover that they have both internalized ideas about Hollywood Indians. Victor refutes Thomas's belief that, as in Hollywood films, "the cowboys always win." Victor also chides Thomas for his friendly trust of Euro-American strangers, has his idea confirmed that Thomas has watched *Dances with Wolves* hundreds of times, and tells Thomas he needs to look more serious and stoic, like an Indian who has just come from a buffalo hunt. Thomas's response reveals that Victor is also a victim of many viewings of *Dances with Wolves,* as he notes that the movie image of the buffalo-hunting Indian is particularly inappropriate for them because of their salmon-fishing heritage. The young men reeducate themselves, and viewers, as they realize that Hollywood images of vanishing nineteenth-century Indians cannot define contemporary Indian identity.

Thomas says, "The only thing more pathetic than Indians on TV is Indians watching Indians on TV" in *Smoke Signals*.

Rather than simply dismiss the continuing influence of media images, Victor and Thomas reenvision themselves by recontextualizing an old image from a contemporary Native perspective. On their way home to the reservation, the two help save a young woman injured in a car accident caused by a drunken Euro-American driver. When they visit her in the hospital, they respond to her friend's compliment that they are "heroes . . . like the Lone Ranger and Tonto" with Thomas's correction that they are more "like Tonto and Tonto." Rather than playing sidekicks to white male heroes in Hollywood films and television shows, they come to see themselves, and invite viewers to see them, as performing good deeds as the protagonists of their own story. The allusion to the Lone Ranger and Tonto duo made popular in both Hollywood and on television reminds viewers that this is a film without a white male hero and suggests that new stories such as this one need to replace old images of Indians. The Tonto reference also alludes to the collection of short stories from which the film was made, Sherman Alexie's 1993 *The Lone Ranger and Tonto Fistfight in Heaven.* The allusion signals to students that they can investigate how stories (and the screenplay) by this Spokane/Coeur d'Alene author have been translated to film, and how the title of the short story collection suggests that contemporary Indian identities can be carved from real differences with Hollywood. Perhaps most important, students can view *Smoke Signals* as an example of how new images of Indians can come from re-viewing Hollywood stories from a Native point of view and how the re-viewing at once informs viewers where they got their old ideas and gives them new ones.

A Thousand Roads

Chris Eyre's 2005 *A Thousand Roads* (forty-three minutes) is billed as "the signature film of the Smithsonian's National Museum of the American Indian" in Washington, DC, where it is shown several times a day to hundreds of visitors.[16] The museum venue is an excellent setting in which to entertain and inform visitors who have come to learn about the history and heritage of Native peoples throughout the Americas. The film, however, is unusual for a museum because it is not about history. Rather than visualize the past, it challenges, and compensates for, the Hollywood-established invisibility of the contemporary Indian. This four-part film tells, in four short fictional narratives, the stories of four very different contemporary Americans: a Mohawk stockbroker in New York, an Inupiat girl from Seattle living in Alaska, a Navajo gang member in New Mexico, and a Quechua healer in Peru. *A Thousand Roads* shows diverse American Indians as protagonists of their own stories in actual locations and roles not imagined by Hollywood. It offers four different stories about unrelated characters to give viewers distinct individuals to learn about and identify with. Created in a collaboration between Indians and non-Indians,[17] all the stories are about contemporary Indians and are told from a Native perspective via the voice-over of (Santee Sioux) narrator John Trudell. Students can explore how, even while ignoring Hollywood, the film revises Hollywood film viewers' expectations as it normalizes seeing Indigenous peoples in a variety of previously unseen settings and roles. The range of different places where the characters live, the variety of lifestyles they embody, and the very different issues they face combine to inform audiences about the vast diversity of contemporary Indigenous identities and their continuing presence across the Americas.

A Thousand Roads is about diverse Indian identities in a twenty-first-century world. Although the four characters all have an Indian identity, it is not a monolithic racial identity. Instead, the film emphasizes how each is distinctly tied to a different cultural heritage. To contrast Hollywood's Eurocentric casting, as exposed in *Images of Indians* parts 1–5, and to add to the film's representational authenticity, its mix of professional and non-professional actors all come from the same cultural heritage as the characters they portray: the Mohawk stockbroker, Amanda Cook, is played by Mohawk actor Alex Rice; the Inupiat girl, Dawn Naageak, is played by Inupiat Riana Malabed; the Navajo gang member, Johnny Chee, is played by Navajo/Omaha actor Jeremiah Bitsui; and the Quechua healer, Don Santos Condori, is played by Quechua healer Honorato Ninantay. Challenging Hollywood's propensity for non-Indian protagonists, here the protagonists are not only Indians, but are Indians from the individual cultures represented. The "thousand roads" of the title suggests that there are many ways, including the four portrayed, that American Indians are living in the twenty-first century and there are many ways in which Indian identity has been and remains essential to Indian survival.

The narrative thread that weaves the four stories together illustrates the evolution of the oral tradition into modern form. In the oral tradition, storytellers pass on, reaffirm, and update important aspects of their cultures to keep both the tradition and the cultures alive. Here the oral storytelling tradition continues in contemporary film form via an off-screen voice-over. Reversing Hollywood's erasure, the storytelling voice in *A Thousand Roads* directly addresses contemporary Indigenous peoples from a contemporary Indigenous perspective. The narrator begins by greeting all Native peoples of the Americas and identifying a common heritage: "Good morning, Indian country. . . . We are all on this one body called the Americas, the land of our ancestors." This greeting is reminiscent of *Smoke Signals*, where the radio announcer proclaims, "It's a good day to be Indigenous" and the protagonists come to understand a common Indian identity based on their salmon-fishing Coeur d'Alene heritage. Here, the narrative voice also reaffirms the presence (rather than the disappearance) of Indians today with his opening (and closing) announcement that "It's a great day to be alive." He explains that this film is also about the importance of reaffirming an Indian identity: "We are a thousand nations strong [and] we Indians are always going home."

Students can explore how the narrative introduction to the first story serves as an introduction to all the stories: "We may feel disconnected from our people and our past, but we're not. . . . We all belong to the story of our people." The first story is about Amanda, a harried Mohawk Manhattan stockbroker struggling with a down market. She leaves her office to give money to a man on the street asking for handouts and they exchange greetings. While she works in the stock exchange and he asks for change, both gain strength from the contact. Together, they represent the diverse range of Mohawk who first inhabited and still call Manhattan home. The second story begins in Seattle, where a mother in the U.S. Army puts her daughter on an airplane to Barrow, Alaska, to live with her own mother while she is deployed overseas. The girl, Dawn, learns about her Inupiat heritage for the first time. She watches villagers share meat from a whale hunt, tastes (and spits out) a frozen whale meat treat, and she eats pizza and plays video games. The narrative voice explains that the whales have been coming here for over ten thousand years, that whale meat "feeds culture and identity," and that "there are no Inupiat without the whale."

Dawn's grandmother tells her, "This is your home too. This is how we are connected: how you are connected to me and to all who came before. Now, let's go eat some pizza." Viewers learn as Dawn learns that her relatives are not ancient relics of the past, but survive as their ancestors did and live in the present.

To enhance viewers' ideas about Indian diversity, stories about an older and a younger female are followed by stories about a younger and an older male. The third story is about Johnny, a seventeen-year-old gang member living in Albuquerque, New Mexico. A juxtaposed shot of Johnny next to Latino teen gang members illustrates, especially for viewers influenced by Hollywood's repeated portrayals of Latinos as gang members, that American Indian teens are as likely as Latino Americans to be tempted into gang life. His mother takes away Johnny's gun and the Navajo community sends him into the countryside to survive on his own. When he inadvertently lets loose a herd of sheep, he must decide if he will drive off with his friends or find his family's sheep. He chooses

An Inupiat girl visits her relatives in Barrow, Alaska, and learns about her whale-hunting cultural heritage in *A Thousand Roads.*

his family and finds his own way by finding and returning the sheep (including one who had wandered farther than the others) to their fold. The fourth story is about a Quechua healer living in the Andes of Peru. He is called on to heal a sick boy living "in a village on the rocks of his Inca ancestors." The narrator explains that Don Santos "has been trained in a tradition of medicine that goes back thousands of years." But, despite his efforts, the boy dies. The child's death reminds viewers that these stories are not romanticized repetitions of Hollywood's Noble Savages. Instead, a market falls, a mother leaves, a gang beckons, and a child dies. Students can analyze these fictional stories as illustrations, for Indians and non-Indians alike, of how important it is for contemporary Indians to reclaim, learn about, regain, and rely on the cultures of their ancestors to sustain them in a twenty-first-century world.

In Whose Honor? American Indian Mascots in Sports

Jay Rosenstein's 1996 *In Whose Honor?* (fifty-six minutes) is a video documentary that examines both sides of the national controversy over the use of American Indians as sports mascots.[18] Focusing on the protests of one graduate student, Spokane Indian Charlene Teters, against the University of Illinois' Chief Illiniwek mascot and logo, Rosenstein also answers *Images of Indians*' call for media depictions representing the realities of contemporary American Indian lives. The documentary shows how Teters's lone protest gave momentum to a then fledgling national campaign to educate fans and convince universities and professional sports teams to discontinue or replace their Indian mascots, logos, and nicknames.[19] Viewers see the controversy through the camera lens of University of Illinois graduate Jay Rosenstein, a non-Indian who, as an avid sports fan, at first accepted the university's Indian representations as mere entertainment. After hearing a talk by Teters, Rosenstein launched his own investigation—on camera. The result: as Teters, other American Indian experts, an offscreen narrator, and university officials and alumni give voice to varying ideas, *In Whose Honor?* reveals how Indian sports mascots and logos are offscreen replicas of Hollywood Indians, perpetuating the same kinds of misinformation and the same contemporary Indian invisibility. Directly confronting the practice of using American Indians as entertaining artifacts, this documentary focuses on the Native perspective of Charlene Teters, who resists contemporary Indian invisibility to at once reeducate audiences and reclaim her own and her children's Indian identity.

In Whose Honor? reveals how Indian sports mascots parallel Hollywood's persistence of vision as real-life replicas of its disappearing Indians. Echoing *Images of Indians'* descriptions of Hollywood Indians, this documentary begins with an intertitle from James Gray's 1940 book about Illinois Indians, *The Illinois*: "It has ever been the way of the white man in his relation to the Indian [to treat him] as a monster until he has been killed off [and then] to sentimentalize him in retrospect as the noble savage." Working from the descriptions and film illustrations in *Images of Indians*, students can explore the various ways sports mascots embody both stereotypes. For example, as savage warriors, mascots inspire fans by signifying that sports events are fierce battlegrounds between teams of winners and losers. As embodiments of noble savages who befriend the good settlers, mascots allow non-Indian fans to think well of themselves in lamenting and honoring the passing of now-dead Indians. Via movie Indians and mascot Indians, honoring friendly dead Indians is an attractive means for non-Indian fans to avoid acknowledging a manifest destiny past that attempted to eliminate Indians and to avoid recognizing contemporary Indian survivors.

The title *In Whose Honor?* both reflects and questions the university's rationale for claiming that its Chief Illiniwek mascot honors Indians. One outspoken fan of the chief, University of Illinois alumnus and Illinois state legislator Rick Winkel, explains on camera that Chief Illiniwek is "an attempt to try to remember a vanished tribe" of Illini Indians, for whom the state of Illinois is named. Winkel's selective historical memory parallels Hollywood's Eurocentric history about Indians, as he says he believes that the Illini were "annihilated, apparently, by an opposing Native American tribe." Combining exposé with reeducation, the documentary juxtaposes Winkel's version to the known history of the Illini, as the voice-over narrator explains that they were "a loose confederation of five or six tribes" whose numbers were greatly diminished in the early nineteenth century because of "wars with other tribes" and "diseases brought by Europeans," but mostly because they were "forced off their land by federal Indian policies" and those remaining were hunted when "a bounty was offered for the killing of Indians in the state of Illinois." Like Hollywood's history of Indians, the history of the Illini for fans of Chief Illiniwek is selectively favorable to sympathetic non-Indians, who are encouraged to innocently lament the extinction of the Illini by other Indians and ignore Indians living in the state.

The Indian mascot Charlene Teters encountered at the University of Illinois while she was a graduate student in 1989 was created much earlier, at the same time Hollywood movies established conventions about movie Indians that remain today. *In Whose Honor?* shows old photos and current video footage of the University of Illinois mascot, Chief Illiniwek, as he is and has been played by successive Euro-American students—all wearing buckskin, face paint, and a full eagle-feather headdress while performing gymnastics at half time—since 1926.[20] Like the Hollywood Indian, Chief Illiniwek and other Indian mascots are dressed in nineteenth-century costumes to invoke images of Indians as relics of the past. Echoing what *Images of Indians* notes in part 2 as the limited wardrobe of the Hollywood Indian, voice-over narration here informs viewers that Chief Illiniwek's costume is, in fact, Sioux, and thus unlike anything Illini Indians ever wore. Like many classic Hollywood portrayals of Indians, Chief Illiniwek is consistently played by Euro-Americans who, in performing a gymnastics routine billed as "an authentic Indian dance," enact their own inaccurately imagined ideas of Indian customs. Having Euro-American students play the role of Chief Illiniwek is akin to what, in part 5, Will Sampson calls acting out "the fantasy of a white man becoming an Indian chief" in Hollywood films. Students can recall *Images of Indians*' objections to Hollywood's Euro-American actors in redface and to Euro-American actors who "out-Indian the Indians" to understand how Indian mascots are additional appropriations of Indian identity. Euro-Americans playing movie Indians and mascot Indians suggests to Euro-American audiences that they are the natural inheritors of the land and suggests to Indians that Euro-Americans, in Teters's words, "control you . . . own you."

In Whose Honor? also addresses the detrimental effects of the university's Indian logo. Rosenstein shows it as a stylized Indian head, in full headdress, appearing on everything from public buildings to letterhead and put on university apparel and other merchandise to bring in revenue. Teters especially denounces its appearance on toilet paper, noting that it sends the message to Indians that "you are not quite as human as we are." Recalling *Images of Indians*, part 2, where Johnny Cash explains that scalping was an accepted practice whereby British and American soldiers were paid for Indian scalps, *In Whose Honor?* includes another University of Illinois student, Karen Strong, who reveals how she encounters the Indian head logo "even in deans' offices," on a daily basis. Seeing Indian head logos on merchandise for sale constantly reminds her that, in Illinois, Indian head logos were placed on businesses to advertise that "Indian men's heads sold for $7, Indian women's heads for $5, and Indian children's heads were $3." Honoring Indians via Indian logos, as Teters and Strong demonstrate, actually dishonors them by continuing to engage in cultural imperialism and to act as if contemporary Indians either do not exist or do not matter.

In addressing the issue of contemporary American Indian invisibility foregrounded in *Images of Indians, In Whose Honor?* documents the perspectives of both Indians and non-Indians. As she recounts the event that launched her protests, Teters describes the reaction of her two children to Chief Illiniwek at a university basketball game. When they saw the mascot perform, her son and daughter both "sank in their seats" and her daughter "tried to make herself invisible." They felt they were "targets" and were embarrassed; in Teters's words, seeing the performance "was a blow to their self-esteem." Akin to seeing movie Indians vanishing into a distant past, seeing replications of movie Indians being honored for having vanished into a distant past invites contemporary Indian children to make themselves invisible as Indians. As Teters's daughter tried to become invisible to those around her because she saw herself "being mimicked," she exemplifies the damaging effect of Indian stereotypes on Indian children described by other American Indian experts. Michael Haney appears on camera to reveal the findings of studies that monitor "the effects of racial stereotypes" on the self-worth of Indian children. He reports their horrifying attempts to disappear: "One in five American Indian youth attempt, not just consider, but attempt, suicide." Teters also cites the reaction of well-intentioned people in the university art department—where she was, ironically, recruited to "add diversity"—to her complaint about the chief. They recommended that she remain silent and invisible, advising her to "just be quiet, get your degree, and get out of here." Student fans of Chief Illiniwek gave similar, if not so well-intentioned, advice to make herself invisible in reacting to Teters's protests with their chants: "Hey, Hey, Ho, Ho / Chief haters have to go" and "Pick another school." To others, Teters was either invisible or irrelevant. When asked to comment on the chief controversy, the then university president simply replies that the chief is beloved as a university tradition, and an alumnus fan insists that the university should "not cave in to out-of-state foreigners."

Teters, however, decided differently. Echoing the strategy of juxtaposing Hollywood images with actual contemporary Indians in *Images of Indians*, *In Whose Honor?* records her resistance to invisibility and loss of self-esteem as she presents herself to the university community as a contemporary American Indian who honors her heritage. Identifying herself as a contemporary Indian to make the invisible visible and to reclaim her cultural identity, Teters began by carrying a sign on campus reading, "American Indians are Human Beings, not Mascots." Although she was "spit on," "ridiculed," and "threatened," she continued and later carried the same message to what the narrator describes as "the big-money world of professional football." Viewers also see Teters's attendance at a talk by the Euro-American student who was the current Chief Illiniwek. As the student holds up the eagle-feather headdress of his costume and explains how he is proud to be the chief, Teters raises a question for him, for the university, and for fans and viewers to consider: "Why is the university involved with some kind of religious ceremony at halftime?" Students can also analyze how, akin to *Images of Indians*' focus on Will Sampson and his concern for Indian youth, Rosenstein's focus on Teters personalizes the mascot issue, inviting viewers to identify with her and understand her need to reclaim her children's dignity and their heritage. She explains to viewers her decision to protest for her children: "I'm standing up for my children," who "were taught to respect the person who has earned the right to wear an eagle-feather headdress" and to understand how "paint is sacred" and "dance is sacred." And she protests to reclaim their heritage: "Our people paid with their very lives to keep what little we have left. The fact that we even have anything today speaks to the strength of our ancestors. And that's what I am protecting." Her ancestors survived the past, and her own and her children's Indian identity depends on a recognition, rather than a Eurocentric appropriation, of that manifest destiny past and their survival.

Rosenstein also shows the widespread effects of Indian mascots on non-Indians to reveal how the issue is of importance to all Americans. As in *Images of Indians*, American Indian experts represent themselves as contemporary Indians and provide Native perspectives to reeducate viewers. Teters explains how the term *redskin* is the equivalent of *nigger*, and American Indian counselor Dennis Tibbetts wonders how people in our nation's capital can refer to themselves as "Redskin fans."[21] As Michael Haney connects half-time mascot music to Hollywood music and Vernon Bellecourt discusses the demeaning and belittling effects of Indian mascots and nicknames on Indians, viewers see stadiums across the country filled with fans playing Indian. Shots include university and professional teams' stadiums filled with fans sporting feathers and painted faces, bands playing and fans listening to Hollywood music designed to conjure up Hollywood images of Indians, and bands and fans waving their instruments and arms in unison to the rhythms of a "tomahawk chop" as they unthinkingly imitate imitation Indians. A topic ripe for student discussion is how sports fans have normalized the idea of non-Indians playing Indian to the extent that they readily participate themselves.

Non-Indian viewers are also invited to think seriously about how offensive Indian mascots and nicknames are to Indians by understanding how they might feel if they were treated similarly. Following part 3 in *Images of Indians*, where Indian comedian Charley Hill questions why the "Cleveland Indians" are accepted but the "Washington White Boys" and the "Cleveland Caucasians" would not be, *In Whose Honor?* offers similar comparisons. The film notes that team names such as the Washington Redskins, Kansas City Chiefs, and Atlanta Braves go unquestioned, but Catholic or Jewish mascots and nicknames would not be allowed, and it asks for equal respect for Indians. Teters comments that other caricatures, such as Little Black Sambo and Frito Bandito, have long been retired,

A Euro-American student performs as Chief Illiniwek, and fans mimic his actions in *In Whose Honor?*

suggesting that it is long past time for Indian mascots to join them. Students can analyze how these analogies recontextualize familiar Indian mascots and nicknames to show them as equally objectionable.

Another recurring issue of importance to all Americans, also addressed in *Images of Indians*, is how entrenched (often unconscious) notions of racial superiority and racial difference underlie support for offensive representations of Indians. *In Whose Honor?* includes interviews with Euro-American University of Illinois officials and alumni to involve viewers in coming to judgment on the race issue. Alumnus Rick Winkel who, as a state legislator, proposed a law that would institutionalize Chief Illiniwek as the official mascot of the university, says, "We have a rich heritage in this country . . . of protecting minority rights, but minority rights are not always right." Having normalized the majority Euro-American point of view as the right view, he claims that it is and should be the deciding view, with no need to take Indian perspectives into account. Similarly, trustee Susan Gravenhorst says in defense of Chief Illiniwek, "The Native

Indians are not as involved as we are in this situation. Perhaps they don't really understand how we are representing the chief. Perhaps they should come to a game. I cannot imagine that the chief . . . could be perceived as a racial insult or a racial slur to the Native American community. To me, it's a compliment." Defending a mascot designed to honor vanquished Indians without knowing the position of live American Indian students on campus (including Charlene Teters) who were attending games and protesting, again suggests the often unconscious thinking by which Euro-Americans see themselves as the presumptive norm and attribute racial difference and a lack of understanding to others.

But not all Euro-American university officials support these Eurocentric views, and new understandings invite change. In an on-camera interview, university dean Leigh Estabrook describes Chief Illiniwek as building on the "racial stereotypes" in the media that she grew up with and says the mascot "perpetuates the old cowboy and Indian myths." She also describes an effect of mascots as encouraging Euro-Americans to think of Indians as outside the normal range of people to associate with. Entrenched ideas about American Indians as a monolithic racial other, as Estabrook suggests, come from normalizing—from internalizing and institutionalizing—racial stereotypes and serve to diminish the humanity of both Indians and non-Indians. Working from an *In Whose Honor?* progress report on colleges and universities that have recognized this collateral damage, reeducated fans, and changed their nicknames and their images, students can examine the continuing controversy for themselves.[22] Most important, students can view *In Whose Honor?* as an exposé of the Hollywood Indian in its offscreen mascot, logo, and nickname manifestations. And students can see how one woman's personal narrative, the story of Charlene Teters, effectively replaces images of imitation Indians with an image of her own making.

Talking Back: American Indian Alternative Media

In the ongoing process of hegemonic negotiations exemplified in these alternative media challenges, entrenched expectations encounter contemporary Indigenous realities. While these media challenges are only a sampling of the many facets of an evolving, expanding, and still not always visible American Indian alternative media movement, they offer students a view into its ongoing issues and some of the means used to address them. They can encourage students to find and to create other films and videos that reappropriate Indian images and represent current issues and the diversity of contemporary American Indian identities to replace the images and change the thinking still encouraged by Hollywood's persistence of vision.

Notes

Unless otherwise noted, all photographs are from the author's collection.

1. *Images of Indians* is a five-part documentary series written, directed, and coproduced by Phil Lucas and Robert Hagopian (Seattle: KCTS TV and United Indians of All Tribes Foundation, 1979). *Images of Indians* was first shown on PBS in 1980; the DVD is now available for sale from the Four Worlds International Institute, at www.4worlds.org/index, and for use from many colleges and universities. The five parts are part 1, *The Great Movie Massacre;* part 2, *How Hollywood Wins the West;* part 3, *War Paint and Wigs;* part 4, *Heathen Injuns and the Hollywood Gospel;* and part 5, *Movie Reel Indians.*

In an essay titled "Promoting Understanding: The Celluloid Contributions of Phil Lucas," author David Delgado Shorter finds the eighty-plus films and television shows of Choctaw filmmaker Phil Lucas, including *Images of Indians,* distinctive in addressing both Indian and non-Indian audiences and in including both the history of and solutions to specific Indigenous issues. Shorter notes that *Images of Indians* was quickly recognized as an important film: it won the Special Achievement in Documentary Film award from the American Film Institute in 1980 and the Prix Italia award in 1981, and it was selected to represent the United States at Input 81. *World Order* 35.1 (2003): 21–29.

2. *Images of Indians* also includes critiques of selected television programs. Cree filmmaker Neil Diamond's more recent documentary *Reel Injun: On the Trail of the Hollywood Indian* (2009; eighty-nine minutes) complements and updates *Images of Indians,* as directors, writers, actors, and activists discuss film depictions of American Indians from silent cinema to 2008. Diamond's film includes a noteworthy segment on the imitation Indian Iron Eyes Cody, and it ends with a brief but important discussion of a number of recent films that students can examine as continuing the American Indian alternative media movement initiated with *Images of Indians. Reel Injun* is available from Kino International at www.kino.com. Other notable (but less comprehensive) documentaries on the topic of American Indian media representations include *Imagining Indians* (Victor Masayesua, 1992) and *Indian Princess Demystified* (Lorraine Norrgard, 1988).

3. For example, the independent documentaries *War Code: Navajo* (Lena Carr, 1996) and *True Whispers: The Story of the Navajo Code Talkers* (Valerie Red-Horse and Gale Anne Hurd, 2002) inform viewers about the essential role of

Navajo soldiers in World War II victories, in devising and using a secret code created from their native language, from the perspectives of the Code Talkers themselves. Hollywood's feature film on the topic is *Windtalkers* (John Woo, 2002). An example of what has changed in Hollywood filmmaking, this film includes a twentieth-century American Indian who gets to survive World War II and return home to his Navajo community. Also an example of what has not changed, this film tells the story of a white male protagonist from his perspective and includes the Navajo Code Talker as his Noble Savage sidekick.

4. Early Pocahontas stories include 1908 and 1910 films. Students can examine the more recent versions: Lew Landers's *Captain John Smith and Pocahontas* (1953), Mike Gabriel and Eric Goldberg's *Pocahontas* (1995), and Terrance Malick's *The New World* (2005). Comparisons reveal how each version updates the story for the audience of its time, and how each is a historical misrepresentation: a ten- to twelve-year-old girl is changed into a voluptuous young woman to serve as a temporary love interest for the white male hero from England who arrives to help create a settlement in the New World.

5. Films of James Fenimore Cooper's novel *The Last of the Mohicans* include 1909, 1911, 1920, 1936, 1946, 1955, and 1977 versions and, so far, end with Michael Mann's 1992 film. As with the Pocahontas films, students can compare available versions to see how each updates the story for the audience of the time in which it was made. Here, students can also note how each version reproduces the same image of a white male protagonist who becomes a Euro-American Indian, out-Indians the Indians he lives with, and embodies the repeated message that he is the natural inheritor of a land where the Hostile Savages are justifiably killed and the Noble Savages dwindle to one "last of the Mohicans." The many films exemplify how repeated versions revamp, recycle, and repeat old images of vanishing Indians in manifest destiny stories told from Euro-American perspectives to promote and popularize ideas favorable to Euro-Americans for succeeding generations.

6. Sequels to *The Paleface* (Norman McLeod, 1948) are *The Son of Paleface* (Frank Tashlin, 1952) with Bob Hope, and *The Shakiest Gun in the West* (Alan Rafkin, 1968) with Don Knotts.

7. For an excellent explanation of Gramsci's theory of "hegemony," and its implications for and applications to popular culture representations, see Lee Artz and Ortega Murphy's *Antonio Gramsci and Hegemony in the United States* (Thousand Oaks, CA: Sage, 2000). Artz and Murphy argue that "because of society's cultural diversity and complexity, hegemony must be continually stitched together at many seams and thus has many points where it may unravel" (28). This "unraveling" is the goal of films and videos in the American Indian alternative independent media movement.

8. The tradition of non-Indians in redface playing Indians continued long after *Images of Indians* was made. Some examples are *Windwalker* with Trevor

Howard (1980), *Running Brave* with Robby Benson (1983), *The Legend of Walks for Women* with Raquel Welch (1984), *Outrageous Fortune* with George Carlin (1987), and (on television) *Dark Wind* with Lou Diamond Phillips (1992).

9. Iron Eyes Cody was influential as a non-Indian who played Indian in movies, on television, and in real life. According to Angela Aleiss, Cody was actually an Italian American who "rarely left home without his braided wig, beaded moccasins, and buckskin jacket." She notes that "his feathered headdress, dark complexion, and braided wig became the embodiment of the noble Indian" when he played "the teary-eyed Indian in the 'Keep America Beautiful' public service television spots in 1971." He played Indian as a child of nature who bemoaned the passing of an America once inhabited by Noble Savages like himself. "Iron Eyes Cody: Wannabe Indian," *Cineaste* 25.1 (1999): 31.

10. The two sequels are *Return of a Man Called Horse* (Irvin Kershner, 1976) and *Triumphs of a Man Called Horse* (John Hough, 1983).

11. In John Ford's *Drums along the Mohawk* (1939), the white male protagonist settler easily outruns three Indians (who chase him but literally fall by the wayside one by one) in a long trek through field and stream to get help to defend a frontier fort from attacking Indians during the Revolutionary War.

In the (eight) film versions of *The Last of the Mohicans*, the last in 1992, the white male protagonist becomes Indian and leads his Mohican companions through field and forest, proving himself physically (in running and hunting) and mentally (in making all important decisions) superior.

12. Eurocentrism refers here to the presumption that Europeans had a historical destiny (a manifest destiny) to colonize the Americas, that Euro-Americans remain inherently superior to those they conquered, and that Euro-Americans and Euro-American civilization epitomize the standards by which others should be measured. It is essential to note that many non-Euro-Americans are Eurocentric and that many Euro-Americans are not Eurocentric in their beliefs. In "Multiculturalism, Race, and Representation," Robert Stam writes, "Multiculturalism is actually an assault . . . on Eurocentrism, [which] . . . permeates and structures contemporary practices and representations even after the formal end of colonialism" and "envisions the world from a single privileged point." Stam notes, "A multicultural view critiques the universalization of Eurocentric norms." *Film Theory: An Introduction* (Madden, MA: Blackwell, 2000), 269.

13. Because the U.S. Census Bureau continues to count everyone in the United States according to racial categories, it perpetuates the mistaken notion that race is a biological reality rather than a social construction. Offering scientific proof that race is not a biological reality, Christine Herbes-Sommers's film *The Difference between Us* (episode 1 in the 2003 three-part film series *Race: The Power of an Illusion*) shows culturally different students sequencing and then comparing their DNA to discover that there are no genes to distinguish any one so-called race from any other.

Tracy Heather's film *The Story We Tell* (episode 2 of *Race: The Power of an*

Illusion) chronicles how, when, and why ideas about race first took hold in the United States. The film explains how racial categories are social constructions that were invented to promote the idea of white (Euro-American) superiority in order to justify enslaving Africans, taking lands inhabited by American Indians and Latino/as under policies of manifest destiny, and ensuring the low cost of Asian immigrant workers and then of all ethnic minorities in a country that also proclaimed freedom and equality for all.

Because race is a social (not a biological) reality, it is important to retain Census Bureau categories in order to record, make public, and bring to an end racial/ethnic inequities in individual instances and institutionalized practices (such as the institutionalized images of Indians in Hollywood cinema). My book, *Teaching Ethnic Diversity with Film*, calls for a public redefining of the term *race* to mean socially constructed categories, or else exchanging it for the term *ethnicity* because ethnicity already refers to socially constructed categories. I define ethnicity as "a more neutral term than race in that, when it defines groups of people in the United States by ancestral origin, it refers to ancestral cultural traits such as language, foods, and other cultural customs and traditions, not inherent human traits passed on, and it does not contend that all members of one ethnic group have any inherent superior or inferior mental, physical, or moral characteristics." Ethnic distinctions also emphasize that "Euro Americans are just another ethnic group," not a norm or standard by which to measure others. *Teaching Ethnic Diversity with Film* (Jefferson, NC: McFarland, 2006), 4–5.

14. *Smoke Signals* was developed at the Sundance Institute, where workshops and mentors guide new independent filmmakers. The film premiered at the 1998 Sundance Film Festival, where it won both the Audience Award for Dramatic Films and the Filmmakers Trophy. Miramax distributed this film, bringing it to public audiences nationwide. The DVD is readily available.

15. John Wayne's attitude toward Indians echoes the "Elbow Room" cartoon that Will Sampson criticizes in part 2 of *Images of Indians*. In a *Playboy* interview, Wayne said, "I don't feel we did wrong in taking this great country away from them. There were great numbers of people who needed new land, and the Indians were selfishly trying to keep it for themselves." Quoted in Gretchen Bataille and Charles L. P. Silet, eds., *The Pretend Indian: Images of Native Americans in the Movies*. (Ames: Iowa University Press, 1980), 101.

16. *A Thousand Roads* is available from the Smithsonian National Museum of the American Indian: www.nmai.si.edu.

17. Scott Garen (non-Indian) and Joy Harjo (Muskogee Creek) cowrote the script for *A Thousand Roads*.

18. *In Whose Honor? American Indian Mascots in Sports* is available from New Day Films: www.newday.com.

19. Students from high schools, colleges, or universities that have considered or gone through the process of changing the names of their sports teams are often schooled on the issue and can connect it with other examples of appropriating

Indian identity that ignores real Indians (for example, in the still-popular child's game of cowboys and Indians, in many Boy Scout activities, historically when the Revolutionary colonists played Indian at the Boston Tea Party, again at some "Tea Party" protests against taxes in 2009, and in New Age use and abuse of American Indian spiritual ceremonies).

20. The film explains that the one absence of Chief Illiniwek was during World War II, in 1944, when a Euro-American woman student played the stereotypical Hollywood role of an Indian Princess, as Princess Illiniwek.

21. That the term *redskin,* which originally referred to Indian scalps presented by U.S. soldiers to the U.S. government for payment, is not understood as offensive is continuing evidence of the invisibility of today's Indians and the obvious need for reeducation. In the documentary film *On and Off the Res' with Charlie Hill* (Sandra Sunrising Osawa, 2000), Dick Gregory explains how Indian scalps came to be called "redskin." Gregory reports that in order to stop those who brought in hair attached to unidentifiable scalps, new directions for Indian scalps called for a piece of "red skin."

22. In February 2007, the board of trustees of the University of Illinois announced that it would discontinue its eighty-one-year-old tradition of having Chief Illiniwek perform at halftime. The announcement meant that the university would then be in alignment with National Collegiate Athletic Association (NCAA) policy. In 2005, the NCAA established a policy that requires colleges and universities with American Indian mascots and imagery to refrain from displaying them during NCAA-sponsored events and that institutions with this imagery would be ineligible to host NCAA championship games. However, while Chief Illiniwek no longer appears at NCAA-sponsored games, alumni who had performed as the chief assumed control of the tradition and can promote his appearance off the playing field, and the Indian head logo remains. Other mascots, logos, and nicknames remain at other colleges, universities, and high schools today. While progress has been made, alternative media education remains essential.

Geographies of Identity and Belonging in Sherman Alexie's *The Business of Fancydancing*

Amy Corbin

Sherman Alexie (Spokane/Coeur d'Alene), one of the most widely read Native American authors, gained a taste of Hollywood through adapting some of his own short stories into the screenplay for Chris Eyre's 1998 *Smoke Signals*, the first Native American–directed feature film to be theatrically released in the modern Hollywood era.[1] After trying his hand at other Hollywood writing jobs that followed, Alexie decided to make his own first film independently, so as to have as much creative control as possible. *The Business of Fancydancing* (2002) was shot for $90,000 on digital video.[2] It played the festival circuit and screened for short periods at theaters in New York, Los Angeles, and Seattle. While reviewers noted the low-budget image quality, some looked past its rough edges to see a conceptually original film that marked a real departure from the more mainstream and uplifting tone of *Smoke Signals*.[3] *Variety*'s reviewer, in particular, praised the film as "adventurous in theme, story structure and cinematic style," as well as "striking" and "imaginative."[4] Alexie purposefully created an atmosphere on set that encouraged experimentation and collaboration among the inexperienced crew—as he told one interviewer, "I essentially tried to do everything I could think of to test myself, and to shoot every kind of scene imaginable. You know, I was never sure anybody would see this, so I didn't worry about it."[5]

The Business of Fancydancing joins a small group of theatrically released Native-directed features that have been reviewed in mainstream publications, including Eyre's follow-up film *Skins* (2002) and Randy Redroad's *The Doe Boy* (2001).[6] While all these films deal with issues of identity—colonialism's theft of Indigenous culture, Native Americans being "unseen" in modern American culture, the mixed-race experience—Alexie's film envisions these issues through innovative use of place and spectator positioning. Alexie conjures up an experience of being in multiple places at once, which invokes the experience of occupying multiple cultures simultaneously. These split mental geographies are felt not only on a character level, but on the spectatorial level, evoking what I call a nomadic viewing experience, in which the visual positioning and structure of the film deny the spectator a constant point of view and therefore simulate a mental feeling of hybridity and contradiction. The nomadic point of view moves between various "insider" and "outsider" positions vis-à-vis particular cultural landscapes—places that stand for and manifest group identities. The cultural landscapes key to *Fancydancing* are the Seattle culture of white art connoisseurs, the Seattle of the "urban Indian" estranged from his tribal identity, and the Spokane reservation in eastern Washington State. Alexie denies the spectator consistent identification with his protagonist Seymour, an acclaimed Spokane poet who now lives in Seattle and has isolated himself from the reservation. Instead, the film also offers the point of view of Spokane reservation residents, who criticize Seymour for using Native exotica and reservation trauma for his personal gain. Intertwined with both of these perspectives are moments in which the spectator is thirdly positioned to be an audience member at one of Seymour's poetry readings, becoming a non-Native consumer of Native art.

In cinema, *point of view* can refer either to a psychological perspective that is based on character identification or to the optical point of view of the camera; I add *cultural* as a reminder that the attitude and position from which a film asks a spectator to view its diegetic[7] world is inherently cultural. While relating the spectator to character and place, the film evokes a relationship with and judgment toward the culture from which those characters and places arise. A nomadic cultural point of view attempts to prevent the spectator from settling into any one point of view—instead reminding us that culture is always seen differently dependent upon where one is standing. The connotation of *nomad* is "constantly wandering," which Giuliana Bruno notes is a particular sensation of spectatorship distinct from that of the traveler, who maintains "home" as a constant point of reference.[8] Teshome Gabriel sees the ever-shifting nature of nomadic aesthetics as a quality that promotes interactivity with the audience and the awareness that culture is, in some sense, fundamentally unrepresentable.[9] With the nomadic metaphor, the spectator is a traveler within the film world and is prevented from assuming a stable place in relation to the film's cultural landscapes—a "here where I am" as opposed to "there."

To contrast with nomadism, we can briefly state that many popular Hollywood films about Native Americans are filmed from a consistent touristic point of view, in which the films assume an audience of outsider non-Natives who pay for the experience of seeing an exotic and romanticized "other" culture on display—*Dances with Wolves* (1990) and *Last of the Mohicans* (1992) being two of the most prominent recent examples. The touristic gaze is invoked not only by having a white man as the protagonist, but also by a camera that seeks visual otherness through dances, rituals, and panoramic scenery. Viewers may feel sympathetic toward the Native characters, but the viewing position remains resolutely outside the Native cultural landscape. Such touristic films market their cultural authenticity to reassure outsider viewers that they are getting "the real thing" (in the case of these films by emphasizing historical research and consultation with Native people on costume, language, and ceremony), assuaging the ever-present doubts in the tourist's mind about his or her inability to access true cultural otherness.[10] Eyre's and Redroad's films offer what I term a dwelling point of view, where cinematic techniques and narrative de-emphasize otherness and offer viewers, no matter their actual racial and cultural affiliations, the virtual experience of being a resident of a reservation community.[11] These films attempt to prevent a touristic gaze—even from non-Native viewers—through the emphasis on psychological depth, humor, "everyday" plot episodes, and an avoidance of deliberate cultural spectacle.[12] While their cultural landscapes are inextricably Native through a bedrock of values such as connection to land and ancestors, they do not emphasize this cultural difference for the display and entertainment of a tourist. They do, however, reveal the heterogeneity of Native communities: *The Doe Boy* by telling the story of a mixed-race adolescent and his efforts to reconcile the different strands of his heritage and *Skins* by contrasting the reservation lifestyles of one brother who works for the tribal police force with another who lives on the alcoholic margins. But these different points of view remain within the cultural landscape of the reservation, and they do not create a spectatorial experience as radically displacing and disorienting as *The Business of Fancydancing*.

Alexie's writing has been criticized by some Native literary critics for its emphasis on hybridity over tribal tradition, its use of popular culture references, and its emphasis on reservation tragedy and nihilism, choices which, some have argued, give white consumers just another, more "hip" version of the noble savage stereotype.[13] These elements of his oeuvre are certainly present in *Fancydancing*, but the purpose of this chapter is neither to celebrate nor to criticize Alexie's cultural politics. Rather, I hope to show how these themes are manifested in the formal properties of *Fancydancing* through cinematic geographies—both the physical and mental senses of place and positioning. Through the use of the above cultural points of view—touristic, dwelling, and nomadic—I approach cinematic geography through a strategy one scholar has called the geography of the text itself.[14] That is, instead of analyzing only the symbolic function of the film's settings, I also ask how a film positions its viewers in relation to the cultural landscapes onscreen. Such an approach is text centered rather than viewer centered; individual viewers will certainly negotiate meanings based on their own identifications and life experiences. Following Stuart Hall, however, I analyze the film's "encoding" through cinematic and narrative techniques and argue that it offers a position of cultural nomadism, in which the spectator "tries on" different points of view and is never allowed to rest in one.[15] In doing so, I see the greater formal experimentation of Alexie's film as an element that enhances the creative repertoire of Native feature filmmakers and also puts itself in dialogue with theories of how film form expresses complex cultural identities.

The Multiple Geographies of Seymour Polatkin

The spectator's experience of nomadism goes beyond identification with a displaced character, but since poet Seymour Polatkin initially appears to be the protagonist (as well as an alter ego of Alexie himself), I want to start first by examining the character himself and his movements—literal and cultural—throughout the film. Seymour lives in Seattle as a gay "ethnic" writer whose work is eagerly consumed by a mostly non-Native audience. Alexie claims to have modeled Seymour on aspects of himself and of lead actor Evan Adams: Seymour clearly experiences Alexie's life of literary fame and performing for a largely white audience, while Seymour's gay identity comes from Adams's life story.[16] Seymour chooses to live in Seattle with a white lover, estranged from the Spokane reservation where he was born—an estrangement that seems to be upheld both by Seymour himself and those he left behind, who resent his status as an absentee spokesman for the tribe. (There is no indication in the film that his sexual identity has anything to do with this friction.) Seymour's childhood friend

Aristotle originally accompanied him to Seattle when they began college, but was overcome by cultural isolation and dropped out. The death of another childhood friend, Mouse, brings Seymour back to the reservation, where he must face Aristotle and his college girlfriend Agnes, who has taken the path opposite of his—from the city back to the reservation.

As is clear from this plot summary, the characters themselves all take journeys back and forth between the reservation and Seattle, making travel between different cultural landscapes a key theme of the film. The film's complex first sequences, which include three different physical settings and varying geographical and psychological proximity vis-à-vis the characters, immediately challenge the spectator to follow a film that is geographically fluid and temporally nonlinear.[17] Such a structure is not just formalist experimentation, but simulates for the spectator the feeling of "trying on" different cultural points of view.

The Business of Fancydancing begins with playful home video images of friends Seymour and Aristotle in cap and gown, celebrating their high school graduation. Arms around each other, each wearing "valedictorian" sashes, they speak to their unseen friend Mouse, who is behind the video camera filming these images. They tease, laugh, and jostle each other, as they speak of their plans to go to college and room together, and "stay best friends forever." Once, Mouse's arm reaches into the frame, and he then turns the camera on himself, to offer his own accomplishments (a GED) and plans (working in the uranium mine) as a self-deprecating contrast to his two friends. The skewed, uncomfortably close perspective of a camera facing its holder soon gives way to visual chaos as the friends start to walk away and Mouse lets the camera tilt downward, producing blurry images of the forest clearing where they stand. The sequence is at once familiar and distancing, a push-pull tension that Alexie uses throughout the film to comment on the experience of never feeling entirely at home in any single place.

The young men's antics before the camera provide potential identification for the spectator, who may recall similar memories of the bonds of high school friendship and the coming-of-age moment that is high school graduation. But such familiarity is contradicted by the framing and context of the images; these images are not an objective, omniscient glimpse into these characters' pasts. The grainy image quality, jiggling motion, and the black frame around the image emphasize that we are seeing a video-within-a-film. This technique inherently forces the spectator to be aware of the act of image making, reminding us that there is a specific point of view behind each shot, and that the image originates from a place that always lies just beyond the screen, fundamentally inaccessible—knowledge that is suppressed in the technical perfection of the classical Hollywood style. The frame of the diegetic camera binds Seymour, Aristotle, and Mouse together in the place of adolescence, but indicates that this moment in time and place is removed from both the characters of the film's present time and the spectator.

The subjectivity of the graduation footage is underscored when Mouse turns the camera on himself, introducing the element of self-examination shared by several of the characters who do not dwell comfortably or unquestioningly in their cultural landscapes. Cultural landscape then becomes psychological landscape as *Fancydancing* cuts to a figure against a completely black background, with no contours to even suggest it is a room. An overhead shot of the adult Seymour in this "no-place" reveals him alone powwow dancing, wearing a simple red T-shirt, jeans, and a colorful shawl. The abstract quality of this setting along with its frequent recurrence throughout the film, not chronologically related to the film's narrative, suggests that it can be read as Seymour's mind or dream-space. Alexie visualizes this mental space as an abstract yet physical space, rather than using more common cinematic techniques of subjectivity such as close-ups, character point-of-view shots within "realistic" settings, and mood music. The dance is gender bending—a man dancing with a female dancer's shawl—and the mix of street clothing and powwow regalia suggests cultural hybridity. While there is clear symbolism to this image, the overhead camera blocks sight of Seymour's face and the shot remains emotionally opaque. So the spectator is in Seymour's head geographically, inhabiting the mind-space as a situated body, but maintains a distinct psychological presence rather than inhabiting Seymour's mind. The effect is that the spectator remains an independent entity and keeps a critical distance from Seymour, from his affiliations and opinions, an element of the nomadic point of view on which I will elaborate below.

Having made a journey progressively further into the spaces of the characters' minds in the film's prologue, the spectator is abruptly repositioned after the credits. The film proper begins with a picturesque shot of the Seattle skyline. Seymour's voice-over starts: "How to write the great American Indian novel,"[18] and these words form a sound bridge from the panorama of the city to an extreme close-up of a book, a hand holding it, and a tie visible behind the hand. With this edit, Alexie defeats the purpose of the conventional establishing shot sequence: we know we are in Seattle, but the exact setting is a mystery because there is no intermediate shot. The spectator may then feel he or she is getting his or her bearings when the camera cuts to a close-up of Seymour's face; he is reading from the book with his eyes darting about, so it appears that he is at a literary reading. A slight glare suggestive of a window is the only clue that something is a little off. Seymour's words continue as a voice-over when Alexie cuts to a black screen with printed text from a literary magazine evaluating Seymour's writing. When the camera cuts back to Seymour, however, it is a long shot situated out on a street looking into the front window of a bookstore where Seymour is seated, reading directly through the glass window to the street.

The street is virtually empty except for one middle-aged white passerby who pauses by the window and stares at Seymour. Seymour makes eye contact with the man and continues to read as if at a normal reading. No one acknowledges Seymour's bizarre placement and the lack of audience. The spectator, like the pedestrian, is thus visually separated from Seymour by the glass barrier. The spectator's perception is also disturbed because he or she has made an inference based on limited information—initially following clues that suggest a literary reading in a conventional bookstore setting, without the benefit of an establishing shot that, in conventional cinema, confirms the spatial layout and relation between characters.

The spectator's incomplete knowledge of the setting, caused by being too close to absorb the whole picture, exhibits a quality of haptic cinema as defined by Laura Marks: "the sense of space is contingent, close up, and short term, lacking a fixed outside point of reference."[19] This spatial disorientation defeats the ideal, objective viewpoint that critics associate both with classical Hollywood narrative and with traditional ethnographic documentaries. In Hollywood narrative, the editing together of multiple optical perspectives combines with omniscience of story knowledge to give the spectator the experience of an all-knowing voyeur; in traditional ethnographic cinema, the voice-over narrator (often described as the "voice of God") provides a sense of outsider authority that translates an "other" culture for the assumed outsider spectator.[20] Placing the spectator into the diegetic setting in a particular, embodied manner without mastery over the space thus dismantles the omniscience of these dominant

Seymour as a Native purveyor of cultural exoticism in *The Business of Fancydancing.*

modes, forcing the film, as Trinh Minh-ha says, to "speak not about, but nearby."[21] (We are also "nearby" but not inside when we observe Seymour's mind-space.) There is thus an inherent sense of relativity between the spectator and the characters in the diegetic world; instead of being the unseen voyeur who has the ideal viewpoint on the action, *Fancydancing*'s spectator is immediately disoriented and must work in order to figure out where she or he stands in relation to the various characters and settings.

The entire film maintains the imaginative movement of these opening sequences: it jumps relentlessly between Seymour at readings, Seymour in intimate moments with his lover Steven in their apartment in Seattle, flashbacks and video footage of Aristotle and Mouse back on the reservation, present-day preparations for Mouse's funeral on the reservation, and dreamlike scenes of powwow dancing and a journalist's interview of Seymour, both in Seymour's mind-space. The film is a collage, the editing style embedding into the structure of the film the idea of multiple cultural identities and points of view on these identities. The film's geographical fluidity, then, becomes a way for the spectator to experience Seymour's struggles to come to terms with these places that represent different cultural affiliations and ways of living. The very physicality of place—you can only be in one place at a time—becomes a metaphor for Seymour's feeling that his different cultures each demand preference. He cannot be at peace with coexisting identities because both the Spokane reservation and arty Seattle lay claim to him in a manner that seems to exclude the other.

Seymour's struggles and displacements are again illustrated through another variation on the looking-through-glass motif later in the film. When Seymour initially arrives at the home on the reservation where people are gathered for Mouse's funeral, he pulls his car into the driveway and sits there. Filmed in long shot by a camera located on the far side of the car (so it looks through two car windows and over Seymour's shoulder), Aristotle leaves the house and walks toward the car, handing Seymour an apple and then walking back to the house. This shot mimics the direction of Seymour's gaze, aligning the spectator with his character, but at the same time, our gaze is partially obstructed by the filter of the car windows. Alexie intercuts this scene with a montage of minor characters gathered on the backyard porch, critiquing Seymour's role as spokesman for the Spokane to the white world, which expands the spectator's view and range of knowledge beyond Seymour. Alexie then returns to a shot of Seymour from outside his car window, as if the group were watching him, although we know he is not in their literal eyesight. Seymour's spatial positioning emphasizes that he is "nearby" but not mentally "home," at a cultural middle point between the reservation "insiders" and the Seattle "outsiders." The nearly invisible barrier of a window teases with the idea of accessibility but at the same time insists on separation.

The spectator is literally on both sides of the car window—optical points of view that enact different cultural points of view—a split that Seymour himself shares. During the funeral service itself, Seymour as a physical entity starts to split: he stands silently in front of the assembled group and then throws his head back and starts screaming. The camera pans around the crowd in a circle; when it returns to Seymour, he is standing calmly and silently, but the soundtrack continues his scream. The man famous for his words can only stay silent or make a nonlinguistic sound, and the separation of his voice and body foreshadows a doubling of actor Adams's body as his character leaves the reservation. Agnes steps up to sing as Seymour leaves the house, and the film cuts to Seymour sitting in his car again, the camera in the first position over his shoulder. Then an image of a second Seymour walks down the path from the front door toward the car, just as Aristotle did earlier. This alternate Seymour leans through the window of the car, mimicking Aristotle's movements, and the camera switches to a reverse shot over his shoulder looking into the car and at the Seymour who is behind the wheel. The camera then cuts back to the original Seymour's point-of-view shot from the inside of the car and keeps the alternate Seymour in view as the car backs out of the driveway. This sequence pushes the symbolism of the invisible window barrier further by visually rendering Seymour's psychological split between feeling like a reservation insider and a visitor from Seattle.

The crosscutting between the funeral service and outside the house is complicated by cuts to a third scene, of Agnes and then Seymour kneeling down in Seymour's mind-space and removing his powwow clothes. Instead of dancing in blended clothing, as he did in the beginning, here he is in a complete fancydancing outfit, a moment that can be read as his sense that a true Native identity is all consuming, and that he must therefore reject it.[22]

The spectator may, however, see the superficiality of believing culture to be clothing, and as simple to remove. Having reaffirmed his sense of Native identity as uncompromising and therefore unacceptable, Seymour is then filmed driving back to Seattle, passing Aristotle walking along the side of a reservation road. More crosscuts between Seymour in his mind-space and Agnes at the funeral follow, before the film settles on its final image: Seymour crawling into bed in his apartment in Seattle, curling up to Steven's back. The two characters' positions prevent them from seeing each other's faces. Thus they experience two different realities instead of connecting with each other; Steven's eyes are open, staring forward anxiously, while Seymour's embrace of his lover evokes a bittersweet feeling of both finding comfort in his partner and contemplating what he has given up to live this life.

Seymour is thus unable to find a coherent self or cultural identity. Being on the reservation reminds him of how he does not fit in there, a feeling most dramatically illustrated by his inability to speak at the funeral. Fluency with words marks his identity and his profession, and this fluency disappears on the reservation. Yet the Seattle of the "alternative intelligentsia"—artistic, multiethnic, gay—does not complete him either; part of him is tied to the reservation, just as his body reenacts Aristotle's movements. Aristotle becomes his alter ego, his projection of himself if he were to stay on the reservation.

Along with crosscutting between several places, unrealistic overlaps of sound and image also evoke the competing calls of different cultural

A shot–reverse shot shows Seymour split into two physical selves in *The Business of Fancydancing.*

landscapes. In one scene, Seymour drives alone through the nighttime streets of Seattle, with a ghostly Mouse playing violin in the backseat. The soundtrack, however, is not of the violin, but of a conversation between Seymour and Steven about whether Steven can accompany him to the reservation for Mouse's funeral. Steven voices his insecurity over Seymour going without him, afraid that the reservation possesses Seymour in a way he can never understand. "You're ashamed of me, aren't you?"

In his “mind-space,” Seymour removes the signifiers of his Native identity in *The Business of Fancydancing.*

The last shot: living with the reality of cultural dislocation in *The Business of Fancydancing.*

Steven asks. Seymour replies, "Yeah, I am. I mean, you're the opposite of rez." Seymour's statement makes people into metaphors for places, which in turn represent the sensation of belonging to a community. In Seattle, Seymour carries "rez" with him, while at the same time, his attachment to Steven represents a cultural-geographic choice: the urban world of gay nightclubs and white-dominated literary readings releases him from the communal bonds and responsibility of the reservation, which he feels weigh him down. Urban life allows him to be free-floating, which, while never completely satisfying, seems his inevitable choice.

This pervasive pessimism about hybrid identities continues in the film's ending. No matter how fluid the film's geography, Alexie had to choose a final shot, and the fact that the final shot is Seymour in Seattle with Steven—having made his choice—underscores a melancholy aspect of the film's message: while one may psychically inhabit many geographies, one can be physically present only in one. This last shot contrasts the different ways the two characters experience the same moment and thus continues the film's interest in perspective. When combined with the spectator's independent observation of Seymour and Steven, the shot offers an assemblage of points of view that are greater than one character, or, more important, than one cultural identity—but instead of unified omniscience, the points of view remain distinct and unassimilated. Thus the nomadic viewing position does not allow an easy exit from the film, a feeling of totality and resolution. Seymour has chosen in which place he will live, and the spectator, having experienced the multiple geographics and cultures between which he lives, understands that either choice, reservation or arty Seattle, results in some loss.[23] But we also see the good sides of both places: while *Fancydancing* does not encourage spectatorial affection toward Seymour's white audiences, it does portray his lover Steven as fairly sympathetic. Since Steven is the prime representative of the hip Seattle art world in which Seymour lives, this depiction renders the cultural landscape of "artistic Seattle" a plausible choice for Seymour. When the film cuts to scenes on the reservation without Seymour, it underscores the strong bonds between the residents that form a true community, which I discuss more below. These varied place-based identifications accumulate and at the film's end, they cause us to consider both the liberating and wearying effects of cultural hybridity.[24]

Nomadic Spectatorship and the Decentering of Cultural Authority

On one level, Seymour is the dominant subject of *The Business of Fancydancing*—it is structured around his life and his poetry, and his similarity to Alexie encourages this reading. The spectator comes to identify with Seymour's conflicting identities by experiencing his traveling, movement that stands for his hybrid experience as simultaneously Spokane, "Native American" (to non-Natives), urban, gay, and a poet. If *The Business of Fancydancing* stuck primarily to Seymour's point of view, the spectator would experience the Spokane reservation as Seymour sees it: a place with good memories of childhood play but also a "prison" for an intellectual Native American who feels the reservation culture limits personal expression. The contradictions and hypocrisies in his Seattle-based writer's life would still be apparent, as Alexie's satire of eager white people flocking to the hip Native writer is not subtle. Showing these circumstances only from Seymour's point of view, however, would make the film primarily about a hybrid subject caught between reservation roots and urban elitism.

But while Seymour's narrative journey from Seattle to the reservation and back is literal, the film's movement (hence the spectator's) both follows Seymour's mental wanderings and departs entirely from him. Consequently, we see Seymour as others see him—arrogant, full of denial, alienated from his tribal culture—nearly as often as we share his vision of reservation life. Alexie undercuts Seymour as protagonist not just to provide an alternate perspective on his character (one that comes from the tribal community's judgment), but as part of his broader project of questioning the artistic representation of culture. Because Seymour is a writer whose work is based on representing his own minority culture to the majority, Alexie must show the instability of Seymour's identity in order to unveil the faulty premises of such cultural display. He then complicates the picture by offering other possibilities for cultural articulation in the form of pseudo-documentary sequences and other characters speaking their truths in contradiction to Seymour's. This jumble of voices is presented as a spatial collage, as Alexie capitalizes on cinematic visuality and editing to create a sense of overlapping spaces that exist simultaneously, parallel and relative to each other, instead of a narrative that moves forward chronologically toward closure.

To return briefly to the scene of Seymour reading his poetry behind the bookstore's window, we can see that from the film's beginning, Alexie calls attention to the act of listening to, reading, or watching art that bears the burden of cultural representation. The disorienting spatial positioning of not knowing where Seymour or the camera is positioned invokes a haptic sense of imperfect embodiment, of being situated without omniscient knowledge. While the surrealism of this moment certainly expresses an element of Seymour's subjectivity—his troubled recognition of his role in profiting from Native exoticism—it also transplants the spectator out of Seymour's head and into the position of a non-Native consumer of Seymour's writing during "National Indian Month" (as a handwritten sign in the bookstore window proclaims). Seymour is like a zoo animal, a curiosity to be exhibited for the consumer who gains self-satisfaction from consuming "multicultural" art. No matter individual viewers' own racial and cultural identities, *Fancydancing* at this moment positions its spectator as an audience member of Seymour's oddly located reading, thus experiencing an unadulterated moment of Native American fetishization.

Alexie places this scene early in the film in order to say from the outset that the performance of a "minority" culture for a "majority" is always fraught with danger. It also functions as a nod to some Native critics who are disturbed at the popularity of Alexie's works that they feel put Native poverty, dysfunction, and alcoholism on display for outsiders. Alexie signals his awareness of the way a Native writer might perform cultural otherness for profit by presenting a caricature of how he thinks his critics see him. With regard to the haptic spatial positioning, this disorientation forces the spectator to temporarily accept a specific position, implicating him or her in its troubling cultural politics, while also revealing the absurdity of this position. So the spatial positioning of *Fancydancing* goes beyond Seymour's nomadic movements; the spectator is not always traversing the film's landscapes "with" Seymour. Stepping out of Seymour's point of view means negating the traditional identification with a main character that most Hollywood films encourage. It also means seeing his nomadic position as cultural, not psychological. The fight for inclusion in the mainstream art world, as Seymour sees it, has to do with him proclaiming himself an individual and reaping praise for his own creations and persona. But Seymour's inspiration, and his fame among white connoisseurs, comes from his tribal community: an interviewer notes that he has traveled around the world and had dinner with "the president, the pope, and Robert Redford," so wonders why 95 percent of his poems are about the reservation. Seymour replies: "Every time I sit down to write a poem, I want it not to be about the reservation, but the reservation won't let me go." Seymour tries to escape the influence of his tribe and his childhood home by proclaiming himself an artist in the traditional Western sense of the individual genius, one whose vision of the world is separated from culture. Yet this stance violates his internal truth, one that places him mentally in both cultural landscapes, even while he resides physically in Seattle. At the same time, Seymour knows that his tacit acceptance of the role of individual spokesman for tribal culture is what has given him fame. His art fits easily into a pantheon of mainstream multicultural art because it denies the polyphony[25] of voices that makes up "culture" in favor of a singular voice that easily fits into the white category of "artist." In doing so, he violates an essential quality of traditional Native American storytelling: that there is no individual author, but a storyteller whose stories come from the tribe and who simultaneously transmits and alters the stories in their telling.[26] While he sees the hypocrisies of his role, he nevertheless accepts it for the notoriety it brings him.

Seymour's ethnic-flavored performances for white audiences can be seen as a type of "autoethnography," in which the native consciously performs culture for colonialist audiences in imitation of traditional ethnographies, which are also "narratives" meant for an outsider audience.[27] Within Native American studies, Seymour enacts what Elizabeth Cook-Lynn calls the "cosmopolitan" in Native fiction, in opposition to the "national," where cosmopolitan refers to a hybrid literary style that inserts itself easily into a multicultural canon formed by Euro-American desires, while the national refers to a commitment to tribal sovereignty without concern for Euro-American expectations or literary conventions.[28] Despite the fact that Alexie's own writing is also what Cook-Lynn would call cosmopolitan, in the film, Alexie interrogates both of those categories, showing that neither is a complete picture. While Seymour can never adopt a purely Spokane identity, neither does his cosmopolitanism ring true. The interconnected geographies of the film undercut Seymour's attempts to divorce himself from the reservation and his cultural origins. Even as he tries to live as an individual artist, free-floating in a Seattle of art connoisseurs and gay nightlife, his status in these "hip," multicultural communities is dependent upon whites identifying him as a representative of Native American culture (seen as a monolith, without tribal distinctions)—all while his art remains inextricably intertwined with family and tribal community.

By briefly noting how Cook-Lynn's notion of nationalism and cosmopolitanism might apply to Native American filmmaking, we can see how *Fancydancing* attempts to use nomadic geography to avoid either designation. Much of Native-directed visual media has been community based, revealing how low-budget productions can give voice to tribally specific, resolutely local discourses.[29] Such films fulfill Cook-Lynn's nationalist principles by addressing community needs first and foremost; a secondary, outsider audience is incidental. A breakthrough film like *Smoke Signals* provides a Hollywood-style coherent and universalizing narrative, taking the genre of the road movie and the theme of father-son estrangement and enacting them with Native characters. These easily accessible narrative elements allowed the film to appeal to white audiences who were interested in multicultural art because it blended a culturally "other" setting with a familiar narrative (while also providing in-jokes aimed at Native audience members). In *Fancydancing*, Alexie adopts a third approach that seeks to break down both of these approaches through an irresolvable collision of points of view that ends up neither prioritizing the tribal nor providing an experience of effortless multiculturalism. His approach is fundamentally dependent on creating a geography that is always shifting and incomplete—a geography that is brought to light by exposing the seeds of artistic creation. In addition to the haptic sense of space that makes us aware of the problematics of consuming art from a different culture, Alexie uses other techniques that invoke geography to suggest how art always emerges out of somewhere—places that represent communities and values. At the same time, *Fancydancing* blurs the physicality of geography by visualizing what overlapping spaces would look like.

One such sequence begins with Aristotle's voice-over recounting a childhood story of the three friends picking green apples from his grandmother's tree. While his adult voice speaks, the camera illustrates his story with a flashback to them as young boys. The camera then cuts to the grown Aristotle in Seymour's mind-space telling the story, and then Seymour continues it in the same space, with the dialogue overlapping. Aristotle also represents a displaced yet embodied reservation presence when he frequently appears at Seymour's Seattle poetry readings, and in one scene, his voice chimes in unison with Seymour's until Seymour's fades away and Aristotle is reading the poem. He then appears in Seymour's bedroom at night as Seymour struggles to write a poem. As Aristotle says the words with him, Seymour starts to tap the notebook rhythmically with a pencil and sing in a traditional style. As the two sing together, Seymour's face shows a rare relaxed smile, as opposed to his false public smile. The act of creation is shared here and Western-style poetry is linked to tribal songs. The overlapping voices enact an aural version of collectivity, just as Aristotle's ghostly appearances in Seymour's life insist upon an artistic and social consciousness that transcends time and place.

Through the frequent intercutting of Mouse's home video footage, Alexie also emphasizes that the Spokane community has the potential to produce multiple artists, denying Seymour his exceptional role as the artistic spokesman. Mouse videotapes his reservation exploits with Aristotle, including playful bantering, consuming alcohol and homemade drugs, and attacking a white motorist. The home videos become Aristotle and Mouse's method of expressing themselves, paralleling Seymour's writing, but in a medium with much less status in dominant culture.

The nihilism of Mouse's attempts at self-expression is underscored by the fact that the images he films are often either self-destructive or destructive to others.[30] After Seymour learns of Mouse's death, Mouse, like Aristotle, becomes a looming presence in his visions and memories, often appearing playing the violin and watching Seymour as he proceeds through his public readings, which are also performances of Seymour's Native American identity. In one instance, Mouse is seated in the audience as Seymour reads to another appreciative crowd of whites. Mouse waves and his lips move, saying, "Good-bye," but his voice is inaudible, the soundtrack dominated by Seymour's words. Metaphorically, Seymour has assumed the role of spokesman for his people, drowning out what is actually a plurality of voices. This scene is the mirror opposite of the ones with Aristotle that show the transformation of a singular voice into a dual one.

The loss of cultural polyphony in favor of one voice recalls the act of narrating culture engaged in by traditional ethnographers. This omniscience is closely related to tourism (anthropology's popular culture cousin),[31] whereby, following the metaphor, Seymour serves as the tour guide or "native informant" to educated whites, giving them access to an "other" culture through an easily accessible conduit and assuring

Mouse and Aristotle try to counter Seymour's published words with their home videos in *The Business of Fancydancing.*

them authenticity. Denying Seymour a central role and the spectator's full identification does more than undercut the practices of conventional Hollywood; it argues that no individual—neither ethnographer, native informant, nor artist—has the authority to represent culture, despite the urges of both Seymour and his Seattle audiences to fit his art and public persona into an individualist paradigm.

Alexie goes beyond arguing for the communal source of Seymour's art; he also constantly juxtaposes Seymour's actions in Seattle with what his childhood friends and college girlfriend Agnes are doing on the reservation. Combining these sequences with those that place the spectator in the position of Seymour's Seattle audiences, we can see that the spectator is able to "try on" several points of view, some concerned with Seymour but some completely separate from him. If we recall the opening sequence of Seymour, Aristotle, and Mouse after graduation along with the frequency of scenes of their life on the reservation without Seymour, we might say that the film is actually more the story of the different paths taken by three reservation young men than it is Seymour's story. That the film's main actor, Evan Adams, argues that "this movie belongs to . . . 'Agnes'"[32] is further evidence that the film in fact belongs to no character and to every character at once, forcing the spectator to be nomadic for the film's duration. So while the film initially appears to be about an individual's psychological journey, it is equally about the differing ways individuals choose to grapple with their cultural heritage and various subject positions vis-à-vis dominant American culture.

The moments when the film becomes most dominantly the story of Aristotle, Mouse, and Agnes are those when Agnes and Aristotle remember Mouse after his death, prepare his coffin, and pray by his body. These scenes are distinct from all others in the film because they are moments of emotional intimacy without the constant reframing and disorientation of other *Fancydancing* sequences. Instead, an emotion that feels universal, grief, becomes the dominant sensation. Here the sense of place as something constantly relative and in motion recedes to the background in favor of that unself-conscious "at-homeness" of dwelling. For a moment, we get to stand still, to feel something purely without questioning how it appears from "over there." It is significant that these scenes of unfiltered emotion and presentness occur only on the reservation; while Seymour always feels alienated on the reservation, the spectator does in fact experience a feeling of being part of the tribal community through virtually dwelling there.

Alexie juxtaposes these moments of emotional intimacy with observational sequences, also on the reservation, that imitate a documentary's attempted objective point of view. In between the shots of Seymour in his parked car in front of the house where Mouse's funeral service is held (analyzed above), Alexie inserts a sequence of a group of friends sitting behind the house commenting on Seymour's return to the reservation. The camera cuts between close-ups to concentrate on individual faces; the sequence of faces, however, gives a sense of group commentary because these individuals are not developed as characters. They represent the community's evaluation of Seymour, similar to the way that tribal communities provide moral guidance to individuals. The isolation of their faces from their surroundings further emphasizes their function more as discourse than individual character. Their comments parallel the moments in which the spectator is positioned as a Seattle audience member of Seymour's readings; it is another position from which to look at Seymour rather than identify with him. Their opinions range from condemnation of Seymour for selling out his culture to compassion for his struggles to be his own person.

Community on the reservation in *The Business of Fancydancing.*

There are several other sequences showing groups of people whom we do not know as characters. They are getting into cars, playing a football game, or dancing in a circle, and are filmed in long shot or using a series of close-ups of several people, in which each individual close-up is not important on its own (they are unnamed minor characters), but rather as one element of a community collage.

Alexie simulates a documentary filmmaking style when he begins one sequence with white text on a black screen asking, "How many funerals have you been to?" The question is followed by an interview montage in which various people respond. The accumulation of responses provides a social, not individual, perspective on the epidemics of depression, addiction, and suicide on reservations. Such sequences recall the deconstruction of traditional ethnographic documentary, as practiced and theorized by filmmaker and critic Trinh Minh-ha. They provide cultural information but negate its status as "the one truth" by challenging "regimes of representation" so that the storyteller's authority is decentered and the spectator must become active in the making of meaning.[33]

Thus parts of *Fancydancing* become a postmodern ethnography, as Stephen Tyler defines it: "a cooperatively evolved text consisting of fragments of discourse . . . none of whose participants would have the final word."[34] When a fictional text incorporates postmodern ethnography into its narrative, it acknowledges that presenting culture to outside viewers is one of its inevitable functions, alongside fiction's preference for psychology, identification, and emotion. Exposing the mechanisms of cultural presentation reveals this outsider position as one of several possible positions in relation to the onscreen cultural landscapes. Such moments of postmodern ethnography are collaged in with the many sequences in which we are aligned with Seymour, or positioned near him without inhabiting him, and with the intimate sequences in which we dwell on the reservation with Agnes and Aristotle as they grieve for Mouse. By continually manipulating the spectator's position, Alexie ensures that the spectator's sense of "here" versus "there," of "familiar" versus "other," constantly shifts. This breaking down of outsider authority has particular importance for Native American stories, since Native cultures have historically been most subject to American anthropology, tourism, and popular myth making. Alexie employs nomadic spectatorship not just as a way to display fragmented individual psyches, but to constantly resituate the spectator in multiple positions that represent diverse perspectives on Native American experiences.

Alexie's experimental techniques reflect a logic that Alexie has described as poetic rather than narrational.[35] If narrative is a fundamentally time-based structure—events unfold in a cause-and-effect manner—*The Business of Fancydancing* instead structures itself around simultaneity and overlapping spaces. The frequent crosscutting, haptic disorientation, sound bridges, and the ghostly appearance of characters in locales where they never literally go (to name just a few techniques of cinematic nomadism) keep a sense of relationality among all the characters and the geographic spaces. No place, not even Seymour's mind-space, exists in isolation. Seymour's ability to make a living as a writer depends on the cultural landscape of artistic Seattle—on contemporary American consumers who have been coached to seek out and praise multiculturalism—while his art could not exist without his attachment to and memories of the Spokane reservation. Reservation residents live their own realities and perform their own art, while periodically entering Seymour's mind-space. The film's visuals and editing continually foreground the act of looking and the relationality between places, which keeps the spectator displaced. The spectator is thus reminded that every cultural landscape feels different depending on where one is standing, and these differences remain rather than being sewn together to form one universalizing point of view. The film denies the spectator a "home base," a spatial position and a cultural perspective that is the default to which others are compared and that enacts a culture's dominant ideology. Instead all cultural points of view are equally relative to each other. This constantly mobile geography suggests that a collage of multiple points of view is the only way to approach any truth. Approaching truth is as far as we get; *Fancydancing* offers no answers to the complex questions of how a hybrid subject can balance competing identities while living in a single place and of how artistic production can be understood as both individual (free-floating) and cultural (spatially rooted).

The Business of Fancydancing makes a significant contribution to the way films about cultural identity can visualize such abstract questions. It demonstrates the fundamentally geographical nature of identity and belonging. Then by destabilizing spectator positioning, Alexie offers a distinct strategy for questioning how a culture can be represented—unraveling both traditional ethnography and the individual ethnic artist as a community spokesperson. By making a narrative film that is realized more through space than time, that is circular, and by turning a story that seems to be about an individual into a communal one, Alexie demonstrates a specifically Native filmmaking aesthetic. In the new diversity of Native American cinema, there is room for the local, the cosmopolitan, and the nomadic.

Notes

I am grateful for perceptive feedback from Brianna Burke, Manon Perry, Henrike Lehnguth, and Amber Nelson at various stages of developing this chapter. Unless otherwise noted, all photographs are from the author's collection.

1. Film historian Angela Aleiss notes that Chickasaw director Edwin Carewe had a prolific career in 1920s and 1930s Hollywood, but did not work with Native actors nor usually make Native-themed films. James Gordon Young Deer worked in the early silent era and claimed Winnebago heritage, but that remains unverified. See *Making the White Man's Indian: Native Americans and Hollywood Movies* (Westport, CT: Praeger, 2005), 1–2, 25, 180n14. *Smoke Signals* is based on short stories in Alexie's collection *The Lone Ranger and Tonto Fistfight in Heaven* (New York: HarperPerennial, 1994).

2. Melissa Olsen, "Alexie's *The Business of Fancydancing,*" *The Circle: News from an American Indian Perspective,* June 30, 2002, 10.

3. Among the positive reviews in the mainstream press are Kevin Thomas, "An Affirming Journey in *Fancydancing,*" *Los Angeles Times,* October 25, 2002, http://www.calendarlive.com/movies/reviews/cl-et-kevin25Oct25,0,2300707.story?coll=cl-mreview (accessed July 14, 2009); Sean Axmaker, "So Many Questions with No Easy Answers in Alexie's Directorial Debut," *Seattle Post-Intelligencer,* May 10, 2002, http://www.seattlepi.com/movies/69814_fancydance10q.shtml (accessed July 14, 2009); Jonathan Curiel, "*Fancydancing* Doesn't Sidestep Indian Issues: Loyalty Conflicts with Success," *San Francisco Chronicle,* August 30, 2002, http://www.sfgate.com/cgi-bin/article.cgi?file=/chronicle/arhive/2002/08/30/DD101497.DTL (accessed July 14, 2009). Elvis Mitchell, "A Poet Finds His Past Is Just Where He Left It," *New York Times,* October 18, 2002, http://www.nytimes.com/2002/10/18/movies/18FANC.html (accessed July 14, 2009), is a mixed review.

4. Dennis Harvey, "The Business of *Fancydancing,*" *Variety,* January 28–February 3, 2002, 33.

5. Aileo Weinmann, "Hold Me Closer, Fancy Dancer: A Conversation with Sherman Alexie," Filmcritic.com, 2002, http://www.filmcritic.com/misc/emporium.nsf/84dbbfa4d710144986256c290016f76e/1adbe1e88680513188256c340015b7b9?OpenDocument (accessed July 14, 2009).

6. Eyre has also produced several made-for-TV movies, including *The Edge of America* (2003) and Tony Hillerman adaptations *Skinwalkers* (2002) and *A Thief of Time* (2004).

7. *Diegesis* refers to the fictional world created by the film, and all the images or sound that come from within it, as opposed to elements like the credits sequence and the musical soundtrack that come from outside.

8. Giuliana Bruno, *Atlas of Emotion* (London: Verso, 2002).

9. Teshome H. Gabriel, "Thoughts on Nomadic Aesthetics and the Black Independent Cinema: Traces of a Journey," in *Blackframes: Critical Perspectives on Black Independent Cinema,* ed. Mbye B. Cham and Claire Andrade-Watkins (Cambridge, MA: MIT Press, 1988), 62–79. Gabriel takes "nomadic" literally in citing aesthetic traits from nomadic groups of people, a move that could become a form of primitivism, but I hope to show that a metaphorical nomadic spectatorial point of view has nothing to do with primitivism, as it is perhaps even more prevalent in art that arises out of cross-cultural contact.

10. The term *tourist gaze* originates in John Urry, *The Tourist Gaze: Leisure and Travel in Contemporary Societies* (London: Sage, 1990), and has been applied to visual media by Ellen Strain, *Public Places, Private Journeys: Ethnography, Entertainment and the Tourist Gaze* (New Brunswick, NJ: Rutgers University Press, 2003).

11. I adopt "dwelling" from phenomenological geography to describe the sensation of being "at home," in a place you do not consciously observe but rather unconsciously inhabit. It originates in the work of Martin Heidegger and was

developed by phenomenological geographers Edward Relph, *Place and Placelessness* (London: Pion, 1976); and David Seamon and Robert Mugerauer, eds., *Dwelling, Place and Environment: Towards a Phenomenology of Person and World* (Dordrecht, Netherlands: Kluwer Academic, 1985).

12. In this scheme, *Smoke Signals* employs a dwelling point of view with traces of touristic satire, in such self-consciously humorous remarks as "This ain't *Dances with Salmon*" and the narrative of exploring white America through the eyes of Natives.

13. See in particular Gloria Bird, "The Exaggeration of Despair in Sherman Alexie's *Reservation Blues*," *Wicazo Sa Review* (Fall 1995): 47–52; and Louis Owens, *Mixedblood Messages* (Norman: University of Oklahoma Press, 1998), 74–82.

14. James Kneale, "Secondary Worlds: Reading Novels as Geographical Research," in *Cultural Geography in Practice*, ed. Alison Blunt et al. (New York: Oxford University Press, 2003), 46.

15. I use *spectator* to refer to the hypothetical receiver of text's encoding, whereas *viewers* refers to the multiplicity of real people who may interpret the film differently according to their own cultural identities and affiliations. The principle is explained in Stuart Hall, "Encoding/Decoding," in *Culture, Media, Language: Working Papers in Cultural Studies, 1972–79*, ed. Stuart Hall et al. (London: Hutchinson Centre for Contemporary Cultural Studies, University of Birmingham, 1980), 128–38.

16. A brief biography of Sherman Alexie can be found in Daniel Grassian, *Understanding Sherman Alexie* (Columbia: University of South Carolina Press, 2005). Curiel, "*Fancydancing* Doesn't Sidestep Indian Issues."

17. Reviewers frequently noted the film's challenging narrative structure; Jonathan Curiel, ibid., wrote that the first ten minutes possesses a "quixotic array of characters and flashbacks that tests patience, but once the viewer understand the movie's cadence and rhythm, the story gets better and better."

18. This is actually Alexie's poem, found in *The Summer of Black Widows* (Brooklyn: Hanging Loose, 1996).

19. Laura Marks, "Video Haptics and Erotics," *Screen* 39.4 (1998): 336. Marks expands on haptic cinema in *The Skin of the Film: Intercultural Cinema, Embodiment, and the Senses* (Durham, NC: Duke University Press, 2000).

20. This account of classical Hollywood techniques is based on general tendencies; there are clearly exceptions, such as detective films that withhold knowledge from the spectator for suspense purposes. See David Bordwell, Janet Staiger, and Kristin Thompson, *The Classical Hollywood Cinema: Film Style and Mode of Production to 1960* (New York: Columbia University Press, 1985). For ethnographic cinema, see Bill Nichols, *Representing Reality: Issues and Concepts in Documentary* (Bloomington: Indiana University Press, 1991), 32–38.

21. A line from her film *Reassemblage* (1982), quoted in Marks, *The Skin of the Film*, 164.

22. Seymour's mind-space is the essence of *space,* as opposed to *place*—as cultural geographers often define it, place is space that is endowed with cultural meaning. It is therefore in Seymour's mind-space that he attempts to strip himself of "culture" and be only an individual.

23. While it does not have to be an either/or choice—one can imagine that a gay multiracial Seattle community would be different than the Seattle of white literary connoisseurs, for example, or that an urban Native community could be an option—Alexie does frame it this way.

24. In his analysis of Alexie's novel *Reservation Blues,* Douglas Ford ("Sherman Alexie's Indigenous Blues," *MELUS* 27.3 [2002]: 197–215) also notes that Alexie does not see hybridity as liberating, though he only cites Alexie's critiques of white people, rather than the melancholy of a character like Seymour.

25. Ella Shohat and Robert Stam, in *Unthinking Eurocentrism: Multiculturalism and the Media* (London: Routledge, 1994), employ this term, derived from Mikhail Bakhtin, to describe the presence of multiple discourses, a more accurate way to represent a social world.

26. Louis Owens, in *Other Destinies: Understanding the American Indian Novel* (Norman: University of Oklahoma Press, 1992), 9, argues that this distinction between author and storyteller is a central problematic of the Native American novel.

27. See Mary Louise Pratt, *Imperial Eyes: Travel Writing and Transculturation* (London: Routledge, 1992); and Rey Chow, *Primitive Passions: Visuality, Sexuality, Ethnography, and Contemporary Chinese Cinema* (New York: Columbia University Press, 1995).

28. Elizabeth Cook-Lynn, "The American Indian Fiction Writer: Cosmopolitanism, Nationalism, the Third World, and First Nation Sovereignty," *Wicazo Sa Review* 9.2 (1993): 26–36.

29. See Steven Leuthold, *Indigenous Aesthetics: Native Art, Media, and Identity* (Austin: University of Texas Press, 1998); and Beverly R. Singer, *Wiping the War Paint off the Lens: Native American Film and Video* (Minneapolis: University of Minnesota Press, 2001).

30. These tragic visions of reservation life are in line with the compassion Stephen F. Evans ("'Open Containers': Sherman Alexie's Drunken Indians," *American Indian Quarterly* 25.1 [2001]: 46–72) and Joseph L. Coulombe ("The Approximate Size of His Favorite Humor: Sherman Alexie's Comic Connections and Disconnections in *The Lone Ranger and Tonto Fistfight in Heaven,*" *American Indian Quarterly* 26.2 [2002]: 94–115) see in Alexie's fiction and poetry.

31. See Edward M. Bruner, *Culture on Tour: Ethnographies of Travel* (Chicago: University of Chicago Press, 2005) on the connection between ethnographic and touristic instincts.

32. Quoted in Meredith K. James, *Literary and Cinematic Reservation in Selected Works of Native American Author Sherman Alexie* (Lewiston, NY: Edwin Mellen, 2005), 85.

33. Trinh Minh-ha, *When the Moon Waxes Red: Representation, Gender, and Cultural Politics* (New York: Routledge, 1991), 2.

34. Stephen A. Tyler, "Post-modern Ethnography: From Document of the Occult to Occult Document," in *Writing Culture: The Poetics and Politics of Ethnography*, ed. James Clifford and George Marcus (Berkeley: University of California Press, 1986), 125–26.

35. Olsen, "Alexie's *The Business of Fancydancing.*"

Teaching Native American Filmmakers

Osawa, Eyre, and Redroad

Angelica Lawson

Feature films written, directed, and produced by Native Americans have increased substantially in the past ten years, and while Native filmmakers have been making documentaries since the late 1960s, there is relatively little information published on how to teach these films. There is a wealth of knowledge contained within these artistic works and educators might find that they can broach a number of topics via Native media. This chapter outlines pedagogical strategies for teaching Native American film[1] from a Native American studies' perspective. I specifically address ways to build teaching units around individual films to educate students about issues of representation and self-representation.

In terms of organization, the first unit focuses on historical information and a selection of key Hollywood films that help guide students in their growing understanding of representation. Each subsequent unit focuses on a specific Native American filmmaker and highlights a single film. I developed these units to present a broad overview of some critical ideas regarding Native American film, in particular, issues of representation. Each unit after the introduction examines Native films in terms of how the filmmakers are resisting deeply entrenched misrepresentations of Native Americans in film and media. I teach both documentary and feature films and I concentrate on the work of three filmmakers whose films are foundational to Native American cinema: Sandy Osawa, Chris Eyre, and Randy Redroad.

I begin this course by contextualizing Native film within the history of American film and the images of Native Americans presented in mainstream film, since many Indigenous writers and directors are reacting to or addressing this history. I then also include a brief introduction to predominate representations of Native Americans in early American literature as well, due to their initial and continuing influence on images in film.

Classroom Unit I: Representations of Native Americans in American Film

Students generally have a good understanding of predominant images of Native Americans in film, purely through their constant exposure to these images in the media, but they may not have the vocabulary or historical context to adequately articulate a strong critical reading of these images. Teaching visual literacy early in the course is a must, and there are several good books with film glossaries that are useful. I particularly like the glossary in Carole Gerster and Laura Zlogar's *Teaching Ethnic Diversity with Film* for its brevity and clarity.[2] To outline key concepts, Jacquelyn Kilpatrick's book *Celluloid Indians* is also a very useful resource for professors wanting to quickly familiarize themselves with the basic trajectory of American literature and its influence on film.[3] In addition, this book provides considerable historical context with an emphasis on U.S. Indian policy as a framework for Native Americans in film. If time is an issue, I strongly recommend Kilpatrick's single chapter, "American Indians and Film in the Classroom," in Gerster and Zlogar's edited volume for a quick overview. The chapter titled "Native Americans and American Film" in *America on Film: Representing Race, Class, Gender, and Sexuality at the Movies* is excellent for contextualizing this subject within the framework of American film history generally.[4] I suggest both chapters as assigned readings in addition to an overview lecture to provide a framework for students.

The one place where I differ from Kilpatrick's work on early American literature and its influence on film is that I spend more time on the captivity narrative. Kilpatrick mentions this in passing, but I feel that a basic knowledge of this category of literature is vital to critically reading films such as *The Searchers* and revisionist films such as *Little Big Man,* which are seminal films for teaching this section. American captivity narratives had great influence and popularity in their day. They were written largely during the sixteenth and seventeenth centuries by colonists taken captive by Native American nations, mainly in the Northeast. I always inform students that during this time, captives were taken by both Native Americans and colonists; however, the phrase "captivity narrative" generally refers to the stories written by colonists "rescued" from Native captivity and returned to their colonial villages. In the early stories, Natives might be noble or savage, but in later versions bloodthirsty savages dominate as editors embellished the stories to add more drama. The underlying threat of miscegenation and the perceived threat of rape kept audiences on the edge of their seats. Taboos against miscegenation would continue well into the early Hollywood film era, as would the general theme of captivity, becoming a recognizable formula in the Hollywood western. Kilpatrick discusses these taboos in her analysis of John Ford's *The Searchers* (1956) in her book *Celluloid Indians.*

Kilpatrick also spends considerable time discussing the frontier novels of James Fenimore Cooper (1789–1851), whose works are thought to have influenced everything from the extremely popular dime novels of the late 1800s to American films. Cooper's *Leatherstocking Tales* featured both bloodthirsty and noble savages as demonstrated in his most famous novel, *The Last of the Mohicans* (1826). While many critics thought Cooper overly romanticized Native Americans, others claimed the bloodthirsty savage ultimately outnumbered the noble savage in his works. Teaching this can help students understand how the "bloodthirsty savage" became a major figure in a later popular American literature, the dime novel.

Both Kilpatrick's and Benshoff and Griffin's work *America on Film* address dime novels and their early influence on American film. Readings from both of these texts will be helpful in the classroom. Once students are introduced to dime novels and recognize that they were playing to the public's interest in westward expansion, the gold rush, and the Oregon Trail, they can understand their influence on early films. These novels featured conflicts between cowboys and Indians and glorified American heroes such as Buffalo Bill Cody. First published by Irwin P. Beadle & Company in 1860, these stories foregrounded Native Americans largely portrayed as bloodthirsty and ignorant, speaking in grunts and broken English, thus validating the ideology of westward expansion and dismissing its devastating impact on Native Americans. The "Indians" in these stories were characterized as barely human, so their defeat by the hero was cause for celebration, not concern. This was also true of the later stage shows created by Buffalo Bill, the star of many dime novels.

Students will likely recognize Buffalo Bill Cody (1846–1917) as a showman, but not necessarily as an actual frontiersman and scout in the U.S. military. Providing this information helps students think critically about the bias Cody brought to his Wild West show, which was established in 1883. The show featured reenactments of the conflicts between

Native Americans and Americans heading west, from a point of view that glorified westward expansion. The show borrowed from the stage, vaudeville, and the circus in an effort to re-create the Old West and targeted both American and European audiences, including kings and queens who sometimes participated in the shows. The Wild West shows further cemented the theme of "cowboys and Indians" in the American imagination and these live shows later became the subject matter of early American films, a point Kilpatrick and Benshoff and Griffin make in their texts.

Naturally, as film technology came to the forefront, popular subject matter reflected the era. Thomas Edison premiered his kinetoscope at the Chicago Colombian World's Exposition in 1893, where he showed *Hopi Snake Dance*, an "actuality" or ethnographic film displaying the "exotic cultures" of the "newly defeated" Native Americans. Despite the terms *actuality* and *ethnographic*, these films were not historically or ethnographically accurate; they were one-sided interpretations of Native American culture that continued the Eurocentric tradition of presenting Native Americans as exotic Others and lesser human beings. Benshoff and Griffin do a particularly good job of explaining this phenomenon quickly and succinctly and their chapter "Native Americans and American Film" in *America on Film* will be especially helpful. With this knowledge students can better understand how an actuality such as *The Parade of Buffalo Bill's Wild West* (1894) could impact the beginning of that popular film genre: the western.

Moving forward from the early days of American cinema's portrayal of Indians, I then introduce students to Hollywood's long relationship with the western. The western is the most typical place to find Native Americans, or, more accurately, "Hollywood Indians." The Hollywood Indian belongs to a fictional group that lacks tribal specificity. For example, one of the most famous directors of westerns is John Ford. His films often feature the iconic actor John Wayne and portray Native Americans as generic tribes. They might be called Cheyenne or Comanche, but frequently the extras were played by Navajos in Navajo clothing speaking Navajo. Ford did not concern himself with historical accuracy and assumed that the audience wouldn't either. Ken Nolley's chapter, "The Representation of Conquest: John Ford and the Hollywood Indian (1939–1964)," in *Hollywood's Indian: The Portrayal of the Native American in Film* does a thorough job of analyzing Ford films in terms of their lack of tribal specificity.[5] Assigning this chapter to students will help them conceptualize how these kinds of films contributed to a historically inaccurate mythology that continues to persist today, despite continued efforts to address it.

In the 1950s the sympathetic western made its debut with *Broken Arrow* (1950) staring Jimmy Stewart, a film now readily available on DVD. This film addressed the impact of westward expansion on Native Americans but still fell into the familiar traps of utilizing the noble savage as part of its formula. In particular, Stewart's wife is an Indian Princess who reinforces the stereotype of the vanishing Native American when she dies tragically but romantically, implying that the two races cannot coexist. There are excellent resources on the figure of the "Indian Princess" in American culture and film, including the much-referenced "The Pocahontas Perplex: The Image of Indian Women in American Culture" by Rayna Green.[6] This article is a solid overview of the concept of the "Indian Princess" and would provide students with key terms and concepts for critically reading the "Princess" stereotype in American culture. Elise Marubbio's *Killing the Indian Maiden: Images of Native American Women in Film* is also an excellent resource for teachers and students alike, in that it specifically addresses this figure in cinema through an analysis of the "Celluloid Princess" and provides students with a vocabulary for analysis and a critical reading of *Broken Arrow.*[7] For substantial information on the topic of the "vanishing race/American," Brian W. Dippie's *The Vanishing American: White Attitudes and US Indian Policy* is a comprehensive resource and would be useful for teachers regarding this topic.[8]

As we continue through this section of the course, I add films such as *Little Big Man* (1970) that illustrate the changes Hollywood made to the western while continuing to embrace the genre's dichotomy of civilization versus savagery. After *Broken Arrow,* filmmakers continued to play with the western genre, but revisionist westerns such as *Little Big Man* often simply inverted the elements of the classic western and kept many of the stereotypes. In this film, for example, the Cheyenne call themselves the "Human Beings," and are contrasted with the amoral townspeople. Yet, like all noble savages, the Cheyenne in this film must vanish. In an eloquent speech Old Lodge Skins (Chief Dan George) says, "There has always been a limited number of Human Beings but there is an endless supply of white men . . . we won today, we won't win tomorrow." *Little Big Man* meets audience's expectations that "Indians," no matter how noble, must vanish in order to make way for "progress" and the future, reinforcing the idea that Indians belong to the past. This film is particularly interesting, though, in that it appears to challenge the myth of the vanishing race when Old Lodge Skins lies down to die, but instead does not die and gets up and walks away from his burial site. Had the film ended with this scene it would have radically challenged nearly a century of Native American representation in film—but it doesn't end here. Instead, it ends with the male Anglo hero (lead actor Dustin Hoffman) telling the story as though there are no Indians left to tell the tale. They have, in fact, vanished.

This myth of the "vanishing race" is a myth that contemporary Native American filmmakers often work very hard against. In an interview, Makah documentary filmmaker Sandra Osawa states, "It's my opinion that we are seen largely as people of the past and largely as people with a problem. I like to show us as very much part of the present and very much part of the solution."[9] Osawa, along with other Native American filmmakers, has tried to address this history by making films about contemporary Native Americans proving that Native Americans have not vanished and are not defeated.

After providing this introduction to representations of Native Americans in mainstream American film, I am able to move on to teaching and discussing how Native filmmakers resist this history with their own independent film productions. I begin this section of the course on Native American filmmakers with a documentary. It is important for students to know that while *Smoke Signals* garnered much attention for being the first feature film written, directed, and produced by Native Americans, Native documentary filmmakers have been producing a solid body of work for over forty years. One of the filmmakers at the forefront of this renaissance is Makah filmmaker Sandra Osawa, whose film *On and Off the Res' with Charlie Hill* (2000), a documentary about an important Native American comedian, initiates the second unit.

Classroom Unit II: The Films of Sandra Osawa

I choose to highlight Osawa for several reasons. One is that she is a Native American woman who has been making Indigenous films for over thirty years, yet there are few resources for teaching her films in terms of book chapters and critical essays. Another is that students truly enjoy her work, especially the film highlighted here, *On and Off the Res' with Charlie Hill,* because of its high quality and interesting subject matter. By their teacher designing a unit around Osawa's films and highlighting one film in particular, students can learn about this important artist and her work.

In this unit I emphasize the filmmaker's artistic response to (mis)representations of Native Americans in film and other media. Though representation is technically not the topic of the documentary, students will quickly recognize that Osawa's selection of specific archival footage and her interview questions for Charlie Hill highlight this topic. Because students have been immersed in images of Native Americans in film from the past century through the introduction and overview, they are especially able to appreciate Osawa and Hill's commentary on this subject. I also begin this and all other Native filmmaker units with biographical information on the filmmakers, which inevitably includes interviews that highlight the filmmaker's own thoughts about images of Indigenous people in film.

For this unit I assign Lawrence Abbott's interview with Osawa in the *American Indian Quarterly* as required reading the night before screening the film.[10] Abbott's interview is especially useful because Osawa specifically discusses her goals and intentions as a filmmaker. She also outlines the origins of her interest in documentaries and how she chooses her subjects. Unfortunately, due to the lack of published material on this very important filmmaker, resources for teaching her work are limited, but Beverly Singer's *Wiping the War Paint off the Lens: Native American Film and Video* is a fine place to start.[11] In particular, Singer addresses the fact that Osawa was the first Native American to produce a television series, in 1975 for NBC, and her book provides an overview of early Native American film and video. This is a good resource for teachers, and excerpts from *Wiping the War Paint off the Lens* may be helpful for students when paired with the interview by Abbott.

In Abbott's interview, Osawa talks about how she first picked up the camera in the late 1960s, "maybe early 70s," when she taught at the Clyde Warrior Institute for Native American Studies in Los Angeles. Before that, she had worked for a recreation program for young people of her tribe, and at one point she decided to have movie nights for the youth: "I tried to get Indian films and couldn't really find anything . . . I searched and searched but learned that there was just nothing there for us. Here we were, a tribe in the Northwest, and there were no images about us." She goes on to imply that this conspicuous absence was connected to issues of low self-esteem in Native peoples. She speaks of an experience in which she wanted to read a poem about the Makahs to a group of high school students, and one student said, "Who would write a poem about us?" Osawa states, "That question always stuck in my mind, the fact that this person didn't think that we were the type of people who were worthy of being commented on, or having a poem written for, or much less having a film about." In this interview, Osawa makes clear her reasons for filmmaking: "The absence of our image was an important factor in motivating me to do something."[12] And so she did.

From the beginning of her filmmaking career, Osawa made it a point to make films about interesting Native Americans who challenged American perceptions about Native people. "I am attracted to unrecognized people, people who are doing important things, but who don't get the recognition they deserve."[13] Her early films focused on Native American activists and activism, but she later moved on to highlight individuals such as jazz saxophonist Jim Pepper in *Pepper's Powwow*. She explains that in choosing unusual subjects for her documentaries, "I like to think I'm opening up the definition of what it means to be Indian by including Indian ballerinas, Indian comedians, and Indian jazz musicians."[14] Yet, there is still an undercurrent of activism in nearly all of her films.

Osawa's *On and Off the Res'* moves away from her earlier documentaries specifically focused on Native American political activism, yet shows Hill, a comedian, as an activist. Other Native American activists including Dennis Banks, Floyd Red Crow Westerman, and Vine Deloria Jr., provide commentary in the film as to how Hill challenges stereotypical media images of Native Americans via stand-up comedy. These comments, along with actual footage of Hill's routines and television shows, establish a critique of those stereotypes for students to consider. A good reading to pair with this film is Vine Deloria Jr.'s chapter "Indian Humor" in *Custer Died for Your Sins*.[15]

After viewing *On and Off the Res' with Charlie Hill* in its entirety, I have the students analyze the film and discuss Osawa's intentions as a filmmaker, as well as Charlie Hill as a subject, in terms of what both are doing to raise awareness about the absurdity of certain Native American images in the media. Students often begin by noting the recurring themes of the film as far as what kinds of archival footage Osawa chooses to include. There is a clear emphasis on footage that addresses stereotypes. For example, in several places, Osawa uses long segments of skits from a Canadian television series called *Indian Time*. In one segment Hill plays a Native American actor who is told by his agent that he will be doing a commercial for deodorant with a Huron name that means "the Lake of the Changing Winds." The agent says, "This is going to be bigger than Mazola, bigger than Pontiac, bigger than . . . than Thunderbird wine!" At this point the agent places a headband with a single feather on the actor's head and hands him a bottle of deodorant. He then instructs the actor to say the name in a low, stoic voice, to which Hill sarcastically replies, "Like my grandfather said it, right . . . and I suppose you want me to do a little rain dance to go with this?" The agent enthusiastically replies, "That would be spectacular!" As the skit continues, the actor refuses to do the commercial because it is too demeaning, but upon learning that it pays $10,000 he reconsiders.

Such segments can prompt discussion of the ways in which American society has appropriated Native American names for commercial products, and how the history of conquest has allowed for such appropriations. This lesson can also raise the question of Native American participation in this kind of exploitation, since the actor in the skit ultimately reconsiders. Students often ask why Native Americans made movies where they were depicted as "savages" or why Native American leaders even participated in Buffalo Bill's Wild West show when their job was to repeatedly reenact their implied defeat. The answers to these questions are varied. In terms of Buffalo Bill's show, Native leaders often took jobs to feed their families during a destitute time, as well as to see the world and attempt to influence people to be more understanding of Native culture. In addition, actors have stated that they have tried to influence more accurate depictions of Natives in the media, sometimes successfully and sometimes not. This complex issue is explored in Michelle Raheja's book *Reservation Reelism* and teachers may find Raheja's work especially helpful regarding this topic.[16]

Students may also be surprised to learn that Native American concerns about derogatory and inaccurate depictions of their people and culture have been voiced since the beginning of film production. Luther Standing Bear, who worked in early film for a time, discusses this in his autobiography.[17] Several other early Native actors spoke up for Native rights, including Jay Silverheels, Chief Dan George, and Will Sampson. Silverheels, who is best known for portraying Tonto in the television series, was not oblivious to the implications of his role as sidekick to the hero. Charlie Hill explores this idea in a television sketch captured by Osawa in *On and Off the Res'*.

In this archival film footage, Hill plays Tonto in "Hero's Heaven" as he negotiates a comeback with the Lone Ranger. Tonto is reluctant, but the Lone Ranger makes some strong offers, such as "equal billing," to which Tonto has little reaction (he wanted top billing). He does get excited, however, when the Lone Ranger says, "Okay, okay, you can have complete sentences in your dialogue." Tonto is thrilled as he replies, "I can say all the pronouns I want?" Students will find the humor in this line as it challenges decades of Hollywood Indians, and they will be able to discuss this critically after having read Kilpatrick's "American Indians on Film" because she briefly explains the significance of the depiction of Native Americans as inarticulate in American film. Connecting film to early American literature, Kilpatrick states, "[American authors] made their Indians inarticulate except for savage grunts and pronoun-challenged pidgin-English, a characteristic wholeheartedly embraced by the majority of Hollywood's filmmakers through at least the first eighty years of film history." Calling this type of broken English "Tonto-talk," she says it was meant to imply "intellectual inferiority."[18] Both Hill and Osawa know this, and by including the skit in the documentary, Osawa compels her audience to consider the absurdity of the lack of Native American characters who speak in "complete sentences."

This documentary also provides numerous opportunities for students to explore the ability of humor to raise audience awareness regarding stereotypes and historical injustice. In addition, by explaining and exploring the power of irony to illuminate Native American issues, students are prepared to move on to the next film in the class. The first feature film for students to view is *Smoke Signals* (1998) by writer Sherman Alexie and Cheyenne/Arapaho director Chris Eyre. Alexie is known for his use of humor, and in particular irony, to raise audience awareness regarding Native American issues, and this is one of many fruitful topics of discussion for this film. Since *Smoke Signals* is likely taught more frequently than any other Native American film, instructors can decide whether or not to screen the film in its entirety or avoid redundancy by screening a few selected clips. The following lesson plans will address both approaches.

Classroom Unit III: Native Feature Films

Smoke Signals is an extremely accessible film for students, and there are several critical essays on this film and interviews with writer Alexie and director Eyre to provide a wide range of options for teaching. *Sherman Alexie in the Classroom* by Heather Bruce, Anna Baldwin, and Christabel Umphrey is a useful book that provides lesson plans and suggestions for teaching this film as well as Alexie's fiction.[19] Although *Smoke Signals* is probably the most commonly chosen Native film for teaching to date, I still continue to teach it because it is an important film historically and a excellent film for discussions on representation. Alexie and Eyre were very vocal regarding how they addressed and critiqued decades of Hollywood stereotypes with this film, and *Smoke Signals* is clearly self-reflexive in this way. Sherman Alexie's published screenplay of *Smoke Signals* can be a useful resource for teachers and students because Alexie provides copious notes regarding filmmaking decisions and production.[20]

For this classroom unit, I give a brief introduction to Native American feature filmmaking before providing biographies of Alexie and Eyre. Kilpatrick's chapter "The American Indian Aesthetic" in *Celluloid Indians*, and Singer's chapter "On the Road to Smoke Signals" in *Wiping the War Paint off the Lens* are useful resources for providing a context and some background on films made prior to 2000. Houston Wood's book, *Native Features: Indigenous Films from Around the World*, provides more extensive information on films made since 1998 and includes an entire chapter on the films of Chris Eyre.[21] Instructors will have to do Internet research for information on the most current Native American films. Film festival Web sites such as the site for the American Indian Film Festival in San Francisco and the Sundance Film Festival can keep instructors current on the latest Native American films, and the Web is also a good resource for current movie trailers.

After providing this background information, instructors can screen *Smoke Signals*, or clips of this film, then have students analyze Alexie and Eyre's response to decades of Hollywood Indian stereotypes and misrepresentation in American film. Christabel Umphrey's chapter in *Sherman Alexie in the Classroom* is a helpful resource regarding this topic since it specifically discusses Alexie's opinions about Native American representations in the media, and it offers additional materials and suggested activities for the classroom. Joanna Hearne's article "John Wayne's

Teeth: Speech, Sound, and Representation in *Smoke Signals* and *Imagining Indians*" also provides an outstanding in-depth discussion of how the "filmmakers strategically intervene in media representations and appropriate media tools for the purpose of visual sovereignty" through music and sound.[22] She specifically analyzes the infamous bus scene in *Smoke Signals*, in which the two main characters, Victor and Thomas, talk about how to be "real Indians." In this scene numerous allusions are made to Hollywood Indians and the western for the purpose of undermining the genre. I often use this clip in the classroom to get students thinking about how music and camera angles influence audience response. This article would be useful for such a discussion as well as provide some background for dialogue on genre and film formulas.

In my class, we look at genre and narrative structure, and explore how Alexie and Eyre consciously chose established Hollywood film formulas to shape their narrative in order to reach the widest audience possible. Alexie and Eyre both address the buddy and road trip formula in several interviews and Alexie also mentions his intention to reach a large audience in his interview with John Purdy in a 1997 issue of *SAIL*.[23] Through the buddy and road trip formulas, and with allusions to the western, the filmmakers are able to frame this screenplay in a way that speaks to a mainstream audience while still critiquing the western.

Because we are discussing narrative we can also look very closely at how Alexie and Eyre build characterization not only through dialogue but also through camera angles and edits. Alexie and Eyre write against the "Vanishing Noble" and "Indian Princess" stereotypes that still dominate Hollywood films today, and they create characters representative of contemporary Native people. I am particularly interested in how Native American women are portrayed in this film, and Alexie addresses this a bit in his screenplay. I also address this topic in my chapter "Native Sensibility and the Significance of Women in *Smoke Signals*" in *Sherman Alexie: A Collection of Critical Essays*, edited by Jeff Burglund and Jan Roush.[24] Analysis of the women in the film provides an opportunity for students to consider the impact of particular camera angles on character development. Close readings of scenes featuring the women reveal that they are strong characters essential to the narrative and to the film's resolution.

In *Smoke Signals* Victor Joseph and Thomas Builds-the-Fire travel from the Coeur d'Alene reservation in Idaho to Phoenix, Arizona, to retrieve the ashes of Victor's father, Arnold. Many of the smaller stories contained within this larger narrative focus on the men's relationship with Arnold prior to his leaving the reservation when they were young. Eyre uses match cuts to indicate the connection between Arnold's abandonment of Victor as a child to Victor's problems in the present. Carole Gerster's discussion of match cuts and other editing techniques used to direct viewer response in her chapter "Film Studies: Teaching Representations of American Ethnicity on Film" in *Teaching Ethnic Diversity with Film* provides an invaluable resource for teachers. I often begin a class discussion on film technique with two or three examples of match cuts from the film to start the students thinking about how edits can direct the viewer and build characterization. They learn quickly and become confident in their ability to analyze the film via edits and camera angles, and this opens the door to a fruitful discussion of the narrative significance of the women in the film.

Thomas and Victor make their physical and emotional journey to retrieve Arnold's ashes with the help of many women, ultimately leading to Arnold's literal and metaphorical return to the reservation. Through this storyline, the film creates a depth and complexity of Native American characters not previously seen in Hollywood film. Although *Smoke Signals* alludes to the Hollywood western and is a buddy/road trip film, it also resists and veers away from these formulas through the female characters. These characters do not operate as a foil to the bonding of the two male characters, which is typical of buddy films, nor are the women diminished by demeaning roles typical of the western. To further uncover this aspect of the film, instructors might choose to have students reflect on the typical images of Native American women in Hollywood westerns and compare them to the women in *Smoke Signals.* Jane Tompkins, in *West of Everything: The Inner Life of Westerns*, comments on the negative images of Indian women in Hollywood film. Referring specifically to the Comanche woman "Look" in John Ford's *The Searchers*, she states, "This woman was treated so abominably by the characters—ridiculed, humiliated, and then killed off casually by the plot—that I couldn't believe my eyes. The movie treated her as a joke, not as a person."[25] Literature and film critic Ellen Arnold argues, "Such images misrepresent the powerful social roles that Native American women historically played in their cultures," adding, "These stereotypes, by influencing public perceptions, also interfere with the recognition of contemporary Native American women's vital roles as cultural mediators, political activists, and leaders of resistance."[26] Alexie, very much aware of the powerful roles Native women have occupied throughout history, purposefully wrote strong women into his screenplay. "When Arlene Joseph stands up to Arnold, she is being the kind of powerful Indian woman I've known all my life."[27]

Smoke Signals also differs from conventional Hollywood films by representing strong women who are not portrayed in opposition to the men. The female characters, far from being an obstacle to male bonding, contribute to the resolution and bonding in the film. This represents a distinctly Native American sensibility. In Native American myth, history, and contemporary life, Native American women frequently serve as creators, healers, leaders, and advisors, contrary to the way they are portrayed in the majority of American myth, history, and the media.[28] *Smoke Signals* subtly addresses this reality, despite its emphasis on male bonding and father-son relationships. The female characters, though not the focus of the film, have an important presence as they serve as advisors, guides, and catalysts for action.

Arlene, Victor's mother, is a catalyst for Victor's identity formation and healing through his journey to Phoenix. As an advisor, she instructs Victor to accept Thomas's help in arriving at this destination and she does this while making her famous fry bread. I often use this scene and those that follow not only to teach my students about the significance of these female characters in the film, but also to teach them visual literacy.[29] In this clip in which Arlene and Victor are talking while she cooks, I have my students pay close attention to camera angles. The director uses an overhead shot each time he focuses on Victor, and a low-angle shot for Arlene. The students comment on how these camera angles present each character in a way that reflects his or her current emotional state. Arlene, who is very strong, looks commanding and stable when shot from a low angle. Her advice seems trustworthy and worth considering as she speaks. Victor, on the other hand, looks small and less secure as he looks up to his mom. The end result is that Victor accepts his mother's advice and lets Thomas help him, which ultimately leads to his journey and the beginning of his identity formation.

From there we watch the fry bread and dinner scene with Thomas and his grandmother—comparing them to the one with Victor and his mother. Thomas is much more secure in his identity, and this is largely because he relies on his grandmother. Thomas's grandma serves subtly as an advisor, but more importantly as Thomas's foundation for his place in the community. This is reinforced onscreen through their actions more so than through dialogue, since the grandmother has little onscreen time. This fact does not undermine her presence, since visually her relationship with and influence on Thomas is clear. Students first compare the scene in which Thomas is cooking dinner for his grandmother, noting that he is standing while she is sitting—yet the director uses less extreme high- or low-angle shots, making them appear more equal. Later, when Thomas and his grandmother are sitting at the dinner table, the students are able to freeze the frame and analyze the mise-en-scène[30] for even further proof of their equal and well-balanced relationship.

Thomas and his grandmother are perfectly balanced in the scene, directly across from one another, each taking up about half the frame. The window behind them frames them equally. Their similar appearance—thick braids and thick glasses—makes them appear as near mirror images as they sit across from one another. When they hear a knock at the door and simultaneously look up, then at the door, then at each other, they are barely able to contain their joy in the knowledge that it is Victor. The staging of this scene firmly establishes Thomas's relationship with his grandmother. They balance and complement each other. There is a sense of strength in this equilibrium that visually places Thomas in a very solid position in terms of identity. The students enjoy analyzing this shot, because there is much to discuss and it builds confidence in their ability to read and discuss the mise-en-scène.

The last female character we discuss is Suzy Song. Victor is in greatest need when it comes to identity formation, and he finds the missing stories that lead to his further development in Phoenix through the character of Suzy Song. Suzy does not serve as an obstacle to the male bonding in the film, which is typically the role of females in the road trip/ buddy movie. She also does not inhibit the lead character's ability to resolve his conflict with his father. Instead, she is a catalyst for resolution. Comparing Suzy's character to the Native women analyzed in Ellen Arnold's "Reframing the Hollywood Indian: A Feminist Re-reading of *Powwow Highway* and *Thunderheart*" can help students understand the significance of Suzy's character in terms of her complexity and uniqueness. Suzy's presence forces a critical turning point in Victor's understanding of his father and himself. She knows that Arnold abandoned his family in part because of the guilt he felt over starting the house fire that killed Thomas's parents. Suddenly, Arnold's actions are explained, and without realizing it, Victor has encountered an important story he needed to know. One way to underscore this is by having students analyze how this is visually represented in the montage that takes place later in the film after the car wreck scene. Images of Suzy and fire and his father pull all the pieces together, culminating in a vision for Victor. After falling unconscious from running an extreme distance, he awakens to a vision of his father helping him up—a first step toward resolution. This is a scene students especially enjoy analyzing, as are the others, which makes this very accessible film one well worth teaching.

Eyre and Alexie's success with *Smoke Signals* immediately led to more opportunities for both filmmakers. Eyre directed *Skins*, released in 2002 and Alexie directed *The Business of Fancydancing* (2002). Neither film had the success of the first film, but clearly a door had been opened. Over the next ten years Eyre became the most prolific Native American feature filmmaker in terms of both directing and producing. Perhaps one of the best, but least known films Eyre has produced thus far is *The Doe Boy* (2001), written and directed by Randy Redroad.

Classroom Unit IV: Randy Redroad's *The Doe Boy*

I present a unit on Randy Redroad's *The Doe Boy* for its originality and the challenge it offers students in terms of a critical reading. This film has not garnered the same kind of attention that *Smoke Signals* has, and no critical essays or lesson plans currently exist on this film. I hope that my approach to the film and suggestions for teaching it here will be a useful starting place for most educators. *The Doe Boy* breaks radically from Hollywood stereotypes, and is perhaps one of the most realistic and most subtly Native American full-length feature films. It does not contain the "sign posts" of Indianness that most audiences want and expect. Perhaps this is why, though it did well on the film festival circuit, it did not pick up a major distributor. Whereas Alexie and Eyre's film frequently reminds its viewers that its contemporary characters are Native American—"We're Indians, remember? We barter!"—*The Doe Boy* rarely does this. There are many moments in the film that express a Cherokee worldview that are not explained. Like a poem in a Native language that does not offer a translation or a glossary in the back of the book, *The Doe Boy* allows itself to be a Cherokee film with no explanation, no translation.

Randy Redroad is a Cherokee filmmaker who grew up in Texas.

The Doe Boy is loosely based on his personal experiences, including the critical moment in the film when the protagonist, named Hunter, accidentally shoots a doe while out hunting with his dad. Houston Wood discusses the significance of this scene to some degree in his book *Native Features*. As a filmmaker, Redroad claims this real-life event came to take on "mythic significance" for him and became the foundation for his first feature film.[31]

The Doe Boy can be a difficult film to teach, but is an excellent example of a film that disrupts mainstream audience's ideas of "Indianness." These are not Plains Indians; the setting is not in the "Wild West" or on a reservation (as with *Smoke Signals*); the characters are contemporary and not frozen in the past. There are characters who respect and reflect their Cherokee ancestry, and those who do not, which is a most realistic portrayal of Native Americans of all tribes. The film depicts a different history from what people think they know about "Indians," and it challenges them to revise what they've "learned" from over a hundred years of Hollywood filmmaking.

I design my class discussions to explore how the film moves away from depicting Hollywood Indians, and instead alludes to a more realistic and tribally specific worldview of a contemporary Cherokee person. The film is largely billed as a "coming-of-age story," though few seem to recognize that it is also a film about balance and ethics, and that it relies heavily on the symbolism of "blood" throughout. One exercise I use is to have students analyze the symbolism in the film as well as the metaphors stated in the repeated voice-overs of the grandfather to determine how these filmic qualities reflect a Cherokee worldview. Blood functions symbolically in a number of ways. First of all, Hunter is a mixed-blood Cherokee who is also a hemophiliac. He claims to have inherited this "whiteman's" disease from his Anglo father, who finds Hunter a bitter disappointment because he is unable to play sports or work with tools. The father's only hope is to take the boy hunting to prove his masculinity, but the hunting trip fails when Hunter accidentally shoots a doe. The film focuses on the relationship between father and son, but it also emphasizes identity, since the father is constantly trying to pull Hunter away from anything traditionally Cherokee. Therefore Hunter's blood signifies many things in the film. A good resource for studying the symbolism and significance of blood in Cherokee culture is Circe Sturm's *Blood Politics: Race, Culture, and Identity in the Cherokee Nation of Oklahoma*.[32] Sturm contextualizes how blood has functioned both symbolically and literally (as in blood quantum) in Cherokee history and discusses its relevance today. This can be a useful starting point for instructors wanting to teach this film.

Students might also explore the theme of balance and ethics in the film, a prominent theme in Cherokee storytelling and life. According to Wilma Mankiller, former principal chief of the Cherokee Nation, "In the old days Cherokee people believed that the world existed in a precarious balance and that only right or correct actions kept it from tumbling. Wrong actions were believed to disturb the balance . . . in our current state we are so very distant from that time when our world had balance."[33] The film seems to reflect this concept in that Hunter's mistake of killing the doe throws everything out of balance and saddles him with the nickname "Doe Boy," a constant reminder of his failure. The experience leaves him angry and disconnected from his Anglo father, who is partly to blame for the incident since he pressured the boy into hunting and then irresponsibly fell asleep under a tree, leaving the boy to hunt on his own.

It is only after Hunter ultimately models himself after the most respected Cherokee hunter in the community and takes his Cherokee grandfather's words to heart—"There is a difference between hunting and killing, you know"—that Hunter's situation improves. As an adult, he finally adopts a more appropriate hunting ethic and things start to move forward in a good way. This is emphasized strongly at the end of the film, when Hunter goes out with a single arrow made by his grandfather and encounters a buck that gives itself up. In this moment Hunter can kill the buck, thus proving his manhood by his father's standards, or he can let it go, proving that there is a "difference between hunting and killing." He lets the buck go and is rewarded for this action when he is able to stop a deep wound from bleeding without Western science's medicine, but simply by going to a creek and rinsing his hand. At this point the mythic qualities in the film become fully realized as Hunter becomes "the good story" that the grandfather narrates at the end of the film.

Students will likely struggle with analysis of this film beyond the universal symbolism and father-son relationship, but that is what makes it so useful as a teaching tool. Too often students learn what they think they already know "about Indians" from movies, and this film challenges them to think differently. The film works in sharp contrast to movies like *The Searchers* and other Ford films that breezily dismiss tribal differences and relegate Native Americans to the time of westward expansion. It creates a new way of thinking about "Indianness" and introduces a very good Native American director in the process.

The work of Native American filmmakers can teach students how to critically analyze both the films that have come before via Hollywood and the films that "talk back" via Native voices. Teaching students visual literacy in reading Native American films can help them understand their significance in terms of self-representation. It is all too easy for most students to take representation for granted, since they have seen some sort of realistic semblance of themselves onscreen—but Native Americans have not. Teaching the films of Osawa, Eyre, and Redroad opens their eyes to how Native filmmakers have responded to misrepresentation and absence in American film. Despite Alexie's pessimistic claims that the door for Native American filmmaking has already closed, Native directors keep making films. At the Sundance Film Festival in January of 2009 Creek director Sterlin Harjo premiered his second feature film, *Barking Waters,* just two years after *Four Sheets to the Wind* was nominated for a Grand Jury Prize at the festival. The enthusiasm for making films independently is a reality, and as Native directors, writers, and producers continue on, the opportunity to teach a variety of works representing many viewpoints will only improve. As a professor of Native American film, I look forward to what the future has to bring.

Notes

1. By "Native American film," I specifically mean films written, directed, and/or produced by Native Americans. I do not include films made by non-Natives with Native subject matter.

2. Carole Gerster and Laura W. Zlogar, eds., *Teaching Ethnic Diversity with Film: Essays and Resources for Educators in History, Social Studies, Literature and Film Studies* (Jefferson, NC: McFarland, 2006).

3. Jacquelyn Kilpatrick, *Celluloid Indians: Native Americans and Film* (Lincoln: University of Nebraska Press, 1999).

4. Harry M. Benshoff and Sean Griffin, *America on Film: Representing Race, Class, Gender, and Sexuality at the Movies* (Malden, MA: Blackwell, 2004).

5. Ken Nolley, "The Representation of Conquest: John Ford and the Hollywood Indian (1939–1964)," in *Hollywood's Indian: The Portrayal of the Native American in Film,* ed. Peter C. Rollins and John E. O'Connor (Lexington: University Press of Kentucky, 1998).

6. Rayna Green, "The Pocahontas Perplex: The Image of Indian Women in American Culture," *Massachusetts Review* 16.4 (1975): 698–714.

7. M. Elise Marubbio, *Killing the Indian Maiden: Images of Native American Women in Film* (Lexington: University Press of Kentucky, 2006).

8. Brian W. Dippie, *The Vanishing American: White Attitudes and US Indian Policy* (Lawrence: University Press of Kansas, 1982).

9. Cindy Stillwell, "Moviemaker Interview: Sandra Osawa," http:www.fargo filmfestival.org/moviemaker-interview-sandra-osawa (accessed May 4, 2009).

10. Lawrence Abbott and Sandy Osawa, "Interview: Sandy Osawa," *American Indian Quarterly* 22.1 (1998): 111.

11. Beverly R. Singer, *Wiping the War Paint off the Lens: Native American Film and Video* (Minneapolis: University of Minnesota Press, 2001).

12. Abbott and Osawa, "Interview," 111.

13. Ibid., 112.

14. Stillwell, "Moviemaker Interview: Sandra Osawa."

15. Vine Deloria Jr., *Custer Died for Your Sins: An Indian Manifesto* (Norman: University of Oklahoma Press, 1988).

16. Michelle H. Raheja, *Reservation Reelism: Redfacing, Visual Sovereignty, and Representations of Native Americans in Film* (Lincoln: University of Nebraska Press, 2010).

17. Luther Standing Bear, *My People the Sioux* (Lincoln: University of Nebraska Press, 1975).

18. Jacquelyn Kilpatrick, "American Indians on Film," in *Teaching Ethnic Diversity with Film: Essays and Resources for Educators in History, Social Studies, Literature and Film Studies*, ed. Carole Gerster and Laura W. Zlogar (Jefferson, NC: McFarland, 2006), 60.

19. Heather Bruce, Anna Baldwin, and Christabel Umphrey, *Sherman Alexie in the Classroom* (Urbana, IL: National Council of Teachers of English, 2008).

20. Sherman Alexie, *Smoke Signals: A Screenplay* (New York: Hyperion, 1998).

21. Houston Wood, *Native Features: Indigenous Films from Around the World* (New York: Continuum, 2008), 125.

22. Joanna Hearne, "John Wayne's Teeth: Speech, Sound, and Representation in *Smoke Signals* and *Imagining Indians*," *Western Folklore* 64.3–4 (2005): 189–208, 190.

23. John Purdy, "Crossroads: A Conversation with Sherman Alexie," *Studies in American Indian Literature* 9.4 (1997): 1–18.

24. Angelica M. Lawson, "Native Sensibility and the Significance of Women in *Smoke Signals*," in *Sherman Alexie: A Collection of Critical Essays*, ed. Jeff Burglund and Jan Roush (Salt Lake City: University of Utah Press, 2010).

25. Jane Tompkins, *West of Everything: The Inner Life of Westerns* (Oxford: Oxford University Press, 1992), 8.

26. Ellen L. Arnold, "Reframing the Hollywood Indian: A Feminist Re-reading of *Powwow Highway* and *Thunderheart*," in *American Indian Studies: An Interdisciplinary Approach to Contemporary Issues* (New York: Peter Lang, 1997), 349.

27. See Alexie, *Smoke Signals*, 160.

28. Arnold, "Reframing the Hollywood Indian," 349.

29. For a good discussion on visual literacy, see the aforementioned Gerster as well as Bruce, Baldwin, and Umphrey, *Sherman Alexie in the Classroom*.

30. *Mise-en-scène* refers to all the elements in a scene and is explained in the Gerster and Zlogar glossary mentioned earlier in this chapter.

31. Wood, *Native Features*, 125.

32. Circe Sturm, *Blood Politics: Race, Culture, and Identity in the Cherokee Nation of Oklahoma* (Berkeley: University of California Press, 2002).

33. Wilma Mankiller, foreword to *Selu: Seeking the Corn Mother's Wisdom* (Golden, CO: Fulcrum, 1994), ix.

“The Native’s Point of View” as Seen through the Native’s (and Non-Native’s) Points of View

Sam Pack

This chapter describes a reception study that I conducted with both Navajo and Anglo viewers using two sets of films about Navajos in order to compare and contrast their reactions to “insider” and “outsider” perspectives of the same subject matter. The first set addresses the forced relocation of Navajo families from their ancestral homeland as presented by a Native filmmaker and non-Native filmmakers. I screened the films to both groups to determine if either was able to distinguish cultural authorship. The second set of films—one a documentary and the other a television drama—chronicles the journey of Navajos who were adopted by white families as infants and then reunite with their biological families as adults. Unlike the very structured nature of the first study, this one replicated a more natural viewing environment. Interestingly, any historical and cultural inaccuracies depicted in these visual reproductions did not detract from the viewers’ enjoyment of the films.

Until relatively recently, studies of audience reception among Indigenous peoples have been all but ignored within anthropology.[1] Debra Spitulnik bemoaned the fact that there was no “anthropology of mass media,” as anthropologists had largely managed to neglect the centrality of mass media in twentieth-century life.[2] This absence was ironic in light of the often-quoted Malinowskian dictum that the goal of ethnography is “to grasp the native’s point of view, his relation to life, to realize his vision of his world.”[3] Anthropologists in industrial countries paid scant systematic attention to the production, distribution, and consumption of mass media in their own societies and even less attention to mass media in nonindustrial societies.[4]

The glaring lack of reception studies within anthropology reflects the unacknowledged assumption that all viewers process information in a similarly unproblematic manner. Studies have demonstrated, however, that there is an intrinsic link between culture and communication and that each culture socializes its members in its own viewing habits and interpretive strategies. Simply stated, the media do not affect all equally or in the same fashion.

The literature regarding the effects of imported mass media in nonindustrial societies oscillates between two diametrically opposed poles. The first, influenced by Marxism, conceives of the media as an extremely powerful force in the reproduction and distribution of a dominant ideology that both reflects and reinforces asymmetrical power relations delimited by race, class, and gender. The other, influenced by cultural studies, views mass culture—in spite of such inequitable power relations—as allowing for active agency on the part of audiences. Of course, mass media are capable of both of these extremes in that they can produce resignation and resistance.

By virtue of relying on self-fulfilling research designs, too many reception studies obscure the agency of their human "subjects." With their preconceived agendas in place, all they have to do is fill in the blanks. Indeed, anthropologists and other researchers have historically employed what I call a "ventriloquist approach" in their studies of Indigenous peoples. By essentially speaking on their behalf, they have rendered their Native subjects as little more than exotic puppets. Within anthropology in recent years, there has been interest in reversing the academic perspective by using Native epistemologies to critique our own assumptions. Dan Rose, in particular, urges a more radical democratization of knowledge that simultaneously de-privileges our academic inquiry while helping to recover ideas and practices from historically marginalized points of view.[5]

Thus, the following study seeks to address and perhaps remedy some of the deficiencies of its predecessors in three specific ways. First, it takes as its point of departure the need to examine the cultural dimension of communicative processes. This is especially important since the dynamics of image interpretation are magnified when the producer of the image and the consumer of the image come from different cultures. Second, this chapter explores the multiple formations and contestations of identity through the experiences of a Navajo family with which I have been closely associated for two decades. Such familiarity is crucial precisely because so much family behavior is private and hidden from public view. Finally, bolstered by the application of an insider/outsider perspective, this study mitigates the objectification of ethnographic subjects by actively soliciting their reactions to two sets of films: *In the Heart of Big*

Mountain (1988)/*Broken Rainbow* (1985) and *The Return of Navajo Boy* (2000)/*The Lost Child* (2000). It is formulated on the premise of not only recognizing but also privileging the voices of Native people in their own mass-mediated representations.

There is also an added significance in focusing on the voices of Navajos in particular because of their participation in a landmark study known as the Navajo Film Project. During the summer of 1966, Sol Worth and John Adair visited Pine Springs, Arizona, to conduct an anthropological experiment by handing film cameras to seven Navajo adults to determine whether the kinds of films they chose to make would reveal something about the ways in which they perceived the world. Interestingly, the underlying assumption was that Navajos had little knowledge of Hollywood film language and an analysis of the films they elected to make and the ways they framed their images would reveal something of the cultural lens through which they perceived the world.

Perhaps the most interesting finding from the Navajo Film Project was the specific ways in which Worth and Adair found the films to be distinctly "Navajo" as opposed to "amateur" or even just "different." Since it has been demonstrated that Navajos produce images distinctively, perhaps it should follow that they *receive* images distinctively as well. In other words, my reception study examines whether there are uniquely "Navajo" viewing habits and interpretive strategies as they specifically apply to watching films.

In the Heart of Big Mountain and *Broken Rainbow* tackle similar subject matter from different points of view. While a Native American filmmaker completed the first, non-Natives produced and directed the second. In 1976 Robert Aibel conducted a reception study similar to Worth and Adair's among Anglo university students to see whether they could distinguish between a Navajo-made film (by Johnny Nelson) and an Anglo-made film (by John Adair) about the same topic (Navajo silversmithing). Although he found that informants could correctly determine cultural authorship, Aibel acknowledges that it would have been "particularly valuable and revealing" to conduct the study with a Navajo audience,[6] especially in light of the comment by a Navajo woman during a screening of the Navajo Film Project films that she "cannot understand English"—despite the fact that all of the films were silent.[7]

The reception study I conducted does precisely what Aibel's did not, as it was undertaken with *both* Anglos *and* Navajos. I originally completed a study using *In the Heart of Big Mountain* and *Broken Rainbow* in an introductory anthropology class I taught at Temple University during the summer of 1998 with eight Anglo college students.[8] Two years later, I repeated the study with five Navajo informants, all members of the Benally family, as part of my dissertation research.[9]

Methodologically, presenting the films to these two constituencies presented a unique challenge because the cultural baggage that each group brought to the viewing was very different. Since most of my students knew little to nothing about Navajo culture before taking my class, it was imperative for me to provide some contextualization for what they were about to watch. As such, I assigned relevant readings and dedicated two class periods to lectures briefly describing the history of the Navajos as well as the issues and ethics of (self)-representation.[10] My Navajo informants did not require such background information for obvious reasons. All five individuals were already familiar with the relocation controversy to varying degrees.

The viewing contexts for the college students and my informants also varied tremendously. All of the students watched the films together in a classroom as part of an assignment. Although I emphasized that they would not be graded for their responses to the films, their participation was undoubtedly motivated by academic concerns. Several of the students, for example, scribbled notes during the screenings. My informants, on the other hand, took these films a lot less seriously. With the exception of Grandma Annie, who required an English translator, the other four family members watched the films individually and at their leisure. They often paused the films to get up and do something else. Several ate during the screenings. None wrote down any notes.

For both groups, I introduced the films by stating that each addressed the same topic—Navajo relocation—from different perspectives. I cued each film to start at a point where the title and the credits would not be visible. I distributed questionnaires immediately after each screening and instructed the viewers to fill them out. Both groups were allowed a brief intermission before the next screening.

The questionnaire was divided into four components. For each film, respondents were asked to provide a summary, describe what they had learned from the film, numerically evaluate ten separate filmic qualities, and devise their own title for the film. After both screenings, they were also asked to explain which was better made, which they liked more, and which film was made by whom. The college students wrote down their answers, and my Navajo informants responded verbally to the questions.

Before discussing the results of the reception study, it is important to emphasize that neither group can be essentialized as constituting a homogenous entity. Both groups exhibited significant differences and contradictions among members. That said, there were also common cultural threads. Although I may generalize findings from each group for the sake of brevity, readers should keep this intragroup diversity in mind.

The first set of films explores the topic of Navajo forced relocation. A highly polished film narrated by actor and activist Martin Sheen, *Broken Rainbow* won the Academy Award for best documentary in 1985. The film details the relocation of Navajo families from their homes in Big Mountain, Arizona, compassionately portraying the devastating impact of coal mining on the forcibly removed Navajo and implicating the federal government's role in creating the Navajo-Hopi land dispute that precipitated the relocation. Navajo-Hopi borders were nebulously defined during the pre-reservation era. Strife between the two tribes resulted in a federal partitioning of the commonly claimed land in 1977. As a result of this ruling, over 10,000 Navajos had to be relocated to government housing in cities off the reservation. Many traditional Navajos whose families had lived on Big Mountain for generations refused to leave. Those who were forcibly removed have had great difficulty adjusting to a radically different way of life. The film makes an impassioned plea that the relocation process be overturned in order to prevent the impending ecological destruction of a sacred land due to coal mining as well as the cultural destruction of a proud people.

Like *Broken Rainbow, In the Heart of Big Mountain* also addresses the forced relocation of Navajos as a result of the Navajo-Hopi land dispute. The major difference is that the latter is made by a Native American filmmaker. Sandra Osawa provides thorough background information for those unfamiliar with the history of the land dispute. The strength of this film lies in Osawa's emphasis on the emotional and human aspects of the issues. She shows how the land dispute has adversely affected the lives of various Navajos from Big Mountain who have become afflicted by alcoholism, mental problems, physical illness, and even death because of their separation from their homeland.

The film is divided into two sections, the first of which focuses on a Navajo matriarch, Katherine Smith, who was born and raised and continues to live on Big Mountain. The second half describes Katherine's daughter, Nancy, who was relocated to a HUD (Department of Housing and Urban Development) house near Tuba City, Arizona. Through these two individuals, Osawa juxtaposes the traditional and modern worlds. For example, although Katherine washes her face from a bin and cooks fry bread on an open fire, her daughter enjoys the amenities of running water and electricity. The dichotomy is overly simplistic, but it serves its purpose.

The dominant description of *Big Mountain* among the Anglo college students was that this film depicted yet another instance of the government mistreating Native Americans. In their questionnaires, most students recycled familiar clichés along the lines of "Oh, these poor Indians." A sampling of the responses:

> Colleen: The film was about the problems brought on by the forced relocation threat imposed by the government: namely, increased death rate, alcoholism, mental problems. The government has created boundaries and split up the land between two groups of people. However, in doing so, they have divided land that is sacred. Because there are no statues or huge churches built on the land does not mean that this is not a place of prayer.

Colleen's comments clearly reflect that she has learned something about cultural relativism. A self-proclaimed devout Catholic, Colleen recognizes that the Navajos' religious beliefs are just as valid as her own.

> Karen: I feel this film was made primarily to generate sympathy. It worked. I felt really bad for these people. What right do the whites have to come in and drive those people from their homes? I greatly admire Katherine and the others who stayed where they belonged regardless of what the government said.

Karen's remarks are interesting because, in the space of only a few sentences, she proceeds from feeling sympathy at the Indians' "plight" to proclaiming admiration for their strength of character.

The majority of the students referenced *Big Mountain* when summarizing *Broken Rainbow*. The general consensus was that the second film approached the topic of relocation in more historical detail.

> Mary: Like the other film, it was about the government trying to take away Big Mountain from the Navajo in order to exploit its resources. Only this

> time, the film gave time to the Hopi to show how they are affected by this as well. Not as much time spent on their bond with the land, but more on the whole litigation process.

But what this film gained in comprehensiveness, according to students, it sacrificed in a personal connection to affected individuals.

In terms of the film's educational value, the students' responses varied most in this category. Some, like Dave, found *Big Mountain* to be a valuable learning tool:

> I really learned a lot from the film because I can understand that the Big Mountain is an important place for the Navajo. I am angry that the government forced the people to move out. I would support Navajo people to have their rights to stay . . . I would like the Navajo to maintain their standards. I really want them to be left alone.

Others, like Mary, were not as impressed:

> I didn't learn a whole heck of a lot. I know from papers I wrote earlier in college that the Navajo religion is based on the land and that each element of the land has its own "spirit," and I knew from the readings that land inheritance was a "female thing." Also, it didn't surprise me that mental illness and suicide was on the rise among the Navajo. It makes sense given what they're going through. The deaths did surprise me, although it can be argued whether that's really based on the relocation or if it's purely medical.

A similar juxtaposition applied to *Broken Rainbow*, which was well articulated by Scott:

> Basically what I learned was a pretty solid history of the Indians in that region. But most of the info about whites taking advantage and manipulating I was already aware of.

As part of their evaluation process of the films, all of the respondents were asked to give a numerical score from 1 to 10 (lowest to highest) for a series of different filmic qualities, including artistic, smooth, intelligible, complete, interesting, funny, educational, good, unusual, and likeable.

On the whole, the students ranked *Broken Rainbow* higher in terms of intelligibility, completeness, and educational value, while *Big Mountain* received a slight nod for being more interesting and unusual. Both films were rated as being evenly artistic and smooth, and none of the students found either of the films to be particularly funny. The students disagreed about which film they liked more or was better made—which I will discuss in further detail later.

For the final component, students were presented the opportunity to demonstrate their creativity by proposing their own title for each film. For *Big Mountain*, titles tended to focus more on the deleterious impact of relocation upon the Navajo: "The Effects of Forced Relocation on the Navajo" (Mark), "The Heartache of Relocation" (Karen), and "Big Mountain and How the People Can't Live without It" (Gena). On the contrary, suggested film titles for *Broken Rainbow* concentrated more on the underhanded tactics of the government: "Manipulation and Destruction of the Hopi and Navajo" (Scott), "The Navajo, the Hopi, and the Government: Whose Land Is It?" (Mary), and "The Government's Destruction of Indian Lifestyles" (Dorian).

Unlike the college students, my Navajo informants spoke in broad generalizations and rarely provided specific examples from the films. For instance, this is the way Isabelle, a middle-aged mother of ten, summarized *Big Mountain*:

> It was about the Navajo people being relocated out of Big Mountain and how it's working on them psychologically. And all the problems they're having up there with their family dying and all that.

Her college-educated daughter, Regina, employed similarly sweeping strokes when describing *Broken Rainbow*:

> This film gave a brief history of the origins of Navajo relocation. Then it also included the Hopis. This one was more spread out to a whole group of Navajos living on Big Mountain.

Such lack of detail may be indicative of their not paying very close attention to the films. But I have noticed that many of the Navajos whom I have come to know have difficulty giving precise answers to vague and open-ended questions like "What did you think about it?" or "What was it about?" Instead, general questions invariably elicit general responses.

Of course, the main reason they did not pay very close attention to the educational value of the two films was because they were already familiar with the subject matter. Although bothered by the travesty of justice perpetrated against the Navajos of Big Mountain, none expressed any surprise, as they have come to expect this type of unethical behavior from the government. Sixteen-year-old Chucky first heard about the issue in his high school class:

> I knew about Big Mountain from taking "Navajo Government" this semester. He [the teacher] didn't tell me about the relocation, though. I got a white guy. He don't know nothing. He just goes by the book. The part I was surprised about was where people died because of it and how it affected their minds and stuff. I felt sorry for the people but, then again, it was expected. Because the government, man, they're always going to do you like that. Sooner or later, they're going to kick us off our land. Watch.

An underlying apathy also characterized their reactions of *Broken Rainbow*:

> Isabelle: I never really paid attention to the relocation because it didn't affect me. It used to be a big thing about ten years ago, but now people kind of just forgot about it. Even when all this was going on, nobody really cared or they would have been out there supporting those relocatees. I don't think the outside people really got involved.

All five members of the Benally family maintained an emotional distance from the issue of relocation since neither they themselves nor anyone they knew was directly involved. But Delbert, an unemployed silversmith, acknowledged that the situation would have been different if he had been *personally* affected.

> Being way over here, I heard it all on the radio and newspaper. I couldn't really do anything about it. What if they come over to where *I* live? "Hey, man, this whole doggone valley ain't yours." That's when you get a little bit more about how these people feel. And it could happen this way, too.

> They can easily say, "Forget about these social services anymore. No more hospitals. Run your own show."

The Benallys' unsympathetic remarks are consistent with the "every man for himself" ethos that I have found to be common among contemporary Navajos.

As a means of evaluation, assigning a numerical designation to various traits seemed to be an entirely foreign concept to my Navajo informants. Unlike the college students, they were not accustomed to isolating specific traits and then ranking them on a relative scale. Grandma Annie, the Benally family matriarch, had an especially difficult time understanding the ranking system no matter how many times and different ways that her son, Delbert, and I tried to explain it to her. Ultimately, I believe she humored me by rattling off an arbitrary series of numbers.

The arbitrary nature of the evaluation is most evident in how inconsistently they ranked the different traits. Delbert, Isabelle, and Chucky all felt that *Broken Rainbow* was the more intelligible, complete, and interesting film, yet they gave higher scores in all three categories to *Big Mountain*. Another interesting tendency was how several of the Navajos supplied two different numerical scores: one for the general public and the other for themselves. So, for example, Chucky gave *Big Mountain* a 7 for being unusual, but quickly noted that it rated only as a 3 from his own point of view. Similarly, Isabelle and Regina both thought the films would be much more educational for non-Navajos.

Asked to propose their own titles for these films, the Navajo informants' responses were predictably uninspired given their generally lackadaisical approach in the viewing context. Unlike the case with the Anglo students, there was no discernible difference between the titles for either film. In fact, Delbert and Chucky gave practically the *same* title for both films. Perhaps this is because the films are ultimately about the same thing in their eyes: how the federal government has once again victimized the Navajos. It is a story they know all too well.

As with those the college students proposed, the titles basically fell into two camps. The first addressed the sadness and heartache of the Navajos: "Brokenhearted Diné" (Grandma Annie), "Emotional Crisis at Big Mountain" (Isabelle), and "The Psychological Effects of Navajo Relocation" (Regina). The second group focused on anger aimed at the federal government and Anglos as a whole: "Screwed Again by Uncle Sam"

(Chucky), "Stealing Indian Lands" (Regina), and "The Corrupt White Man" (Delbert). Significantly, the two camps were almost equally divided according to gender lines, with the female viewers responding more emotionally and male viewers responding more angrily.

When asked which film is better made, each group of viewers provided responses that reflected their own cultural biases. Although the college students unanimously agreed that *Broken Rainbow* was the much slicker production, such evidence of its higher budget did not necessarily translate into superior overall quality. Scott elaborated on the pluses and minuses of each film:

> For entertainment value, [*Broken Rainbow*] was made a lot better and gave more of a historical background. But the film was done in the "voice of God" method with the narrator speaking for the people. While [*Big Mountain*] was not very artistically pleasing, it did seem to be more believable. So as far as an ethnography, [*Big Mountain*] seemed to have less flaws.

Similarly, Dorian hailed *Broken Rainbow*'s "informational nature and multiple perspectives," but ultimately decreed that *Big Mountain* was "more anthropological" because of its focus on individuals rather than groups.

The Navajos unanimously nominated *Broken Rainbow* as the superior film in terms of production quality. Compared with *Big Mountain*, this film was longer, more detailed, and more informative. Taken together, my informants easily gathered that the documentary was the more expensive film to make. *Broken Rainbow*, observed Grandma Annie, "looked like it cost a lot more money." For Annie, there was a direct correlation between cultural value and its monetary counterpart.

Surprisingly, several of the students who decided that *Broken Rainbow* was the better-made film nevertheless liked *Big Mountain* more. Karen, for example, sided with the Oscar-winning documentary as the superior production because it was "more informative and educational," whereas *Big Mountain* was "only about one woman and her life." Yet when it came time for her to cast her vote for the film she found more appealing, Karen preferred the smaller production precisely because of its human touch:

> I enjoyed [*Big Mountain*] better because it was on a more personal level. I know the view of one person does not represent all Navajo, but I

> sympathized with her. [*Broken Rainbow*] was too full of facts and statistics. It doesn't matter to me that their sheep are a gift from the Holy People—I could care less. I was interested in how relocation affected their everyday lives and [*Big Mountain*] showed that well.

Dorian, on the other hand, had the opposite impression:

> While I feel [*Big Mountain*] was better made, the second provided me with more information that was obviously lacking in the first. I needed things to be placed in a historical timeline and the second film provided adequate info mixed with varying opinions and imagery. [*Big Mountain*] acted as a more focused version of [*Broken Rainbow*].

As these divergent comments illustrate, there is no accounting for personal taste.

Perhaps because of their greater familiarity with forced relocation, the Navajos were far more critical of both films' content. In contrast to the college students, my informants were not as susceptible to the emotional underpinnings of either film that portrayed the relocated Navajos as helpless victims. Through the reservation grapevine, Isabelle had heard that the Big Mountain residents were offered a significant economic incentive to move:

> Those guys received funds to build brand-new houses and they also got moving expenses. There's a lot of other people that had their arms wide open to the money. You know how Navajos are. Ninety-nine percent of the time, they're thinking about the money.

While the goal of both films was to elicit sympathy for the displaced Navajos, several of the informants viewed the financial settlement resulting from the relocation as a blessing in disguise for those involved. Perhaps because neither film showed this perspective, the Navajos did not express a strong preference for either. They seemed to agree with Chucky's one-word response when I asked him which film he liked better: "None."

Finally, the all-important question: Is there anything uniquely "Native" about Osawa's version? Other than smaller production costs, is *Big Mountain* really that different from *Broken Rainbow*? Would a casual observer or even a fellow Native be able to tell the difference? Thus, for the final phase of this reception study on *Big Mountain* and *Broken Rainbow*, respondents from both groups were asked to determine which film they thought was made by a Native filmmaker and which was made by a non-Native filmmaker.

The majority of the college students based their judgments on aesthetic quality rather than content. Several students (Scott, Dorian, Gena) attributed the personal nature of *Big Mountain* as being a Native quality. Others (Dave, Karen, Colleen) cited the strong anti-white stance of *Broken Rainbow* as being characteristic of a Native American filmmaker because he or she would be understandably upset at the harsh treatment of his or her people by whites. In other words, there was no clear consensus as all of the students felt strongly that *their* perception was the correct one.

My Navajo informants, however, experienced much less uncertainty in determining cultural authorship. For them, the simple fact that *Broken Rainbow* looked like it was so much more expensive to put together necessarily meant that it had to have been made by Anglos. By comparison, an Indian could never gather enough funding to travel to all those different places, much less hire a famous actor to serve as a narrator. Furthermore, "all those politicians and businessmen wouldn't have talked to no Indian" (Isabelle) and "only a white man would do that much homework" (Chucky).

Sufficiently impressed by the "Native" filmmaker's privileged status, none of the students noticed or cared that Osawa is Makah and not Navajo. Operating under the apparent assumption that all Indians are essentially the same, my students did not attribute any importance to the tribal dissimilarity even after I specifically brought this fact to their attention. As an Indian, Osawa seems to be granted the preordained right to speak for all other Indians.

In contrast, the fact that Osawa is not Navajo made a significant difference to my informants. Delbert, for instance, attributed the glaring omissions in *Big Mountain* to his conclusion that the filmmaker, although perhaps an Indian, did not know enough about Navajo culture to make a thorough and convincing film:

> They should have put a little bit more about what the Hopis thought about it and what the U.S. government really had to do with it. The United States government is not something you mess around with. I think at the time Peter MacDonald was chairman and I feel like he sold the people out.

> They didn't say anything about what the council's reaction was. It should have been more about getting the whole tribe involved and asking them what they thought about it. That film right there was just about one person. What they should have done was they should have got another family that had a mother and father and see what the father thought about it. And the kids, they come back and just feel sorry. They should come out and speak. It seemed like this family just kind of folded.

Regina also speculated that the individual behind *Big Mountain* was not from the reservation:

> I think he was an urban Navajo. He probably based the film on just a few relocates that he may have interviewed, but not a lot.

After I informed her that the filmmaker was actually a Makah and a woman, Regina thought for a moment to choose her words: "Then I don't think she should have made this film." What this statement suggests is that Osawa, as a non-Navajo, does not have the *right* to make a film about Navajos.

Quite the opposite of the structured nature of the first reception study, the second study involving *The Return of Navajo Boy* and *The Lost Child* was based entirely on observations of a natural viewing environment. Instead of watching my Navajo informants individually watch a videotape, taking notes during the screening, and then asking a series of prepared questions afterward, I decided just to "go with the flow" and see what happened. No tape recorder, no list of questions, no notepad—not even a pen. For *The Return of Navajo Boy,* I simply inserted the tape into the living-room VCR during a time when the trailer was full of people and, within minutes, a crowd of curious onlookers began to assemble in front of the television. I did not limit viewing to my five Navajo informants but opened access to whoever was interested in watching the documentary. Various people came and went and came back again.

The Lost Child was screened during even more informal circumstances. One evening, when a large group of people came over to play cards, Isabelle suggested that I "play the tape," ostensibly as supplemental entertainment. So while a couple of dozen people were crammed together around a makeshift gambling area, the made-for-TV movie played in the background (or foreground, depending on one's perspective). Every now and again—between shrieks of laughter, cheering, and cursing over the card game—various members of the Indigenous delegation would sneak a peek at the television to follow along with the plot. Granted, such divided attention seems far from ideal for a purported reception study, but this is the way the Benally clan typically watches TV as a group.

Analogous to *In the Heart of Big Mountain* and *Broken Rainbow*, *The Return of Navajo Boy* and *The Lost Child* also tackle a similar subject matter: the abduction of Navajo infants by outsiders and their subsequent reunion with their biological family as adults. But this is where the comparisons end. While the former is a heart-wrenching documentary, the latter is a cheesy television drama.[11]

The Return of Navajo Boy chronicles a serendipitous chain of events that began with the appearance of a 1950s film reel and eventually led to the reunion of a long-lost brother to his Navajo family after four decades. The Cly family has a long and storied history in pictures. For nearly a century, family members appeared as unidentified Indians in countless photographs and films shot against the backdrop of Monument Valley. But it was the sudden appearance of a 1950s silent film reel called *Navajo Boy* that would affect the Clys the most. Bill Kennedy, the son of the man who shot the original footage, wanted to return the film to the people in it. The Cly family matriarch, Elsie Mae Begay, delighted in seeing herself as a young girl, but she also sadly recognized her infant brother, John Wayne Cly, who was adopted by white missionaries and never heard from again. Amazingly, John Wayne read about the return of *Navajo Boy* in a newspaper article and learned that the Clys were the family he had never known. Suddenly, *The Return of Navajo Boy* takes on a literal tone.

The Lost Child also follows an individual's path to self-discovery, but this Hallmark Hall of Fame presentation ultimately gets lost in trying to do too much. Although based on the autobiography *Looking for Lost Bird: A Jewish Woman Discovers Her Navajo Roots*, by Yvette Melanson and Claire Safran (1999), the film's fish-out-of-water narrative still feels like a stretch. The movie is about a Jewish woman living in Pennsylvania who discovers that she was stolen at birth only to learn in middle age that she is actually a full-blooded Navajo. Like most screen adaptations, there are numerous discrepancies between the book and the film.[12]

After learning of her roots, Rebecca (played by very Italian-looking actress Mercedes Ruehl) uproots her family to move to the reservation. While she retraces her ancestry and adapts to her new family, her Anglo husband and two daughters experience bitterness and prejudice from the locals. In fact, after continual teasing, her older daughter is assaulted at school by a male student. At this point, the film suddenly switches gears altogether by turning Rebecca into a crusader. (Needless to say, none of this occurred in the book.) While the first half is an almost interesting portrait of birthrights and cultural clashes, the rest of the movie is reduced to a predictable fix-the-system melodrama.

Perhaps it is unfair to compare these two films, as one is a documentary and the other a Hallmark special. We are talking about apples and oranges—or, more appropriately, fry bread and Wonder bread. Although *The Lost Child* was inspired by a true story, the producers have taken obvious creative liberties and fictionalized certain parts in order to package the film for mass consumption. But herein lies the problem. By virtue of being telecast on broadcast television, *Lost Child* reached a much larger viewership than *Navajo Boy*, a documentary distributed by PBS. As a result, the inaccurate or "wrong" version is more likely to shape the general public's attitudes about Navajos in particular and Native Americans in general.[13]

In spite of the chaotic circumstances surrounding the screening of *The Return of Navajo Boy*, the documentary was compelling enough to captivate the attention of nearly everybody who originally sat down to watch it out of curiosity. Such a high retention rate is exceedingly rare for most television programs or videos, as it is customary for certain viewers to watch only for a few minutes before losing interest. At the documentary's heartrending climax, when Elsie Mae is finally reunited with her younger brother after forty years, there was *complete* silence in the room. Intermittent sniffling and eye rubbing soon followed. As I looked around, I noticed that even the men were choking back tears.

The key to the documentary's appeal among the assembled viewers was its authenticity. Members of the Benally family could identify with and literally relate to the film's "characters." (The Clys are clan relatives of the Benallys.) Everyone recognized familiar locations such as the new museum at Window Rock and Richardson's Pawn Shop. (In fact, a brief shot of a photograph of an elderly couple at the pawnshop shows my research assistant's girlfriend's grandparents.) Isabelle and Regina saw people in the documentary whom they knew. Grandma Annie remarked that one of the older ladies shown speaking at the museum bore a striking resemblance to her. Tom and Todd elbowed each other during scenes of "rez kids" playing outside as these idyllic images surely reminded them of their own not-so-distant childhood.

Isabelle referred to the Monument Valley Navajos depicted in the documentary as "hard-core traditionals" because of their remote living conditions. In one particular scene involving footage of the original Navajo boy happily riding around a desolate canyon on a horse, Jerry (who is about the same age now as that boy was then) asked his mom if "that's how it was back then" and whether she ever experienced those types of moments herself. Ironically, the documentary includes a scene of a young Navajo girl clad in a basketball jersey looking at old postcards of her relatives and inquiring of her grandmother, "Did you always put your head in a bun?" and "What did you do for fun?"[14]

Grandma Annie particularly enjoyed this film because a large portion of the dialogue was spoken in the Navajo language. But she was also able to follow along with the parts in English with only minimal translation. (Later, she stated that this was "the first movie I ever understood.") At the conclusion of the documentary, Grandma Annie's comment was simple but fitting: *Nizhoni*, the Navajo word for "beautiful."

However, *Navajo Boy* did not garner unanimous praise. Isabelle objected to the powwow music at the beginning of the documentary because powwows, a ceremony of the Plains Indians, are not culturally indigenous to Navajos. Nate voiced disagreement with scenes of a Yeibechei song and dance not so much because it is a sacred ritual but more because the ceremony is performed only during the winter months and not intended to be shown at any other time. (This viewing took place during the summer.) Regina, who had already seen the documentary at a screening sponsored by Fort Lewis College in Durango, Colorado, expressed mixed feelings. Although she found the reunion deeply touching, she resented the fact that John Wayne Cly was abducted from his family in the first place: "It was the white man who took him away and the white man who brought him back." Meanwhile, the members of the Cly family spent four decades with their lives shattered.

The Lost Child elicited very different reactions. Although the movie depicts a similar scenario—a Navajo baby adopted by Anglos returns to her Navajo roots as an adult—members of the assembled card-playing gathering immediately dismissed it as inauthentic. Scattered throughout the screening were frequent protests of "Those aren't Navajos!" Trisha ridiculed the actor who played Yazzie, the Navajo father, for the way he tied his hair as well as his loosely fitting concha belt. The most vocal scorn, however, was reserved for the characters' persistent mispronunciation of common Navajo words. They would repeatedly say "Dee-NAY" instead of "Din-EH"—the name Navajos traditionally call themselves. The actors even pronounced the more mainstream tribal moniker as "NAH-vah-ho" when no self-respecting "NAY-veh-ho" would verbalize it that way. Similarly, the characters kept referring to the Navajo girl's puberty ceremony as a "keynalda" when it is supposed to be enunciated "ki-na-al-DAH."

The assemblage also took issue with the movie's "corny" New Age dialogue, from Rebecca's sappy testimonial, "I don't know why I walk the path I walk, I only know I have to" to Aunt Mary's melancholy proclamation that Rebecca's biological mother's "spirit returned to the Great Creator." None of the Navajos in the room talk in these aphorisms or know of any other Navajos who speak in such a manner. When Rebecca's daughter begins attending the reservation school, her classmates tease the blonde-haired girl by calling her "cornhead." The gathering suddenly erupted in laughter, as they had never before heard such an insult. For the rest of the evening as well as for the next several days, the members who were present at this screening would teasingly call one another "cornhead" (or "corny" for short).

Although *The Lost Child* thus played to a steady soundtrack of mocking laughter, none of the onlookers appeared angry or offended by the inaccurate representation of their culture. Rather, it seems as if they have all become immune to these mass-mediated stereotypical portrayals. The Hallmark special is just more of the same standard fare. Whether Indians are depicted as cold-blooded murderers in the old westerns or as noble victims in newer films such as *Dances with Wolves* (1990), none of these misrepresentations are taken personally. Whenever I ask members of the Benally family why they react to these films in such a detached manner, they give me the same answer: "It's so stupid." In other words, they seem to be saying, why get hot and bothered over something so trivial that you have no control over anyway? Parenthetically, such dismissive apathy also applies to their attitudes about the Native American sports mascot controversy.

It likewise makes no difference if Native Americans are the ones controlling media representations of Native Americans. My Navajo informants were as equally oblivious to *Smoke Signals* (1998) and *Skins* (2002) as they were to *Black Robe* (1992) and *Thunderheart* (1992). Although

Skinwalkers (2002),[15] for example, is a film about Navajo medicine men directed by Chris Eyre (Cheyenne/Arapaho) and starring Indian actors and actresses in all of the primary roles, none of these individuals are *Navajos*—and their tribal ignorance is clear from the onset.

The recruited Navajo spectators disagreed with the basic premise of the film: since medicine men are the only ones with the power to repel the witchcraft caused by skinwalkers, they have no reason to fear them as the movie shows. Their criticisms of the film ranged from the anecdotal (for example, Jim Chee's "non-Navajo" wood-chopping technique) to the more factual (for example, again, the mispronunciation of Navajo words).[16] Yet none of these discrepancies seemed to prevent them from enjoying the movie. The Navajo viewers did not nitpick about these details, much less act offended by the inaccuracies. In fact, they seemed surprised and even somewhat grateful that their culture was even portrayed on film at all. It is important to remember that Navajos have not experienced too many cinematic moments of seeing a familiar landscape or hearing their language (albeit not enunciated correctly). As the saying goes, beggars can't be choosers.[17]

This does not mean that the Navajo viewers in my study did not challenge the rights of both Anglos and non-Navajos to undertake such films. In varying degrees, they displayed an awareness of the wider historical contexts that problematize the filmmakers' narrower points of view. But, as my reception studies have confirmed, the viewers' criteria for production evaluation are not the same as those for enjoyment. The reported reactions of viewers suggest a window into what criteria are most salient for their enjoyment, engagement, and evaluation, as well as what factors contribute to the point of view that they express.

In conclusion, reception is never a matter of passive acceptance but always a process of creative adaptation and unintended consequences. Meanings constantly shift and are subject to multiple interpretations. It is in this process of negotiation that different, alternative, and even oppositional readings are possible. John Fiske has argued that media texts contain an "excess" of meaning within them. Like a jigsaw puzzle with too many pieces, media contain the raw materials for multiple interpretations. Although many of the components of a television program, according to Fiske, will fit together into one relatively consistent interpretation that is likely to be the dominant interpretation, lots of bits and pieces around the edges of the program do not quite fit, and the dominant interpretation cannot completely contain them.[18] Thus, media texts are structured in such a way that they facilitate, and perhaps even encourage, viewers to "read against the grain."

Since their inception, every form of mass media has become an easy and convenient target on which to blame society's ills. As is always the case, cultural change results from numerous factors instead of a single one. Rather than causing the breakdown of Native traditions, I found that media consumption provides an expanded frame of reference by introducing Navajos to peoples, places, and things they would likely never see or know otherwise. Indeed, mass media present viewers with the imaginative resources to envision virtually infinite possible lives.

But different audiences receive media messages in different ways. The majority of Anglo viewers are usually able to contextualize—or compartmentalize—what they are viewing based on their past experiences. So while they may be enthralled with images of the luxurious lifestyles depicted in *Desperate Housewives*, for example, they also know that suburban life is rarely so extravagant. The key difference, however, for the Navajo viewers in my study is that they lack such a competing frame of reference. Most members of the Benally family have limited firsthand knowledge about life outside the reservation. The media serve as their primary, if not only, means of learning about the outside world. Viewers are drawn to the screen for more than just the entertainment value—it presents them with a rare opportunity to compare their own lives with the televised images of foreigners. Analyzing the differences gives them new perspectives not only about other cultures but, more important, about their own way of life.

My findings might therefore be interpreted as a glimpse of film as a mode of cultural exchange in a period of rapid social change. Viewing these images transformed not only their perception of the outside world but the ways in which they perceive themselves and their positioning vis-à-vis the dominant society. Watching their cinematic counterparts provided these real-life Navajos with a clearer understanding of how they are seen through the eyes of the mainstream population, thereby expanding their frame of reference for what it means to be "Navajo."

Notes

1. Surprisingly, at least the *idea* for reception studies of "Native" audiences is not new. Half a century ago, Anthony R. Michaels wrote: "The time may be

approaching when social anthropologists may have to devote some attention to the cinema-going habits of certain native populations, if all aspects of culture are to be considered in fieldwork." Cited in *Research Films in Biology, Anthropology, Psychology and Medicine* (New York: Academic, 1955), 231.

2. Debra Spitulnik, "Anthropology and Mass Media," *Annual Review of Anthropology* 22 (1993): 293. In the intervening years since Spitulnik's lamentation, anthropology has decisively thrown its hat into the field of media studies, as evidenced by the recent publication of Faye D. Ginsburg, Lila Abu-Lughod, and Brian Larkin, eds., *Media Worlds: Anthropology on New Terrain* (Berkeley: University of California Press, 2002.) The volume is a collection of essays addressing current research in the emergent subfield. The editors of *Media Worlds* underscore the importance of an ethnographic analysis of media in their introduction: "We now recognize the sociocultural significance of film, television, video, and radio as part of everyday lives in nearly every part of the world, and we bring distinctive theoretical concerns and methodologies to our studies of these phenomena" (1).

3. Bronislaw Malinowski, *Argonauts of the Western Pacific* (New York: E. P. Dutton, 1922), 25.

4. Harriet D. Lyons, "Television in Contemporary Urban Life: Benin City, Nigeria," *Visual Anthropology* 3.1 (1990): 422.

5. Dan Rose, *Living the Ethnographic Life* (Newbury Park, CA: Sage, 1990), 1.

6. Robert Aibel, "Communication, Cognitive Maps and Interpretive Strategies: Filmmakers and Anthropologists Interpret Films Made by Navajo and Anglos" (master's thesis, Annenberg School for Communications, University of Pennsylvania, 1976), 48, 27.

7. Sol Worth and John Adair, *Through Navajo Eyes: An Exploration in Film Communication and Anthropology* (Bloomington: Indiana University Press, 1972), 130.

8. Located in the heart of Philadelphia, Temple University boasts an extremely racially diverse student body. However, this class was taught at the Ambler campus, which is predominantly white.

9. All names have been changed to protect the informants' identities.

10. Readings included a chapter from Clyde Kluckhohn and Dorothea Leighton's *The Navaho* (Cambridge, MA: Harvard University Press, 1951); Jay Ruby's "Speaking for, Speaking about, Speaking with, or Speaking alongside—An Anthropological and Documentary Dilemma," *Visual Anthropology Review* 7.2 (1991): 50–67; Kirin Narayan's "How 'Native' Is a Native Anthropologist?" *American Anthropologist* 95 (1993): 671–86; and Richard Chalfen's "Navajo Filmmaking Revisited: Problematic Interactions," in *Native North American Interaction Patterns*, ed. Regna Darnell and Michael K. Foster (Quebec: Canadian Museum of Civilization, 1988), 168–85.

11. For teaching purposes, these two films constitute ideal companion

pieces. They share many similar scenes, including the adoptees not feeling fully accepted by their adoptive families, references to feeling like "something is missing," finding their biological family through extraordinary circumstances, fears that they will not be accepted by their new family, an emotional reunion, and the lost birds "feeling whole" for the first time.

12. As Jeff Zucker, president of NBC Entertainment, has recently conceded: "All made-for-TV movies based on fact have some fiction in them" (Howard Rosenberg, "History Rewritten to Make Us Feel Good," *Los Angeles Times*, June 30, 2003, E1, E4).

13. This is humorously displayed in a scene in *Navajo Boy* when Anglo teenagers from Missouri visit a souvenir shop on the reservation and inform the Navajo shopkeeper: "We're studying the Indians because we just got finished reading *Bury My Heart at Wounded Knee*." These girls think they understand Navajo/Indian culture because they read a book or watched a movie.

14. This is an example of the flip side of the common argument that visual records taken by outsiders are documents of colonization. Sometimes, as in the case of the postcards, these are the only remaining visual records to give testimony to the past. Hopi filmmaker Victor Masayesva explains his debt of gratitude to photographer Edward Curtis: "I wouldn't know my grandfather if not for photography, because I never met him and I saw him in [a photograph of] a Snake Dance. So that's how I've met him" (Fatimah Tobing Rony, *The Third Eye: Race, Cinema, and Ethnographic Spectacle* [Durham, NC: Duke University Press, 1996]). Similarly, the National Inuit Brotherhood of Canada highly recommends Robert Flaherty's *Nanook of the North* (1922) because the organization believes the quasi-documentary "excited great pride in the strength and dignity of [the Inuits'] ancestors and they want to share this with their elders and their children" (Harald E. L. Prins, "American Indians and the Ethnocinematic Complex: From Native Participation to Production Control," in *Eyes across the Water*, ed. Robert M. Boonzajer Flaes [Amsterdam: Het Sinhuis, 1989] , 80–89). In a remarkable display of prescience, Edmund Carpenter predicted that Indigenes would one day learn about their own history through such "exploitative" films (*Oh, What a Blow That Phantom Gave Me!* [New York: Holt, Rinehart, and Winston, 1973]).

15. The film is adapted from the Tony Hillerman novel of the same title, which is part of a long-running series about the adventures of Navajo tribal officers Jim Chee and Joe Leaphorn. For those who do not know, a skinwalker is a Navajo witch who is capable of causing great injury or even death to unsuspecting victims. According to what I have been told by my informants, skinwalkers are medicine men who have chosen to use their considerable knowledge and powers for causing evil. A person becomes a skinwalker by committing an unspeakable act such as incest or murdering a family member. Skinwalkers are believed to have supernatural powers, such as the ability to take the form of an upright wolf and travel far distances in a short period of time. They get their name from wearing the skins of wolves or coyotes.

16. Perhaps what the Navajo viewers found most unbelievable was the purported claim that Joe Leaphorn did not know the meaning of *bilagaana*, the Navajo word for "Anglo." Every Navajo, no matter how assimilated or urban, knows this particular word—especially somebody who lives and works on the reservation.

17. Similar feelings were expressed about *Windtalkers* (2002), a feature film about the role of the Navajo Code Talkers during World War II. Although Navajo moviegoers who eagerly anticipated the movie's release were disappointed by the many inaccuracies, they were happy just to have this story told at all. Ironically, it was the film critics who were the most incensed by the Navajos receiving the short end of the cinematic stick.

18. John Fiske, "Television: Polysemy and Popularity," *Critical Studies in Mass Communication* 3 (1986): 398, 404.

The Dirt Roads of Consciousness

Teaching and Producing Videos with an Indigenous Purpose

Beverly Singer

I have a favorite ceramic sugar bowl, handmade in New Mexico, that I bought at an upscale garage sale on Santa Fe's eastside. For over twenty years it has been a keeper; I love it. The colors and design reflect my life—an abstract desert landscape with pale blue skies and hues of gold and brown with a swathe of green. It reminds me of the northern Rio Grande valley and the foothills near my village of Santa Clara Pueblo, located east of the Jemez Mountains. At the time I purchased the vessel, my future hung in the clouds as I agonized over how to support my life on earth with part-time teaching and nothing substantial on the horizon. I was living in a mobile home on a tract of land my father had willed to me at the pueblo. But the substance of what I wanted to do was precarious. "Enough," I said aloud to myself upon returning to my mobile home with that sugar vessel. That prompted an immediate shift in my thinking.

I let go of worry and broke through a paralysis of fear and longing, of wanting to create and produce films. Having spent two years in film school, I needed contact with other filmmakers and instinctively knew where this could happen. Remembering the scenario, my decision took hold and circumstances changed soon thereafter. Within four months I had moved to New York City to begin connecting with others also in search of creating truth through films, art, and conversation.

It was the stories I heard while growing up at Santa Clara Pueblo that inspired me to make films and to become a teacher. The stories were about different places in the surrounding community where certain events happened, about individuals who were good hunters or potters, and about others who experienced life in profoundly subtle ways. One particular story that I retell is how my life intersected with Hollywood during the summer of 1969. With paid permission, Warner Brothers Studio executives chose to make a movie by setting up their filming location in my community. They had purchased the rights to the book *Nobody Loves a Drunken Indian*, written by non-Indian writer Ruth Bebe Hill, and opted to make an "Indian film" about a group of Indians who liked to booze it up. While out on one of their adventures, they set out to organize an "Indian protest" led by now-deceased actor Anthony Quinn in the title role of Flapping Eagle, after which *Flap*, as the film was released in 1970, was named.

Many of us from the pueblo took to visiting the film set of *Flap* each day that summer. One day about a week into the middle of the filming, an inebriated older man from our community, whom I will call "Mud," crossed the barricade onto the set and stood below the crane where the director was perched. Mud was wearing a breechcloth and had painted his bare chest with mud; he wore a leather headband with a turkey feather shoved askew in the band. I'm not stretching the story either by adding that he carried an authentic Pueblo bow and arrow. Getting the director's attention, he lifted his arm with the bow and arrow and announced, "I'm here to be in the movies. Make me a star."

I was stunned at the ridiculousness of his appearance but, though I recall everyone present kind of laughed, he was reflecting our own Hollywood-obsessed behavior. The experience taught me the lesson of discernment, and of guilt about being in awe of Hollywood. The opportunity to work on the film created jealousy for those chosen as film extras. Mud however, was the reality—an Indigenous rebel, albeit drunk—about whom the film studio, with its imitation story and title character, wasted its money. The movie closed in theaters very soon after its release. Being an impressionable preadolescent, I was struck with the Hollywood production; it was literally a five-minute walk to the film set from my parent's home. In fact, my entire community was starstruck, and many wanted to be cast as a movie extra. But my star was the film director, who sat on a crane wearing a classic beret and used a megaphone to call "Action!" for the filming to begin.

I began filmmaking studies in the early 1980s. By this time, selected government-sponsored programs offered American Indians the opportunity to learn and participate in video documentation initiatives to collect oral histories of elders and record Indigenous languages. After the Occupation of Alcatraz Island by the group of Indians of All Tribes from November 1969 to June 1971, the years following witnessed a watershed of Indigenous activism, an impetus that included a filmmaking movement among Indigenous peoples that brings us to the present moment. Based within my experience of that period as a college student, I recognized teaching as a storytelling art and a skill that incorporates knowledge combined with abilities to help others learn how to think, to carry out an idea, or follow a quest as in research, or to speak and write without fear. With family support and plenty of mistakes, I succeeded in my goal of completing several college degrees and learned how to balance my Pueblo thinking with non-Pueblo expectations. My years of practice as a filmmaker and teacher has been a continual integration of this balance.

I have been a witness to a history of North American Indigenous film and video production that I view today as passing from a first phase of experimenting with ways to convey unmistakably Native voices to a second where, building on that groundwork, some filmmakers are focusing more intensively on emphasizing Native languages and independent narratives. As individual stories were shared through film and video, a kind of recovery and reconnection with a missing link between our ancestral past and our present occurred; each story gave voice and significance to and about Indigenous people.

One example of this, a video I produced in 1994 titled *Hózhó of Native Women*, was shown at the 1995 Sundance Film Festival as part of the Native Vision in Cinema program.[1] The video features Indigenous women organizers talking about individual and community wellness at a Phoenix conference attended by two thousand Indigenous women. Cecelia Fire Thunder from the Pine Ridge Reservation in South Dakota presented the keynote address. She is not only the first woman to have been elected president of the Oglala Sioux Tribe, but also the first to be impeached by the Oglala Tribal Council. She was impeached in 2006 for her declared intent to create a Planned Parenthood clinic at Pine Ridge Reservation in response to legislation passed by the state of South Dakota virtually banning all in-state abortions. Fire Thunder remained steadfast in her belief that American Indian reservations are sovereign territory within the United States, as promised by the federal government. She said Indian reservations should be subject not to state laws but to their own sovereign laws. When the Oglala Tribal Council impeached Fire Thunder, they also issued a ban on all abortions on tribal land.

A decade earlier, in the video I produced, Fire Thunder says (in her keynote) that in spite of the violence, suffering, and grief experienced by our people, we are still proud to be "Indian." She also said that it is our responsibility as Indigenous people to help each other to heal and to act like real Indians again—to be good to one another. Her call to "be good to one another" is a reminder of the fractured history of reservation systems, broken promises, and failed federal policies that led to the 1973 American Indian Movement standoff in her homelands at Wounded Knee, South Dakota, with the FBI and the U.S. military in an attempt to call attention to the history of broken treaties and further expose corrupt tribal leadership, which produced a climate of mistrust and fear, particularly among tribal peoples in South Dakota.

Between 1986 and 2000 I happened to have been in the right place at the right time with access to a group of filmmakers such as Randy Redroad (Cherokee), Harriett Skye (Lakota), Dean Bear Claw (Crow), and Chris Eyre (Cheyenne/Arapaho) walking the streets and riding the subways of New York City with me during the fourteen years I lived there. Bear Claw, Eyre, and Skye were enrolled at New York University. One afternoon after a presentation at NYU, Dean and I walked along Sixth Avenue (also known as Avenue of the Americas) talking about Indigenous languages. He said, "Crow believe words in themselves have meaning, and when we speak Crow, we are responsible for those words—they follow us." This principle of words following us is applicable to any language and is a profound teaching that brings speaker and listener into a relationship based on trust, that sense of knowing you are with someone whom you can know intimately. In relationship to the significance of a film or video documentarian's role as a patient listener, one is able to cultivate and capture the speaker's words that will follow them. Most uniquely, this principle also applies to the language of filmmaking as an ethical consideration.

Thinking back to when I began making films, my early works show a lot of talking heads because I was listening to their stories as I filmed the speakers. As a rule, Indigenous people never explained themselves in films, were never allowed to go on and on about what they thought on camera: how they felt, what they wanted, what they saw, what they would change or hold on to if given the opportunity. Entertainment filmmakers do not have time for "deep listening" or breadth and depth of thought. This deep listening, or filmic pause, exemplifies (demonstrates) an Indigenous sense of time, and perhaps space. It does not fit the linear movie template concerned with moving the plot forward to the end of the story, just as the opening sequence is about harnessing attention from the first frame. Indigenous stories are generally not linear.

Teaching from a Native Film Perspective

I begin my story above by acknowledging America's "Indians" in commercial movies where we still find Indians normally presented as aggressive/hostile people who, as a body politic, are seen as infidels impeding national economic development and social progress. In particular, classic western movies upheld European and American colonization dispossessing Indigenous peoples of their lands and resources. "Indians" in feature movies were looked upon as a construct in the minds of filmmakers whose view of Indians represented political expediency intended to keep Indians controlled by the military and regarded as social illiterates. The following retrospective regards my use of films and videos produced over a twenty-year period by Indigenous film and video makers finding their voices while working from community-based perspectives.

I have been teaching at the University of New Mexico (UNM) for nine years, teaching in anthropology and Native American studies. My undergraduate course offerings for the Department of Anthropology include a course titled Indigenous Peoples of North America and another called Culture Study of Indigenous Video. For these courses, I draw from the well of films and videos produced by Indigenous film and video makers who signify their Aboriginal or Indigenous identity. I believe that Indigenous-produced works need to be used in university settings to sophisticate the conversation about concerns and questions that directly affect Indigenous peoples' lives physically, emotionally, intellectually, artistically, spiritually, theoretically, and politically. What follows are my thoughts on some of the Indigenous films I teach, what I see as their importance in the classroom, and how they relate to the courses and students I teach.

Métis filmmaker Loretta Todd's *Hands of History* (1994), directed for the National Film Board of Canada in 1994, highlights the artistic achievements of Joane Cardinal Schubert, Doreen Jensen, Jane Ash Poitras, and Rena Point Bolton. Todd focuses on nuances in each artist's work, their inspiration reservoir and artistic achievements. She also explores how First Nations art is relevant to all aspects of Native cultural life in comparison with standard European art history approaches that—in particular—obscured women's art. I also recommend her film *Kainayssini Imanistaisiwa: The People Go On* (2003).

Apache/Diné filmmaker Dustin Craig's video, *I Belong to This* (2003), a shorter-length work produced for a PBS series called *Matters of Race*, is both a self-portrait and a representation of those of a younger Indigenous generation who hail from federally defined reservation communities as inheritors of change and who traverse reservation boundaries. Craig identifies himself as White Mountain Apache and Navajo. His wife, Velma, is Navajo. They have three children and a fourth on the way. The work presents varying contemporary Indigenous moments on the White Mountain Apache Reservation in Arizona as Craig transitions from his life in the city of Phoenix and returns home to visit his parents. He questions his own politics of identity, an "Indian" identity that is abated under government policy and laws impacting all Indian tribes, including his own White Mountain Apache Reservation. He and Velma take part in community ceremonial practices that his parents want him to emulate. On camera, they share their feelings of independence in being able to make their own decisions about their children and the extent to which they will participate in White Mountain Apache community life and ceremonial practices. In my lectures, I tell students to look beyond the identities imposed through government-defined blood quantum and explore the messiness of Indigenous identity Dustin Craig's story presents. There are no categories that fit any Indigenous society, nation, or community. But for bureaucratic infrastructures like political organization and health and education services, being classified by a title functions as though it implies entitlement, when actually it undermines and erases the meaning of being human.

Students and the public at large may wonder, Why offer a degree in Native American studies? In large measure, the Western academic canon does not regard Indigenous histories or peoples as significant; much is ignored or not considered relevant and, as reexamination demonstrates, deficient research was a frequent outcome with regard to studying "Indians" with no benefit for the people. Given the brief time I have with students enrolled in university studies, it is critically important for me to avoid rehearsing the model of criminality and victimization seen in traditional academic narratives about Indigenous peoples. There, "Indians" always occupy the background, or are positioned at the margin of "society." Instead, I privilege the complexities of Indigenous history, voices, and stories. In contrast, I am able to use films made by Indigenous peoples to move beyond the status quo narrative of colonial rhetoric and theory.

For example, a documentary such as *On and Off the Res' with Charlie Hill* (2000), by Makah filmmaker Sandy Osawa, can have a secondary effect in teaching from an Indigenous-based perspective. Osawa's films are intrinsically political, and in this portrait of the Oneida comedian Charlie Hill, we become his audience. His humor is lucidly spiked with overt commentary directed at the American imagination and ignorant views of "Indians." Hill extends himself outside the comfort zone for "good Indians" when he says that he will start respecting America or the U.S.A.—which he calls "Europe Junior"—when the government acknowledges its history of broken treaties and promises to Native people and treats its women as equal citizens. Student reactions to Charlie Hill differ depending on several factors. Especially when most of the class is non-Native, they tend to share the view that Hill's humor is reverse racist commentary. This is where staying power as a scholar is critically useful in making connections between everyday language we speak and know in uncharged contexts versus charged popular language that victimizes. When students (or anyone) respond with racial finger pointing, they are not ready to explore possibilities outside their own safe public postures. As a teacher, I encourage them to identify their own stories, to make an intervention into their own personal experiences and what they've been taught about life in America, and to explore a change of positioning. Sandy Osawa's film moves beyond being a film about Charlie Hill and is an opportunity for challenging our perceptions.

With respect to being a professional comedian or a filmmaker, these are unlikely professional aspirations for Indigenous people because they compel us to behave contrary to family and communal expectations that we should succeed in business, law, or medicine. To a large extent, filmmaking and comedy are not conventional choices but self-determined pursuits. Questions arise from inside and outside one's own community about what we do. Indigenous peoples have become accustomed to outsiders looking at us, but when we look at ourselves, the same surface assumptions exist in Indigenous societies. From a community perspective, this work has to do with breaking traditional silences. More to the point, film practices bypass older forms of Indigenous knowledge and philosophy passed down through oral storytelling practices intended to protect meaning. Although I also consider older storytelling practices as having been silenced by business, law, and medicine—just as these professions supplanted Indigenous subsistence agriculture, hunting, and gathering practices, turned Indigenous lands into property and ownership deals, and introduced foreign medicine, bringing sickness and disease models into our systems that affected not only our bodies but our way of thinking about life. Why, then, can't films be a way to go back, look at ourselves and identify the old ways that have weight, depth, and truth, and to counter the contamination in our life today? That kind of filmmaking takes skillful crafting; that's what each film opportunity allows you to do, to process your story. Celine Parreñas Shimizu (UC–Santa Barbara) writes about Asian American visual exploitation in films and suggests that in spite of a confusing bombardment of stereotypes that affect who you can imagine yourself to be, they can be resisted.[2]

Smoke Signals (1998) is one of the few commercial films I showed to one class many years ago. As an independent feature film, it functions like a Native American demonstration project, since no other film directed by, written by, and featuring an entire Native American cast has since been produced in the United States and distributed to theaters worldwide. I recall when, eleven years ago, Miramax Films purchased its distribution rights and began Chris Eyre's film-directing career. Sherman Alexie, whose success as an author had already established his visibility, wrote the screenplay. Not since *Smoke Signals* has another Native American film made it to the Cineplex. The most recent independent film, *Frozen River* (2008), released by Sony Pictures, features Heather Rae as a producer. Heather, a Cherokee, began her career at the Sundance Institute. From 1995 to 2001, during the time *Smoke Signals* was in production, supported by Sundance, she was director of the institute's Native American program.

At the time of the film's release, the class discussion centered on the truth of the character portrayals—particularly Thomas Builds-the-Fire, portrayed by Evan Adams, who is Coast Salish. In the film, his role as storyteller seemed disconnected to people in the community, but strangely, Thomas's meek and nerdy or "innocent" nature seemed to resonate with film viewers. The story was an amalgamation of plots and scenes applicable to any small community where death, grief, and bereavement happen, but with particular scenes—such as one where Tantoo Cardinal saves the feast by halving the fry bread in the air to feed everyone—that served as deft segue. As mentioned, *Smoke Signals* launched a Native American film career for Chris Eyre, who established himself as a director; his work includes the PBS series *We Shall Remain* (2009). Sherman Alexie already had a major literary career. He went on to direct his own independent film, *The Business of Fancydancing* (2002), with limited distribution by Outsider Pictures. In my view, Alexie's film was a truer-to-life, community-based story on an emotionally raw gay subject.

Isuma is the first Inuit-owned production company, founded in 1990 by Inuit Zacarias Kunuk and non-Inuit film producer Norman Cohn, who together coproduced *Atanarjuat: The Fast Runner,* which won multiple international awards, including the Cannes Film Festival's Golden Camera Award in 2002. *Isuma* is a word from the Inuktitut language meaning "to think." Based in Igloolik, Nunavut, the company's goal is to produce community-based media that preserve and enhance Inuit culture and language, using film production as a means of economic development in Igloolik and Nunavut. Telling authentic Inuit stories to Inuit and non-Inuit audiences worldwide is the cornerstone of Isuma's enterprise. Isuma has produced over twenty documentaries since becoming an independent production house and is in production on a fourth feature-length narrative film. Such continuity of purpose and determination to focus on one's own community and build a repertoire of films demonstrate authentic achievement.

A dynamic feature of Aboriginal film and video produced in Canada is a reflection of using art to negotiate politics. Recent productions pointedly take their cue from explorations to emphasize Indigenous language recovery and memory of ancestral linguistics. Editor and now film director Kevin Lee Burton is Swampy Cree from Canada. Although I have not used it in the classroom yet, his recent video *Nikamowin* (2007; Song) anticipates the energy currently circulating around the Indigenous languages movement, to relearn or revitalize respect for speaking, writing, and protecting Indigenous ancestral authority in our own words. *Nikamowin* can be previewed on MySpace, where it is tagged as "Aboriginal," "Cree," "experimental," "Indigenous," "language," and "Native."[3] Sans quotation marks, Burton describes his work as a linguistic soundscape comprised of the deconstruction and reconstruction of Cree narration dances with various manipulated landscapes. This audiovisual experiment begs questions of how languages exist, emerge, and survive.

Finding My Talk: A Journey into Aboriginal Languages (2000) is a seminal documentary by Paul M. Rickard—also Cree—who produced it with two non-Cree, George Hargrave and Janice Benthin, for the Aboriginal Peoples Television Network in cooperation with Rickard's own production company Achimist Films and Nutaaq Media, Inc. Rickard's video is about his Cree-language roots and contains interviews with Indigenous peoples working to revive and preserve First Nations languages in Canada.

Horse You See (2007, eight minutes), directed by Melissa A. Henry, a Navajo from Gallup, New Mexico, has her own company, Red Ant Productions, and uses the Navajo language in this short video. It takes the unique perspective of Ross, an actual Navajo horse, who transmits his own precise essence to audiences entirely through a Navajo perspective of subjectivity and self-definition as a living being. I asked Henry to present *Horse You See* at the America Studies Association Conference in Albuquerque in November 2008. Following the screening, the audience, mostly academics, seemed filled with surprise, but had few comments about the production. Clearly they knew what they had seen and heard, but were unable to find a familiar comparison—the most logical connection was an attempt to relate Ross to the television series *Mr. Ed.* The series was about the eponymous Mr. Ed, a talking horse who shared his secret with architect Wilbur Post. The syndicated comedy aired from January 5, 1961, until September 4, 1966. Henry was born well after that television program ended and grew up on the Navajo reservation without access to television.[4]

I also work with students to create film. In my Video Research Methods class students are given access to a digital video camera and computer editing equipment in a hands-on learning environment. While the goal is to produce a short video of anthropological interest, my objective is to get students to organize their project as a story that demonstrates not only a skill but shared learning in working with whomever their subjects are. One memorable video was a true collaborative effort on the part of Nicole Kellett, a PhD student in anthropology, who worked with the Sacred Alliance for Grassroots Equality (SAGE Council). The SAGE Council is a people-of-color-led organization committed to social change and self-determination based in spiritually centered movement that honors Mother Earth and all peoples. Kellett documented the SAGE Council's 2002–3 work to protect the Petroglyph National Monument, threatened by the construction of two major freeways. The freeways would fast-track an enormous amount of change on the far west side of Albuquerque, where unplanned development and sprawl would inadvertently disenfranchise people part of the local community—namely, people of color. The SAGE Council used this video in its campaign to raise community awareness beyond the city of Albuquerque and traveled with it to gain support.

To a separate end, during the summer of 2006, I offered a two-week session, Native Americans in Film. Of eleven students, only two were not from Indigenous communities. I worked with the class to produce a documentary about the Native American Studies program at the University of New Mexico. The video is titled *Season of Transformation: Decolonizing Education at the University of New Mexico* and highlights the discourse of decolonizing methodologies that promote self-determined education, community-based research as taught within the program at UNM. The video can be viewed online at www.unm.edu/~nasifo/stories.html.

In summing up my overview of the use of film and video as a teaching method, I am thinking of new songs for old stories shared by Indigenous peoples. I question the documentary recordings made by explorers, missionaries, patrol officers, and early historians and anthropologists and ask why they are still revered as evidence supporting prevailing views of us. The new songs I hear are a metaphor for telling actual stories in our own languages, expressing and communicating our own identities as we walk the dirt roads of consciousness in being comfortable with cameras as well as in our ceremonies.

Notes

1. Among the other films shown in the Native Vision in Cinema program were *Real Indian*, by Malinda Maynor (Lumbee); *Forgotten Warriors*, by Loretta Todd (Métis/Cree); *The Gift*, by Gary Farmer (Cayuga), filmmaker and actor from the Six Nations in Canada; *A Nation Coming*, by Kent Monkman (Cree) in collaboration with choreographer Michael Greyeyes, also Cree from Canada; and *Usual and Accustomed Places*, by Sandy Osawa (Makah). In 1992, the Native Vision in Cinema was programmed separately by the Sundance Film Festival. By July 2004, the Sundance Institute's Native American program coordinator Bird Runningwater, a member of the Mescalero Apache Nation, announced that Native American films would be integrated with other festival selections, rather than being confined to a separate section. This decision suggests that Native American films were attaining a level of achievement on par with any other film accepted at Sundance.

2. I reference Professor Parreñas Shimizu's work here only as it relates to ways in which Native filmmakers have resisted being stereotyped, but for full

discussion of her analysis of Asian American visual images in films, see Celine Parreñas Shimizu, *The Hypersexuality of Race* (Chapel Hill: Duke University Press, 2007).

3. http://vids.myspace.com/index.cfm?fuseaction=vids.individual&VideoID -24488426; *Nikamowin* is distributed by www.vtape.org (accessed August 13, 2008).

4. As part of a new project about a recent generation of indigenous film and video makers, I have begun a series of interviews that include one with Henry, who discusses her childhood influences in detail. I interviewed her on January 24, 2009, at the University of New Mexico bookstore café.

Section Three

Conversations with Filmmakers

Introduction to Section Three

Everyone loves a great story: to be included in other people's stories, to imagine oneself as part of their world. Learning is never more engaging then when peoples' stories lift you out of the classroom or theoretical realm and into the heart of their reality. Section 3 offers us the opportunity to immerse ourselves in filmmakers' stories. Here we elevate the volume and strength of the personal voices reflected in the previous sections. Five interviews highlight the individual philosophies, perspectives, personal stories, and voices of six filmmakers. Many of the theoretical questions posed in section 1 and the elements of these filmmakers' work analyzed in section 2 are answered, made more complicated, or challenged completely by the filmmakers themselves. In this concluding section of *Native Americans on Film,* the theoretical and analytical are reframed by the practical and the personal.

The personal aspect of this section is fostered through connections based on family, friendship, and colleague relationships between the interviewers and the filmmakers. These relationships allow for a level of insight into the filmmakers' personal lenses—what drives them, inspires them, and frames their worldview on film. Our diverse group of filmmakers—Sterlin Harjo, Blackhorse Lowe, Shelley Niro, Sandy Osawa, Randy Redroad, and Mona Smith—illustrates a range of aesthetic influences, purpose in storytelling, and genres of filmmaking: documentary, narrative, and video. The love of media as a mode of storytelling and artistic form characterizes both the interviewers and the filmmakers. Our authors—Joanna Hearne and Zack Shlachter, Jennifer Machiorlatti, M. Elise Marubbio, Saza Osawa, and Elizabeth Weatherford—represent a variety of disciplines ranging across the fields of academia, filmmaking, and law; but all have in common a deep respect for Native film.

The interviews provide a snapshot of Native film history across three generations as the filmmakers talk about their connection to community, their inspiration for films and who inspired them, and their beginnings in film production. The filmmakers bring to the table aspects of what it is to be a filmmaker and/or a Native filmmaker. In some cases this means emphasizing community needs, in others it is the celebration of storytelling, and in some it is the political act of reframing stereotypes. Sandy Osawa and Mona Smith ground their works in Native community needs. For Smith, this has taken on a very localized meaning in terms of projects that promote health, wellness, and history in Minnesota; most recently she has focused on "Dakota subject and Dakota-controlled media." In Osawa's work, community is also pan-tribal, with shared issues such as land and treaty rights central concerns. Shelley Niro, Sterlin Harjo, Blackhorse Lowe, and Randy Redroad shape narrative shorts and feature-length films from personal stories, poems, events, and regional locations near to their hearts. As Joanna Hearne and Zack Shlachter's introduction to their interview with Sterlin Harjo and Blackhorse Lowe points out, this approach emphasizes characters who are "ordinary people 'who just happen to be Native American.'" All create characters or represent Native Americans who refuse to be confined by Hollywood stereotypes: for example, a mixed-heritage hemophiliac (*The Doe Boy*); a "mature female detective . . . who runs the reserve café/cabaret" (*Honey Moccasin*); young lovers and "families in transition" (*5th World* and *Four Sheets to the Wind*); a jazz musician (*Pepper's Pow Wow*), and a woman with HIV (*Her Giveaway*). These strategies work to overtly and subtly reorient mainstream ways of thinking about Indigenous people and Indigenous film.

Taking shape across the interviews is an image of the complexity of politics woven into Native identity and its connection to the act of filmmaking. Issues of representation and voice, frameworks and models for empowerment through film and media, and the politics of defining what is Native film surface in various concrete and illusive forms throughout the section. Once again questions come to the fore, with answers as divergent as the categorizations for Indigenous films on Houston Wood's Indigenous film continuum (section 1) about the role of Native film; about the politics of identity and self-definition as a Native filmmaker; about the parameters of Native film sovereignty; and whether or not these are issues of the same magnitude today as they were in the past. However, at the core, each of our filmmakers seems to agree that representing Native people must be done differently than what Hollywood has offered us.

Across the interviews and of paramount importance to counteracting Hollywood representations or mainstream media hegemony are issues that include: paying homage to important cultural/sacred landmarks in tribally specific narratives, providing insider perspectives on Native characters' lives and stories, developing contemporary Native characters, highlighting the strong role of Native women in community, acknowledging and respecting the influence of both non-Native and Native filmmakers on one's craft, and a love-hate relationship with the term *Native filmmaker.*

This ambiguity toward the term exemplifies the multifaceted reality of being Indigenous and a filmmaker in the twenty-first century. If one chooses to work within one's community, "Native filmmaker" excludes one's tribal identity, homogenizing it into a pan-tribal Native one. The term may, however, facilitate working across tribal communities on a pan-Indian or pan-Indigenous level and reflects recognition of global Indigenous sovereignty. For those filmmakers working in feature-film circles, the term can represent a growing contingent of supportive colleagues whose experiences reflect one's own, such as the difficulty of breaking into mainstream Hollywood and distribution circles. For others who also work within the mainstream media arena, "Native filmmaker" elicits a host of questions about intent and reductionist labels. Randy Redroad, whose work crosses many of these areas, suggests that the filmmaker must ask, "Does he or she want Spiderman to be an Indian? Or to be the Indian director that makes *Spiderman*?" The question may then become: Is it always the film industry that creates the boundaries involved in being a filmmaker who is also Native?

The question posed above has everything to do with personal choice, but it also speaks to the issues of Indigenous film sovereignty. Michelle Rahcja's chapter in section 1 introduced the concept of visual sovereignty as a "creative act of self-representation that has the potential to both undermine stereotypes of Indigenous peoples and to strengthen the 'intellectual health' of communities in the wake of genocide and colonialism" (quoting Robert Allen Warrior). Randolph Lewis, in his seminal work on Alanis Obomsawin, similarly presents the idea of the cinema of sovereignty, which embeds "authority, autonomy, and accountability in the representational process" in the hands of Indigenous communities and filmmakers.[1] Thus, an important aspect of reclaiming media representation is about controlling the point of view of the story, the stories that are told, to whom they are told, and how they are told. A number of our filmmakers express this political act of reclaiming and challenging national public memory through their narratives. According to Mona Smith, "Listening to Dakota people is an extremely radical act"; for her, the documenting of voices silenced by the mainstream takes on great cultural weight and significance. Similarly Sandy Osawa's documentaries spotlight those whose artistic or political actions have been overshadowed by non-Native interests and intend to "take dead aim at the stereotypes that have frozen our lives in the past and made us irrelevant in the present and future." Shelley Niro's narrative films aim to flip the stereotypes, refocusing the cinematic gaze to that of a sovereign gaze—one that empowers Native subjects, provides sensitive representations of women and gays, and elevates Native epistemology. Such acts of talking back result in the forceful repositioning of Native media as center. Randy Redroad reminds us in his interview, however, that the problem with talking back is that you confine yourself within the paradigm: "We aren't imagining ourselves outside it." To move forward you must imagine yourself outside it. These filmmakers clearly also embody the ability to do so.

Note

1. Randolph Lewis, *Alanis Obomsawin: The Vision of a Native Filmmaker* (Lincoln: University of Nebraska Press, 2006), 180.

"Pockets Full of Stories"

An Interview with Sterlin Harjo and Blackhorse Lowe

JOANNA HEARNE AND ZACK SHLACHTER

Sterlin Harjo (Seminole/Creek) and Blackhorse Lowe (Navajo) are part of a dynamic new generation of filmmakers who have bypassed Hollywood in order to make low-budget portraits of families in their home communities. Unlike the self-conscious, direct engagement with media stereotypes that characterized films like *Smoke Signals* (Eyre, 1998), Harjo and Lowe tell stories about ordinary people "who just happen to be Native American." They describe their films as "regional" and "personal," but their cinematic influences are also global and historical, from French New Wave and American independent filmmakers (Jean-Luc Godard, John Cassavetes, Terrence Malick) to contemporary Japanese and eastern European filmmakers (Katsuhito Ishii and Emir Kusturica). This fluid engagement with both far-flung avant-garde film movements and the particularities of Native languages and homelands informs the films' stories about Native young people leaving and returning home.

Blackhorse Lowe's first feature film, *5th World* (2005), screened at the Sundance Film Festival and other festivals internationally (including the National Museum of the American Indian's First Nations/First Features Festival). He has also directed short films in English and Navajo; his newest short film, *Shimásání*, screened at the April 2009 Tribeca Film Festival in New York. Sterlin Harjo premiered both of his feature films, *Four Sheets to the Wind* (2007) and *Barking Water* (2009), at the Sundance Film Festival, where lead actress Tamara Podemski (Salteaux) won the Special Jury Award for Acting for her role as Miri Smallhill in *Four Sheets to the Wind*. His short film *Goodnight, Irene* (2005) also screened at Sundance and received Special Jury Recognition at the Aspen Shortsfest. In 2006 Harjo was selected as a United States Artists fellow and won the Creative Promise Award from Tribeca All Access; in 2004 he was among the first group of Sundance Institute Annenberg Fellows. Both Harjo and Lowe received Media Arts fellowships from Renew Media, and both have participated in symposia and other events at the National Museum of the

American Indian film festivals and screenings. They have each combined formal training (Harjo at the University of Oklahoma's Film and Video Studies Program, Lowe at Scottsdale Community College) with festival-based support structures like the Sundance Institute, but their most important schooling has come from hands-on experience with their own feature-film projects. Making films locally also enabled Harjo and Lowe to combine professional actors and crew with nonactors—often family members and friends. Their ambivalence toward labels like "Native filmmaker" shows us the ways that Native cinema is a heterogeneous rather than a unified category, one that means different things to different people—a critical construction, a set of institutional and festival structures, and a community of individual artists.

Four Sheets to the Wind and *5th World* are love stories about young people leaving and returning home. They are films about families in transition, about generations moving between languages and between big cities and rural reservations. In both films, central scenes of traditional community life—a Creek funeral service in *Four Sheets to the Wind* and a Navajo family gathering and sheep butchering in *5th World*—communicate visually and narratively the warmth as well as the limitations that come with close ties to a tightly knit community. Finally, both films are love songs to particular places, and powerfully foreground parental storytelling to frame young protagonists' relationships to homelands in specifically familial terms.

Four Sheets to the Wind raises and dispatches two of the most pervasive cinematic stereotypes about Indians in its first scene—the "vanishing" Indian and the New Age spiritual Indian—with an image of a young man (Cufe Smallhill, played by Cody Lightning, Cree) dragging a dead body (Frankie Smallhill, played by Richard Ray Whiteman, Euchee/Creek) across a dirt road, while a voice-over narrator tells a story about Rabbit and Bear in the Muscogee language. That Frankie Smallhill also turns out to be the film's narrator underscores the dynamics of silence, speaking, and listening in the relationships between restless young adults and a bilingual, boarding-school-educated older generation. The film focuses on Cufe, a young man coping with his father's suicide and his desire to explore the world beyond his small-town home by visiting his troubled sister Miri in the city of Tulsa. Strong character acting by performers such as Jeri Arredondo (Mescalero Apache) and Jon Proudstar (Yaqui) amplify the playful humor in the script's portraits of small-town social relations, which Harjo renders with beautiful economy and affection. Much of the action is also centered on (equally humorous) hipster foibles in trendy spots around Tulsa. The film's rural locations—fishing ponds, open pastures, and isolated houses—invite us to fall in love with Oklahoma's verdant landscapes, and Cufe Smallhill's movement between these worlds asks us to recognize the allure of both urban cosmopolitanism and quiet country communities.

5th World follows young lovers Andrei (Sheldon Silentwalker, Navajo) and Aria (Livandrea Knoki, Navajo) as they hitchhike from Phoenix, Arizona, across the Navajo reservation toward Shiprock to visit family. Their teasing and affectionate relationship develops both from their immersion in popular culture and film and from their background in the Native American Church (they share childhood stories about peyote meetings at one point). Made with an incredibly small budget (about $20,000), *5th World*'s experimental strategies provoke strong reactions from audiences. The story structure, editing, and sound are nonlinear and fragmentary. Lowe makes extensive use of long shots, long takes, and pans and tilts across the desert landscape and Arizona sky. This contemplative pace, accompanied by a soundtrack that includes Lowe's own relatives telling stories about traditional Navajo courtship, as well as original music by Corey Alison, is interrupted and punctuated by montage sequences that give the film the feel of old home movies. At the center of the narrative is the tension between traditional and contemporary ways of falling in love, and Lowe's inspired use of his parents' storytelling as a framing and interwoven soundscape combines the conventions of voice-over with flash-forward to lend Andrei and Aria's story both historical depth and emotional immediacy. The discussions between Andrei and Aria about love, cultural heritage, and pop culture veer from the serious to the romantic and hilarious, and their occasionally meandering dialogue reflects Lowe's penchant for improvisation and the film's hyperrealistic feel. Stunning landscape shots link the film to the work of directors such as Andrei Tarkovsky, though Lowe also used these sequences in a practical way to qualify the film as feature length. Much of his approach is formed on the set, and he says the tricks he employs aren't anything he could have ever learned at film school—for example, smacking one of his lead actors in order for the right feeling of anger to come across in a scene. Like Harjo's,

Lowe's work is featured at top independent and Indigenous festivals internationally, but finding a life for the films outside of that circuit has proven difficult.

The following interview was conducted in March 2009 at the University of Missouri's KBIA radio station studios (we edited the interview for both length and readability). The filmmakers discuss aspects of their feature films as well as production financing and film distribution, their cinematic influences, their work with Native actors, their mentoring through the Sundance Institute film and writing labs, and their views on the relationship between Indigenous and mainstream cinemas. They also articulate some of the challenges independent filmmakers face in financing and distributing films on Native subjects. Currently, most articles and interviews with Sterlin Harjo and Blackhorse Lowe come from Internet publications and newspaper sources. We hope to provide a resource for students and scholars that will facilitate our collective close attention to these innovative writer/directors who are just beginning their careers. Their originality of vision, stylistic experimentalism, and regional filmmaking in a global context promise us good viewing for a long time to come.

Joanna Hearne: Sterlin, I want to invite you to tell the story of how you came to make *Four Sheets to the Wind*.

Sterlin Harjo: The first idea that I had was the opening scene: you see a dirt road and a young man dragging a dead body across the screen. What was interesting to me was that opening scene and then trying to piece together what led us to that point. Mainly I wanted to write about where I was from. When I first started writing the script, I was living in New York. I don't know if it was nostalgia for home, but New York was a really good place to write a movie about Oklahoma. A lot of it was wanting to—without making it cheesy—show different aspects of life where I come from. The further I get away from *Four Sheets to the Wind*, the more I realize that it's pretty personal. I went from a small town and I went to the University of Oklahoma, which isn't a metropolitan city by any means, but it's a bigger town, it's a college town. I was exposed to music and all these things and got in with a group of friends who were into books and reading and music. It was just kind of like culture shock, and so I think *Four Sheets* is about that experience, from when I was young and just leaving home.

The narration is done by the father, who is dead in the first scene, and you find out at the end of the film that he narrated the movie and he's been telling you this story. People have done that before—*Sunset Boulevard*—and I just think it was a cool tool to use a dead person as a way to tell the story. And it's also in another language. Throughout the whole film people talk about the character of the father being really quiet—the irony of it is that at the end of the film, you realize this quiet person has told you this whole story. And that came from—I remember I was at this church, it was a Christian church, but it was a Creek Christian church and it was at a funeral. And the Creek Christian churches are usually out in the woods, out in the country, and there was this guy there that I knew for a long time and he was a preacher but I never knew him as a preacher, I just knew him as a person. And I knew him as a really timid, kind of quiet person. He's an older man. I saw him outside and he was talking to people that were English-speakers, and he was still very timid and quiet and not very sure of himself. And then we all went inside the church for the funeral and during the funeral he preached, but he preached in the Muscogee language, which is the Seminole-Creek language, and all of the sudden he became alive and he was really animated and loud and confident and talked a lot. So I realized he wasn't a timid person, he was just more comfortable speaking in his first language. That was the idea behind the father narrating the story.

So I wrote the script and the biggest thing that happened for me was I got into the Sundance Writers Lab and Directors Lab. And it was like a workshop—it's a yearlong process, but really it's just a month and two weeks. You work with professional writers and creative people and you hang out and talk about your work. And you also shoot scenes and you're just encouraged to take chances, things that you wouldn't normally do when there's a lot of money riding on it and you're actually shooting film. I made a short film called *Goodnight, Irene* because I didn't want to make a feature film right out of the gate. That showed at festivals and was pretty successful, and then I got the funding for *Four Sheets to the Wind*—pretty easily, actually, but it was a very low-budget film. I just made another film called *Barking Water* and the two films were made very differently. *Four Sheets to the Wind* was my first film. I was working with a Los Angeles producer, and so he wanted to make a film the way a lot of Hollywood films get made. There was a big crew and we had a schedule. Which is a great way to work under certain conditions, but it's just not one way I like to work. And so when I made my next film, I really did the opposite—I worked with a small crew, we could change things if we wanted to, we could improvise.

JH: How much was it made for?

SH: I made *Four Sheets to the Wind* for $200,000. That is not a lot of money if you have a big crew and you're doing this big machine of a thing. People make short films for that much, so it was really difficult and we shot in eighteen days. You have all these ideas of how a scene is going to look and what shots you're going to use, but when you only have eighteen days, a lot of that goes out of the window and you just have to hold the camera still and shoot one take. But it was also a good experience because you had to find ways to be creative within that schedule.

JH: What did you feel like you were learning?

SH: I think the biggest thing I learned making *Four Sheets to the Wind* was to have confidence in choices that I make and in myself, because it was my first film and I was really nervous and listening to too many people. But when I did go for it on *Four Sheets to the Wind,* things felt better and things turned out better. And that was mainly in a schedule sense, how rigid we were. Working with the actors in *Four Sheets to the Wind* was really rewarding because we worked really close together, and for one of them to get an award for their performance was pretty great. It was like me and the actors were really like a family. On my next feature film, *Barking Water,* it was just having confidence, because there's not a dragon that's going to jump out at you and eat you at the end of the shoot. It was a learning experience in the sense that physically and emotionally you're exhausted by the end of it. So that was just the biggest thing, was like pacing yourself and learning how to deal with the schedule and spread yourself out for that amount of time.

Zack Shlachter: How did you get into filmmaking?

SH: Growing up, I just loved movies. My dad and I would watch films a lot—and [my parents] never told me I couldn't watch an R-rated film. We watched war movies together, we watched everything. Also when I was a kid, I would always listen to people, older people, talk, and I was always the one that would ask older people to retell stories that I had already heard. It wasn't the story that I wanted, it was how they told it. I think that helped a lot with telling stories, just seeing how the different ways people tell stories—sometimes they lie and sometimes they stretch the truth or sometimes they leave things out. I just grew up loving telling stories, but the main thing I wanted to do was be a painter. I never had a backup plan—I always wanted to be an artist. Then when I went to the University of Oklahoma, I was enrolled in the painting school and three films came out—*American Beauty*, *Good Will Hunting*, and *Smoke Signals*—none of which are my favorite films by any means, but I watched them at the same time. One thing they have in common, they're really personal and a couple of them are regional. It just got me thinking, "Maybe I could do that, I could write scripts about where I'm from." Before that I'd started writing scripts but they were copying people, like trying to do the next *Usual Suspects*.

So that's when I started writing screenplays and then I sent my first completed script to the head of the Film and Video Studies Program at the University of Oklahoma, Dr. Andrew Horton, and he liked the script enough that he encouraged me to take Intro to Film and Video Studies. So I took that class and it was with a teacher named Misha Nedeljkovich and he just had really good taste in films, some of the first films that he was showing us—I think I saw *Stranger than Paradise, Dead Man*, some John Cassavetes films, and French New Wave. I really fell in love with that side of it—movies that do things that I didn't think you could do with film. That's when I changed my major. And then I just started watching as many things that I could watch and found what I liked best.

ZS: Blackhorse, could you talk a little about your experience?

Blackhorse Lowe: My parents are pretty much the same way as Sterlin's parents: if it came in the house, everyone watched it. My first experience was watching *Blue Velvet* at age six or five and seeing Dennis Hopper on top of Isabella Rossellini and screaming, "Mommy!"—and asking my mom, "What the heck is this movie about?" And she's like, "Oh, you'll understand one day." She didn't really worry that it was warping my brain or anything—I would grow into it and understand all these darker things about the human brain and the soul. So I'm just like, "Alright." Watching *Road Warrior* and then *The Exorcist* and *The Man Who Saw Tomorrow*—it was like, "Oh, cool, the world's gonna blow up." Having all this access to all these different movies and coming from a family of cinephiles who would watch *The Good, the Bad, and the Ugly*, *The Wild Bunch*, and *Sophie's Choice*, that was always in my childhood. But my big thing, like Sterlin, was painting and drawing and doing photography. When I first went to college, that was what I was primarily going for. Until I got a media job, and that's where, "Oh, you like movies, right?"—"Yeah"—"Well, here's a digital camera, here's Final Cut Pro, here's Adobe Premiere. Teach us how to use this stuff." It really put the hook in me that I could come away with something that had more energy and vitality than painting ever did. In terms of actually communicating an idea or telling a story, film did it very quickly, so it was just very immediate in that way. So that's what I dug about it and once I started making those short films and teaching myself about lighting, how to use the camera, reading various screenplays, I started going on my own and just creating my own little movies. Most of them were just really short and personal and going specifically from stories that I heard from my grandmother and my grandfather about someone being arranged to be married back in the '30s—and the family was given ten sheep and a deer hide and the bride ran away. And they spent like a whole day trying to look for her, so they could drag her back to get married. So that was the basis of one of the very first short films I made, called *Happy Boy*, which was shot on video, all primarily in the Navajo language, trying to do a 1930s movie with $500, a crew of three people, and a digital video camera. But we were still able to make it and do an original soundtrack. Once we got that made, it was just like, "Oh, cool, you don't have to go to Hollywood, you don't have to go to a school in order to actually make something."

So that was where I began from and from there kept making short films, a lot of really bad ones. But it's all just a learning process and I'm just consistently trying to learn from as much as possible, from doing a movie with $10 and a couple friends and actually doing the short film I just shot recently with $45,000, having a crew of twenty to thirty people—people from New York and LA with various professional expertise, and me just writing the story. After doing that in New Mexico for a while, I went to Phoenix, to Scottsdale Community College, where they had a film studies program. But I never excelled at any of the classes, I was more interested in the making and not so much the teaching because a good portion of the teachers there were former Hollywood people who were very resentful of their past experiences and then being booted out of LA. So all you got was—three-structure story act, and just really trying to press their ideas of what a film should be. And from that, it became like, "Oh, I don't need that—I just want the tools, I just want to learn how to make my vision and make my story." And the beautiful thing about that is that it was a $50 deposit to use any gear that you wanted, from sound to 16-millimeter cameras, and at the time they had a local postproduction house where you could take a hundred feet of film, give them $50, they'd process for you and put it on tape and just watch it and cut something together. So that was just my experience of just like doing it as opposed to seeking actual proper education from a film school or anything like that, and a lot of my thinking is just try it and fail, just keep learning and keep going forward and see what I could pull from it.

JH: How did you come up with the idea for *5th World*?

BL: Previous to *5th World*, I'd done a short film called *Shush*, which had shown at Sundance in 2004 and a couple other festivals, and I was doing the festival circuit at that time and also working in Phoenix and just traveling a lot during the downtimes. I was really listening to a lot of Sea and Cake, and Ugly Casanova's album had just come out then, so when I was going to different festivals I was driving a good portion of the time. I'd come off a relationship. I just took all those things and fused them all together. It was like, "Well, I haven't seen a good love story in a while." I really wanted something soft and naturalistic that kind of just flowed—about love. I wanted to test myself and see what I could do with that subject matter. So that became a forty-five-page screenplay, and we went back to the original investors of *Shush* and we showed them, like, "We've got this small script, it's purely an experiment, we could make it for $20,000." And they were like, "Oh, okay, here's a check—good luck!" So, you know, twelve days, a two-man crew and two actors—we just took to the roads of Arizona and New Mexico and shot it along the way, pretty much in order of how the script is written, because everything is geographically laid out, how the scene develops and grows as you go throughout the film. Luckily we got into Sundance in 2005 under the American spectrum, and once we found that out we really tried to make it as best work as possible—which is really funny because we never really had the forethought to think about advertising or the business aspect of that movie. "Let's just make the movie to make the movie"—and to test ourselves and get it out there. Totally unexpectedly, people liked it—or hated it enough—either way, it got screened at different places. It still draws interest. But now with experiences I've had, I want more money, I want a more professional, slicker look. If I make something, I really want it to have this certain level of professionalism to it.

JH: How did you choose the specific locations?

BL: When I was writing it, at the time I was living in Phoenix. I'm originally from northwest New Mexico, this small town called Farmington, and there's a highway that goes from Flagstaff through Kayenta and into Farmington. So I would always go along that way on the weekends either for ceremonies or just to go visit family when I had some off time, and I was always really taken away by the landscape through there—Monument Valley, Elephant's Feet, all these really cool landscapes—and a lot of it really tied into the creation stories, how we believe our holy people came out of all these different experiences, but also a lot of tragedies and all these other things back in the day. And also at the time I was really heavily into Terrence Malick—*Badlands* and *Days of Heaven* and [*The*] *Thin Red Line*, which was just landscape and very naturalistic—and Andrei Tarkovsky, with these really long, beautiful shots of people in landscape. The landscape told you the story as opposed to the people, or there was a combination of both. So I was really interested in that—and with the story we had written and with the budget that we had, it was the only way we could really get away with making a feature film.

JH: What are some of the most important locations?

BL: I think once you get into the New Mexico portion toward the end, there's Shiprock. In terms of the mythology or the belief the Navajo people have in those certain locales, holy people originated from that area and there are all those stories about monster birds and the hero twins that went and saved the Navajo people from enslavement by other beings or animals. I tried to at least pay reference to it in some way. That, and it just looked pretty, too.

JH: You were telling your actors to mention certain films at certain times, and I thought of [*The*] *Grapes of Wrath*. We've been talking about [François] Truffaut and French New Wave and we've been talking about Terrence Malick. What about John Ford?

BL: They do talk about Monument Valley and all the films that were shot there. *Black Cloud*. Well, it was one thing for me to just like openly trash other Native films in my movie and make fun of them, but at the same time, too, pay reference to that landscape, the many other movies that were shot there. You always hear, "The first Native blah blah blah"—

SH: "First Native that made a Native film with Native parents."

BL: You're always "the first." The thing about that portion was I wanted to pay reference to all the movies that were shot in that area—*2001*, *The Searchers*, *Grapes of Wrath*. The whole movie is cinephiles referencing other movies and other pop references and music and everything else. With John Ford, I like his movies—beyond his very narrow vision of what Native Americans were, but that was like the '40s and '50s, so it's not like I'm going to bad-mouth him. They're still really solid movies. Those movies were made then, these are the movies we're trying to make now out of this area, trying to make it our own again and just cinematically own it.

JH: How did you decide to frame the beginning of the film, with your parents' storytelling as a sound flash-forward over the images?

BL: Well, my dad just tells everything, every experience he's ever had from growing up in boarding school to being in rodeo to being an artist and just all these different things. And my mom, her one story is meeting my dad and falling in love. And then he's always just like, "What? I don't remember that." And then they get mad at one another 'cause they don't remember certain details. One story I would always hear at peyote meetings was how they met. He first saw her when he was ten years old at a traditional ceremony; the next time he saw her was at a high school basketball game; the next time he saw her after that was at college on campus. That's where the foundation of the movie kind of began—just that story. But the opening of the movie, in terms of how it was made, that wasn't planned—it didn't come to be until like a week before we had to actually give it to Sundance so they could screen it. Because at the time I was working with different types of openings, some more heavily dependent on Navajo creation stories and talking about coming into the *5th World* and what that represented—and kind of being didactic to a certain degree. And when I was working with my mom and dad, I heard that one sequence about her just talking about remembering my dad—and I had the images of their wedding and everything. So as soon as I put those two together, they just meshed—and all of the sudden I just had a bit more of an emotional pull and punch right at the beginning and led you into this story. And it was just really good to show how I think Navajo love stories are contemporary and what it was like in the past. It was very traditionally oriented, and now people don't ask who their clans are or where the people come from or anything like that. It's just very immediate, as opposed to my parents—and I don't know if it's just them trying to teach us something—but they were a lot more respectful of one another and really wanted to understand, "Who are your people? Where are you from? Are you related to me, and, if you are related to me"—not to give away anything in the movie—"I can't have anything to do with you."

ZS: That's a big issue in the film, and it seems to matter a lot more to the men, both to John, who has the "Tale of Injun Woe," and to the main character, Andrei. In both of those situations, the women are either indifferent or a bit perplexed by it. Perhaps Aria for a different reason, she doesn't really come from that background.

BL: I guess it really depends on how you were brought up. Navajos are sort of diverse. You can have Mormon, Christian, Baptist, atheist, Scientologist—whatever—but also very traditionalist Navajo who also blend beliefs in Christianity. The male characters, and the family, were very traditional. How does that clash with people who weren't brought up with that? And when it came to clans, to a certain degree it's my experience of going out with Navajo girls and then finding out a couple of weeks later I'm related to them by some sort of clan. This very attractive woman turns out to be your sister or your cousin or something—it's just like, "Oh, man." And me being brought up traditionally, it's just a giant no-no. But I just loved the traditional past and the present of thinking in new ways and showing them clashing against one another.

ZS: Both *Four Sheets to the Wind* and *5th World* draw upon a lot of different influences from your upbringing in your home communities—what's been the reaction there?

SH: People back home, in my community, respond really well. I was at our ceremony, a stomp dance, last summer, and a lady was like, "You know, I really liked that film—you made that?" And I was like, "Yeah." And she was like, "Yeah, I liked everything but the ending." One of the funniest things is I've met so many Creek and Seminole people back home that tell me that they really liked the movie, but their family will burn copies and pass it around. So, it's sort of like this Creek-Seminole, Oklahoma, Indian hit—that they burn and pirate for each other. So it's really cool that they're burning these DVDs and passing them out and stuff.

I have sort of a love-hate relationship with the whole "Native filmmaker" thing. Sometimes I'm like, "I hate this—what is this? What are you talking about?" But at the same time, I learn to be proud of it. What really made me proud of it is just meeting people like Blackhorse and Taika Waititi from New Zealand and all these other Indigenous filmmakers. We're all sort of rooting each other on, and it feels like you're a part of something. And a lot of us are regional filmmakers. I couldn't imagine myself going to LA and trying to make movies, it would just be gross—it's not why I want to do it. After being broke for a good three months or something, you're like, "What am I doing here in Oklahoma, editing promotional videos and training videos and trying to make a living and then making these low-budget movies on the side?" But then you go back and you read interviews with Truffaut or Godard or whatever, and there used to be this type of filmmaking that was really respected, that was lifting a finger to Hollywood and the standards of the blockbuster movie industry. I don't want to make huge-budget films right now—you know, I will hopefully. I mean, I would make *Watchmen 2* or whatever.

BL: I'll make 3.

SH: I've had final cut on all my films, I've had complete control over everything, and I get to make films in Oklahoma, and do them the way I want to. No one's telling me what to do differently. That's what's exciting about it.

BL: Actually, when we did screen [*5th World*], I think [the community members] were more baffled than anything, just because the stylistic quality of it and the influences it came from—Malick, Tarkovsky, [Stan] Brakhage. Most Navajos are like most of the American public—all they watch is commercial cinema. Unless they live in a major city or are artistic, they wouldn't watch foreign films or anything like that. So when they saw the movie, they were just like, "What the hell is going on?" And a lot of them just want to see the same old Native movie of this one proud person sharing their experiences and these spiritual matters and whatnot—

SH: Making flutes.

BL: Eff the flute. But yeah, when we did show there, other than college students at [the University of New Mexico] who saw it, maybe two or three appreciate it for what we were trying to do, but most of them were kind of, "So what?" And it's a very specific movie, too—it's not like I made it with the idea of pleasing all audiences or trying to think about one segment of the population. No, it was just my own need to make something at that time and do that story, so a lot of people were just baffled by it. It's very much my personality up there on the screen and my personality doesn't really mesh that well with most other Navajos, so they didn't really take to it that well. One filmmaker from Canada, Shane Belcourt, was like, "Oh, that was the movie that made me want to go make my movie." So in a small way, that was really cool—that your movie influenced somebody else to go make a movie.

SH: Well, *5th World* was done on such a low budget, no one could believe that it was done that cheaply. And one of the craziest things about the whole Native cinema thing is that none of us knew each other—until probably that year at Sundance—

BL: 2005, yeah.

SH: All of the sudden we're surrounded by other like-minded filmmakers who are interested. You know, back home you throw a name like Terrence Malick out in the air and it just falls from the mouth to the ground. It's a hard thing whenever you're like, "Well, I think I'm the only person doing this that I know." And then once we all became friends and started screening our films together at Sundance, it was like, "Wow, there's other people out there." So it became a community.

BL: That's the part of the label of Native filmmaker I'm proud of—Taika Waititi, Sterlin Harjo, Lisa Jackson, and all these people. But if it wasn't for them, I would hate being labeled "Native filmmaker." Because when I began it's like, "Oh, 'Native filmmaker'—what's a Native filmmaker?" Then I started watching the movies and was like, "My God, they're fucking horrible!" I mean, most of them are just these didactic pieces about our struggle and historical trauma, which never really applied to my existence—or the cinema I was interested in at all.

SH: And whenever I talk about Native cinema, that's really where I pick up—when I met these guys. The films before that, I can't even stomach most of them. Even *Smoke Signals* I wasn't a big fan of.

BL: I hate it.

JH: I was going to ask about *Smoke Signals.*

SH: When it first came out, I remember feeling really good. "Oh, there's Indians onscreen!" But then after that, once I got into films and I started to want to make them, I didn't like it very much. It was cool to go to Sundance and I started meeting all these filmmakers, where there were experimental films being made and it didn't feel like I was watching a film that had its audience in mind. The only reason I say "Native cinema" is because there's nothing else to really call it, except there's a bunch of Indigenous people making films and all of the sudden it's like something new is happening. And we have a lot fresher stories. Right now, it feels like Hollywood is scrambling for stories. We have our pockets full of stories we can tell. The other side of it, too, is that we're influenced by all these filmmakers. I keep going back to French New Wave—it's probably just because I just read Godard's interviews yesterday—but if you think of how they were so influenced by American cinema, a lot of the classic filmmakers, and they incorporated that into their own style and their sensibilities. We could do that, or we can make films that don't have a Native person in them at all. When I first wanted to be a filmmaker and an artist, I didn't ever say, "I want to be a Native filmmaker"—I just wanted to make film.

JH: When I first watched *Four Sheets to the Wind,* I saw Cody Lightning getting into the father's pickup truck—all grown up. It seemed like a conversation with *Smoke Signals.*

SH: Well, it is about a father-son relationship. But it's funny because no one ever realizes that's Little Victor. Because he's grown up, he's got curly hair. But it's funny because whenever I was casting for that role, I remember saying, "I'm not using the usual suspects of Native film—I'm not going to use the *Smoke Signals* actors, I just want to find some new, fresh faces." Somebody kept mentioning Cody Lightning to me. I was like, "Man, he's probably like thirteen, what?" I hadn't seen him since *Smoke Signals*—I thought he was this little kid. Then I actually met him and hung out with him at Sundance, and he had a beard and was grown up. And also he's really funny and really cool. The most common young Native man role is like "Angry Native," that's oppressed by society and has to get revenge and has this chip on his shoulder. And so for all of the auditions for Cufe Smallhill, the main character, that's what they would do: this tough Native guy. At Cody's audition, he was just a regular guy. I was like, "Wow, that's so radical, he's just acting like a regular person." So that's why I cast him. But I think that it's a father-son story and the comparisons should stop there.

BL: Actually, me and [Cody] were thinking of doing a follow-up on Little Victor, twenty years later—still trying to get into festival parties and bars, as that star, but how he is now, which is bearded, long-hair, kinda overweight. "Oh, it's Little Victor!" Little Victor, twenty years later, still trying to live off the glory.

SH: You should call Little Victor "L-I-L Victor."

BL: He moonlights as a rapper.

ZS: You have both said that you don't anticipate working with Hollywood. You would like to have a big budget, but the kinds of films you make, both in terms of the style and also, for better or worse, the characters in your films, aren't the kinds you see in Hollywood movies. It's getting cheaper to make films but it's very difficult to get them distributed. How do those things influence the way you are making your movies now?

SH: The new film that I want to make is, by Hollywood standards, a low-budget film. It's hard to get films distributed today. So far, *Barking Water* hasn't sold. The economy's bad and it's a hard movie—it's about two old Indians, on the road. It doesn't necessarily scream the big bucks. Luckily, I've had two financiers on two films that were like, "I just want to make this film." They didn't even want to see a cut of the film. The first time they saw the film was the premiere at Sundance. So I've been really lucky. But it's all been a learning experience of trying to find where I can get those two lines to cross: make films that I want to make with characters that I want to make with sensibilities I want to make, but also make money.

JH: How did you find those mellow financiers?

SH: I have no idea. I just got really lucky.

BL: I've been fortunate with the short film I shot—we were given $30,000 from the New Mexico Film Office. New Mexico is one of the bigger states, along with Louisiana and a couple of other states in the U.S. where a lot of film productions from Hollywood go through—so once that happens, a lot of the money [the states] make from those films, they turn around and give to the local filmmakers. So, I was fortunate enough to actually get a portion of that money to do that short film for $30,000, as well as get a Panavision film package for that and shoot on bigger formats. But that was just one specific case—with everything else, I've just been lucky in finding really cool people who were willing to give me their money and their trust and try to make something out of that, not really think so much about the business end. For right now, how can I make this work financially as well as artistically and try and find some sort of balance? As opposed to just making it and then just being frustrated and poor for two years on the festival circuit.

SH: Yeah! It's time to learn how to make the money also.

BL: So just trying to figure out, "How do I make it fly in the business without being in LA?" Without selling your soul—yet. But I think it's definitely on the horizon sometime. I would definitely not pass up the chance to do a big-budget feature because that would be just one hell of an experience.

ZS: You were saying that self-distribution is something that you're looking into.

BL: I was living up in Boise for a little while [and] I was staying on Heather Rae's couch. She made this movie called *Trudell,* which is a documentary about an American Indian Movement political figure. She had taken a service deal on her documentary, she paid a company to distribute her movie to small college towns and different venues where she knew she could draw an audience and get support. She also had a decision on the marketing of the film, the art of the film, how long she was gonna do the theatrical run, setting up a screening at IFP [Independent Feature Project] in New York, or IFC [Independent Film Center] theater in New York, then paying these people to support her and knowing all these different channels to distribute her movie. After a certain time—I think it was two or three years—she was actually able to make all of her money back that she had put in the movie, pay off a good portion of all of her investors, and then turn a small profit for herself. So that was just like, "Wow." She didn't go the Hollywood route or wait for an offer from some giant distributor, or like a smaller house. She just took it all on her own: "I know how to sell this movie, I know how to do it right." Another friend of mine, named Shonie De La Rosa, did a really low-budget movie—called *Mile Post 398*—with primarily all Navajo characters. It's about an alcoholic and it's not the faces you would usually see in cinema at all. He knew he wasn't going to get big distribution. He was smart about it and was like, "I'm just going to market the hell out of it, do a small theatrical run but all on special reservations and show it there to the community who understands what this movie is about." He was able to take all that good press and do a small DVD release. After that, he got into Blockbuster and Hastings—just regional stuff—but out of that he got it distributed, he got it shown, people knew about it, newspapers picked up on it. People were like, "Oh, *Mile Post 398*, I know that movie." He really knew how to market and sell it himself, by himself, through self-distribution.

SH: Yeah, I mean, *Four Sheets to the Wind* I haven't made a dime off of. It's in Blockbuster and everywhere—I haven't seen any of that. Someone told me, a friend was at a powwow and there was a guy there that had bought probably twenty *Four Sheets* DVDs and was selling them at $40 a pop, making all this money off of it. Man, that's what I want to do.

BL: Self-distribution, that's the way to go for me right now—either the service deal or doing it all yourself. Just from hearing the horror stories from different filmmakers: "Yeah, they took my movie but they butchered it, they recut it, they decided they were going to hold on to it and just not do anything with it at all, and just do a small theatrical run and end up on the Starz channel at midnight," and just really abuse their work and all their time and effort and love poured into this thing for three years. That's basically what it is—it's just all business when it comes to that. And no one's really aggressively looking for what's the latest, newest Native Navajo, Seminole-Creek movie. In terms of massive amounts of people, no one's like, "Ah, I want to see something Indian!" Even I don't!

JH: What was it like to direct your family?

BL: Well, with *5th World* I didn't direct my family—I just let them be. Because once I direct them, they start acting, and once they start acting, it's just really downhill from there. When I was working with my mom and dad on the sequence when Aria and Andrei get picked up by [his] aunt and uncle, when I directed them, it was just like, "Just think of them as my cousin Leonard or Cathy—just think about them like that. That type of relationship, that type of history you have with them. People who are really close to you and you know each other so well. Just act like that. I'm not giving you any lines, you guys just do your thing." But once I actually gave them some sort of—well, I didn't give them full range. "I would like you guys to talk about this and that, which pertains to this particular scene. But also when you work with my actual actors, I want you to lead them in this way, I want you to push the conversation in this way. I want you to somehow organically make the scene happen." Which is why long takes are so good, it just kind of came out, like, "Oh, thank God." But that was with *5th World.* With this short film that I shot—the 1930s period piece, *Shimásání*—my mother plays the grandmother in the movie, a $45,000 movie. I don't have time for being like, "Oh, just let the camera roll and see what happens." No, I need this portion to connect to this portion to connect to this portion, so I really worked my mother after that point. "This is not *5th World,* this is not anything I've done beforehand. I'm gonna be hard on you, I want this emotion at this point and I need it to cut with this here. And I don't have ten takes to do it in. I have to get this shot and then I have to get this shot before the sun goes down." So it was really a different working environment, but she was just so stoked to do it, she was actually reading acting books—which is really funny.

JH: Which ones?

BL: I have no clue. She was like, "I've watched *Rebecca*"—was reading Hitchcock. I was just like, "Wow." Which is a cool thing, but sometimes it becomes annoying because you've grown up with these people. . . . The thing about it is you're this big person on set who's trying to direct everything creatively and just get stuff that you need done, but your mom's still your mom. Good manners go out the door once I have thirty minutes to get two more shots that I absolutely need for the movie. The other good side of working with family is they're very supportive, they're very loving, but it goes both ways. But in terms of watching movies, I think my mom and maybe my sister like my movies, as opposed to my dad, who's like, "Eh, when are you going to do an action movie?" But he enjoys the process. He always ends up in them.

SH: I worked with family—well, I worked with them on *Four Sheets,* too, but with *Barking Water,* they're a huge part of it. It's the same thing. You can't give them exact lines. I worked with 90 percent nonactors in *Barking Water* and you can't give nonactors lines. You have to just say, "I need you to say this." You can give them a line but they'll probably make it sound like they're acting. It's funny because I'm so nervous working with family. We were shooting at my grandma's in *Four Sheets to the Wind.* We were also shooting at my family's house in *Barking Water.* You have crew that's used to tearing places up and it was raining outside and getting mud everywhere, so you're stressed out, you're ruining your parents' house. My dad's always mad that I cut him out.

BL: So is mine.

JH: Were the actors in *5th World* also basically improvising?

BL: No, that was a controlled improv, actually, because before we went into production we had a month of rehearsals, which was just going through character history, background, and also going over what I'd written over and over and over again. Because I knew we were doing long takes, so it was just like A to B, where we have to go in terms of the emotions of this scene and what I'm trying to communicate. So once we got down this is what the scene is and this is what the words . . . "Some of the dialogue I need, but you can add your own flavor to it—but just as long as it sticks to this idea." And they understood that, so once we got out to those locations, since we only had maybe four takes at each place, they knew the material down cold, they knew what they had to communicate, they knew exactly at what line I specifically want them to say or what reference to what movie I want them to make because of those rehearsals. And with twelve days, a certain limited amount of film, and a small, small amount of money, it was just like, "Let's make the errors part of the movie, but make an error within this type of context."

JH: Sterlin, when you say you shot documentary-style, what do you mean? Were you giving the actors general directions?

SH: Yeah, I would give them general directions. We had one boom mic in this scene, for this specific scene. They knew the main characters, my family did. And it was a scene where my aunt was cooking fry bread and they were just supposed to be hanging out. And in the script it just says, "They hang out and talk." But they know the actors and I knew that they would talk and have stuff to talk about. I would give them general directions, like, "Alright, tell a story about this"—because I know all of them, so I could just reference little things. "Alright, tell that story about when you got pulled over by the cop and ran for it." But we had the camera just floating and one boom mic, just sort of picking up dialogue—like a doc.

ZS: Tell us more about it.

SH: *Barking Water* is about this couple that's been in this forty-year on-and-off relationship and the movie starts with the man dying in the hospital, and the lady, Irene, comes back to him one last time. He doesn't want to die in the hospital, he wants to go home and die and to see his daughter, and so she breaks him out of the hospital and the whole movie is about her trying to get him home before he dies. Throughout this road movie—and it's funny, too—you see glimpses of their relationship and what went wrong, I just wanted to tell a relationship story that was truthful, especially about old people. No one ever deals with the older people. My first short film that really got any play was *Goodnight, Irene*—it's about this old woman that's in a hospital, or waiting in the waiting room with these two young guys in an Indian clinic all day. It's just about this old couple, she's trying to get him home; it's just about who they see and what happens. It's Richard Ray Whitman and Casey Camp-Horinek, and one's an activist and one's an artist. They get small bit parts, they play spirits or, like, a warrior in the background, on the horizon, on horseback. It was really just written for them. But I wanted to tell a truthful story. I know a lot of people from my community, and my grandma in particular—they don't want to die in a hospital, they want to go home where they're comfortable. So I wanted to tell the story about that, too.

JH: How did you learn to direct actors?

SH: I don't know, it's just something I've always been good at. It's definitely my strength. With *Barking Water,* it was a pretty big challenge because it was a lot of nonactors—just trying to find that balance. I love working with trained actors and nonactors and having them in scenes together because things come alive. And I really think I can get a decent, believable performance out of anyone. I really love working with actors. I could get you to act. Some actors you have to beat a performance out of them, sometimes you have to trick a performance out of someone, sometimes you just have to leave them alone. Every actor's different. A lot of preproduction—sometimes the beginning of shooting—is deciding what kind of actor they are.

BL: With most of my films I use nonactors and primarily all Navajo, so a lot of them aren't really trained. They've done newspaper ads in Phoenix or Albuquerque, or they've done some short film where they were a background extra. So they have a decent idea of what goes on in a film set, but in terms of acting it's always really difficult. I usually just like to hang around with them a lot, especially if they're Navajo, and find out what their personalities are and see what I can pull from their backgrounds and histories to hopefully use it and put it into the script and find out what exactly they can do or not do.

ZS: A lot of filmmakers have background in photography or art. You guys have experience all over the place and then came to film, but how do think that those have influenced the way you make films?

SH: I think they have—it's like visual art. But it was just like, all of the sudden you find film and it's like, "Wow, I can put all this stuff into that." Because I like music, too—I don't get to put music into my paintings. I listen to music when I paint but I want to put all this stuff together. I love painting; I still paint.

BL: A lot of my movies take notice of things I've learned from painting or just music and creative writing, just blended all together. But for me, it was like a natural progression, to learn about colors and compositions. I didn't really come from literature or classic storytelling. Storytelling for me was my parents telling nonlinear background stories of where they came to be.

SH: I still owe money on a loan that I took out to buy a computer and learn how to edit and make music videos. That's how I started just trying to do it. And so I feel like I'm pretty fortunate to have made my first feature film when I was twenty-four and I still have all this time to learn. That's the coolest thing about it, that it's such a learning process—we just keep getting to explore different ideas and getting better. I don't think I could ever not like one of my friends' films because we know each other's stories so well and we know each other's struggles so well that we know it's such a learning thing. "Oh, Blackhorse wants to make a movie about . . . unicorns . . . alright . . . He's learning something with that. I'm sure it'll be great!"

BL: Now I'm going to put in a unicorn sinking somewhere, it'll be one of the drug trip sequences.

SH: So, that's what's exciting about having a group of friends making films—not in Hollywood. We're all learning.

Wrestling the Greased Pig

An Interview with Randy Redroad

M. Elise Marubbio

I first encountered Randy Redroad's (Cherokee) work at the Museum of the American Indian's Film and Video Center in New York City in late September 2001. The museum sits on the corner of Battery Park at the tip of Manhattan, just blocks from Ground Zero. Army and National Guard, who were camped out in the park and patrolled the area, along with the lingering smell of the destroyed buildings and the debris-polluted air heightened the sense of danger, anxiety, and surrealism of the moment. As I viewed his early award-winning short films—*Haircuts Hurt* (1992) and *High Horse* (1994)—the reality of this particular moment in time and the still-fresh images, smells, and memories of 9/11 continually refocused my interpretation. What on initial watching appeared as gentle vignettes of various characters' lives in the city—a haircut, fishing, working as a bike messenger, an encounter with a kinsman—filtered through the lens of reality outside the museum's doors, resurfacing as complex narratives about the residual effects of acts of terrorism on Native peoples: removal, forced assimilation, racism. The poignancy of the filmic and temporal moment remains etched in my psyche.

Randy Redroad's savvy ability to weave quiet stories of everyday people with layers of political and social commentary continues to mark his more recent work. Films like *The Doe Boy* (2001) expand on issues of identity and identity crisis, while *133 Skyway* (2006) chronicles the effects of homelessness, poverty, and alcohol on a talented musician, played by Derek Miller. This short film's visceral reflection of urban homelessness, survival, and friendship, like *The Doe Boy*, also imbeds elements of Native worldview in subtle and untranslated filmic moments offering textual readings to a variety of Native and non-Native audiences. It is, perhaps, this ability to bridge communities of viewers with stories that resist the grandiose and embrace the quotidian that most clearly highlights the power of his work.

A world traveler who has shown his work globally and to a diversity of audiences, Randy Redroad embodies the complexity that is the Native American and Indigenous cinema movement. Resistant of terms such as *Native filmmaker* and Native or *Indigenous aesthetic*, which he finds confining and often obfuscatory when applied academically, he sees himself as one of the "architects of an emerging cinema and part of a relatively small family of makers who, more often than not, support each other." He has no qualms taking on academic intellectuals, forcing them to expand their ideas and concepts of what is Indigenous or Native American film, reminding them how absurd it is at this point in Indigenous cinema's incubation process to perform a "C-section" in an attempt to find an Indigenous aesthetic, encouraging them to see the amazing differences within a filmmaker's body of work and across regions, continents, and communities of Indigenous film.

A self-proclaimed collaborator, cowriter, and writer for hire, he embraces the eclectic and various possibilities offered by ever-expanding film industries, moving easily across genres that include Canadian television—*Moccasin Flats* (2003), the "first all-Native produced television series in North America"; documentary—his work with Heather Rae and Russell Friedenberg on *Out of the Blue: A Film about Life and Football* (2007) and *Family: The First Circle* (2009); comedy—*Ibid* (2008); drama—*The Doe Boy*; and narrative shorts—*133 Skyway*, *Haircuts Hurt*, and *High Horse*. Redroad's films have won awards and critical praise around the world, including the Sundance NHK International Filmmakers Award and a nomination for the Independent Film Producers/Gotham Open Palm Award for Outstanding Directorial Debut. His honors also include a Rockefeller Fellowship (1994).

In 2008 Randy Redroad came to Minneapolis to participate in a collaborative program between Independent Film Producers Minnesota (IFP) and my project—the Augsburg Native American Film Series (ANAFS). I screened Randy's film *133 Skyway* and chaired a panel for IFP's Director's Conference that included Redroad, Georgina Lightning, and Christine Walker.[1] A lively debate emerged during our group discussion around the term *Native American filmmaker* and the confines of such a term. Randy and I continued our conversations over the next year when he returned to Minneapolis in November 2008 to host the ANAFS screenings of his films *The Doe Boy* and *133 Skyway* and to participate in another IFP event in June 2009. The following written interview, which took place over the summer of 2009, stems from our discussions.

Elise Marubbio: Randy, your early works—*Haircuts Hurt* and *High Horse*—were filmed in New York City in the early 1990s and to me recall the history of assimilation of Native peoples through their themes as well as their sense of ennui and cultural confusion. Could you tell me more about what inspired these first films and what your intent was with each?

Randy Redroad: Both films deal with fractured identity and are kindred aesthetically and in terms of what they meant to me at that particular time in my life.

High Horse is about Indians who don't know how to be Indians—the kind of Indians Vine Deloria called "ethnic Indians," meaning there is no cultural base. The character I play learns his language from a cassette tape. He measures his face against an old photo of Red Cloud, to whom he bears no resemblance and suffers by comparison. He lives in a tent in an East Village apartment. He is in exile.

The film presents identity as perpetually nascent. That's what an identity crisis is: a transient fog. You have no footing. You are rendered a voyeur, an actor in your own life. Someone is going to see through and expose you. Like a nonsmoker trying to smoke. He looks silly and a real smoker knows it. It's a psychologically tortured way to live. This was very personal to me. I am a cross-legged academic sports freak who barely got out of high school. A half-Cherokee redneck with an Afro. I'm allergic to horses. I don't fit. I'm sensitized differently. I'm not enrolled, so I'm not an Indian. I'm a half-breed, so I'm not an Indian. I didn't grow up on the rez, so I'm not an Indian. If I take the Indian test, I fail. Who wins? The "real" Indians? No. The colonizers? Probably. Because if I'm not an Indian, there is one less Indian and that is the point of extermination. Now what?

Of course, I filtered all of these personal feelings through a certain historical lens particular to Manhattan and endeavored to stretch the themes beyond Indians by including the African American characters. In retrospect, I think I stretched the canvas too far.

Haircuts Hurt gives a cultural context to what is an iconic moment in many kids' lives: the First Haircut. That part is not an "Indian" thing, but the rest is. The film was inspired by the experience of an Apache family in Texas, who happened to be friends of my mother. Their son was kicked out of elementary school for wearing his hair traditionally long. There was a lawsuit, a nasty fight, and every imaginable expression of racist intolerance. Eventually, the school challenged the identity of the parents. One of them wasn't enrolled. If the school board could establish that one parent wasn't a "real Indian," they could dispense with the claim that the son's long hair had cultural/spiritual value. He would just be obstreperous, a hippie. They were trying to wipe him out. One less Indian. The family eventually moved away to spare their son any more pain. So I reduced that story to allegory.

High Horse and *Haircuts Hurt* offer solutions to identity crises within superficial Native aesthetics that I now realize are powerless without cultural provenance. There is no wholeness to be found in the casual adoption of aesthetics. It's a cloak that has no lining. Can you catch an Indian girl with a flute? Not if she's into rock 'n' roll and loves her rich white boyfriend. But as a younger man, I had invested these aesthetics with a redemptive, healing quality I later discovered was the stuff of romance. Both films end with acts of resistance, which are not only stands against colonialism but also against the kinds of rigid identity criteria Indians impose on each other.

EM: What do you mean when you say you "stretched the canvas too far"?

RR: With *High Horse*, I wanted to make a larger, more universal comment on dislocation by including the African American characters, which really only served to repeat the main theme, already omnipresent. The film is too long as a result, languorous where it could have been vigorous, the result being the ennui you insightfully discerned.

EM: You mention that *Haircuts Hurt* and to a more abstract degree *High Horse* are allegorically based on your experiences or those of close friends. I know that *The Doe Boy* and some of your future film ideas grew directly out of family stories. Are most of your films drawn from such inspiration?

RR: This is something I've considered carefully over the years. Being a little older, I now have the benefit of looking back and taking more intelligent wild guesses as to what I was up to.

The theme of identity runs through all of my work until *The Doe Boy* as well as through *Blue Suede Indian,* my hitherto not produced screenplay about an Indian Elvis impersonator. *The Doe Boy,* however, is the only film that was semiautobiographical. There are other themes and motifs tethered to my personal life, which have made recurring appearances. For example, there is a flute player in both of my short films and one in my feature, a broken record of a motif that my dear friend Blackhorse Lowe has described as "those fucking flutes." My first instrument was the cedar flute, so this choice was more personal than stereotypical, but still—three times? To make all this appear even more repetitive, there was an extended caesura in my work between *High Horse* and *The Doe Boy,* a period of several years. During this period, I apparently could not imagine my way out of the handful of themes that had obsessed me since the beginning, and as I recall, did not even try. What the heck? Was I so limited or solipsistic that I could not conjure a story that was not lifted from scenes of my life?

The simpler answer is that I write what I know. My family has been an inexhaustible source of eccentricities, life lessons, and characters. If I chose to, I could have a long, prolific career and never look elsewhere for inspiration. Families are just weird. The larger they are, the weirder, because as with any group, the "talent" pool expands with the number. In a family of three, you may or may not have a three-hundred-pound pyromaniac porn-addicted gay truck driver. But in a family of thirty-three, you probably do! In my family, we have that guy. He is my uncle on my father's side, the white side—so it's not limited to the Indians. My uncle is the inspiration for my film *Tearjerker,* which I hope to shoot this winter. It's not about me and not really about him at this point, but he inspired the character.

I left Texas when I was nineteen. My entire family still lives there. For years, I was "the weird one," living in New York City in my black clothes with the roaches and drug dealers and strange roommates. I would come back to Texas and they thought I was from Mars. But guess what? They were from Neptune, which is farther from Earth. I always had a notebook and could not write fast enough to keep up with their lovably crazy behavior, which persists to this day and even cinema strains to describe. The one with the notebook is usually not the weird one.

Another reason certain themes persisted in my work is that short narrative films, more often than not, are suggestive of feature films and are made as a kind of calling card. That's why funding panels are so much kinder to experimental work, generally, even when it sucks. Experimental work doesn't so loudly announce its limitations with the more "professional" form it evokes. In my case, short films were not adequate containers for the themes I was then wrestling with. I had more to say.

Over the last several years, my attention has moved away from the obviously personal to myriad other places: a pot comedy with a werewolf in it; a septuagenarian road movie; a television pilot about a maverick female detective who protects children. I've been a collaborator, a cowriter, and a script doctor. But to some degree, my storytelling is still culled from my life experience and the people I've met. I just don't know how else to do it.

EM: You and I have rambled through our favorite vampire films—*The Hunger* (1983), *Fearless Vampire Killers* (1966), *Innocent Blood* (1992), and *Lair of the White Worm* (1989), which, while not exactly a vampire film, conforms to the list—reveling in our love of the tawdry and comic aesthetics of this genre, so I know you have a penchant for these along with werewolves, as the screenplay you mention suggests. But which filmmakers and/or genres most inspire you? Or do you have a favorite?

RR: I can't say I'm inspired by a particular genre because there are both timeless classics and piles of elephant shit within every genre—just follow the *Terminator*, *Indiana Jones*, and *Star Wars* franchises for evidence. As a film fan, I am the first one in line at *The Dark Knight* (2008), but would never go see *X-Men* (2000). I can't explain that. I loved *The Hangover* (2009) and loved *Wedding Crashers* (2005), but wouldn't see *Father of the Bride* (1991) or *My Best Friend's Wedding* (1997), even if seeing them were the only way to save the world from an alien invasion. It's mysterious what pulls one in and what does not. I love a popcorn movie. I love foreign films. I love romantic comedies, action, sci-fi. I love the good ones and hate the bad ones.

There are bodies of work by filmmakers that have meant a lot to me and single films by makers that have meant as much. Mike Leigh's triptych of *High Hopes* (1988), *Life Is Sweet* (1991), and *Naked* (1993) has had a profound influence on me. He manages to blend realism with absurdity, to be an actor's director and still somehow proceed with the eye of a painter. Terence Malick inspired me, especially the way he disappeared for all those years. Films like *The Squid and the Whale* (2005), *No Country for Old Men* (2007), *Dirty Pretty Things* (2002), and *Old Boy* (2003) have reminded me how beautifully brutal cinema can be. A film like *The Departed* (2006), which I've seen fourteen times, reminds me how flawed a master of the art can still be. I just love movies. Going to the movies is a hopeful act. It really is, unless you're a mean-spirited critic or your girlfriend talked you into seeing *Beaches* (1988). You're spending the money and you're taking the time, you're making a choice, not flipping channels and sampling thirty flavors. There is alacrity there, which is why it would be such a tragedy to kill the theater experience: we'll just be a world full of flies that buzz around but never land.

EM: Your answers to my questions provide a wonderful insight into your world and hint at who is the man behind the camera. You have done a wide assortment of filmic work, including television—*Moccasin Flats*—music videos, drama, narrative shorts—*133 Skyway* comes to mind—that showcase your music, writing talent, cinematographic eye, and directorial skill. You are also an extremely well-read person who can talk widely on theory or politics one moment, vampire and horror films the next, and tie it all together with a sardonic critique of popular culture. I have come to know you also as a very witty guy; much of your humor is situational, a tad dark, and certainly off center. This works well to bring the audience into your humor in films like *Cow Tipping: The Militant Indian Waiter* (1992), which you wrote with Cochise Anderson. Such a wide variety of films and themes—do you have a favorite project?

RR: As with lovers and employers, it's probably wise to be fondest of your current one. Right now, my favorite films are still screenplays—*Tearjerker* and *Geezers*, cowritten with Russell Friedenberg. *The Doe Boy*, as firstborn, has a special place in my heart. With *133 Skyway*, we achieved a high level of craft, poetics, and drama with first-time actors and a truncated writing process. We also achieved a running time that made it nearly impossible to program. *Moccasin Flats* was made quickly under duress, personal and professional, and in the middle of a grasshopper and mosquito invasion. It became an award-winning Canadian television series and a feather in my cap.

The documentary work I've done with Heather Rae and Russell Friedenberg—*First Circle* and *Out of the Blue*—presented an entirely new menu of challenges. Documentary is a different animal for reasons that aren't elusive. Life keeps happening. Which part is the story? When do you stop? *Ibid* was the most interesting in terms of process, because I came in at a later stage and it was truly a product of the DIY digital age, made with too many cooks in the kitchen, left on the stove too long, frozen, thawed, then microwaved. Somehow, it was still delicious.

EM: I want to expand on two things you mention above, and I'll start with your statement that "documentary is a different animal for reasons that aren't elusive. Life keeps happening." Would you expand on this statement a bit, build us a scenario if you will?

RR: With documentary you are dealing with accretion rather than architecture. A narrative feature is based on a script and everyone has a copy and a set of plans on paper and, though things can change, the changes don't alter the overall plan, there is a shape there you are always moving toward. In contrast, many documentaries must have a shape imposed on them out of infinite possibilities. With *First Circle* we followed two drug-addicted parents around for two years. Their children had been taken into state's custody and they were working their case plans, determined to get them back. They were each doing well, getting healthy, off drugs, and employed. We thought the film was finished and even had a hopeful ending. A few months later, they both fell off the wagon and the state moved to terminate their parental rights. So we "finished" the film again, this time with a tragic ending. A few months later, as we were preparing to lock picture, one of the parents was back on the wagon and fighting to get her kids back, the other parent was in jail and his son was up for adoption. Making that kind of documentary is like being in a fight with a pissed-off drunk who lives with you. You are always wary of the haymaker out of nowhere.

EM: Your answer to that question elucidates the complex ethics of documentary, the telling of people's stories, and the politics involved in telling or bearing witness. Would you also tell us about the process of *Ibid*—what was your role here and what makes this film such a delicious product?

RR: *Ibid* had been shot and edited for over a year when I became involved. It was made with a wonderful cast of local Boise filmmakers and a combination of professional and first-time actors. It looked amazing, had great performances, manic energy, and great style, none of which I had anything to do with. In spite of all these attributes, the film wasn't working. It was confusing, overlong, and disjointed. It pissed you off to watch it, because you knew a great film was in there somewhere. Russell Friedenberg is like a brother to me, so I was able to say to him that I thought the problems were in the original script and could not be fixed by cutting—something no filmmaker wants to hear a year and a half into a project. I convinced him to write new scenes, to bring a clearer storyline to hang the craziness off of, to fly his actors back in, to spend more money. He was all for it, truly dedicated.

EM: We've talked about the term *Native filmmaker* and how confining that can be. While you reject that term, much of your work focuses on Native folks in everyday ways—not accenting, per se, their heritage—I'm thinking of *133 Skyway*, but in other examples your work is Native specific—*Moccasin Flats* and *The Doe Boy*, for example—would you comment on this?

RR: I don't reject it as much as resist it. And I don't resist it, except in conversations with academics. In the personal realm, being a Native filmmaker means that I am one of the architects of an emerging cinema and part of a relatively small family of makers who, more often than not, support each other. I've made great friends and lost a few. I've traveled the world, projected films off churches in the mountains of Mexico and in meeting houses on the *marae* in Aoteora. I've met revolutionaries in Chile and blonde Sundancers in Germany. It's a cherished part of what makes me "me." I'm also a fan. When I started there was Chris Eyre, Shirley Cheechoo, myself, and a few others. It's not like that anymore, the page has turned. There are some real badasses out there: Sterlin Harjo, Cedar Sherbert, Maerta

Mita, Blackhorse Lowe, Laura Milliken, Taika Watiti, Warwick Thornton, Dega Lezare. I cheered the birth of the Sundance Native Forum and cheered again when it was discontinued. We graduated. The cream rose.

Over the last fifteen years, the term *Native cinema* has grown from a focus on the States to a focus on North America to an international embrace we finally call *Indigenous cinema*. That was thrilling to witness and to the credit of the globetrotting Bird Runningwater at Sundance and to no small degree Elizabeth Weatherford and her crew at the Smithsonian, who first put Cherokees and Bolivians in a room together. It's the antidote to "One Less Indian."

I watched academics, some of them Indians, contort their psyches in ways that would make an acrobat wince, racing to establish a Native aesthetic, often to the exclusion of what they saw with their own eyes. While the academics were studying me, I was studying them, and they are fascinating. Only by looking at a large body of work and with the benefit of hindsight can you begin to untangle the myriad themes, patterns, politics, subtext, metaphors, and informal elements that run through the films of even a single filmmaker, much less a globe full of them. And even then, half the time the maker will be surprised by your conclusions. Just look at the eclectic body of work of Blackhorse Lowe. How does *Shush* relate to *Floating* or *Shimásání*? Why jump to conclusions? Let Native cinema come to term. Why give it a C-section? I understand why it's important. We need to be able to talk about Native film, write term papers and books on it, teach it, put it in social and historical perspective. There are careers at stake, a power structure!! God forbid we proceed without the anthropological gaze. Would we even know we were alive?

As for my own work, again, I write what I know. *Tearjerker* has no Indians in it, but is intensely personal. I edited a documentary for Heather and Russell about the Boise State football team called *Out of the Blue*—no Indians. Just jocks. How is that kindred to *The Doe Boy*? Am I even the same guy? How does *Ibid* fit in, where my role was unconventional but influential? I'm a storyteller, not always an auteur. I like chess and football. It's all one thing to me: music, writing, editing, directing, telling jokes. It's just me around a campfire, with my inhaler, of course, night after night, armed with a hopefully expanding filmic vocabulary, more and more experience, a life-accruing mass. Sometimes, I'm with Indians.

EM: Thank you for resisting the pigeonholing by academics. You and I talked about this on the IFP panel, how academics, myself included, through our desire to explore the theoretical impact of Indigenous media and to write about it as a way to help our colleagues and students push further into new realms and ideas, all too often interpret through lenses that confine the filmmaker or the fluidity of work. I think it's important that we are kept humble and honest about that. So thank you for reminding us that "contorting our psyche" can truly warp reality.

Many of my students grapple with the fluidity and diversity of Native film—approach, genre, Hollywood style, community focus, social issues–oriented, nonlinear, etc.—wanting a simple answer to the question: What is Native cinema? This becomes a very political question, particularly if one is using film as a way to talk back to Hollywood and mainstream representations of Native people or is using it in a strategy of media sovereignty, if you will. As someone who has grappled with the identity question as well as having worked in the industry on Native film projects, how would you answer the question?

RR: So how do we catch the greased pig called "Native film" from the safety of our classroom and name it? And who are we to name it? First of all, I think theorizing about what one is doing or would like to be doing is a vocation for those with time on their hands. It's a privilege. It doesn't mean one grew up with advantages; one may have suffered greatly. But if, for whatever reason, you find yourself in a position to ask questions about representation without worrying about where lunch is coming from, you're already a different Native filmmaker than the kid in Chiapas or Bolivia dodging bullets and U.S.-made helicopters or the kid at Pine Ridge trying to document an Elder's last words. We ought not kid ourselves about simple definitions. You'll always be a sellout to somebody, inauthentic to somebody else.

I find "talking back" to be a slippery slope as well. We have to be careful or we can end up dignifying what we're battling, because we aren't imagining ourselves outside it. When my nephew was fourteen, he decided the best way to rebel against my sister's Christianity was to buy the Satanic bible and leave it where she could find it. I was quick to remind him that Satan is part of the Christian story and he wasn't rebelling at all. If you embrace the notion of Satan, then you are embracing the notion of sin, and somewhere a Christian just smiled because you need saving. That's elementary logic. Now, worship a petrified cicada and you might be on to something original. Want to portray Indians differently? Then portray Indians differently. Just do your thing. Your thing may be conventional or unconventional, that's okay. You're still an Indian. Your thing may be documentaries; your hero could be Asian. That's okay, you're still an Indian—except to the people who say you're not. No simple answers.

EM: I have to admit that from the safety of the classroom that greasy pig does slip through our fingers. Your answer gets at a number of important issues that I'd like to pull out a bit more: "Indian" as a signifying label that confines filmmakers, and the politics of storytelling.

Let's start with the latter. I'm thinking particularly about the politics of Indigenous media as cultural survival tools in a "globalized" economic world that reacts to Indigenous sovereignty (media, political, social, cultural, you name it) with acts of violence and erasure. We know that there are a growing number of Indigenous communities globally using film/media for very politically personal reasons. Igloolik Isuma Productions, Inc., which uses film in a counter-hegemonic reaction to ethnographic film, but also as a means for strengthening traditional Inuit cultural history comes to mind, as does the Center for Cinematographic Training and Organization of Indigenous Audiovisual Communicators of Bolivia, which chose to discontinue distributing its work outside its communities. These are very different strategies for telling one's stories, and when positioned alongside more conventional productions marketed to U.S. or Canadian markets, force us to realize the real difficulty of catching "the greased pig called 'Native film.'" This is amplified for students whose access to Native film often is the video store or YouTube or the few films their teachers may have been able to acquire, often at great cost. So the question broadens to who tells the story, who decides who receives the story, whose stories are told . . . and as consumers, what right do we have to decide what types of films Indigenous filmmakers should be making?

RR: I think we're back to the greased pig. I can't answer that question, but I'll try to chip away at it.

I've observed that often when people consider Indians, they seem to be searching for some kind of commonality of values, ethics, or approach that doesn't exist. It's interesting that Isuma, who are dedicated to culture, history, tradition, education, and community, made *The Fast Runner*, a film funded by the National Film Board of Canada—in other words, the government. The film is far and away the most internationally lauded and commercially successful Native film, well received in all the conventional realms and, in my opinion, a masterpiece, the gold star of Native cinema to date. Isuma's second feature, *The Journals of Knud Rasmussen*, had a $6 million budget, one the Bolivians have surely never dreamed of. So, this is hardly the Bolivian model, which is more closely married to national politics, though historically, the most well-known Bolivian filmmakers, for example, Jorge Sanjines, worked for governmental organizations for at least part of their careers, navigating complicated issues of control. There is a new breed of Bolivian filmmaker (Jose Sanchez H., Adriana Montenegro) who studied film in the United States and there will always be armies of politicized guerilla filmmakers working in their own communities. Hello, greased pig. To limit distribution to one's own community doesn't make sense to me personally, but then again, it doesn't have to, which bears on the last part of your question, which I think also answers the question: Who are we to decide?

EM: As someone who does not limit his media to one community, do you find that you have to market yourself differently depending on the project or on funders, positioning yourself across shifting lines of mainstream-independent-Indigenous film?

RR: I'm really just a hustler. I do what I do to get the job. This summer I cut a feature film in New Mexico, taught a six-week music camp in Idaho, sat on an IFP panel in Minnesota with a senior programmer at Sundance and a Harvard professor, cut a Fox Movie Channel piece for *Night at the Museum 2*, and did an adult filmmaking workshop in Idyllwild, California. My Indianness never came up, though my Afro did. Between directing efforts, my living has been eclectic, a farrago of different things, and I'm thankful, in this tough economy, not to be so specialized. Still, *Tearjerker* was announced in *Variety* recently and they referred to me as Native American filmmaker Randy Redroad, a term which couldn't begin to grasp me or the film, which isn't about Indians at all. But, that's okay—again, it's part of me. As for marketing myself, I feel that we do so with our personalities and the quality of our work. Again, the scripts that I'm getting the most attention for at this stage, *Tearjerker* and *Geezers*, aren't about Indians. In the end, I don't want people to stop trying to label me—it's too much fun arguing about it.

EM: I mentioned an issue earlier about the term *Indian* as a signifying label, which you addressed a bit in your last answer. Do you have some final advice about working with and outside of Hollywood?

RR: First, understand what Hollywood is. Even "Hollywood" is changing with the new markets and new technology. If an Indian wants to break into Hollywood, what does that mean? Well, who's the Indian? Does he or she want Spiderman to be an Indian? Or to be the Indian director that makes *Spiderman*? What are your goals? Is it the work? Or is it the fame? Is it the business? Or is it the frame? If you are an experimental or nonlinear storyteller, why on Earth would you want to be in Hollywood? Just do your thing and understand that your audience will be smaller, more specific. Don't show a three-hour silent film about rez dogs as metaphors for displacement and wonder why there are three people there and one of them is snoring. If your focus is your community, be in your community. There is a different level of responsibility if you are speaking for your tribe and using traditional elements and there are no easy answers there either.

The best way to market yourself is with hard work and audacity. If you have that, you have a lot. If you're young, you have energy and it's infectious. Study your craft, live some life. Film is that rare medium where there is a bloated reverence for storytellers who are young. It's backwards. Storytellers should be old and shriveled with their boobs and balls down by their knees. We can see that they've used them and they can tell us how. Why do I need a twenty-three-year-old to tell me about life and love? They don't know where their elbow is! I would just say, don't think too much about where you fit in. Have some fun, listen, and hopefully find a community of supportive peers, in school or not, and some kind of mentor. If you're a pissed-off revolutionary and want to make films that dismantle

> the entire system, you're not the first. I'm all for you. I mean that. I wouldn't care if a comet hit right now. We've earned it. I just hope the world doesn't end before your premiere. Making a film is a self-fulfilling prophecy, no matter who you are. "If you build it, they will come."

Note

1. A Native Perspective on Filmmaking, the IFP MN 9th Annual Producers Conference: South by Minnesota, Minneapolis, April 26, 2008.

An Upstream Journey

An Interview with Sandra Osawa

SAZA OSAWA

Sandra Osawa has been working as a filmmaker longer than any other American Indian in the country. She is also my mother and I have been lucky enough to travel with her and my father, Yasu Osawa, to many parts of Indian country since I was eight years old. At a young age, I never thought the work my parents did was special. It was not until later that I realized that my mother, and really both of my parents, had unique gifts that they cultivated all of their lives to make them into master storytellers; my mother shaped stories through words and thematic concepts while my father followed those concepts by finding ways to bring them out visually.

My perspective on my parents' work was helped by an internship I had at the National Museum of the American Indian's film department, where I previewed all the Indigenous film that had been cataloged. While there I was able to gain a unique perspective on Indian films and I was also able to see some of the many accomplishments of my parents in an overall context. To me, my mother's films stood out for their depth and clarity and painstaking research. They had layers of themes and addressed hard political issues. They were refreshingly clear of stereotypes in music, font styles, graphics, and choice of subject matter. They came across as contemporary and fresh and highly engaging. I had not paid a lot of attention to her films beyond what I had observed on my own travels, so it was eye opening to see the impact of her work in context with other films. Still later, in law school, I had tangible evidence of the important work my mother was doing when her work was screened for our classes. Films like *Lighting the 7th Fire* and *Usual and Accustomed Places* address the treaty right to fish in Wisconsin and in the Northwest. Even years after their creation, they remain the best all-around presentation of these issues and are used in many college classrooms across the country. Recently, I was the associate producer on her latest production, *Maria Tallchief*, and was able to experience the relentless and demanding pressures that she felt trying to do a low-budget film on such a legendary figure. Rather than compromise, my mother took the production to the absolute limit. She realized there would be no other complete documentary of Tallchief, and she wanted it to be as good as she could possibly make it. While working with her, I realized that my mother's artistry comes from her ability to draw on a life full of experience and interests—her love of politics, poetry, and great orators come to mind—to tell complex stories with great depth but also simplicity and humanity.

Although it seems that she is not as well known as she should be, like many of her subjects, I have no doubt her work will be studied for many years to come. She has had to overcome many funding and distribution obstacles in making her documentaries because her work does not fit the mold of a typical Indian documentary. The goal of her work has been to take dead aim at the stereotypes that have frozen our lives in the past and made us irrelevant in the present and future. Her strong foundation in her own culture has provided her with deep insights and sensitivity toward Indian issues in all parts of Indian country. With her cultural and political awareness, and the ability to tell complex stories from a very human perspective, she has helped fill the gap in the mass media's depiction of American Indian people.

I believe her place in history is solidified for many reasons. For example, she was the first independent Native American to produce a television series. She did this in 1974 when she began work for KNBC for a ten-part series she both wrote and produced called *The Native American* (which aired in 1975). There was no other Native American doing production work at this level. The series garnered her an Outstanding Producer's Award from the station and also led to an unprecedented move by the station to return the copyright back to her due to her own contributions of time and money. She continues to work to retain copyrights to her productions and is unique in that regard.

My mother was initially interested in producing and writing feature films, and to that end she sold an original dramatic work to *Visions*, part of KCET TV, whose mandate was to look for new scriptwriters. The series folded before her script came up for production, but she was able to join the Writers Guild of America based on the sale of her script "Upstream at Medicine Creek." She speaks of this period in the 1980s as a time when opportunities became very limited as a real conservative wind took hold for the next thirty years.

Shortly after, our family moved to Seattle. She thought she could work anywhere, as she had compiled so much experience. She soon realized that the independent world of film was very closed at the local television stations. No minorities were working at key levels. A good ten years passed while she volunteered here and there and tried to find a way to work. Gradually my parents started investing in their own camera equipment and found a way to complete their next major six documentaries, all of which have aired on PBS. They formed their own company, Upstream Productions, influenced by the title of my mother's first dramatic script. Along the way, she has been honored with awards such as the Native American Filmmaker of the Year, and with grants from Rockefeller, the Ford Foundation, the Corporation for Public Broadcasting, and many others. Her films have been featured three times at the Sundance Festival and at the Margaret Mead Festival, the Amiens Film Festival in France, the National Museum of the American Indian, the Taos Film Festival, and the Munich Film Festival.

I interviewed my mother in the summer of 2009 at our home in Seattle after I had just finished law school and completed the Washington State bar exam.

Saza Osawa: What was the first documentary that you made after the KNBC series and how did you come to that story?

Sandra Osawa: The first documentary that I made with Yasu was *In the Heart of Big Mountain.* When I first heard about Big Mountain I was really alarmed that there was a whole tribe of people being forced to move from their traditional land. That story stayed with me because I kept thinking, if this was a land dispute in Maine and these were rich, wealthy, white citizens, you can bet there would be no forced removal of anyone. But, because these people were Indigenous people, the Hopi and the Navajo, there was this forced relocation.

Saza: So how did you get to Big Mountain?

Sandra: I had begun reading a little bit about Big Mountain, as much as I could, and there was this MIT study that studied forced relocation on Indigenous people everywhere around the world. In summary, what they found was whenever they moved Indigenous people, there was a great deal of trauma: there was alcoholism, increased suicide rates, depression—many, many, many social factors entered into

Sandra Osawa. (Courtesy of Upstream Productions)

this. I wanted to see if we could document some of the aspects of trauma that I suspected was going on in Big Mountain in order for lawmakers to know that when you pass a law, it's not just a law, it affects people's lives in tangible ways.

Saza: How did you pick Katherine Smith (the Navajo matriarch highlighted in *In the Heart of Big Mountain*)?

Sandra: I had been reading about her a little bit. She was one of the Navajo matriarchs who was very active in the protests. It happened to be just fortune that I landed in her path or she landed in my path because our guide for Big Mountain didn't show up. It's very difficult to get around there if you're not from there. We had a flat tire on our old Volkswagen van and Katherine Smith's niece came to help us. She helped us to get our tire fixed and we were telling her what we wanted to do, a documentary to document the relocation issues. She took us then to Katherine Smith.

Saza: One of my favorite things about your programs, this one in particular, is the music. How did you pick the music?

Sandra: I had been wanting to do something on Indian music for some

Kate Smith with lambs in *In the Heart of Big Mountain.* (Courtesy of Upstream Productions)

time, so I had been slowly gathering different Indian musicians. When we got to Big Mountain, I had Sharon Burch's tapes with me and I played them for Katherine toward the end of our visit. I asked her which one she liked and she picked the one that we used for the opening. Sharon sings in Navajo so I wanted a Navajo to select the music. I think the music is really a big part of all our films. We pay attention to music because the music that has been used on most Indian documentaries is really so horrible, so stereotypical that I've always had a conscious desire to upgrade the music and the sound. This worked out really well and her voice is very powerful.

Saza: Sharon Burch's music was good. It was simple and conveyed the strength and spirit of that documentary. Even though it was only a half hour, you packed a lot of stuff in there. My favorite statement in that movie is when Katherine Smith says, "All of my life, I'll always be thinking of this place."

Sandra: That actually is the real center of the film. At Big Mountain, we found that the concept of Mother Earth was no cliché. It was very real and very much a part of all the people at Big Mountain. When

Katherine Smith was moving around the place where she grew up and talking about the place and how she would always, her spirit would always be there, we purposely wanted to capture that visually, with the colored pattern of her skirt going through the weeds and also with the sound, the breeze, just to carefully make that statement come out as strong as possible. I think I agree with you that that is the center and power of the film.

Saza: I also remember her daughter saying, "I feel like I'm just waiting for some good news that will help the people of Big Mountain."

Sandra: That particular statement in the film is partially a religious statement and a hopeful statement. You know the Good News is what they talk about in the Bible as well. The Good News also has a very sorrowful component because the Good News did not ever come for that family. It did not ever come for the people of Big Mountain. In a sense this half-hour program is very short and sweet and sorrowful, but it also has strains of strength in it. Many, many people have covered this issue. You probably know there was an Academy Award winner on this same issue. In fact when that won the award, when *Broken Rainbow* came out, we thought, "Oh, well, it's been done; we don't have to do it." But when we saw that film we realized, "No, we still have to do this." The Academy Award–winning film wasn't really our take on it. The outcome of that is that when Katherine Smith would go to, say, the United Nations to speak about Big Mountain, she would take our film, *In the Heart of Big Mountain.* I realized we really hit the target because it spoke to them, it was real to them, and it was useful. We got our own award in a sense. It wasn't the Academy Award, but our own award was the stamp of approval from the local people there.

Saza: What was your next documentary after *In the Heart of Big Mountain?*

Sandra: It was *Lighting the 7th Fire.* But right before we did *Lighting the 7th Fire* we did *The Eighth Fire.* There was an NBC bid that was put out; they wanted the producer to do something on treaty rights for the NBC programs on Sunday. Unfortunately, after we bid on it, they lost half their budget. I had a very top-notch associate producer at the time and she suggested we do the program for half the money but we retain all shooting rights to the footage. So wherever we went we could keep that footage and turn it into another film. We did work on *The Eighth Fire,* which I think was very well done. It aired on NBC and it involved treaty rights in three parts of the country: the Northwest, the Black Hills area, and Wisconsin. With that being aired we started to think of which area we should concentrate on because we had so much footage in each area. And somebody sent us some footage from Wisconsin. We looked at this outrageous footage. It was white people screaming racial epithets at all the Chippewa people there along the riverbanks and it was so shocking that it brought me back to how things were in the Northwest in the '60s. I felt that we had to find a way to do this because it was happening now. We basically wrapped all our existing footage that we had shot around the Great Lakes area and we decided to go out and gather some more.

Saza: Lighting the 7th Fire was very legal because you got more into the treaty rights and the legal history of the spearfishing conflict in the Great Lakes area. Was that done on purpose or was that just the nature of the subject?

Sandra: Not too many Indian producers were doing political films here in the U.S. I think we were one of the few to do really overtly political films. It really stems from my interest in politics. I was also involved in the fish-ins here in Washington State so I was very interested to do something on treaty rights—so here was this prime opportunity. I took it to the max because I really wanted to research the legal issues in terms of the line of resistance. You know how some people do film and they just center it on what's happening now, but I wanted to go back in time and give a legal background, a little thumbnail sketch. We were able to do that and give you a fuller legal history in terms of the spearfishing rights issues in Wisconsin. Then we were able to give you, with the help of the great people that we interviewed, many of the layers of conflict—the economic issues that were there, the underlying racial issues that were there. That's something I want to do in each film. I want to give you a little more than just the surface look. It's when you go deeper and give people more depth that you're really going to help solve problems.

Saza: You open with that beaver shot, which Dad was lucky to get. I'm wondering how much of this is preplanned before you go out shoot-

Lighting the 7th Fire: protesters at the fishing boat launch area. (Courtesy of Upstream Productions)

ing? Documentary filmmaking seems kind of like a crapshoot because you never really know what people are going to say, so how do you shape it up?

Sandra: That's the real difficult part. We really didn't find some of the people until the very end. It is kind of a crapshoot because you never know if you're going to run into the right people. Always the goal is to try to figure out who we can get that will really represent more of the community voice as opposed to the "official" voice. There were many, many struggles in *Lighting the 7th Fire* in terms of people. There was one person that we tried forever to get. He was a spiritual man there. We really wanted the spiritual aspect to the story because, after all, the whole title *Lighting the 7th Fire* became a title because I read a prophecy in a newsletter I subscribe to and it had the Ojibwe prophecy called the 7th Fire. The 7th Fire basically talks about a time when traditions would come back and people would be healed. When we grappled with the story, I realized that was what was going on around the lakes there in Wisconsin. We wanted to find a religious person to speak about this age-old prophecy. Someone guided us to this person and we tried and tried and tried but for whatever reason we couldn't get in the interview. When we finally got the interview, his dog wouldn't stop barking. We could not use the footage that we had when we brought it back because talking about spiritual concepts with the dog barking just didn't work.

That's an example of something we didn't get. However, we were able to find another man, as you said, the one who opened the program. On his own he wanted to take us to this site where the falls were, this spiritual site. We went there and he had his pipe and on his own he began his prayer, which he allowed us to film, and spontaneously there appeared a beaver in the creek. We were able to get that spiritual aspect that I wanted, not in the way I thought we would, from the man who is regarded as a spiritual leader there, but in other ways—from the landscape, the ice melting from Eugene Begay, our opening person, talking about the different ceremonies that they have there. We were able to fill in this very strong spiritual aspect, which I saw all around me when I was there.

Saza: So your next documentary was *Pepper*? *Pepper's Pow Wow* is another favorite of mine because of the music.

Sandra: Why was that?

Saza: I think mostly because of the emotion of it. I'm thinking of Karen Knight. And I think Dad opening with tree, that long shot of the tree going up and hearing those old hymnals, it just grounds the piece. You hear Jim Pepper but you begin with just pure emotion, just the tree and singing.

Sandra: I'm glad you were able to see that because Yasu and I grappled with the opening for probably several weeks. We couldn't find a way to get into the story of Jim Pepper and we struggled and struggled and struggled. Somehow when we were shooting, this large tree was located right on the church grounds where they sang the traditional version of "Witchi-Tai-To." It was a hymn that they sing all around Oklahoma, especially around Creek country. It was such a powerful tree and I kept asking Yasu to shoot this tree. I didn't really know how we were going to use the tree but I felt it was really important. And when we got back into the editing room and we were playing some of the music we happened to have the "Hallelujah" song on and we were running through footage. Somehow this tree appeared and when we saw that and heard the song, it was perfect. We just knew immediately that was the one. That was the visual that was going to go with [the] opening song. Many things happened when we were editing. For example, when we were editing I was lucky to call Jim Pepper's close friend in Europe and I was asking him, "You know, we're having a hard time with what songs to highlight because there's so many, many good ones." He said, "Well, I can tell you one thing, his favorite song was 'Hallelujah' and we went all around Europe and he never got tired of putting that song in . . . I got tired of it but Jim Pepper never got tired of it, and he would always reach for that and put that in, and we played that wherever we traveled." And I said, "Oh, that's really good to hear because that's the one song we're going to use to open with."

Saza: That's a good story.

Sandra: Yeah, so it was almost like Jim Pepper was finding a way to speak to us even though he had passed on. I felt really happy and satisfied to know we were on the right track.

Saza: What I thought was good about that documentary is that Jim Pepper had such a strong personality that you were able to have a strong show, with him leading the way, even though you didn't have a lot of interview time with him.

Sandra: Jim Pepper was so charismatic. I guess that word is overused but he was such a strong personality, as you say, that he when he came on the screen you were riveted to him. He was also so articulate that what he had to say, you really wanted to hear. Lots of musicians aren't also speakers but he happened to be both. For example, when he talked about music being a healing force, it comes from the four directions. I mean he just had a way of speaking, of joining words together that was really poetry in itself.

Saza: You didn't seem to be intimidated by the subject of jazz even though that was a new film topic for you.

Sandra: There was a group of Indian college students that got together in what was called the Workshop on Indian Affairs in Colorado. Among the top Indian youth leaders at the workshop, there was a strong interest in jazz and that's how I became influenced by jazz at an early time in the '60s. So when Jim Pepper came along it didn't really faze me that he was a jazz musician. Then when I heard him

I thought that no one was doing what he was doing. He was the only one that I ever heard who was mixing jazz with Indian themes and Indian music. I thought he was very important from the get-go and I was disappointed that he didn't seem to have a large following in the United States. When we would film him in places there would be small crowds, and I thought if people understood more what he was trying to do he'd be a lot more successful, and people should hear him anyway. I appreciated jazz but I gained an even deeper appreciation after doing the program because I realized that jazz musicians are kind of like independent filmmakers. They're almost totally ignored and in the background but they're doing very, very important work.

Saza: Can you talk a little bit about the Brooklyn performance that you taped, and some of the highlights and your obstacles with that?

Sandra: The very last scene in *Pepper's Pow Wow* takes place in Brooklyn in an outdoor park. There they were performing some of Jim Pepper's compositions that he had created for a full orchestra. The full orchestra was playing. We had gone through the trouble of getting everything cleared. We got there, however, and there appeared these guards who were walking around the audience and they came up to us and they said, basically, "No filming." They made Yasu shut his camera down. I'm a practicing Buddhist and I began chanting that we would have the ability, and somehow the means, to tape this very important concert because I didn't think that it was ever going to be performed again. This was actually a memorial to Jim Pepper right in Brooklyn, his hometown, where he lived and played for so many years, so I wanted to get this. Somehow or another, it was kind of a magical moment where the breeze came up and this man, this guard, kind of walked away and disappeared into the crowd. Then I looked at Yasu and the red camera light was on. He was getting it. We put that camera on and proceeded to tape the entire concert.

Saza: That was an important concert to get. It's a good thing that whatever blockage was there was wiped away. That footage was so impressive, with Karen Knight and the band members, that whole event.

Sandra: I think when you hear Karen Knight's voice at the end it's very, very haunting. She was of course mourning Jim Pepper, who had just passed away so recently, and was a longtime companion, and here she had to get up and sing this song. I think her struggle to sing is evident in the visuals and in the song. It's kind of a triumph of her own character that she was able to carry on and do this without breaking down completely. There's a lot of beauty in that last concert scene. Even though you may or may not know the full context of what's going on with Karen and what's happening, there's a lot of power in the music as a whole. As Don Cherry said at the end of the documentary, "His music will not die." That seems to be the case—the power of film was to uplift Jim Pepper's legacy and life; I'm now confident that Don Cherry, in his memorial tribute to Jim, was absolutely right. His music will not die.

Saza: You talked about when you were making this film people opened up to you. You could have shaped the documentary following his lifeline or some other formula, but it seemed like all these interesting jazz musicians who came forward to talk about him really pushed this to be shaped in a way that was not just a note-for-note retelling of his life, but really more about his legacy.

Sandra: That's true. Jim lived a very rich life because he had so many friends. I was just taken aback and overwhelmed because everyone wanted to talk and they had many, many stories that they just had to share. You could just see his life, the way it was lived, because people around him had such rich memories of him. It's true that they really led the shaping of story and we allowed that. Luckily we had sense enough to allow that to happen to where we didn't just say, "No, we're set on doing this and we want to do this chronologically and we want this and this." Instead, we were relaxed enough to let the flow come in and let the story be told the way people who knew him best wanted it to be told.

Saza: Then after *Pepper's Pow Wow* what did you work on?

Sandra: It was *Usual and Accustomed Places.* We went back to a project that I had started back when we were doing *The Eighth Fire.* We went to the three treaty sites; one of them was the Northwest. Of course I always wanted to do something on fishing rights in the Northwest so I began a project, which was a mammoth project. To give one quick example, I knew I wanted to go to all the treaty sites where they signed the treaties in the Northwest. Well, little did I know that those sites were not documented. There were no documented sites to say, "Here's the flag, here's the place where they made the treaties." So it took a number of years, just combing through archives, talking to tribal people, asking, "Where was your treaty signed?" That small wish to show where the treaty sites were represented took several years of intense research. I realized more with *Usual and Accustomed* than with any other project that our history has not been documented. We do not know our history because we have not told our history, and it's been told in the point of view of non-Indians who often did not bother to say someone's name next to a photograph, to say someone's tribe—of course to say someone's age would be too much to ask. I was left with all this undated, no face, no name, material that we needed to personalize. That was one of the biggest efforts in *Usual and Accustomed*, to try and personalize it. It's a mammoth undertaking. We do sell *Usual and Accustomed* part 1, and it goes up to 1920. The next quest is to try to tell the Boldt decision story, the decision where we won a court victory in 1974 in which we were finally able to be guaranteed 50 percent of the harvestable salmon.

Saza: I see *Usual and Accustomed Places* as one of your biggest and most personal projects because it combines the politics, the legal aspects, our own tribe and history here, archives and culture. It's really multilayered. Also, you have really good music to open it up. It sets the tone there. It's not contemporary but it's really powerful and deep.

Sandra: The music in *Usual and Accustomed* is really powerful and that has an interesting story in itself. For years I had been trying to get a recording of my grandfather Chief Jongie Claplanahoo's music. He was always known to have had lots of gatherings in his home at which they would sing. And the minister lived across the street and he would come and tape-record all the Indian people, my grandfather and all the relatives singing. I was always wanting to hear this because they had said they had done some tributes to my mom as well. Every so often I would see this minister's wife and I would ask, "Is it possible to get a copy of the music and to hear the music?" This started when I was in college. She would always say, "Oh, it's somewhere, it's buried somewhere in boxes." I would sort of get the brush-off. Finally, as we were beginning work on *Usual and Accustomed Places*, I got a lot more determined and I asked Helen Peterson, one of my relatives who was a very close friend of the minister's wife, if she could help me get a copy. I think in fact, coincidentally, they were at a restaurant and I asked the minister's wife if I could listen to a copy and she gave me the same story, "Well, it's in boxes and I'm not sure where I could find it." So I went away again and I thought, "Well, I've lost again." I was getting into my car when Helen Peterson came running out and said, "If you can bring your tape-recording equipment we can meet you at the house and you can record the music." We were able to record one entire concert of my grandfather singing one evening with my grandmother. Now this was in the 1950s when this was recorded, so the music you hear in the opening of *Usual and Accustomed Places* is from the 1950s and it's a very rare period of time in which we still had great, great, great singers. They still had such authentic, strong voices. It's very real music. Our singers, in my opinion, are some of the best in the country and our music is some of the best in the country because it has such an uneven beat. And it's complicated. It's also complicated to dance to because the rhythm is uneven; it's not just a steady beat as you hear often in Plains' music. In the Northwest, you never know what kind of beat you're going to get and as a dancer you've got to be ready to dance with that drum. So it's very invigorating music and I'm glad you noticed that that is so powerful because that's really your own heritage, singing through the years. It was a long struggle to get that music to really now be a part of history and to be alive.

Saza: Usual and Accustomed Places seems like it was the most research intensive of your documentaries. It seems difficult to have that much research and pare it down to something that is palatable.

Sandra: I think that is partly what has slowed the project down, because of the very heavy research materials. We have thousands and thousands of slides and stills, many interviews that haven't been edited. So part of it is that we have so much material that, really, you need to put it into a book and a film. In my mind it does represent the most important work I've done, just in terms of my own cultural background, my own history, and the depth of research that I've undertaken. It's staggering. It's a very staggering project that I hope to finish. That remains a big goal of mine.

Saza: I just want to now ask you a couple of questions about *Maria Tallchief*. Why do you think you chose Maria as your next subject?

Sandra: Again, it was back to the group of college Indian students who went to summer school in Boulder, Colorado. There happened to be some Osage students there and they would sometimes talk about these famous ballerina sisters. I thought that was very intriguing because I never really heard of American Indian ballerinas before. That stayed in my mind and years later when I met Elise, Maria Tallchief's daughter, at the Fishtrap writer's session in Oregon, I asked her if her mother had ever had a full documentary done on her and she said no. I asked Elise if she would be interested and she said, "Well, why don't you call her?" So that's really how it started. I didn't really know anything about ballet, but after many, many years of reading and studying everything I could, I got a little bit up to speed in terms of having some familiarity with the subject. Maria Tallchief was actually a legendary figure and very well known, especially to a certain generation, so she was a little exception to the rule because basically I'm interested in untold stories. I soon began to realize, however, that she did fit because no one had ever gathered up her archival dance clips. I could see why, because it was all stuck. You had copyright issues galore. The fact that we are able to show you the clips we did is a miracle and, I think, a testament to sheer perseverance. The last two clips we wanted to show you were *Orpheus* and *Nutcracker.* I could not tell the story without *Orpheus* and *Nutcracker*—when you see the film you'll see why. I persisted until we were able to get those locked in. Then the story seemed to flow because we were able to use her dance clips as a way of her speaking to you. She's not necessarily a speaker like Jim Pepper was but she's an artist, she's a dancer. We wanted you to see her dance and feel her emotions, what she was all about by watching her dance.

Saza: You mentioned some of the difficulties of getting some Maria's archival dance clips, but I also saw some other difficulties in making this documentary. It was a long process and it seemed like, opposite of Jim Pepper, that the story didn't evolve from the subjects themselves, but really this documentary was shaped differently. I think that change was a new process for you. How did you find working with Maria?

Sandra: Well, it was a little intimidating to work with Maria on this, first of all, because she's such a legendary figure. It was difficult for me to get past the public figure of Maria and get into the person of Maria. I think, like any superstar, she was naturally very guarded and also, she admits in her interviews, she's a very shy person. I am also a very shy person. I think two shy people together was bound to be a little bit of an obstacle. I realized that toward the end I would have to step forward. One of my friends in New York said, "You have to tell your story. This documentary is your *Firebird*." That stayed with me because I realized I had to insert my own interpretation of Maria. Working with her for seven years, I had to now step forward and say, "This is what I see." As I stepped forward, I think the story began getting stronger because I realized history, ballet history, had been told from the point of view of George Balanchine and Lincoln Kirstein and the men involved, but had not been told from her point of view and had not included the many contributions she had made to the discovery of ballet in America. That became one of the points of view I inserted into the story as a filmmaker. My intent was to bring out her story more and also to bring out her cultural background. I think even though she didn't necessarily speak of her cultural background in depth, I felt like I discovered she had very deep roots in her own life there in Fairfax, Oklahoma. I talked about her ability to observe and be observant, which helped her throughout her entire life. Her first memories of dance were of course Indian dancing. I strove, as a filmmaker, to make those points come out. I wanted to do a tribute to Maria, not that she was important because of what man was in her life; although Balanchine had a strong influence in her life, she certainly brought her own gifts to the table and I wanted that to be clear. I hope that does become clear in the sense that she will have her rightful place in history.

Saza: I liked all the people we met in Fairfax, Oklahoma. I liked Raymond Redcorn saying that he remembers Osages pointing to their vests and asking car dealers if they could make the car in those colors. I liked Harry Red Eagle saying, "Washka," which he said means "Do your best."

Sandra: Well, you were the one—I always call you eagle eye—you were the one who pointed to Harry Red Eagle and said, "Interview him, interview him." Talk about accidental things or finding just the right people to come and help be a voice. He was the one who knew about dance and knew about traditions of when you Indian dance.

"Washka, washka" is "Do your best." We were able to put that over some of Maria's dancing. You could say she personified that goal of "do your best" because all her friends and dance colleagues have told us over and over in interviews that Maria gave nothing but 110 percent of her best every time she went out. I was glad when the cultural aspect of "do your best" really blended with Maria's ballet dancing. So I was really glad to have his voice present.

Saza: We forgot to talk about *On and Off the Res' with Charlie Hill*. You did that one before *Maria Tallchief*, right?

Sandra: *On and Off the Res' with Charlie Hill* also stems from a long quest in wanting to see us addressed in more than stereotypical ways. I'd always wanted to [do] something with the theme of Indian humor. I remembered Charlie Hill because I had been around Los Angeles when he was first starting to do stand-up comedy and I thought he would be a good vehicle, because he started so early, he was around in the '70s, and he'd been persevering. In a sense, he was an innovator and a leader in this regard. Again, this program was with the intent to go after a gap. You know, Indians weren't seen as funny and you know, average, typical, living in typical houses; we show Charlie Hill living in a typical house and his friends and family and the fact that he had a family that had succeeded. His grandmother was an actual MD, a physician. So there were many points to Charlie's story that really fit in with my kind of themes that I like to drive home, that we are not just a bunch of losers. We are successful, creative, alive people who are also very artistic. Charlie Hill was just the perfect vehicle for me and I was finally able to do this show that touched on Indian humor.

Saza: Do you want to wrap up by saying anything about your work overall, what it is you've been trying to do all these years?

Sandra: Hmm . . .

Saza: You've kind of said it all along, that you have these untold stories that you want to tell and you think they've been largely ignored by history and that's there's some rich history here. When you don't have the full history, that's another way to sideline people, to sideline women or American Indians and not recognize the full contributions that they've given to humanity. So you don't get to see them as full people. I think your documentaries are full because they en-

On and Off the Res' with Charlie Hill: illustration depicting comedian Charlie Hill. (Artwork by Michael Horse; courtesy of Upstream Productions)

compass some legal aspects, historical aspects and culture, personalities of the area, and all the different places that you've been. Do you want to talk about that?

Sandra: I like to do stories where I feel we are omitted and erased from the picture. That makes me feel that we are more complete. When I tell stories about an American Indian ballerina or an American Indian jazz musician or an American Indian stand-up comedian, I feel like we are doing a fuller portrait of American Indian people than what you would normally see in a more traditional story about our lives. I think this sets me apart because I deliberately seek out stories that are not known or not told or not fully discovered. That really keeps me going because I feel like I'm filling this gap that I saw way back when I started in media back in the '70s. Wherever you would go on Indian reservations there was always humor, strength, spontaneity, love of life and, of course, love of land and particular places. These aspects of our character never did really come across, so that really motivated me too. Whenever I tell a story I want to make sure the fullness of our character and our lives comes across so it's a bit more real.

We have more and more Indians coming into media (and you did the associate producing on *Maria Tallchief* so you have an appetite and an interest and awareness in telling stories and how important these are). Numbers alone won't help us grow stronger, however. We grow stronger as long as we're not just doing these stories to become famous directors. We're not doing these to become rich. If you are, you really don't belong in the category of Indian filmmakers. I think you really need to be committed to a purpose and a mission. You need to be conscious of why you are doing each story you do, why you are doing your edits this way, why you are doing your filming this way, why you are doing your narration this way. You have to be filled with a powerful mission basically to right the wrongs that have been done to us, as Indian people, in the media. When you do this and when you have this powerful feeling, then you can call yourself an American Indian filmmaker. Until then, I don't think you have that right.

Video as Community Ally and Dakota Sense of Place

An Interview with Mona Smith

Jennifer A. Machiorlatti

Mona Smith is a Sisseton-Wahpeton Dakota whom I met in the early 1990s, when she was producing work for the Minnesota American Indian AIDS Taskforce. These early videos interweave Native worldview with current health issues, gender identity, sexuality, and sexual orientation, as well as inspiration and Native philosophy in healing. I wrote about two of her videos, *Her Giveaway: A Spiritual Journey with AIDS* (1988, twenty-one minutes) and *That Which Is Between* (1989, eight minutes), which are pioneering and moving videos addressing HIV and AIDS from alternative perspectives (other than Western medicine and disease approaches).[1] Ms. Smith's early video work in this subject area also includes *Honored by the Moon* (1990, fifteen minutes).

These videos have screened at national conferences, festivals, and on regional public broadcasting. They are held in many university, school, and video libraries across the United States. In recognition of the many ways her video, installation, and Web-based art/communication have contributed to communities, Mona has received awards and acknowledgments on the community level (Community Artist of the Year, National Museum of the American Indian), the state level (Minnesota States Arts Board Community Cultural Partnership Grant), and the national level (National Council on Family relations).

I first interviewed Mona in 1992. Sixteen years later, we were able to meet again in Minneapolis for a documentary digital film and book project titled *Matriarchal Voices: Native and First Nations Women in Film and Video* that I had been working on over a six-year period. Her work has moved from single-channel video to interactive, with recent creative contributions in installation and Web site formats. Smith feels that this interactivity better represents the Dakota way of communication, which is more of a dialogue within the community, than one "teller" being responsible for the community's stories. This focus on community is where

Smith has centered her work, from early HIV/AIDS awareness videos to her recent work on the pilot *Bdote Memory Map*[2] with the Minnesota Humanities Center and on a Bdote video podcast for the *Telling River Stories* project at the University of Minnesota.

I conducted the following interview with Smith in the fall of 2008 in Minneapolis.

Jennifer Machiorlatti: How did you come about using video? Tell me about how you came to this medium.

Mona Smith: From 1977 to 1983 I was teaching and loving it. It was at the point where I had to decide whether I was a scholar, and whether I belonged in the academic world or not. They offered PortaPak classes (that definitely sets me in time) for teachers to use video in their classrooms.[3] And I took the class and fell madly in love. Interestingly, when I was in high school, theater was my love but I thought in the back of my mind, "I want to be a film director." But I had forgotten about it all along, didn't know how to go about doing that. And so after the PortaPak class it helped me decide that I needed to leave college teaching. So I slowly did and became an account executive for a little independent production house. And it was so small, and working the way three-quarter-inch videotape houses did at that time; within three weeks of being hired as an account executive, I had commercials on the air.[4] Cheesy commercials. From there I was able to move into the subject matter and focus of my life that I wanted, which was working on Native-focused video, and the first Native project that I did was a very small piece for the Minnesota Women's Indian Resource Center called *Heartbeat, Drumbeat* and that was it, that was completely it, my fate was sealed. That was 1983 or 1984.

So I went along making various Native-focused media, health-focused—we did one of the first Native HIV videos in '88, called *Her Giveaway: A Spiritual Journey with AIDS*, and that was an incredible experience. I remember the day. Nan, my editing collaborator, and I saw it for the first time all together and we jumped up and hugged each other. We felt really good. We had done justice to Carole La-Favor's (Ojibwe) story and to the need for educating about HIV. And we liked it, so we were happy. Then there were many more shows that have taken me lots of places and taught me all kinds of things that I may not have learned otherwise.

The next turning point I would say was when I got a phone call from the Minnesota History Center saying, "Do you want to do a room?" And the earth stood still. Three years later, we were putting together a room—an installation slash exhibit called *Cloudy Waters: Dakota Reflections on the River.* What it taught me was that an installation was the way to express Native ways of being in a way that I always hoped for but didn't understand how to make happen. I knew that the Web was one possibility for expressing the nonlinear nature of Native and particularly Dakota way of being. Having a room meant I could adapt traditional ways of teaching—that the choices were in the visitors' hands, just like they are in life—what you hear, what you take in, what you see, what you spend time on is your choice. The installation showed me a new possibility of using video and audio for expression.

JM: Let's go back to early video works. You had some national distribution. Did you find that your target was to work more nationally or locally or both?

MS: My focus is not the media world; my focus is Indian country, and whatever that meant. I didn't really know how to chart this career; I only knew how to do the work as it emerged, as it came to me. We made *Her Giveaway* for the eleven reservations in Minnesota. That was quite clearly our market. A prime collaborator on the show really thought that there was a possibility that this might be the only HIV education that reservations would get. But within two months after it was released, it was in Sweden and Brazil and other places around the world. So it found a market because of the AIDS epidemic and because Carole's story was one that people of all kinds could connect with. That taught me that my best choice in these projects was to make them as particular as I could. Marketing has never been my strong suit, and distribution has usually been in the hands of collaborative partners, i.e., clients. We've done more than one national project; probably the biggest was for the CDC on community health workers around the United States. I didn't do the final edit of that show because their needs were different than mine. Since then, I believe that I've taken a long path to where I am now, which is work that is about . . . this place. I remember that it was not that many years ago I would tell people my dream is to focus on Dakota people and Dakota media. I didn't think that was possible even seven or eight years ago. And now that's pretty much all I do. By and large, all my work is Dakota focused . . . and this place, this, one of our sites of genesis.

JM: What do you mean by Dakota media?

MS: Focusing on Dakota subject and Dakota-controlled media. Living in the city we're a multinational community. And quite clearly our numbers are weighted heavily in favor of the Ojibwe. There are many more Ojibwe-Anishinaabe in Minnesota because of our history. The Dakota were exiled from Minnesota, were ethnically cleansed after the 1862 war. So there are only a few thousand of us in here in this place.

JM: Is there a large community you can draw on for stories? Let's talk about this place. The urban area that has a rich history for Dakota. For example, Franklin Avenue . . . it has history in the founding of AIM, correct?[5]

MS: Earlier than AIM or the European/Americans, Franklin Avenue was a Dakota trail. The confluence of the Mississippi and Minnesota rivers is a very sacred place to the Dakota people. Pike Island, which is an island at that confluence, is the place where the Mdewakantonwan Dakota tell us is the site of origin. It's often described as the Dakota Garden of Eden. It's also the center of the beginning of the *wasicun* [European] settlement here in this area. Pike Island is the site of the first treaty with the Dakota, when the land theft started officially. That was in 1805. Dakota people lived in this area all over. Our villages were very fluid, but sites were named and located. We buried our people here. We met each other here. We lived here. Our territory ran all the way into Canada and traveling to New Orleans, what is now New Orleans. But this is the center. This was one of the most sacred and crucial places for us. It is also the site at Fort Snelling, which is at the confluence, Fort Snelling after the war of 1862, those Dakota who surrendered—most of whom had no role in the war—were marched here from Morton, Minnesota—lower Sioux agency—to a concentration camp at Fort Snelling and were held over the winter there. Hundreds died. They were put on boats and forced down the Mississippi and up the Missouri and out of the state. Governor Ramsey made a very clear statement that all Dakota must be exterminated or driven from the borders of the state of Minnesota. It's hard for modern people to hear that and not define it as genocide.

So for Dakota people this a very exciting time to be a Dakota person, in this place, because Dakota people are coming back here, back home. Slowly, bit by bit. Sometimes we're importing elders from Canada—where many of our people went after the war. Maybe ten years ago a man, Glenn Wasicunna, had come to Minnesota as a teacher of the language. He and I talked for an afternoon about what it meant to him to come back here. And that this was a place he had always longed for and feared. Canadian Dakota are often frightened to come back here. It was into the twentieth century that farmers in certain parts of Minnesota would shoot at Dakota if they were seen. There was once a bounty. And the legacy of that bounty on Dakota lives continues. So it's a very difficult history of Dakota people here. And a wonderful time of transformation and healing. That is taking place here at the site of our genesis.

JM: Do you think that art, film, media . . . is a part of that?

MS: I hope so. One way that we may be a part of it is hopefully expressing Dakota point of view about the place to a non-Native audience. Hopefully in ways they can actually hear and let in. I see it as only a piece of all the work that needs to be done and all the expressing that needs to be done. I just said to somebody the other day, who was kind of complaining about the way one Dakota person chooses to express the notion of this being the site of our genesis and genocide. My answer to that is that Dakota people communicate every way. We write, we talk, we teach classes, we sing songs, we write poetry, we tell jokes, we're tremendously congenial, and sometimes we're really angry. We try every which way. And in my opinion, we need all of those ways. The media that I do and hopefully now putting some of it on the Web, is another way for me to put—as a partner has described it—unmediated voices on the Web for people to hear Dakota voices. In my opinion, listening to Dakota people is an extremely radical act.

JM: Talk about the Web site a bit.

MS: One of the primary Web projects that is very close to my heart comes from an installation I did at Ancient Traders Gallery (see image on page 328) . . . and when I say I did . . . I mean lots of help in that "I," both technical and those offering their voices—all the way to mechanics who cut a police car in half. It was an installation at the Ancient Traders Gallery that was about this as an Indian place. That very often through the twentieth century, probably from the 1950s on, the term *city Indians* was seen as something ironic. Indians who weren't really Indian. And when you look at this area as Dakota homeland, as our place, then it becomes a lot less ironic. We're here where a city grew up. One part of that installation was a stylized map of this area where I had historic photos showing various stages of sites in the area and then we had the Dakota names for various places in the confluence area, the Bdote area. And we invited people to add with Post-it notes their own stories on the wall.

My dream was to do that map on a Web site, but the funding and time wasn't there. The Minnesota Humanities Center liked the idea and saw it as a potentially useful thing for teachers teaching about Native people. They provided the funds through grants to do the pilot version, which is on the Web now. And have sought funds for the next version, which we're in the process of doing now and is more interactive, less page oriented.[6] You click on Pike Island and an elder will come up and tell some stories about it, some information about it. I have a dream of doing the *Bdote Memory Map* in a larger version, first of the Mississippi from Itasca to New Orleans. Another part of the dream is to help Native people and partners, allies with those partners, in various areas around the country who want to look at their own place. If you're going to use place as a lens, on this continent you have to start with the Indigenous people. You can't separate the place from the Indigenous people who lived there. So that's my largest dream.

JM: What a great project! Also to be able to express the movement and choices of where you/we go is not that linear experience you talked about. It is that web that is woven and woven, like stories and voices . . .

MS: Yes. One of the things I've learned most deeply about traditional storytelling and traditional education is this very deep understanding of human psychology that says, "What you tell needs to change given the circumstance and you can't control what the listener, the visitor, the participant takes in." So you tell it differently at different times.

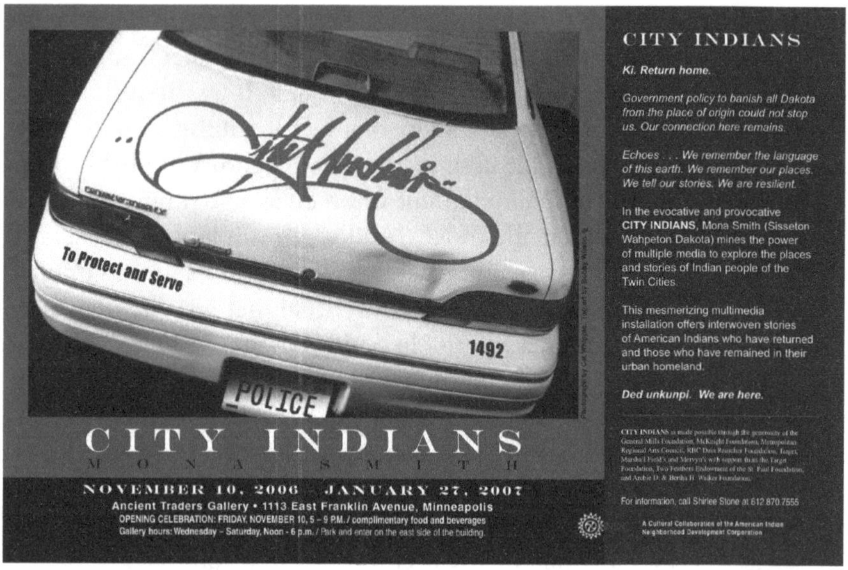

Ancient Traders Gallery poster *City Indians.*

And it's heard or seen differently at different times. So the Web for me really gives that choice and really gives something that people can go back to again and again. On Monday, this piece is going to strike you the most. Something will happen to you Tuesday. On Wednesday, you're going to go back and hear that same story in a different way. We're inviting visitors to visit these sites and give us—in text, photos, or video—their own stories. My primary goal is for Dakota people to place their stories to enhance that notion that it isn't a "was" our place. It "is" our place. That came home to me when I heard an elder from Sisseton speaking at Fort Snelling at a workshop for teachers. He said, "You know, sometimes people get upset—because the white people say they own this. But that's only on paper, we know that spiritually this is ours . . . and that is forever."

JM: When you were growing up, were you told traditional stories?

MS: I grew up in a small, largely wasicun town[7] . . . I say outside of the culture, but have since learned that my mother and her sister carried on Dakota values and ways of doing things. For example, the Dakota family structure . . . your mother's sister's children are your sisters and brothers, not your cousins, as they are in the white way. And

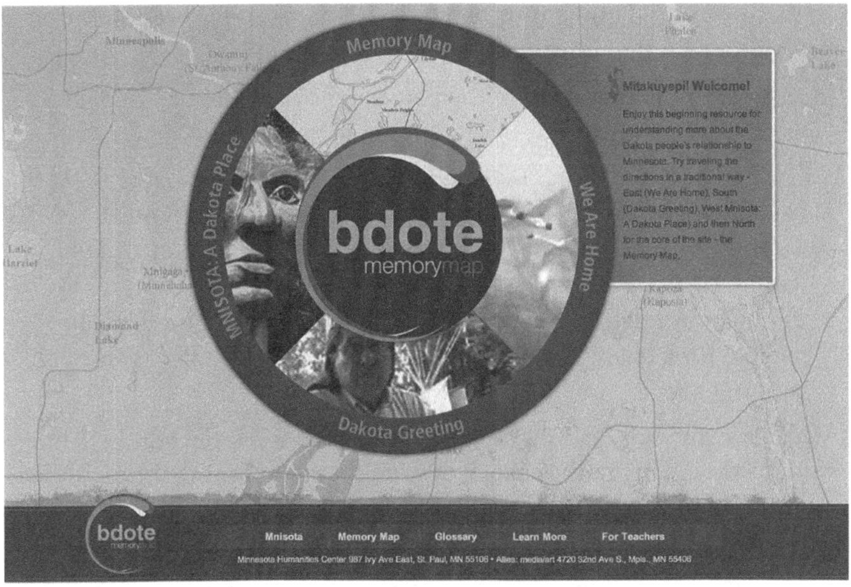

Mona Smith's *Bdote Memory Map*.

your mother's sister is like another mother. My mother was a modern mid-twentieth century woman. She traveled for her work when I was little and I lived with my auntie and my brother and sister, who are my cousins in the non-Native way. My mother was orphaned at an early age and was raised on the Crow Creek reservation in a mission school—a boarding school, which became an orphanage for her and her sisters when her mother died when she was eight. So often when I speak in public, I inform people that I was raised by a woman who was raised by nuns and priests. Not by Dakota elders. We lived in a small wasicun town on the river in Red Wing, Minnesota. It is traditional Dakota homeland, and when I look at our history, my mother, her sister, and me have all been led—not knowing what we were doing, but moving toward different parts of Dakota homeland. I, without knowing what I was doing, have moved very close to the Bdote, the confluence of the Mississippi and the Minnesota rivers. So it's a sign that it's where I am supposed to be and what I am supposed to be doing. But I was not raised with traditional stories; I was not raised with ceremony. I was raised with Powwow and we visited Sisseton rarely when I was young and occasionally relatives would come from there to visit us. I was fairly confused in childhood—that way. I was definitely bicultural.

JM: Do you think that's part of the cultural recovery themes or objectives within your work?

MS: Yes. One of the things that eased me, because in my early life I felt "not enough." As I learn our history, it's a natural given of what's happened since the war—being disconnected from your Dakota family is . . . certainly not universal but not at all uncommon. We're finding our relatives all over the continent and bringing Dakota people back together now. So my family history is not uncommon and not outside the forces of history.

JM: When you were getting into film and video work, did you look to any other Native filmmakers, or were there many at that time? Now we have so many emerging filmmakers.

MS: Yeaaaah! My first hero that was leading me into filmmaking just passed on. And it wasn't a woman and wasn't a Native person. It was Studs Terkel. Studs Terkel's books led me to whisper in my heart, "This is what I want to do, and I want to use a camera. I want to bring the voices of Native women in particular, but Native people to a place where other people can hear." Because again, the primary message of mainstream USA is for Native people to be invisible . . . to be past. So anything we do to make visible is radical. So first it was Studs. But then after a few years of doing stuff, what is now NAPT [Native American Public Telecommunication] had a conference in Santa Fe for Native filmmakers. I was so excited and went down and met maybe thirty or forty Native filmmakers. Of course, the two elders at that point—who are about an hour older than me—were George Burdeau and Phil Lucas. But because I came to video late—it wasn't my first career—they were certainly my elders too. They were serious role models. Their work, the work they do was not precisely the work I wanted to do or the way I wanted to do it, but that didn't matter. As a matter of fact, the reason I called my company Allies has to do with Phil. Because Phil talked about how you cannot do this media production work without allies. So being that "allies" is one translation of the word *Dakota*, and in honor of the non-Native people who have to be part of the work, I do it to make it happen. I was also honoring those allies in naming my company Allies: media/art. And George and Phil tell the story of Phil calling George when he found out there was another Native filmmaker and George, I believe, was working with CBS at that time and he called him and he was nervous because here he was going to be competition, and he was nervous about it. And George just said . . . "There are enough stories for every Indian person on this continent to pick up a camera."

JM: When was that?

MS: Like 1985, '86 . . .

JM: Was that before Turner's *The Native Americans*?

MS: Yes. Then I got to meet Victor Masayesva. I should not have started down this path. Names . . . Dan Jones . . . and D. R. Gary Farmer. He was introduced by Victor as the biggest Hopi who ever lived because he was doing Hillerman then and he was playing a Hopi and to all the Indian people Gary was an odd choice for that role.

JM: Do you work with any next-generation filmmakers?

MS: I am on the board of Migizi Communications here in Minneapolis. They have worked with Syd Beane and worked out internships with Fox in Los Angeles. They send young Native people out there every summer for two weeks to learn about the industry. My future is . . . I see so much hope in the Internet for Native people. It suits Native people. We are of imagination, as is the Internet, so it is perfect. I work with young people in that I invite their participation in these sites. We will be doing training for doing media for the Bdote sites. Generally my work has become much more intimate that it used to be. It's "crewless." The term that I love, I've become a *preditor* . . . a producer editor. It used to be when I started in the business, I was not allowed to touch the equipment. I was the concept person on the phone, the liaison, the interviewer, and then working with the technical artist to make it happen. Now I've had to learn Final Cut Pro.[8] I do shoot sometimes but with a little prosumer camera. I prefer just shooting nature. I don't like shooting interviews. Audio, which is my primary love of media, I am doing more audio interviews on my own and audio editing. *Cloudy Waters* was extremely about the audio—so much so that I use the primary and surround-sound nature sounds as a piece by itself and I use that when I go speak with groups.

JM: I remember carrying around those PortaPaks. When I first worked in broadcasting I couldn't even press the play button to watch my field tapes. I had to have a union engineer or technical person do that for me.

MS: Yes, exactly. I frankly crave those days. Now, I try to do this from the way Native people teach me . . . how to be Dakota. For example, all elders are shot from a lower angle and I do not interrupt people when I am shooting. Which makes for a lot of tape to go through for editing. That's how I try to learn and when possible I hire the best technical artists I can to work with.

JM: I have read a couple of articles that talk about IAIA [Institute of American Indian Art] and how they teach production and they do prayer, bless equipment and such . . . and some other Native filmmakers have talked a lot about protocol when in the community. Do you do anything like this?

MS: Well, I think there are a few significant anecdotes about how I see producing video, as a Dakota pursuit is different than other documentary or filmmakers of any kind. One that has always stuck with me was when we were doing *Her Giveaway*, there's a scene where the camera—it's a point-of-view shot into a bar—and I choose to shoot on a Sunday morning, because in those days, Minneapolis had a lot of street people with alcohol problems and I was trying to avoid having a camera around folks who were intoxicated. It was a conclusion I had come to that I would never record a Native person intoxicated. Carole LaFavor and I used to argue about this. She would say, "You have to show the truth," and I would say, "No, I believe in the old way, that you are locking someone in space and time." In that sense you are taking their spirit when you shoot them. So it needs to be a voluntary gift. Not locking them in time that way. It wasn't easy, because there were intoxicated people on the street, who in ways that I wouldn't have predicted, wanted to be on camera and had things to say and they wanted me to record them. Not recording them was not as easy as I had hoped. Another example, I have a few collaborators I have worked with during the years. I have them shoot elders from a lower angle out of respect. This has been confusing for them. I obviously won't shoot ceremony. Sometimes I am more conservative than the folks involved with the production on the other

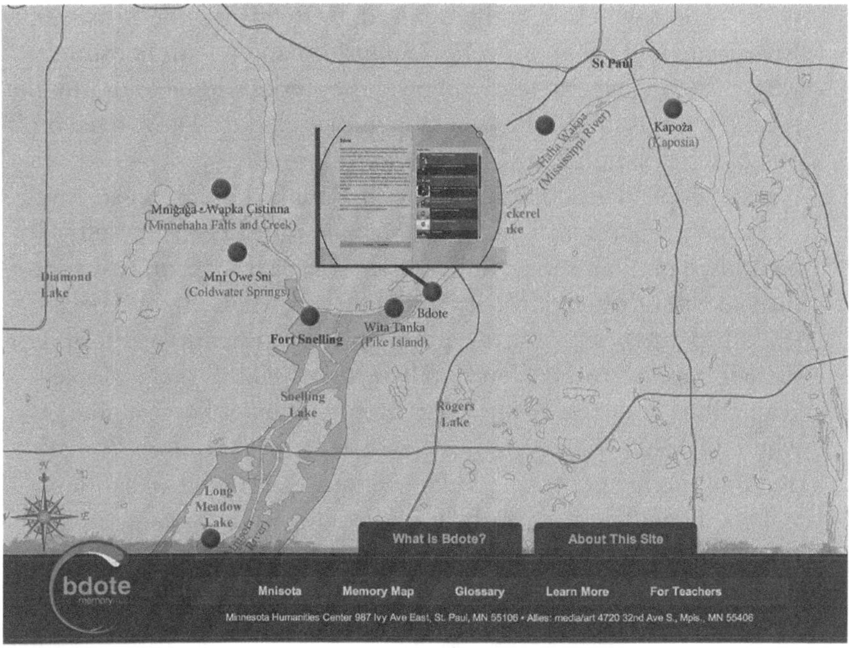

Cloudy Waters Web site image.

end of the camera, but I prefer to be wrong that way. I won't shoot pipes . . . I certainly do not find fault in other people who do. Because I think we are in a time of transition where protocols are also changing, but those are important things for me.

JM: Is there anything that you want to share that I didn't ask?

MS: I just think it's really important to recognize all the people who make the work possible. Very often I get to be the point person and I am sure I get some blame and discredit. But I often get the goodies for others' work. My husband, my collaborators and institutional partners, and absolutely, certainly . . . the people who always sign those release forms and allow me to gather the gifts they give and their person stories and knowledge. It just couldn't be done otherwise.

JM: Who are some of your institutional partners?

MS: The University of Minnesota has been a great partner, especially Pat Nunnally of the *Telling River Stories* project. We're just at the beginning of collaborating together, but he is making sure the stories of the people who live, and have lived, by the river—the Mississippi River—are told. That project is in transformation. I am not sure where they're going to land in how those stories will be told. Another good partner is the Minnesota Humanities Center. They've become one of the best non-Native sources for information for teachers on Native people. Particular in Minnesota, but that vision is expanding. They are my partner in the *Bdote Memory Map*. The site itself will be housed on their server, and workshops for teachers on how to use the site will be offered by the Humanities Center. I am also occasionally partners with a very controversial mainstream organization, the Minnesota History Center. Their history with Dakota people is appalling . . . to be clear. Their interpretation of Fort Snelling, where Dakota people were hung, where people were imprisoned, and that was the center of military action against the Dakota have not been handled well. Birthday parties at the Fort Snelling, school tours that never mention the Dakota history. However, my experience with some of the staff members at the history center has been good. *Cloudy Waters* was one example. They absolutely let me do—with their technical expertise and their technical artist's help—do things that there was no way I could do without them. Also they're in transformation with learning how to work with Dakota people and some good things are happening there. For example, using new technology, new media, doing podcasts that are presenting the voices of Dakota elders as a way to learn about the site at Jeffers, Minnesota, which is petroglyphs which are thousands and thousands of years old and very sacred. They do a good job protecting that site and interpreting that site. We're in discussion on another project of using cell phones and cell phone tours of Dakota sites in Minnesota. This is a way to bring more unmediated voices of Dakota people to other Dakota people. Also the Oceti Sakowin, which is a group of Dakota people, of all communities, of all Dakota tribes that is starting to come together, and that provides political action and ceremony. We just had a wonderful ceremony where elders could speak at the site of the concentration camp this last Sunday. They're involved with a lot of different kinds of healing work with Dakota people. And they have been very generous in allowing me to shoot events and helping bring elders for me to record.

JM: For someone who got into this early, you have a lot of longevity, stamina. You've done video, installation, and into new media now. For some Native filmmakers there were one or two pieces—that was it. They are valuable, but their media careers were shorter. I give you credit for this new work—podcasts, Web work . . .

MS: I am one of those weirdoes that really loves learning new software. I like that. I don't ever learn it deeply enough to become an expert but I learn enough to understand the vocabulary of new media. And for me the Internet, since I first saw that I could visit city information sometime in 1982 or '83 with prodigy Internet service. It has always struck me as a home for Native people in the modern world. We can work on it at the times that suit us. We create community of imagination. Which is what we are anyway. And it can help us get together. We are making connection as Dakota people in places where we're not in the same room—that are long lasting. I think our future is there.

Notes

Research funding for this interview provided by the WMU Faculty Research and Creative Activities Grant. Unless otherwise noted, all photographs are from the author's collection.

1. My previous publications on Mona Smith include "Consideration of a Native American Aesthetic: Mona Smith and Activist Video Voice," *Michigan Academician* 39.4 (1998): 371–86; "Consideration of a Native American Aesthetic: Mona Smith, Community Leadership and the Activist Video Voice," A *Leadership Journal: Women in Leadership—Sharing the Vision* 3.1 (1998): 67–76 (a revised version of the first article); and "'Children, Welcome to Your Past': Native and First Nation Film and Video as the Enunciation of Interdependence," in *Ethnic Media in America: Building a System of Their Own*, ed. Alice Tait and Guy Meiss (Dubuque, IA: Kendall/Hunt, 2005), 128–51.

2. Available at http://web.mac.com/alliesms/Memory/MEMORY_MAP_.html (accessed June 15, 2009).

3. PortaPak is a field video "kit" popular in the 1980s–90s before the release of digital equipment.

4. Three quarter inch tape stock was considered a professional field tape stock (analog) and used in news, commercials, public service announcements, college video/film programs, and independent production. The tape case is six to

eight inches long, five inches deep, and two inches high. A "three-quarter" house refers to a production company (house) producing on professional-grade analog video (three-quarter-inch tape).

5. AIM is the American Indian Movement. See http://www.aimovement.org (accessed June 15, 2009); and Joane Nagel, *American Indian Ethnic Renewal: Red Power and the Resurgence of Identity and Culture* (New York: Oxford University Press, 1997), 129.

6. *Ded Unkunpi*—Dakota for "We are here"—is located at http://web.mac.com/alliesms/Allies/Ded_Unkunpi.html (accessed June 15, 2009). Also see the *Bdote Memory Map* at http://web.mac.com/alliesms/Memory/MEMORY_MAP_.html (accessed June 15, 2009).

7. *Wasicun* in both Lakota and Dakota Sioux (variously spelled *Wasicu*, *Wašicun*, *Wasichu*, *Washicun*, or *Washichu*) means "non-Indian," and is also used to refer specifically to Europeans. Also see http://www.native-languages.org/iaq20.htm (accessed August 18, 2009).

8. Final Cut Pro is the Apple video-editing software.

The Journey's Discovery

An Interview with Shelley Niro

Elizabeth Weatherford

A gifted photographer, bead worker, painter, multimedia artist, and independent filmmaker, Shelley Niro explores the complex world of Native people and community story in the light of being part of the twenty-first century. With remarkable insight and often with humor, her work is intended to deflect and even comment on the customary stereotypes of Native people as represented in art and film. One of her strategies is to confront negative or clichéd notions and turn them upside down, reclaiming their kernel of insight while reframing them into positive characterizations. Niro's work reflects close ties to her community, family, and friends, creating a feeling of welcome and closeness in her audiences. Niro's work is in the "here and now," and she is equally comfortable with presenting the contemporary search for self-awareness of a young Native woman and the ways that traditional Mohawk knowledge serves contemporary people.

Since the 1990s Niro has been working in the field of photography, often with multiple-panel works—almost a prototype for a film—and in 1992 directed her first short film, *It Starts with a Whisper.* This was the year that Shelley and I first met. As was true for everyone working in Native cultural activities, that year, springing from the hemispheric awareness of the anniversary of Columbus's first voyage, was one in which creating work and presenting the arts was an act of protest and of positive energy about the present-day world of Native America. The National Museum of the American Indian (NMAI) combined forces with other Native organizations in New York City to present a unique film exhibition, Wind and Glacier Voices. Shelley was invited to show her work, and came to introduce it. We have been friends ever since. In 1997 she was invited to be a guest selector for the NMAI's Native American Film + Video Festival, an event that selects and screens more than one hundred new works from Indigenous directors and communities throughout the Western Hemisphere.

Niro is a member of the Turtle Clan, Bay of Quinte Mohawk. She was born in Niagara Falls, New York, in 1954, and raised on the Six Nations Reserve at Brantford, Ontario. A graduate of the Ontario College of Art, she also studied at the Banff Center for the Arts and received her MFA from the University of Western Ontario. Her work has been exhibited in galleries and museums across Canada and the United States, and she has had fellowships and residencies at major educational and cultural institutions.

In 1998 *Honey Moccasin* combined elements of melodrama, performance art, and "whodunit" to question conventions of film narrative and of ethnic and gender identity. The film, starring Tantoo Cardinal and Billy Merasty, with others in the cast from the community, was set on the "Grand Pine Indian Reservation" ("Reservation X"). The scene was set for a confrontation between the crusading café owner and private investigator Honey Moccasin and the errant drag queen/powwow outfit thief Zachary John. One of the first films to try to reinvent Native cinema in terms of pop culture, and to play with the ironies, it won festival awards and is recognized as a modern Native film classic in its irreverence and its deep appreciation of the strength of community.

Niro also continues to produce exciting exhibitions in photography and media arts, sometimes shown in unusual circumstances. In 2003 she was selected to be the exhibition artist with IA3[1] at the Venice Biennale, in which she showed her video *The Shirt* (a piece that in fact exists in multiple formats), a sly indictment of all that has been stolen from Native peoples, casting for it Hulleah Tsinahjinnie, the noted Navajo photographer. In 2007, again in Venice, she was part of the Requickening Project, which offered a display of Indigenous knowledge to contribute to a conversation invited by the Biennale's curator Robert Storr. For this she projected nightly her piece *Tree*, in which a young Earth Mother wanders through scenes of environmental loss and grieves over the changes she encounters until she is changed into a tree.

Niro's awareness of history is sharply represented by her confronting bitterness over the constraints placed upon Indigenous people and turning it into a vision of having power over the present. Her sense of social awareness is expressed in her care about creating strong female and gay characters. Her films often follow a journey of discovery in which her heroines and heroes uncover what is truly important. Frequently, the discovery is triggered by music or dance. At the center of her films is awareness that artists search in just this way, and through their creativity can sustain a view of autonomy, independence, and meaning that supersede the past and actually invent the future. Her portrayals of artists and musical performance not only enliven the works with interesting characters and scenes but also give a dimension to the autonomous and unique space that art inhabits. And by being so close to her community, she insists that highly contemporary Native art is not an elite system but one that the community can own and claim for itself. Niro's work is full of care for her characters, and in situations of deep emotion—anger or grief—she shows how humans reach for resolution and continuation. This could be in history or through experiences more intimate and personal.

In 2009 Niro premiered her first feature film, *Kissed by Lightning*, at the imagineNATIVE Film & Media Arts Festival in Toronto. Thus we got the chance to speak together in Toronto (our interview was initially conducted long distance by phone). Much of our discussion focuses on thoughts following the enthusiastic reception of the film.

Elizabeth Weatherford: As we begin to talk about you and your work, I'd like to start with asking about what influences your filmmaking.

Shelley Niro: It really comes down to what influences me when I'm trying to make something. I really believe that music is a big part of that influence, and I always think about music when I'm trying to write something, or to think about an idea. If you're listening to a song, you can't listen to half a song, it has to be a whole song, it has to start, it has to end, and it has to be able to get you from one place to that ending, and it has to be a satisfying experience, or you will not dedicate yourself to listening to that song 'til the end.

Yeah, it's storytelling, you know, and you have to have a story, and you have to finish that story, and if you're doing your job right, people will want to use the story 'til the end, but I think about music quite a bit when I'm trying to think of an idea.

EW: It sounds like you're composing film as if you're composing music. In listening you make some connection to how you structure the work you do. Music is not just what you listen to when you're working, as I was first thinking, but it offers a kind of model for how things work.

SN: And when you're working on your own, like when I'm doing a painting, I think, "Okay, nobody has to see this painting but me."

But when you're thinking about film, the audience is such an important factor. There is nobody who makes films just for themselves; you have to really think about people that are going to be watching this, and you have to put so much care into every frame that you're thinking about. You [can't not care about] what people think at this point, you have to really try to develop your images and your dialogue and your composition. And there's so much love put into making something.

EW: Who is the audience you imagine for your work? Do you make the work for them?

SN: When I first started it was for my family, for my sisters and my brother. I wasn't really doing it for my parents, because they didn't really get it anyway.

EW: But your mother's been a key figure in some of your images.

SN: She was always a great participant in the work, and she loves to be creative in that area. I guess that's my dad, my dad was like, well . . . He'd go, "I guess you like what you're doing, I don't get it, but you seem to do a lot of it."

EW: So your first audience when you started making film was your family. And already we see that imagining family as an audience is also imagining a critical audience with opinions about your work, who may or may not know your intentions. What happens to your sense of audience as your work has gotten more recognition?

SN: The audience has become further away, my audience isn't like my face anymore. I know they're out there, I know they're going to be seeing this, and I have to be able to make something for the people on the fringes. It's become a much more abstract audience. . . . But they're still in the room, this is what I think is interesting.

EW: You have an audience, not just one, you have different people who come to your work for different reasons, or walk away with different stories. But as you're a First Nations artist and filmmaker, do you think a Native audience has a primary place in this?

SN: We've been screening my newest film quite a bit to see if people are getting the stories and to see if there're little things that catch their eyes that make them go, "What?" So I've been trying to show the work to people as much as I could.

EW: Talk about your process for being in your community, making films with stories that are familiar, and being accountable, and living there too. Community screenings are a kind of an invitation for commentary, but not every filmmaker does them, much less a filmmaker who lives there with neighbors who are the same people whose commentary they've solicited. . . . Or to put it another way, showing it to the community you're not only preparing them for the fact that the film is going to come, but you're also soliciting comments that help you understand what you did.

SN: I expected people to say, "Oh, who do you think you are that you can do that?" But once I showed something to the community I would find it like it's really positive and people are really happy it's done. Of course they do not understand the labor-intense work that has to go into making it—for them it's entertainment, they're so conditioned to going to the movies, clunking down their ten bucks, and coming away? My screenings, you don't clunk down ten bucks, you just come.

But they've always been very generous, very kind. Somebody once, when I first showed *It Starts with a Whisper*, got up and said, "What's that all about?" but this is an elderly man. So he didn't get it, but even my own father, he watched it about five or six times, and he goes, "I think I'm getting this." Understand that movie, you know.

EW: That was your first film?

SN: Yes, it was made in 1992.

EW: It starts with a tragic reality, this lovely young woman Shanna, like you a Bay of Quinte Mohawk, who represents from the outset a sense of the cultural memory. In the way of tragedy, but also survival, it offers several levels of wisdom. There are the three aunties with a kind of Native "savvy." And there's Elisha Harper, who is an embodiment of elderly wisdom itself. That trajectory is so special in this film. And there is the coming to awareness that is the young woman's own path to wisdom. And it is rich with all the details you put in, the Busby Berkeley–style dance number and the stars in the sky, the fireworks in the sky. How did that film come to be, and what was in it that moved you to commit to being a filmmaker?

SN: Back in 1992, film was something that I never would have even imagined I would be able to make. It's like saying, "Okay, I want to

Toby Burning as Shanna in *It Starts with a Whisper.* (Courtesy of Shelley Niro)

be an astronaut," and it's like, "Yeah, right!" Because it will never happen, because you know for one thing, economically it is so beyond my scope. I never even considered it until I met a filmmaker, Anna Granau, from Toronto, whom I approached to make a film with me. I think once I went through the steps of making this film, seeing the actual steps that had to be done to make a film, I realized that you can make a film, anybody can make a film. You take one step at a time, and it's in knowing the results you're going to get each time you make a step. It opened my eyes so wide! So *It Starts with a Whisper*, it really shows you can do anything if you meet the right person and are shown how to do something, and you can really do it.

I've always envied people in film because you're really encasing those people in something so that you can see them in their youth forever. To a certain extent, Native people have never had that kind of opportunity and that kind legacy. When we were kids watching TV, we were so hungry to see Native people's images in film that when somebody was even pretending to be a Native person we just got so excited. Someone was playing this Indian guy who obviously was not Indian, but he was wearing the makeup and for us it was just so exciting! We were happy to see somebody who was just trying to be what we were, because the other version of Indians was through westerns—not a contemporary version at all.

I guess *It Starts with a Whisper* really laid out a foundation for me.

EW: How did the film express your 1992 thoughts?

SN: At that time, I was just starting out as an artist. 1992 was going by quickly. So I thought I'd have to do something in such a way that, when the film ends, it really bounces us into the future. It will take us from midnight 1992 into the next millennium of time thinking, "So we've been through this time period, and now we're going to go into the next time period, when we're going to do great things."

EW: That's great, because it does end that way, it ends with a kind of splendid New Year's. Your next film was *Overweight with Crooked Teeth*?

SN: That film was based on a poem written by my brother Mike. I always admired that poem, which was funny and serious and has many levels and layers. The film was done with no budget at all, which is so obvious, because I just had that desire to do that. We did it in a couple of days, and a really fast editing job.

EW: What's already begun to show up in these two films is your great sense of having characters who embody extremely contradictory aspects, who go against stereotypes, like the very unnoble Mohawk in the poem and your film. Can you tell us a little bit about the way you turned the poem into a film?

SN: When I read it, I felt the cultural humor there. The question is, "Well, what were you expecting, anyway?" At that time [the photographer Edward S.] Curtis was someone everybody was talking about, what he did about Native people, how he posed them, all this sort of thing. I thought, "This is right up the alley for deconstructing Curtis and his photographs." When I read the lines, I felt we could break this down, even poking fun at Native people themselves, even the great leaders Curtis photoed, because they carry so much weight with their well-known names and their history, and the image of them he perpetuated. We did the video, not really to be a rebel or irreverent—we just wanted to have a good time.

EW: It's a razor's edge you walk along when you're playing with somebody's beloved stereotype. You get pretty close to what might be really problematic for somebody, and then by your own nature you've got the humor to turn it into something people would like to laugh with. *Honey Moccasin* was, I think, close to this film in production, and it's obviously close to what we're talking about. The characters strongly express a number of different kinds of outlooks, or ways of being in the world. There's the gorgeous mature female detective, played by Tantoo Cardinal, who runs the reserve café/cabaret. And the likable cross-dressing thief with the telltale trail of feathers. They're both typecast and portrayed against type. That's what's so interesting, it's very experimental. You play with how a movie character acts and works, and then keep going to what you can do with it after you understand that. So do you want to talk to me a little bit about how you created the characters?

SN: I started writing that right after *It Starts with a Whisper* finished. At that time we were getting very close to the fiftieth anniversary of World War II. AIDS was a much-talked-about subject, and people from my father's generation considered it a "gay disease," sort of say-

Tantoo Cardinal in *Honey Moccasin*. (Photo by Jeff Thomson; courtesy of Shelley Niro)

ing, "Well, they deserve that." And I thought, "Here we are, close to the fiftieth anniversary of World War II, a war intended to counter the evil in the world, but now, after just looking at a community where a lot of death and disease were passing, there doesn't seem to be any kind of generosity there for the people." I was researching at the American Museum of Natural History, where I read about the berdache. In traditional times and in numbers of tribes in the West, there were transgendered men who dressed like women. They were considered to be powerful medicine people, people of high significance to their communities. But when the missionaries came, they started to label the berdache as evil, and this influenced the people to no longer accept them. I just started thinking about how these things link together, so I came up with the character played by Billy Merasty.

I made this environment where the bad and the good were within the whole Native community. Up until that point, the white guy was the bad guy, the Indian was the good guy, and then we made the story from there—I wanted bad and good within the Native community. I also wanted to have a lot of fun with it too. When the character of Jackly John ends up putting on a jingle dress, I thought, "I'm going to get into trouble here, because he's wearing this dress that is considered to be the dress of healing in Native communities and people are going to say, 'How dare you take our symbol and do this to it?'" And I thought, "This film is really about healing, and this man is putting on this dress." It's my way of saying that we have to heal ourselves, so I wanted to make that dress symbolize that.

EW: Another character in the film that is so compelling is the artist, Mabel Moccasin. In her performance piece she presents deeply troubling themes, but she also expresses this with poetry and aesthetically. In this way you introduce a whole other level. It is not humorous, but the historical and painful story is told through beauty—a beautiful young artist, her framing of it into something visual, with creativity so palpable, being able to have others pay attention to the most difficult of subjects. How much of your own thinking about being an artist does that reflect?

SN: That's kind of like the thing that's inside the thing—the film's stories are all one story. It's simply another story about healing something that's sort of invisible. The forgetting of the past, the berdache

Billy Merasty and Bernelda Wheeler in *Honey Moccasin*. (Photo by Jeff Thomson, courtesy of Shelley Niro)

reality, is like forgetting other parts of our history, as we wish to avoid knowledge about some of the pain. But then, I think you go ahead.

EW: You put your artist in the position of the one to be actually presenting tough truth, tough history, in a reflective way, right? But in an artistic way that must be viewed and felt.

SN: Right. Each character combines some good/bad things, each character is not a completely anything, they each are complex.

EW: As a media artist I think you've been involved with the Biennale in Venice a few times. How has being in that kind of arena had any impact or interest for you?

SN: I was asked in 2003 if I would be interested in doing something. I agreed because I think it's always important to have Native representation, especially outside of North America. It just opens the crack a little bit more, kind of like lifting up the side of a tipi and saying to people, "Come on! Hurry up! Jump in here! Come on!" So it feels like we're making a little ripple somewhere. The piece is *The Shirt*.

Another short media piece, *Tree*, was made possible in this way. I was approached by Roberto Arriganelo (now deceased), who was the executive director of a group in Toronto called LIFT/Liaison of Independent Filmmakers of Toronto. He invited me to make a short film for a program called New Horizons in Cinema. The support was limited but they could provide me any kind of camera and film I wanted to work with. I wanted to make a black-and-white, 35mm film and that's what I got. My thought is to show how Mother Nature would come from the lake and walk toward the city. Of course she's dismayed by everything she sees. It was the female version of that famous America the Beautiful campaign, and she too sheds a tear at what she sees.

EW: You often leave us with serious messages about memory and forgetting. But frequently you make this accessible through humor, the presence in the films of serious fun. I'm thinking in particular about *It Starts with a Whisper, Honey Moccasin*, and your new feature, *Kissed by Lightning*.

SN: To me humor is one of the most important ingredients in a film. I appreciate humor when I see it in other peoples' work. And in my own films—it has to be original, if it's not original it may be not funny enough. Or is it going to be so funny that people are going to be a little bit shocked?

EW: You take some surprising turns in some of your scenes. For example, in *It Starts with a Whisper*, when Shanna, on a serious quest for her own identity, gets carried off by her aunties, they won't let her remain pensive, and through their banter and ultimately the show-stopping musical number they perform, they show her one facet of life she seems to be missing. In *Kissed by Lightning*, you've used humor in a couple of different ways, in the way you portray and also contrast your characters.

SN: The character of Mavis is very serious. She's in a state of sadness where she can't really express emotion or absorb anyone else's emotion. She's in a kind of cocoon. And then there's the character of Bug, who is trying to get her attention, going through a kind of courtship ritual around her. But as he's doing this he's humble, and it's really about balance. Bug is trying to balance himself out by getting this woman to become part of his life. He becomes an object of humor in the film because he's always bumping into things and breaking things, even ends up breaking himself a bit. In the film we can witness her state, and then we can sort of relieve ourselves through seeing him, because he's so charming and so lovable that your heart wants to protect him, even as you know he's going to be crashing somewhere soon again.

EW: You have included characters in your films who are serious artists. Since you're an artist, working in a lot of different forms, what does it mean to include an artist as your character? In your new film the central character, Mavis, is a dedicated painter whose work is central to the plot. In other films, like *Honey Moccasin*, you have a key moment in which something that engages us in thinking more deeply is introduced through the vision of an artist, Mabel Moccasin, the artist who does a performance piece in the community's café. You've actually given your characters some of your own life.

SN: To me artists are like magicians. It's having the ingredients and trying to figure out how to mix them together to make them react with each other. I like pulling apart that whole experience of making something and what the artist is thinking, and how they're living their life, and then you almost get to see a little bit of the end product. Mabel is interesting because what she does is get her community, make the film and then show it to the community. Of course they're all there to see themselves in the film. As she's doing this, she's incorporating them into the work, but then she's also teaching them something. They're not really sure about what exactly she's teaching them, but they really like that she's included them.

EW: That reminds me of how you described your audience for your films earlier. You said something very similar to what you heard people say at your screenings in the community, "I don't know, but I really like it." Also, *Honey Moccasin* is set on a reserve. Mabel's presentation is to the "café society" on a reserve. You're holding up for scrutiny the idea that it's only in a city away from the reserve that you'll find an audience for contemporary arts. This community is so robust it's into the contemporary arts, too. This is flipping a stereotype about contemporary Native community, addressing a notion that a general audience needs to think about—the stereotype that reserve life is one thing, and life outside it is another, absolutely different thing, and that artists may not fit in.

I also wanted to mention how impressive it is to find out that when the artist produced an exhibition of paintings based on the story of the Great Peacemaker, all the paintings were actually done by you!

SN: Mavis was going to complete these paintings and take them to New York. Years ago, it would be interesting to have another artist do the paintings, because I felt, "What would another artist paint? How would they paint them? What would they consider to be the important painting to say this painting?" But we can't afford to pay another artist to do these things. The paintings had to have some kind of substance to them, and I really had to work fast on them. I would paint, go to a production meeting, work on the script, work on scenarios. I had so little time to work on the painting, but it became kind of fun and interesting at the same time, because it was done so fast. I had to pretend I was somebody else painting the paintings. "Okay, what would Mavis paint?" You're totally inventing somebody, you're becoming that person. So it was fun, a lot of fun.

EW: The subject matter is something that obviously fits with your character. Mavis is going through a personal journey and she's accompanied by the Peacemaker—a man who journeyed throughout the Haudenosaunee territories to teach about peace—through her work, as well as finding the connection there to her husband.

SN: Mavis is kind of an atheist, she doesn't believe, hasn't paid attention. But now that she's trying to remember her husband, she's making permanent the memory of her husband. Since these stories were important to him, she's become the conduit of that whole spiritual journey, so in a way she's sort of using her body to express this stuff. Initially she's not really attached to it because she wasn't brought up that way. But the act of telling the story opens up new avenues for her.

EW: In a way you're also describing the conduit a filmmaker is. You don't have to have lived the life of your characters to make your characters have lives, but you have to be empathetic to their lives.

SN: Exactly.

EW: In constructing a character you construct a whole person. So you got inside that Mavis, as well as made her up as a whole person.

The other artist in *Kissed by Lightning* is of course Mavis's deceased husband, Jesse Lightning, the musician, who was to some people, as the young girl describes him at some point, "'centric." He's this brilliant composer and violist who is no longer there, but whose presence is felt deeply. And in the movie we have a compelling sound track which includes his compositions as well as other interesting traditional and nontraditional music. Would you talk a little bit about the artist/musician and about the music that you were drawn to for this film's score?

SN: When I first started writing this years and years ago, I was thinking at the time of Jesse Lightning being a cellist. But the solo viola, it's interesting and cellolike. And it's like a voice. Did you know that the viola in an orchestra is called the "Peacemaker" because it's in between the violin and the cello?

EW: It's true about the voice of the viola. It's a resonant, bittersweet voice, that sound.

SN: It is a lonely pursuit. In our culture I think it was Handsome Lake who said violin music should be restricted, as it's something that's coming from the West—to be banned really. This was about not accepting new technology, that technology has to stop here. But in life it doesn't stop, it goes on. And for the film I needed to use the viola because I just had such a strong picture of this man playing his viola, and the music.

EW: That's interesting, because Jesse is a man who is also talking to his wife, Mavis, about the work of the Great Peacemaker and Hiawatha, and whose compositions are themed to fit in accord with the Peacemaker's messages. Even though that seems to be by custom a prohibition, obviously there's built into your story that such a transgression of custom can actually work to serve a higher purpose. It's an understanding that rules may not cover all occasions, and that meanings are not overtaken by new technology, but can be amplified by them. In your films I think you present not only the bigger picture, the Law of Peace, the big thing. You also always seem to have within the works characters who are elders, who might be seen to be the best spokespeople for traditional outlooks. But your elders generally say to people, "This is the present, go forward from now, into the future." Elders in your stories are not pulling back, pulling everybody to only come back to the old ways nostalgically, but are so grounded they can see the way to the future.

SN: This works because they're saying, "Just remember where you come from, you can go ahead, just remember your history."

EW: A great example of this is the scene in *Honey Moccasin* in which it's the elders who put on the hip and experimental fashion show that allows the young people to imagine new forms of dresses and outfits.

SN: Yes, somebody stole all their stuff, and then stole all the stuff that they make their stuff with, and the elder says, "Yeah, you lost all that stuff, but you still have your brains, just use something that your brains can think of." It was really a reference to language and history, and all those family and clan ties, which may be gone. But we still have our brains so that we can keep going, and we don't have to give up so fast.

EW: And the brains make us creative. This was another form of artistry you referenced, because they end up making these wonderful outfits with weird materials, very punk looking and interesting. This is about how one embraces the present possibilities and doesn't turn away from what looks like an extraordinary shift from what is considered traditional. Maybe tradition is about change, tradition isn't about anything static.

I think also of the great-grandmother in *Kissed by Lightning* who takes Mavis aside and says to her, "You're rooted here." She demonstrates this by pointing out that she knows all about Mavis's and Jesse's and Bug's families that have been in the Mohawk territories for generations. And then she gives Mavis advice, her permission to go forward into her future, to embrace what's right in front of her. This is about choosing to love Bug, but it's also about letting the past take its special place but not dominate. You have made what we might consider the avatars of the past, the elders, be the ones who are most progressively pushing the younger people—who are a little confused and don't know exactly which way to go—to give them a path, and give them permission to go on it.

SN: That's right.

EW: I would love to hear a little bit more about how you chose Kateri Walker to play the role of Mavis. Did she feel comfortable playing the role of a Mohawk woman?

SN: Even though she's supposed to be Mohawk, her character is kind of universal, a woman in grief who is trying to find her way through the

Kateri Walker (Mavis) and Eric Schweig (Bug) in *Kissed by Lightning*.

Kateri Walker as Mavis Dogblood in *Kissed by Lightning*.

world. Her role is really about family, and trying to find that family, and make that family. She's missing the family that she almost had, and she can't get over that to go on.

EW: You directed her to move into a life where she could smile again, she's so sad as the film starts. When Mavis and Bug are in that coffee shop in upstate New York, where the people are so cold to them, a singing group comes in who are African American, and they urge her to sing and also generously give her a song. By the situation she is compelled to participate, and then to feel some joy. Well, I think it's the sense of each film of yours I've seen, a strong sense of how one becomes aware through joy, art, humor, play, and unexpected encounters.

SN: The singers have a lot of impact on Bug and Mavis. When she tells them that they're Mohawk, the singers immediately honor the fact that this is the land where once upon a time the roots of the Mohawk people were. [In this scene the singers also express gratitude for the participation of the Mohawk in the Underground Railroad that helped African Americans find freedom from slavery.] Their interest sparks in Mavis interest in some things that she had never really paid much attention to before.

EW: This film has strength because of the thread that connects people's feelings with the presence of history that lies everywhere and simply needs to be noticed. As they cross the Mohawk territories, you really feel the arbitrariness of that border [the international border between Canada and United States, across which Haudenosaunee people are supposed to be able to pass freely, according to the Jay Treaty]. You permit us to see the difference between what people live with and what the original territories actually are for First Nations people. Even if you're not necessarily there anymore, it's always where you've been, where your roots are. Even better, there are people living all around within the upstate New York part of the Mohawk lands that are Mohawk and they are remembering the whole.

You've done something very special in the way you present the notion of the territories, this larger space that has been the Mohawk space and still is, even though it's now penetrated by towns and highways that are not Mohawk necessarily. You even introduce a mythical aspect, a wonderful way to say the territories are eternal; some people obviously from the eighteenth century pass through the land and are seen, to their amazement, by Mavis and Bug. It is such a lovely idea, to demonstrate what these lands contain in terms of Bug and Mavis's own history.

SN: You know, they are outside at night, and they're lost. And they can feel that the spirits are reaching out to them. They can see these warriors of the past at the moment of their being lost, too. [During the time of colonial strife in the region, many Mohawk left to go north into what became Canada.] Maybe their village left while they were gone to war, so they are still wandering, wondering where everybody is. And Mavis and Bug, sitting in the van, are a little lost, too.

EW: The film is about a young woman who is lost in her own life, and a people, from whom she comes, now in a place in Canada called Six Nations Reserve, but who once fully inhabited this very place. It comes together when Mavis opens her gallery show in New York City. She's showing these very personally significant as well as culturally significant paintings. Not only are there New York buyers and critics, but three of the warriors are now in the gallery with her, and one of them stops and puts his hand on her shoulder. These men of the past are looking intently at her works, and like the insiders they are, they are in deep and animated discussion in front of the paintings. I liked that very much. The sense of the gallery show as a place for the artist to feel comfortable was interesting, too. Strong, in her own terms, it can be a positive place to end her journey. It means stepping forward into an unpredictable world dominated by another cultural sensibility that Mavis—an artist, a woman, a Mohawk—might have, and finding that it's okay.

Being a woman filmmaker from your own creative perspective—does it make, what kind of impact do you think it makes on the films you choose to do?

SN: When I first started making art and films, I had a personal manifesto: my art is going to be like this, this, this, and this. One of the things was, "In my films I'm going to have a female protagonist, because female Native roles are so limited. And I will really stay away from clichés. And I will try to be as inventive, and make it as much fun, as I possibly can." I think of films I admire—*Blazing Saddles* is one of them, such a smart, funny film which got so many points across about racism and was hilarious. If [Mel] Brooks can do it, I can do it too. You need to set up your boundaries, and your own rules.

EW: I know when you say set up your own rules, in one way it's a kind of conceptual thing that an artist does, it's not that you say, "These are my limits" but you say, "These are my priorities." You work in a lot of different art forms, how do you know whether you're going to be painting or making a photographic series or a film? You've got so many talents, how do you know where to use them?

SN: I think it just depends on the image—would this image be stronger painted, would it be smarter as a photograph—so it's sort of making those little decisions as they go along.

EW: So next, do you think you'll be making film right on the heels of this, or do you think you'll do something else?

SN: I'm going to do something else for a year or two.

EW: I think that's a reflection of how you work as an independent artist. That is, you're obviously highly regarded in the industry in Canada. [The new films' producer Telefilm Canada is] a very significant organization to be interested in you as a filmmaker. But you really function autonomously as an artist most of the time, and that allows you to choose to not always be a filmmaker.

SN: That's probably the best thing I do for myself is not to be only a filmmaker. If I could make a new work only every five years or so, I would not be happy. This is why I've got to do my photos, more paintings. Maybe I could make a film a lot faster if I totally devoted my time and effort to it, but I don't think I would be artistically satisfied by that.

EW: You're a filmmaker, you work in the world of Native arts, and you work in the world of arts and film in general. Where do you think this field is going? What do you think lies in the future for First Nations independent film?

SN: When did Native films start getting Native, twenty years ago? I remember going to those first few film festivals, and the same twelve people would be there. Since then it's totally taken off and gone in every direction you can think of. That's so cool, because we were just so hungry just to see ourselves onscreen. For us, David Steinberg was a major hero when we were kids, because he'd be on TV doing all these crazy things. But since he had black hair, we'd think, "Oh, he could be an Indian!" We were so hungry for role models of any kind that we attached ourselves to anybody. And now we don't have to do that, we don't have to pretend they're us, just because they have dark hair.

Concluding Remarks from Elizabeth Weatherford

The field is really diverse now. Back in the first days, for a lot of filmmakers it was crucial to make documentaries, which were about inscribing Native cultures into history. It was very serious, and a big obligation that filmmakers took on themselves, and there's still a great stream of it. Alanis Obomsawin was speaking recently about documentation work she did when she was quite young and how important it still is, because, as she noted, every community should have access to its own history, its own film version of its own history.

But since the first works were produced, so many things have happened. Now there are experimental media arts and horror films and funny films and feature-length documentaries and narrative films. In thinking about the multiplication of genres, I think about what Shelley Niro's special contribution has been. From the beginning she spun together films drawn easily from a variety of genres and tones—humorous, artistic, nostalgic, seriously presenting the past and the inroads of the present, and the present's possibilities. As Shelley Niro did in *It Starts with a Whisper,* she can open with a reference to the decimations of the past, ironically stage a dance number, and end with fireworks and a highly joyful look into the future. What I love in her work is she didn't stake a claim, she opened a doorway into lots of alternatives for making film. I think a lot of this next generation of filmmakers are taking one or the other of these genres and moving forward. Shelley Niro is an ideal "elder." She has a good sense of lingo, and the path she can guide us to is almost mythical.

Notes

Unless otherwise noted, all photographs are from the author's collection.

1. IA3 is a collaboration of Indigenous artists and curators specifically organized for showing works during the Venice Biennale. Initially called the Native American Arts Alliance, the initiative is now named the Indigenous Arts Action Alliance and continues to challenge the contemporary art curatorial world to incorporate the works and outlooks of contemporary Native artists.

Acknowledgments

Native Americans on Film is the creative outcome of a long-standing friendship and collegial dialogue about Indigenous film, nurtured by our mutual respect and philosophy of life and learning. Our dialogue grew to include an extended family of educators, scholars, filmmakers, and artists whose voices are highlighted in this volume.

Native Americans on Film began as a conversation about the need for a collection of essays that provided the Native American and American Indian studies' approach to film. As often happens, the idea began to take on concrete weight in a most sideways but fortuitous fashion. In acknowledgment of our journey, we would like to extend our deepest gratitude and thanks to those who have encouraged us, helped with editing, participated in conversations, and included their voices in any and all versions of this project: Gregg Britton, Amy Corbin, Jennifer L. Cauthier, Carole Gerster, Sterlin Harjo, Pauline Harris, Joanna Hearne, Angelica Lawson, Randolph Lewis, Blackhorse Lowe, Jennifer Machiorlatti, Shelley Niro, Petra Lina Orloff, Sandy Osawa, Saza Osawa, Sam Pack, Michelle Raheja, Ann Reagan, Randy Redroad, Zack Shlachter, Beverly Singer, Mona Smith, Carla Taunton, Elizabeth Weatherford, and Houston Wood. We also extend our gratitude to Anne Dean Watkins, Bailey Johnson, Ila McEntire, Robin DuBlanc, and all the staff at the University Press of Kentucky for their belief in our project, their respect for our process, and their commitment to Native film and media.

We also would like to thank the following journals and presses for their permission to reprint key articles in our theoretical section: The Continuum International Publishing Group for Houston Wood's essay, "Dimensions of Difference in Indigenous Film," which was originally published in Houston Wood, *Native Features: Indigenous Films from*

Around the World (New York: The Continuum International Publishing Group, 2008); The Johns Hopkins University Press for Michelle H. Raheja, “Reading Nanook’s Smile: Visual Sovereignty, Indigenous Revisions of Ethnography, and *Atanarjuat (The Fast Runner)*,” *American Quarterly* 59:4 (2007): 1159–85, copyright 2007 The American Studies Association; and *Post Script: Essays in Film and the Humanities* for Jennifer L. Gauthier, “Dismantling the Master’s House: The Feminist Fourth Cinema Documentaries of Alanis Obomsawin and Loretta Todd,” and Carla Taunton, “Indigenous (Re)memory and Resistance: Video Works by Dana Claxton,” from *Post Script: Essays in Film and the Humanities. Native American/Indigenous Film, Special Edition*, guest editor, M. Elise Marubbio, *Post Script: Essays in Film and the Humanities* (Texas A&M University–Commerce) 29.3 (Summer 2010).

Selected Filmography

In conceptualizing this collection, we imagined a resource guide for teachers, academics, students, and general readers. Part of that resource includes this filmography, which provides a listing of the Indigenous films discussed throughout the edition. It also theoretically continues the conversation about what constitutes an Indigenous film and an Indigenous filmmaker, a primary theme throughout the book. Some of the films listed are not Indigenous in subject but are made by Indigenous filmmakers. Others are Indigenous in subject, based on Indigenous writers' works, or collaborated on with Indigenous people, but are not directed by Indigenous filmmakers. By including such variety, we hope to encourage further debate among your students, colleagues, and friends.

Many of the films are available in DVD format for home use through such outlets as Blockbuster, Hollywood Video, and Netflix in North America (Region One). "DVD" follows these entries. A few of the international films are available for home use only on VHS. Educational and theatrical distributors are listed with the titles; some of these also distribute on DVD for home use. Those wishing to purchase for school uses should work with their libraries to procure copyright permission. In some cases for films from Canada, such as *Atanarjuat*, educators will need to go to Vtape (www.vtape.org/catalogue.htm). Further purchasing information is provided for those films only available from either small or region-specific vendors. Some films are labeled "not currently available," but readers should be aware that older titles are frequently being reissued. We highly recommend that readers refer to the Native Networks Web page; its master list of films, filmmakers, and distributors provides valuable information on these and other Indigenous films as well as film festivals.

Los angeles de la tierra/Angels of the Earth. Directed by Patricio Luna (Aymara). 2001/2003. For information on the English-language version, contact the National Museum of the American Indian at fvc@si.edu.

Atanarjuat: The Fast Runner. Directed by Zacharias Kunuk (Inuit). 2002. DVD. Available from Vtape at www.vtape.org. At Isuma.tv there is also a portal site for Indigenous media, which has many other works and clips that can be viewed online at no charge.

Barking Water. Directed by Sterlin Harjo (Seminole/Creek). 2009. Information available from Indion Film at www.indionfilm.com.

Before Tomorrow. Directed by Marie-Hélène Cousineau and Madeline Ivalu (Inuit). 2007. Available from Vtape at www.vtape.org.

Beneath Clouds. Directed by Ivan Sen (Gamilaroi). 2002. DVD and VHS. Available from http://www.roninfilms.com.au.

A *Bride of the Seventh Heaven* (Jumalan Morsian). Directed by Anastasia Lapsui (Nenets) and Markku Lehmuskallio. 2001. Available from http://www.ses.fi.

Buffalo Bone China. Directed by Dana Claxton (Lakota). 1997. Available from Vtape at www.vtape.org.

The Business of Fancydancing. Directed by Sherman Alexie (Spokane/Coeur d'Alene). 2002. DVD. Available through FallsApart Productions at www.fallsapart.com.

Cow Tipping: The Militant Indian Waiter. Directed by Randy Redroad (Cherokee). 1992. Available from Third World Newsreel at distribu tion@twn.org.

The Doe Boy. Directed by Randy Redroad (Cherokee). 2001. DVD. Hollywood Video and Netflix.

Eagle vs Shark. Directed by Taika Waititi (Māori Te Whanau-a-Apanui). 2007. DVD. Available through the New Zealand Film Commission at www.nzfilm.co.nz.

Family: The First Circle. Directed by Randy Redroad (Cherokee), Heather Rae (Cherokee), and Russell Friedenberg. 2009. Not yet available.

5th World. Directed by Blackhorse Lowe (Navajo). 2005. Available from L. Blackhorse, blackhorse_films@hotmail.com.

Finding My Talk: A Journey into Aboriginal Languages. Directed by Paul M. Rickard (Cree). 2000. Available from Shenandoah Film Productions at www.shenandoahfilms.com.

The Flying Head. Directed by Shelley Niro (Mohawk). 2008. Available from Vtape at www.vtape.org.

Forgotten Warriors. Directed by Loretta Todd (Métis). 1997. Available through the National Film Board of Canada at http://www.nfb.ca and Vtape at www.vtape.org.

Four Sheets to the Wind. Directed by Sterlin Harjo (Seminole/Creek). 2007. Information available through the Film and Video Center: AllenW@si.edu.

Goodnight, Irene. Directed by Sterlin Harjo (Seminole/Creek). 2005. Available from Indion Film at http://www.indionfilm.com.

Grand Avenue. Directed by Daniel Sackheim. 1996. VHS. Available at Blockbuster.

Haircuts Hurt. Directed by Randy Redroad (Cherokee). 1992. Available from Third World Newsreel at distribution@twn.org.

Hands of History. Directed by Loretta Todd (Métis). 1994. Available from National Film Board of Canada at http://www.nfb.ca and Vtape at www.vtape.org.

Harold of Orange. Directed by Richard Weise. 1983. Available from VisionMaker Video at www.visionmaker.org.

The Heart of Everything That Is. Directed by Dana Claxton (Lakota). 2000. Available from Vtape at www.vtape.org.

Her Giveaway: A Spiritual Journey with AIDS. Directed by Mona Smith (Dakota). 1988. Available from Women Make Movies at www.wmm.com.

Her Sugar Is? Directed by Dana Claxton (Lakota). 2009. Available from Vtape at www.vtape.org.

High Horse. Directed by Randy Redroad (Cherokee). 1994. Available from Third World Newsreel at distribution@twn.org.

The Hill. Directed by Dana Claxton (Lakota). 2004. Available from Vtape at www.vtape.org.

Honey Moccasin. Directed by Shelley Niro (Mohawk). 1998. Available from Women Make Movies at www.wmm.com and Vtape at www.vtape.org.

Honored by the Moon. Directed by Mona Smith (Dakota). 1990. Available from Women Make Movies at www.wmm.com.

Horse You See. Directed by Melissa A. Henry (Navajo). 2007. Available from Red Ant Films at http://red-ant.net.

Hózhó of Native Women. Directed by Beverly Singer (Tewa Pueblo, Navajo). 1994. VHS. Available from Women Make Movies at www.wmm.com.

Hunger. Directed by Shelley Niro (Mohawk). 2008. Available from Vtape at www.vtape.org.

I Belong to This. Part of *Matters of Race* (PBS). Directed by Dustin Craig (Apache/Diné). 2003. Not currently available.

Ibid. Directed by Randy Redroad (Cherokee). 2008. Available at Amazon .com.

Images of Indians. Directed by Phil Lucas (Choctaw) and Robert Hagopian. 1979. Available for sale from the Four Worlds International Institute at www.4worlds.org/index.

Imagining Indians. Directed by Victor Masayesva Jr. (Hopi). 1993. Available from Electronic Arts Intermix at www.eai.org.

Incident at Restigouche. Directed by Alanis Obomsawin (Abenaki). 1984. Available from National Film Board of Canada at http://www.nfb.ca and Vtape at www.vtape.org.

In the Heart of Big Mountain. Directed by Sandy Osawa (Makah). 1988. Available from Upstream Productions at www.upstreamvideos.com.

Is the Crown at War with Us? Directed by Alanis Obomsawin (Abenaki). 2002. Available from National Film Board of Canada at http://www .nfb.ca and Vtape at www.vtape.org.

Itam Hakim, Hopiit. Directed by Victor Masayesva Jr. (Hopi). 1984. Available from Electronic Arts Intermix at www.eai.org.

It Starts with a Whisper. Directed by Shelley Niro (Mohawk). 1992. Available from Canadian Filmmakers Distribution Centre at www.cfmdc .org and Vtape at www.vtape.org.

I Want to Know Why. Directed by Dana Claxton (Lakota). 1994. Available from Vtape at www.vtape.org.

The Journals of Knud Rasmussen. Directed by Norman Cohn and Zacharias Kunuk (Inuit). 2006. DVD. Available from Vtape at www.vtape.org.

Kainayssini Imanistaisiwa: The People Go On. Directed by Loretta Todd (Métis). 2003. Available from National Film Board of Canada at www.nfb.ca and Vtape at www.vtape.org.

Kanehsatake: 270 Years of Resistance. Directed by Alanis Obomsawin (Abenaki). 1993. Available from National Film Board of Canada at www.nfb.ca and Vtape at www.vtape.org.

Kissed by Lightning. Directed by Shelley Niro (Mohawk). 2009. Available from Vtape at www.vtape.org.

The Land Has Eyes (Pear ta ma 'on Maf). Directed by Vilsoni Hereniko (Rotuman). 2004. DVD. Available from www.thelandhaseyes.com.

The Learning Path. Directed by Loretta Todd (Métis). 1991. Available from Icarus Films at http://icarusfilms.com/cat97/k-o/learning.html.

Lighting the 7th Fire. Directed by Sandy Osawa. 1995. Available from Upstream Productions at www.upstreamvideos.com.

Llanthupi Munakui/Loving Each Other in the Shadows. Directed by Marcelina Cárdenas (Quechua). 2001. For information on the English-language version, contact the National Museum of the American Indian at fvc@si.edu.

The Māori Merchant of Venice (Te Tangata Wahi Rawa o Wenit). Directed by Don C. Selwyn (Māori Ngati Kuri and Te Aupouri). 2001. Not currently available.

Maria Tallchief. Directed by Sandy Osawa (Makah). 2007. Available from Upstream Productions at www.upstreamvideos.com.

Mile Post 398. Directed by Shonie De La Rosa (Navaho) and Andee De La Rosa (Navaho). 2007. DVD. Available from www.sheepheadfilms.com.

Moccasin Flats. Directed by Randy Redroad (Cherokee). 2003. Available from Big Soul Productions at www.bigsoul.net.

My Name Is Kahentiiosta. Directed by Alanis Obomsawin (Abenaki). 1995. Available from National Film Board of Canada at http://www.nfb.ca and Vtape at www.vtape.org.

Naming Number Two (No. 2). Directed by Toa Fraser (Fijian). 2006. DVD. Available from www.arovideo.co.nz.

Naturally Native. Directed by Valerie Redhorse (Cherokee/Sioux) and Jennifer Wynne Farmer. 1998. Available from Red Horse Native Productions at www.naturallynative.com.

Ngati. Directed by Barry Barclay (Māori Ngati Apa). 1997. VHS. Avail able from www.arovideo.co.nz.

Nice Coloured Girls. Directed by Tracy Moffatt (Aboriginal Australian). 1987. Available from Women Make Movies at www.wmm.com.

Nikawomin (Song). Directed by Kevin Lee Burton (Swampy Cree). 2007. Available from Vtape at www.vtape.org.

Ofelas/Pathfinder. Directed by Nils Gaup (Sámi). 1987. DVD. Carolco Pictures.

On and Off the Res' with Charlie Hill. Directed by Sandy Osawa (Makah). 2000. Available from Upstream Productions at www.upstreamvideos.com.

Once Were Warriors. Directed by Lee Tamahori (Māori). 1994. DVD. Fine Line Films.

133 Skyway. Directed by Randy Redroad (Cherokee). 2006. Available from Big Soul Productions at www.bigsoul.net.

Our Nationhood. Directed by Alanis Obomsawin (Abenaki). 2003. Available from National Film Board of Canada at www.nfb.ca and Vtape at www.vtape.org.

Out of the Blue: A Film about Life and Football. Directed by Randy Redroad (Cherokee), Heather Rae (Cherokee), and Russell Friedenberg. 2007. DVD.

Overweight with Crooked Teeth. Directed by Shelley Niro (Mohawk). 1997. Available from Vtape at www.vtape.org.

Pepper's Pow Wow. Directed by Sandy Osawa (Makah). 1997. Available from Upstream Productions at www.upstreamvideos.com.

Radiance. Directed by Rachel Perkins (Arrernte/Kalkadoon). 1998. DVD. Available from www.ezydvd.com.au.

Richard Cardinal: Cry from the Diary of a Métis Child. Directed by Alanis Obomsawin (Abenaki). 1986. Available from National Film Board of Canada at www.nfb.ca and Vtape at www.vtape.org.

Robert's Painting. Directed by Shelley Niro (Mohawk). 2011. Available from Vtape at www.vtape.org.

Rocks at Whiskey Trench. Directed by Alanis Obomsawin (Abenaki). 2000. Available from National Film Board of Canada at www.nfb.ca and Vtape at www.vtape.org.

Samoan Wedding (Sione's Wedding). Directed by Chris Graham. 2004. DVD.

Seven Songs from the Tundra (Seitsemän laulua tundralta). Directed by Anastasia Lapsui (Nenets) and Markku Lehmuskallio. 1999. Not currently available.

Shimásání. Directed by Blackhorse Lowe (Navajo). 2009. Information available from Film and Video Center, AllenW@si.edu.

The Shirt. Directed by Shelley Niro (Mohawk). 2003. Available from Vtape at www.vtape.org.

Sitting Bull and the Moose Jaw Sioux. Directed by Dana Claxton (Lakota). 2003.

Skins. Directed by Chris Eyre (Cheyenne/Arapaho). 2002. DVD.

Skinwalkers. Directed by Chris Eyre (Cheyenne/Arapaho). 2002. DVD.

Sky Woman with Us. Directed by Shelley Niro (Mohawk). 2002. Available from Vtape at www.vtape.org.

Smoke Signals. Directed by Chris Eyre (Cheyenne/Arapaho). 1998. DVD.

Sonam, the Fortunate One. Directed by Ahsan Muzid. 2005. Not currently available.

Spudwrench: Kahnawake Man. Directed by Alanis Obomsawin (Abenaki). 1997. Available from National Film Board of Canada at www.nfb.ca and Vtape at www.vtape.org.

Ten Canoes. Directed by Rolf de Heer and Peter Djigirr (Yolngu). 2006. DVD. Available from www.ezydvd.com.au.

Te Rua. Directed by Barry Barclay (Māori Ngati Apa). 1991. VHS. Available from www.arovideo.co.nz.

That Which Is Between. Directed by Mona Smith (Dakota). 1989. Available from info@alliesmediaart.com.

A Thousand Roads. Directed by Chris Eyre (Cheyenne/Arapaho). 2005. DVD. Available at http://www.nmai.si.edu/subpage.cfm?subpage=shop&second=cds&third=AThousandRoads.

Tree. Directed by Shelley Niro (Mohawk). 2006. Available from Vtape at www.vtape.org.

Trudell. Directed by Heather Rae (Cherokee). 2005. Available at Appaloosa Pictures, www.appaloosapictures.org.

Tushka. Directed by Ian Skorodin (Choctaw). 1996. Information available from Film and Video Center, AllenW@si.edu.

Usual and Accustomed Places. Directed by Sandy Osawa (Makah). 1997. Available from Upstream Productions at www.upstreamvideos.com.

A Video Book. Directed by Beverly Singer (Tewa/Navajo). 1994. Available from Third World Newsreel at distribution@twn.org.

Vigil. Directed by Rebecca Belmore (Anishinabekwe). 2002.

Warrior Chiefs in a New Age. Directed by Dean Bear Claw (Crow). 1993. Available from Film and Video Center, AllenW@si.edu.

Waterspeak. Directed by Dana Claxton (Lakota). 2000. Available from Vtape at www.vtape.org.

Whale Rider. Directed by Niki Caro. 2001. DVD.

Yolngu Boy. Directed by Stephen Johnson. 2001. Not currently available.

Contributors

Eric L. Buffalohead is associate professor and chair of the American Indian studies department at Augsburg College in Minneapolis. He received his PhD in cultural anthropology from the University of Minnesota with a specialization in North American Indians and a minor in American Indian studies. Eric teaches courses in American Indian history, contemporary American Indian issues, American Indians in film, and cultural anthropology. He is an enrolled member of the Ponca Tribe of White Eagle, Oklahoma.

Amy Corbin is an assistant professor of film studies and of media and communication at Muhlenberg College, where she teaches courses in film history, genre, and American film. She holds a PhD from the University of California–Berkeley, and writes on race and cultural geography in American film. Her current book project, "Traveling Spectators: Cinema, Geography, and Cultural Difference in America," theorizes the geographical relations that are inherent in film spectatorship and the way these relationships reveal racial and cultural hierarchies, grounded in a case study of the post-1960s era and its images of Indian Country, the South, the inner city, and the suburbs. She has published an essay on the representation of southern white heroines as multicultural leaders in 1980s film in the volume *Southerners on Film: Essays on the Hollywood Portrayals since the 1970s*.

Jennifer L. Gauthier is associate professor of communication studies at Randolph College (founded as Randolph-Macon Woman's College in 1891) in Virginia, where she teaches courses in film studies, rhetoric, and cultural studies. She has published in *TOPIA: The Canadian Journal of Cultural Studies*, *CineAction*, the *Canadian Journal of Film Studies*, the *American Review of Canadian Studies*, the *International Journal of Cultural Studies*, and the *Quarterly Review of Film and Video*. She has a chapter on Māori filmmaker Barry Barclay in *Global Indigenous Media: Cultures, Poetics and Politics* (2008).

Carole Gerster received her PhD in literature and critical theory from the University of Minnesota and studied American Indian film at the University of California–Berkeley. She currently teaches film and ethnic studies at the University of California–Santa Cruz. Her article "Powwow Highway" is in *Studies in American Indian Literatures* (1991) and her essay "Reclaiming Indian Identity" is chapter 3 in *Screening Culture: Constructing Image and Identity* (2003). Her own book, *Teaching Ethnic Diversity with Film: Essays and Resources for Educators in History, Social Studies, Literature, and Film Studies* (2006), details ways to incorporate films by and about African Americans, Asian Americans, Latino/a Americans, and American Indians into high school and college curricula. It includes an essay on the film history of American Indians and numerous suggestions for teaching current and recurrent Indigenous issues with film.

Joanna Hearne is assistant professor of English and film studies at the University of Missouri. She is the author of *Native Recognition: Indigenous Cinema and the Western* (2012) and Smoke Signals: *Native Cinema Rising* (2012). She has also published articles on Native cinema, animation, and westerns in journals such as *Screen* and in the collections *Global Indigenous Media* (2008) and *Hollywood's West* (2006).

Angelica Lawson is an assistant professor at the University of Minnesota in American Indian studies. She specializes in literature and film. Dr. Lawson was the Charles Eastman Dissertation Fellow at Dartmouth College in 2003. She is Northern Arapaho from the Wind River Reservation in Wyoming.

Jennifer A. Machiorlatti, PhD, is a media artist and teacher who has exhibited her work at national and international film festivals and on the Web. Her writings on Native filmmaking have appeared in the *South Atlantic Review, A Leadership Journal—Women in Leadership: Sharing the Vision, Afterimage, and Ethnic Media in America.* Machiorlatti teaches media and cultural studies, video/digital production, and intercultural communication at Western Michigan University and is currently working on a documentary film project on Native and First Nations women in film and video.

M. Elise Marubbio is an associate professor of American Indian studies at Augsburg College in Minneapolis and director of the Augsburg Native American Film Series. Her publications include articles on the representation of Native Americans in Hollywood film in *2003 Film and History: CD-ROM Annual,* the *Journal of American and Comparative Culture, Polemics: Essays in American Literature and Cultural Criticism,* and the forthcoming volume *Skin Flicks: Native Studies Scholars Look at American Indians in Cinema.* She was guest editor for

Post Script: Essays in Film and the Humanities, special edition on Native American film (2010). Her first book, *Killing the Indian Maiden: Images of Native American Women in Film* (2006), won the Peter C. Rollins Book Award.

Saza Osawa is a member of the Makah Tribe. She graduated from the University of Washington School of Law and has been admitted to practice in the state of Washington as well as the Quinault Nation and the Tulalip Tribes. She currently works as the assistant prosecutor for the Tulalip Tribes in Washington. Prior to law school Saza spent several years working for Upstream Productions, the company founded by her parents. She was associate producer of the nationally broadcast documentary *Maria Tallchief*.

Sam Pack is an assistant professor of cultural anthropology at Kenyon College. His research interests address the relationship between media and culture and specifically focus on an anthropological approach to the production and reception of television, film, and photographs. Dr. Pack is currently revisiting some of the themes explored in this chapter in a manuscript titled "Television through Navajo Eyes: Situating Reception in Everyday Life."

Michelle H. Raheja is an assistant professor in the Department of English at the University of California–Riverside. Her areas of specialization are Native American studies, visual culture, and early American literature. Her newest work is *Reservation Reelism: Redfacing, Visual Sovereignty and Representations of Native Americans* (2011).

Zack Shlachter cast his lot at a young age with the family trade—writing—when he began freelancing for alternative weeklies in North Texas out of high school. He earned an undergraduate degree in history at the University of Missouri and has written for print and public radio over the years. After volunteering for a rural sustainable development NGO in India and resuming work as an arts journalist in Texas, he will next pursue graduate study in South Asian history at the School of Oriental and African Studies.

Beverly Singer is Tewa and Diné from Santa Clara Pueblo, New Mexico. She received her PhD in American studies at the University of New Mexico. She is currently associate professor of anthropology and Native American studies and director of the Institute for American Indian Research at UNM. Her recent video *The Answers Lie Within* (2009) documents a historic exchange of forty-two Native American artists hosted by southern African artists and designers from communities in Botswana, Mozambique, Lesotho, Swaziland, South Africa, and Zimbabwe. Since 1979, she has produced over thirty films and videos including the orientation film *Who We Are* for the opening of the Smithsonian National

Museum of the American Indian in 2004. Her seminal publication is *Wiping the War Paint off the Lens: Native American Film and Video* (2001).

Carla Taunton is an assistant professor at NSCAD University (Nova Scotia College of Art and Design). She is an alliance member of the Aboriginal Curatorial Collective and is committed to Indigenous solidarity work.

Elizabeth Weatherford is the founding director of the Film and Video Center of the Smithsonian National Museum of the American Indian, which is headquartered at NMAI in New York City, and of NMAI's international Native American Film + Video Festival. With support from the Ford Foundation, nearly a decade ago she launched the Film and Video Center's bilingual Native Networks/Redes Indigenas Web site—the only existing space on the Internet exclusively dedicated to Native American and Indigenous film, video, radio, television, and new media. Ms. Weatherford wrote the 1980s catalog *Native Americans on Film and Video* and has published articles on Native film and media in journals and encyclopedias including *Aperture*, *Videoforum*, *Native America in the 20th Century: An Encyclopedia*, *The Native American Almanac*, and *American Indian Magazine*. She has been an adjunct professor on the faculties of New York University's Program in Media and Culture, the School of Visual Arts, and the New School, and she is currently a research associate with NYU's Department of Anthropology.

Houston Wood has lived for decades in Hawai'i, working variously as a farmer, high school teacher, university professor, and writer. His *Native Features: Indigenous Films from Around the World* (2008) examines over fifty feature films. Wood's other work includes *Displacing Natives: The Rhetorical Production of Hawai'i*, which focuses on visual representations of Oceania, and *The Reality of Ethnomethodology* (with Hugh Mehan), an early book in social constructionist theory. Wood is currently a professor of English at Hawai'i Pacific University.

Index

Italic page numbers refer to illustrations.